BETWEEN SILVER AND GUANO

BETWEEN SILVER AND GUANO

*COMMERCIAL POLICY AND
THE STATE IN
POSTINDEPENDENCE
PERU*

BY PAUL GOOTENBERG

PRINCETON UNIVERSITY PRESS
PRINCETON, NEW JERSEY

Library of Congress Cataloging-in-Publication Data

Gootenberg, Paul, 1954–
Between silver and guano : commercial policy and the state in
postindependence Peru / Paul Gootenberg.
p.   cm.
Bibliography: p.
Includes index.
ISBN 0–691–07810–6
1. Peru—Commercial policy—History—19th century. 2. Peru—
Economic conditions. 3. Peru—Politics and
government—1829–   . I. Title.
HF1525.G66   1989
380.1′3′0985—dc19   88–35722
ISBN 0–691–02342–5 (pbk.)

First Princeton paperback printing, 1991

Publication of this book has been aided by the
Whitney Darrow Fund of Princeton University Press

CONTENTS

CONTENTS

STATISTICAL APPENDIXES

PREFACE

THIS BOOK was written by accident, which helps explain its form. By this confession, I do not mean to deny many years (and many reams) of archival research. Rather, the present book sprang from an attempt to distill something of substance from a mass of evidence, far too much to confine to an initial conference paper. Thus, most of the arguments here remain self-consciously sparse in the embellishments—background materials, source quotations, quantitative series—that enhance (some would say clutter) most historical work.

In its broadest scope, this larger research concerns Peru's nineteenth-century incorporation into a liberal world economy. Two detailed historical studies inform this book, and complement, or support at times, some of the synthesizing assertions found here.[1] The first, my master's thesis, examined economic and statistical aspects of this incorporation process, how the nineteenth-century Peruvian economy responded to the challenge and threat of closer contact with external markets. The reactions of Peru's artisans and industrialists received special due, not just in their economics, but in their lively political and ideological productions as well. The second study, my doctoral dissertation, dealt with the sociology of elites, foreign and Peruvian, as they clashed and accommodated (or just plain interacted) in making economic policy. It addressed the empirical gap between traditional historiography and dependency theory (that is to say, between internal and external theories of change), and there one finds full treatments of the foreign interventions, merchant politics, and finance systems sketched here. In the following chapters, I follow one overriding theme: how the social underpinnings and politics of Peru's early protectionist regimes gave way by 1850 to the free-trade alliance behind the guano-age state.

Why choose these problems and for Peru in particular? Originally, my research was inspired by the broad questions raised about Latin American history by the dependency school. These issues of republican economic-policy formation uncannily never received much scholarly follow-up after the well-known dependency polemics of the 1970s.[2] How did regions of the world largely shielded from international commerce until the late eighteenth century, become, by the late nineteenth century, part and parcel of a liberal world economy? What were the effects of novel free-trade policies and expanding exports on their economies, social groups, and political systems? My hope was that empirical research would prove valuable to those who call such transformations "development" and "integration" as well as to those who prefer the terms "underdevelopment" and "subordination" (or any of the euphemisms in between). Until recently, the gap between schools of thought on trade regimes widened to unbridgeable proportions, even as historians vaunted the centrality of the nineteenth-century experience for modern Latin America. Some view freer trade as simply growth and investment, where others see only exploitation and disinvestment.

Nineteenth-century Peru, at first regional capital to a preliberal Spanish bullion empire, became the liberal Peru of the Age of Guano, a boom-and-bust export experience that has held the morbid fascination of economists and historians for quite some time. That interest, while making Peru a natural choice for case study, has never been translated into intense historical research (perhaps because of the notoriety already earned by empire and guano). Nineteenth-century Peru still remains the least-worked of the major national histories of the republican era, a dark age within the Latin American dark ages. Perhaps, then, other historians of Peru will benefit from the wider historiographic findings of this book. Once I realized the extent and richness of the untapped archival materials, my research expanded, then divided into several studies and myriad subthemes. The principal theme here remains, as the title suggests, Peru's dramatic transition between two forms of "world economy": from the tottering colonial one, based on a political extraction of precious bullion, to the liberal economic one based on expanding bulk trade in mundane goods such as guano.[3]

Friends often ask me as a matter of course whether there are any "lessons" for today in the recondite study of nineteenth-century trade policies. My usual reaction is to deny vehemently claims of direct relevance and to rationalize the intrinsic pursuit of history or the finer distinctions of social science. For example, commodity trade was the chief integrative factor in the nineteenth-century world economy; however, even with all the publicized quandaries in the external sector, that same cannot be said of today's Latin American economies, which are fused with the world economy mainly through large transfers of technology and finance. For most countries, tariff policy is simply not the burning (nor unambiguous) issue it was even twenty years ago, much less a century before. There is a world of difference between the nineteenth-century process of entering the world economy (and the conflicts this sparked) and what by the twentieth century are primarily reactions to an already forged dependency (and to the societies it had spawned).

Lately, though, I have come to soften this disclaimer, particularly when glancing at the Andean region. The grisly age of caudillos may be distressingly relevant to the 1980s. New crises of governability, insuperable external imbalances, and ideological ferment have all recently rocked the Andes. Yet each country, in its own way, appears in startling regress to its nineteenth-century model: Chile, with the return of prae-torian centralism and its reversion to quaint nineteenth-century free-trade doctrines; Bolivia, with its bout of massive instability following in-complete revolution; Peru, with a northern nationalist-populist center enveloped by rural disintegration and rebellion; and Ecuador, which some say never left its caudillos far behind. The nightmares of the dead, it seems, have returned. Thus, many of the themes broached in this book may strike followers of contemporary Peru as déjà vu: talk of debt mora-toria, autarky, Pan-American alliances, and balanced national develop-ment on the one side; on the other, the disgruntled flexes of foreign pow-ers—in this case, the same power Peru faced in the 1820s! The resemblance was unintended; the relevance, I think, is real.

Of course, books do not really happen by accident. Along the way to this one, I incurred almost as many debts as the guano-age state (see Chapter 5). Foremost are debts to three wonderful people—John Coatsworth, Rosemary Thorp, and Friedrich Katz—my teachers, advis-ers, and friends in graduate school, to whom I owe, in effect, my whole way of thinking about the social world. Malcolm Deas and Ralph Austen (among others) also broadened my intellectual perspectives. In some sense I do hold them all responsible for the errors of my way, though not, of course, for any of the particular errors in this book. I am especially grateful to my teachers for the faith they had in me during a time when, in myself, it was lacking. Shane Hunt, true to his legend in our field, has been a model colleague from the start. JoAnn Kawell I recall for first sparking my interest in the economic history of Latin America. I also thank Albert O. Hirschman and the School of Social Science of the Insti-tute for Advanced Study, one of the few places on the planet where a scholar has the free hand and encouragement to let a book develop on its own. While I was there, Lucille Allsen courageously word-processed the entire manuscript, corrected my accidental grammar, and graciously told me when to stop.

Over the years, generous research support has been provided by the Rhodes Trust and St. Antony's College, Oxford; the Searle Graduate Fel-lowship Program and the Center for Latin American Studies of the Uni-versity of Chicago; the Fulbright-Hays Doctoral Dissertation Research Abroad Program; the Social Science Research Council; the American Council of Learned Societies; the Institute for Advanced Study; and the Mazer Fund for Faculty Research of Brandeis University. Praeger Pub-lishers lent permission to use a portion of Chapter 2, previously pub-lished in *Guiding the Invisible Hand: Economic Liberalism and the State in Latin American History*. The staffs at archives and libraries on three continents lent their help far beyond the call of institutional duty. I men-tion here only the Sterling, Regenstein, and Newberry Libraries, the

U.S. National Archives, the Public Record Office (London), the Archives du Ministère des Affaires Etrangères (Paris), the Archivo General de la Nación (Lima), the Biblioteca Nacional del Perú, the Instituto Riva Agüero, the Archivo Municipal de Lima, and the Biblioteca Denegri Luna. In Peru, there have been and are so many encouraging colleagues and friends, it is hard to call this study my own. I especially thank Alfonso Quiroz (my comrade of the archives and pioneer of nineteenth-century history), Gabriela Ramos, Christine Hünefeldt, Marcela Calisto, Carlos Indacochea, Marisa Remy, Luis Miguel Glave, Margarita Giesecke, Alberto Flores Galindo, Miriam Salas, Mariana and Franklin Pease, Scarlett O'Phelan, Heraclio Bonilla, Daniel Cotlear, Gabriela Vega, and my gracious friend Patricia Wieland.

During the revisionist stage at Brandeis, Robert Schneider and Julio Ortega proved true and rare colleagues. I owe much to Charles Purrenhage, the copyeditor, whose calling and improvements to the text seem more than accidental. Richard Salvucci, Shane Hunt, Stanley Stein, Florencia Mallon, Frank Safford, David Holtby, Sandy Thatcher, Nils Jacobsen, Charles Walker, John Coatsworth, and Albert O. Hirschman all read, and rectified, portions of the manuscript.

BETWEEN SILVER AND GUANO

Quito

COLOMBIA
(NEW GRANADA)

ECUADOR

Guayaquil

Tumbes

R. Amazon

PIURA

Paita

CAJAMARCA

AMAZONAS

BRAZIL

Cajamarca

LA LIBERTAD

Trujillo

Highlands

Yungay

Coast

Huaraz

Huánuco

ANCASH

Cerro de Pasco

Chancay

LIMA

Junín

JUNÍN

Callao

Huancayo

CUZCO

Lima

Huancavelica

Cañete

Ayacucho

BOLIVA
(UPPER PERU)

Chincha Islands

Pisco

Cuzco

Ica

PUNO

AYACUCHO

Chala

Lampa

AREQUIPA

PACIFIC OCEAN

Puno

Lake Titicaca

Arequipa

La Paz

Camaná

MOQUEGUA

Islay

Moquegua

Cochabamba

Ilo

TACNA

Tacna

Arica

TARAPACÁ

Iquique

Cobija

CHILE

PERU circa 1830

0   100   200   300

MILES

CHAPTER 1

Introduction: From Nationalist Elites to a Liberal State

BY HIGH NOON, Saturday, the twenty-third of August, 1834, the gratings were locked tight on the swank boutiques along Lima's normally bustling commercial boulevard, the Calle de Bodegones. Around the block, from Mantas Street to Santo Domingo Square, a pall hung over the emptied storefronts of scores of *limeño* shopkeepers. Instead of customers, crowds of tense merchants milled in the plazas. Their *sambos*, black slaves, readied themselves with brickbats, should anyone dare break the peace, or venture out to sell or buy. Yet this was no day of rest for merchants, but one of action, political action.[1]

ORBEGOSO OFFENDS

The "movimiento mercantil" of 23 August—a general strike declared by Lima's merchant guild—was in progress. José Tiburcio Roldan, the *consulado's* elected chief, had warned his foes. His threat, borrowed from Chilean friends, was action "by reason or by force" if the new government of General Luis José de Orbegoso refused to heed their call. Ostensibly, the Peruvian merchants were out to destroy the hated "casas de martillo," public auction houses run by Thomas Eldredge and Samuel Tracy—two obstreperous Yankees whom the august Catholic consulado preferred to smear as "Jews" and "queers" instead. Ever since March, President Orbegoso had tried to elude the merchants' mounting petitions, pleas, and pressures (most recently, from the rostrum of Peru's National Convention itself) against the foreign auctions and their "ruinous" price falls. This on-and-off struggle had obsessed merchants for more than a decade now. The *martillero's* hammer continued to clang, and the merchants resolved to turn from reason to drama and force instead. That Saturday, not a single store opened for business in Lima. Merchant leaders—Roldan, Larrainzar, Oyague, and Oliveira—led a solemn procession of their followers through the streets of the capital to surrender their keys, en masse, to Lima's English, French, and North American trading houses, in the traditional sign of bankruptcy. Anxious liberal publicists and officials knew, however, that auctions seemed but a pretext for Lima's livid merchants. To free traders, the strike was a "scandalous uprising," a "motín comercial," a veritable "revolución mercantil" hatched to smash the whole array of liberal reforms enacted during Orbegoso's brief and beleaguered reign. Merchants were a "mob of *chapetones* out to suck our last blood of Independence."[2] If Orbegoso failed to move resolutely and to jail these "subversives," his days were numbered. In this the liberals proved right.

Trouble had been brewing since February 1834, when yet another Peruvian revolution brought to Lima its first openly liberal government since the merchants had chased Bolívar out of Peru some eight years earlier. For Orbegoso, nothing worked as planned, neither with his free trade nor with his treasury. In March, Orbegoso had to shelve his first liberal tariff, swamped by a flood of political complications. One was his acceptance of a 79,763-peso loan from the national merchants' new Ramo de Arbitrios lending bank. This desperately needed cash came with strings attached: no revocation of the six-year ban on cotton textile imports, nixing Orbegoso's last hope for fiscal salvation. Meanwhile, Lima's foreign merchants, including Tracy and Eldredge (who paid modestly for their auction rights), would not supply the funds Orbegoso required to move his liberal program, even as they prodded for more and more liberal concessions. In May, the north's coastal planters, millers, and merchants even forced Orbegoso to reverse step and dispatch a mission to negotiate a protectionist trade treaty with his illiberal nemesis, Chile.[3] Liberal dreams were floundering.

As the fogs of winter enveloped Lima, the assaults against the auctioneers and their liberal promoters grew only hotter. In July, the consulado attacked before the full National Convention: no liberal giveaways to foreigners. "We are the only ones," Roldan reminded sympathetic delegates, "who contribute to the upkeep of the state; everything comes from our sweat; we Peruvians carry the rifles that uphold the laws of the land."[4] This time, they would supply the rifles to overturn simply the liberal laws they abhorred. Peru's president responded meekly with constitutional technicalities about "freedom of industry." He also confessed what everyone in this hostile (and inveterately nationalist) Congress already knew: his attempts to lower tariffs had done nothing to stem the bankruptcy corroding the regime, whose debt to foreigners from customs and mint advances now soared uncontrollably to more than 400,000 pesos.[5] In mid-August, national merchants and nationalist officials blocked Orbegoso's next effort to lower prohibitive textile duties. Even the presence of two handpicked British merchants on the tariff commission, and the usual behind-the-scenes arm-twisting by U.S. and British diplomats, failed to do the trick. Instead, an uproar of backlash against "foreign meddlers" played right into nationalist hands. Liberals roundly denounced protectionists in Lima's polemicized press: nationalists were not even trying to make tariff policy anymore, but simply to starve Orbegoso of all funding and support.[6] The strike of 23 August drove this point home.

From the interior, a far greater threat loomed by August. The armies of Gran Mariscal Agustín Gamarra, combined with those of the *caudillos* Bermúdez, La Fuente, and Salaverry, were again on the march, the same nationalists thought to be vanquished six months before. In Lima, accusations flew that the merchants would stop only at reviving their "routine of privileges, prohibitions, and monopolies; pining for antiquity and making war on the auctions." Surely, as many hinted, the protectionist ire had now turned into war against Orbegoso himself; that is, into direct support for the spreading *gamarrista* insurgents, now joined by motley provincials and the usual artisan types.[7] Orbegoso had no monies or allies left to prosecute this civil war, nor as yet a single liberal promise fulfilled.

In September, the Consejo de Estado, the strongest authority in the land, hammered out a compromise on the auctions, sensing "this most alarming agitation" around them. Orbegoso desperately embraced this plan to regulate *martillo* sales, and expunge all foreign retail shops to boot. The consulado rejected the ploy, especially after the Consejo declined the merchants' hefty $6,000 bribe to halt the auctions altogether.[8] A small band of breakaway merchants, led by the maverick liberal Miguel Rivera (and suffering one reprisal after another for their liberal deviancy), fought back with lawsuits to annul the election of the "traitorous" consulado leadership. The usual threats and slanders flared, yet never a final verdict. For by October, even the legendary *mercachifles*, Lima's mulatto streethawkers, gossiped about how the top merchants were actively fueling an unstoppable revolution in the provinces.[9] In December, Orbegoso fled Lima to battle the rebels in the far south, on the last turf to find the liberal faithful. The south, as usual, would not suffice. On New Year's Day, 1835, Lima's remaining militias mutinied to the cause of the fiery limeño Colonel Felipe Salaverry, the nationalist caudillo just past adolescence. This was a not unexpected present for Lima's nationalists. Yet an unprecedented round of bloodletting ensued, as Salaverry's men summarily executed the last loyalist sergeants of Callao.[10]

As the new year began, so began a new regime. Abandoned liberals damned the merchants who helped topple republican Peru's first true liberal experiment, "those monopolists who also want to monopolize our government!" Roldan barely bothered to reply to his critics, who "if they are men at all, . . . [are] fags and liars unfit for human society."[11] All this mudslinging was gratuitous. For by then Salaverry had already banished the auctioneers, sealed his exclusionist trade pact with Chile, restored full import prohibitions, prosecuted foreign retailers, returned consulado favors in kind, and mounted a bitter crusade against all the foreigners rewarded and implicated in the crushed liberal regime. Another topsy-turvy nationalist reign had begun for Peru, and the mayhem, epithets, and violence would persist unabated for years to come. But all this turmoil was about something: Peru's entry into the world economy.

LIBERAL PERU AND THE HISTORIANS

Until recently, economic policy in Peru was synonymous with "export liberalism." No other economy of Latin America matched Peru in the fervor, simplicity, and tenacity of its liberal orthodoxy. And no country appeared so thoroughly dominated by the liberal politics of its export elites. For six decades after 1900, the "oligarchy," Peru's coterie of coastal planters and their urban kin, sustained a legendary capacity to deflect the nationalist and protectionist alternatives that by 1930, elsewhere in the region, had already corroded export liberalism. Peru's "liberal state"—in our economic sense alone—served mainly to facilitate unimpeded relations between national export elites and overseas interests and markets, ensuring the oligarchy its lopsided share of the fruits of Peru's open economy.[12] The liberal complexion of Peruvian elites, moreover, dates as far back as historians usually venture. Liberal hegemony, by an even narrower Lima "plutocracy," appeared in full flower by the 1850s, fertilized by the renowned free-trade bonanza of the Age of Guano. As in the modern export experience, the fleeting benefits of the nineteenth-century boom reached few others in Peruvian society. Guano, then, makes our textbook case of export riches gone wrong.

Historians assign a special analytic significance to this, Peru's unbroken chain of elite liberalism. Incorrigibly liberal elites, they argue, locked that country into frustrating long-term cycles of intensifying dependence on foreign markets, finance, and technology, a growth syndrome that only exacerbated Peru's already marked disparities of income, power, and culture.[13] Small wonder that Peru is also the paradigm of a country hobbled by its allegiance to free trade.

It is difficult to imagine a Peru without liberalism, a Peruvian state not run by and for powerful liberal elites. Yet, while overlooked, one such period did exist: the three-decade interregnum between independence and guano prosperity. From 1821 to 1852 (when a radical and durable free trade finally triumphed), Peru ranked as one of the most protectionist regimes in the hemisphere, armed with a complex array of nationalist economic strategies. Import bans and prohibitive tariffs shielded local craftsmen, farmers, and factories from the wave of cheaper imports that came with independence; foreign merchants faced an intricate network of nontariff barriers that hamstrung their maneuvers in the local economy; and the nascent Peruvian state tried every trick at its disposal to steer national development away from full dependence on the expanding world economy. Nationalist, even xenophobic, currents pervaded all strata of Peruvian society, translating into zealous policies and practices that kept foreign and liberal interests at bay. In the postindependence era, Peru's notorious liberal state and elites were nowhere to be found.

Peru's protectionist debut began mildly in 1821, with independence, although in the mid-1820s foreign occupiers, notably San Martín and Bolívar, had tried to reverse this trend with their quixotic proclamations of "free trade." By 1828, Peruvian nationalists and *políticos* had installed a full protectionist regime instead. Protectionism meant total bans on such common consumer imports as textiles and flours, 90-percent sumptuary tariffs for handicrafts, and ever-rising specific duties (100–200 percent) on agrarian staples. This "prohibitions" fervor was backed up by a gamut of navigation acts and commercial subsidies, repression of foreign-trader rights, and a comprehensive scheme for a regulated regional commercial system (with Chile) insulated from Atlantic markets. Through some dozen vociferous tariff debates until the late 1840s, the national thrust of trade policy held firm (although the vacillations and turmoil of Peru's weak state undoubtedly blunted its effect). Protectionism withstood major liberal counterattacks in 1832, 1834, and 1836–38 when liberal (20–40 percent) tariffs were briefly imposed, again from abroad.[14] Nationalist agitation and trade policies reached their zenith between 1839 and 1841, with the autarkic dreams of the Gamarra Restoration. Some tariffs, notably on rustic textiles, now seemed obsolete; but the regime redoubled its efforts to favor national enterprise over pariah foreigners, particularly with its stress on native monopolies. By 1845, though, the venerable penchant for nativist exclusionism and prohibitions was waning. But novel strains of protection—privileges and impromptu 40-percent duties for new factories (and steeper effective ones for artisans and shippers) as well as the "Peru first" guano-export monopoly—now came to the fore. Between 1848 and 1852, sharp struggles broke out between Peru's last protectionists (winning momentary success) and a new breed of Peruvian export liberal. In the end, the liberals were to triumph with the uniform 20-percent Manchesterian free-trade laws of March 1852. It was fully three decades since San Martín had heralded a free trade for Peru.

In many respects, Peru's initial protectionism seems to be just one instance of a wider, still unstudied phenomenon: the prolonged resistance of postindependence elites and states, across Latin America, to the new possibility of free-trade integration with the rising North Atlantic economy. Peruvian protectionism found important counterparts from 1820 to 1860 in Mexico, Colombia, Bolivia, Argentina, and Paraguay, to name some obvious cases. Larger trends were surely working against the new commercial order glimpsed in the 1820s with the collapse of Spanish mercantilism. The political turmoil, depression, and war capitalism that bedeviled nearly all the new republics weakened incentives for would-be export sectors to press for liberalism. Similar balance-of-payments crises prompted emergency stabilization measures, with profound protectionist effects. In most countries, neomercantilist ideologies and monopolies still enjoyed prestige as stopgap fiscal remedies (or among colonial corporate cliques, such as artisans and merchants, who survived independence with greater viability than their liberal foes). In some areas, local interests emerged with a new freedom to voice their own policy needs, often at odds with the cosmopolitan liberals in capitals and ports. Yet, beneath the era's chaotic nationalist policies, a conflict was sharpening between hoary colonial economic norms, practices, and interests (all of which enjoyed a postindependence resurgence) and those, Bourbon-inspired, which by the 1870s would definitively pull Latin America into a liberal world economy. It was, as one historian puts its, Latin America's "long wait" between colonialism and, as many now see it, the "neocolonial" order. Few analyses deal with this thorny and protracted transition from colonialism to liberalism.[15] Even so, recent theorists and historians alike now regard this shift as the portentous change of the nineteenth century—the groundwork for Latin America's modern, dependent, and export societies.

For Peru, the historiography downplays the early protectionist regime, even as a sign of this inherently conflictual process of forging new relationships to the world economy. An extended bout of protectionism fits poorly with recent "dependency" interpretations of the era, which depict liberation from mercantilist Spain as the springboard for Peru's rapid and inevitable subjection by British free-trade imperialism. In this scenario, early British "control" over Peru's weak economy, and diplomatic pressures unleashed against an even feebler state, crushed local opposition to incorporation into a British liberal world order. The protectionist decades also contradict a broader (and by now conventional) view of Peruvian elites as congenitally impaired for the tasks of modern nation-building. Peru's infirm ruling cliques and state, so the argument goes, were incapable of economic nationalism or, for that matter, any form of national development. They proved all too willing to accommodate to the needs, profits, and coercions of North Atlantic capitalism—at the expense of broader and long-term national interests. With this liberal propensity ingrained from the start, the quick adoption of free trade now stands as the first open expression of the long, unnational legacy of republican elites.[16] Their liberal compact would bring compounding ruin and disgrace to Peru as the century unfolded: from the squandered opportunity of guano resources to the disastrous denouement of war with Chile. And when historians do recognize signs of postindependence protectionism, it is as-

8

cribed to struggles by beleaguered underclass artisans, their quixotic attempts to survive the flood of imports unleashed precisely by this furtive liberal matrimony of local and foreign elites.

This interpretation—and analogous ones crop up for all of Latin America—sacrifices a complex reality. It also unwittingly sacrifices our power to explain the key historiographic problem of the postindependence era: the origins of Peru's liberal dominant class and state. Their presumed liberal proclivities are, at base, projections back in time of the characteristics requiring explanation, the zealous free-trade plutocrats, policies, and polity of the high age of export after 1860. In fact, Peru's colonial elites were notoriously illiberal. And, as this book will show in some detail, the stance of Peru's first republican elites was that of defiant economic nationalism, challenging the odds favoring accommodation with the liberal world economy well into the 1840s. Pugnacious popular artisans (and others) did leave their mark on policy; but this occurred because of the wider social context provided by the equally aggressive protectionism of elites—landed, commercial, and military-bureaucratic. Perhaps this elite protectionism merits attention for its historiographic novelty, all the more so because it seems a surprising form of nationalism that defies (as well) many current assumptions about the interests, visions, and behavior of Latin America's nineteenth-century elites.[17] But above all, exploring Peru's early nationalist elites is the only way to grasp the actual conditions behind their dramatic shift to liberalism in the 1840s: that is, how the enduring liberal state was born. In short, how did the genuine liberal hegemony of Peru emerge?

In strict historiographic terms, it should not really surprise us that Peru's founding elites were so protectionist. Elsewhere, historians have long catalogued and chronicled a wave of early "conservative nationalisms" after independence. These ranged from the aristocratic industrialism of Lucas Alamán (Mexico) to the nativistic intransigence and agrarian protection of rustic caudillos such as Juan Manuel de Rosas (Argentina). For the most part, these movements were read as outcrops of the region's colonial heritage, as a conservative reaction to new tremors of social mobility and trade. In Peru, the weight of this colonial heritage is indisputable. Peruvian elites ranked among the most conservative—economically, politically, and socially—in all of America. They resisted independence to the bitter end, as if a hyper-royalism could turn back the clock on dangerous Bourbon liberals and reverse any local reverberations of the Atlantic's newfangled commercial and political revolutions.[18] As will become clear, the influence of these archaic elites—planter aristocrats, consulado monopolists, sierran industrialists—lived on in an independent Peru; and, at least in part, this explains the protectionist surge until 1845.

9

Colonial mines (and minds) remained the mainstay of Peru's economic and political currencies. Nevertheless, the following pages aim at more than filling in another case of nostalgic nationalist conservatism. Colonial legacies operated in novel surroundings. Their mutation into palpable strains of nationalism, and then into a process of genuine liberal-national state-building, should draw as much historical concern as the force of blanket colonial continuity. In fact, historians need most to explain those shards of "colonialism" that would endure into the republican age. In the end, we may decipher new meanings and contributions from the early conservative movements.

The other (and main) historiographic referent here is the more abstract one of "dependency." If dependency is indeed dead, as some historians have chimed, it certainly weighs in on the brains of the living. All of our recent textbooks on republican Latin America, for example, embrace dependency notions, by osmosis or design. Yet, as one historian ironically notes, this revisionist reversal is a simple one. The old villains of history—the conservatives and erstwhile "barbarians" who obstructed liberal Progress, including free trade—have suddenly become its new heroes. And *al revés*: the old modernizers, particularly liberal Europeanized thinkers, have become the century's *malinches*.[19] The dependency rehabilitation of such freakish characters as Dr. Francia of Paraguay—who are now held to offer nineteenth-century Latin America its most viable and progressive path to development—should alert us that revisionism has gone astray.

There is, to be sure, more to dependency views of modernization and Europeanization than this simple somersault implies. These are the problems that make study of Peru's protectionist phase worthy in a broader conceptual and comparative sense. What the dependency school actually operates from, with its unconditional condemnation of export liberalism, is a glaring yet unstated counterfactual argument: that "autonomous" nationalist regimes should have been preferred, on any number of economic, social, and political grounds, over the elite export models that ultimately triumphed in the nineteenth century. Specifically, nationalist commercial policies, if pursued from the start, would have spurred enduring diversification and technological advance, greater social welfare and equity, and stronger and more "national" polities.[20] At least this is what is implied by dependency writers who blame free trade (and kindred liberalisms) for most of the ills of nineteenth-century development—as it was actually to occur under liberal auspices. Thus the early nineteenth century becomes Latin America's great lost opportunity to join the North Atlantic track of self-sustaining development. Indeed it was, in some sense, for recent research proves that by standard economic indicators (per capita income or economies of scale) it was during the nineteenth century that most of the region fell so dramatically behind the rest of the West. (Controversies here are endless. Was liberalism at fault, or protectionism? Was either possible or relevant?)

Fortunately, the real "conservative-nationalist" regimes that flourished prior to Latin America's full incorporation into the world economy (1850–70) can serve to draw out, and perhaps even test, the covert dependency hypothesis. What were the early nationalist possibilities like, and about? Was there a truly alternative political economy of elites? Was it viable in the face of countervailing pressures, and was it socially and economically "progressive"? Peru, a more credible case than Paraguay, is also the striking one for counterfactual analysis. The extremity of its policies and shifts, from radical protectionism to an equally drastic free trade—not to mention its secular decline ("underdevelopment") from a diversified colonial core to a dependent marginal monoexporter—is unmistakably clear. Peruvian clarity will help us to understand, if not interpret, the rash of other nationalist regimes that dotted the early republican land-scape.[21] The analysis may prove ambiguous, for we are dealing with more than villains and heroes, whatever their preference for trade.

One political dimension of current dependency views of Peruvian elites is worth underscoring here: "caudillismo," that ferocious political instability which without question was the birthmark of the new republic. No part of independent Latin America was without its caudillos, but Peru's trial with political factionalism was particularly severe. From 1821 to 1845 Peru endured at least twenty-four major regime changes—for a messy average of one per year—accompanied by untold hundreds of wars, ranging from barracks revolts to all-out internecine and international carnage. The new scholarly views attribute this chronic instability directly to Peru's imputed lack of viable nationalist—or liberal—elite projects at political independence in 1821. Lacking a "hegemonic" dominant class, Peru fell apart, and power fell into the hands of squabbling apolitical military chiefs for thirty-odd years. Postindependence politics became, in the words of one historian, an "utter chaos," a meaningless personalistic scramble for spoils.[22] Politics, on this view, makes sense only with the stability of the guano age, from 1845, when elites lined up in a coherent state as junior partners in the British exploitation of Peru.

Actually, politics made sense all along. This book, above all, aims to make intelligible, not dismiss out of hand, the patterns, terms, and meanings of postindependence politics. Elite trade politics were primordial to Peru's initial difficulties in forming a cohesive state, and played an equally active role in the consolidation of the stable Peruvian state of the guano age. If anything, the value of recognizing the commitments and struggles of elites over trade policy becomes evident: we are now able to elucidate these dimly understood aspects of Peruvian political development. Several ways to go about understanding politics and state-building are elaborated below.

Caudillismo, however chaotic, did pass through discernible stages in Peru, and these ought to be borne in mind as our analysis of its politics unfolds.[23] From 1821, though nominally independent, Peru slogged through three more years of fierce fighting between entrenched royalists and patriots until imported auxiliaries under Simón Bolívar vanquished mainland America's last Spanish forces in late 1824 at Ayacucho. These Bolivarians stayed on, seeking to impose a centralist (and utopian liberal) stability on Peru. They soon faced concerted resistance from local military chiefs (and congresses), mostly former allies of Bolívar himself. By 1827, the aroused "Peruvians" forced the Colombians from Peru—marking the nation's true independence—and, besides making war on neighboring Bolivarian states, broke into arcane political struggles among themselves for ultimate control of Lima. Civil politics, and society, decayed. Between 1829 and 1834, one of the dozens of Peruvian strongmen, Agustín Gamarra of Cuzco, emerged to dominate the executive, although literally scores of insurrections, breakaway movements, and border wars marred Gamarra's conservative reign. In 1834 and 1835, full-fledged civil wars carried in alternating regimes (of Orbegoso and Salaverry) until, by 1836, these caudillo conflicts generalized into a bloody Pan-Andean conflagration. Bolivia's liberal General Andrés de Santa Cruz marched in to conquer this fractured Peru and to impose order from without in the Bolivarian shadow of the Peru-Bolivia Confederation (1836–38). By the mid-1830s, all semblance of parliamentary politics was lost. Two invasions by Peruvian irregulars (and Chile) followed, until by 1839 Gamarra's assorted chiefs seemed again firmly in command. However, between 1841 and 1845, after Gamarra's death at arms, the Peruvian state simply disintegrated, engulfed in an unrelenting, devastating, and byzantine cross-country contest for national dominance. Out from this mayhem finally stepped General Ramón Castilla, who by 1845 had set out to consolidate Lima's central rule, buttressed by his pacification of regional caudillos and an incipient pact with reborn civil elites and institutions. Although Castilla's era of rapid state-building (which lasted into the 1860s) had its own share of troubles, by 1850 it was feasible at last to speak of a unitary Peruvian state. And, as with San Martín's long-delayed free trade, it was some three decades since the Liberators had first declared a "Peru."

The turmoil of tariffs and titular authority was coeval—if not otherwise tied—with sharp changes in Peruvian trade. Late viceregal Peru was basically an antiquated, controlled imperial entrepôt. In typical years, nearly $8 million in upscale European imports flowed (in theory) through Spain and its privileged *peninsular* diaspora in Lima. In return, Peru's silver mines, increasingly concentrated in the nearby Cerro de Pasco district (after the 1770s separation of Upper Peru), supplied all but a trifle of overseas returns, although Lima's *criollo* merchant community also plied some $1 million in agricultural staples up and down the coast, particularly with Chile. The year 1821 surely marked a break with this closed system, and contained the germ of a new venture into the world economy. By 1825, most of the Spanish traders (with their credit) were banished, swiftly replaced by the agents of the shift to direct North Atlantic supply. Some twenty to thirty of these British, U.S., and French wholesale houses set up shop in Lima alone, still Peru's commercial capital.[24] Subsequent statistics on the new trade patterns and partners are difficult to untangle. Yet one unmistakable trend, a radical fall in import costs (at least 50 percent in the 1820s alone), shook Peru's colonially sheltered producers and price structures to the core.

By the mid-1820s, Peru absorbed, in what was decried as an import "flood," $4–5 million in diverse foreign manufactures. Goods worth perhaps $1.5 million came from Britain (chiefly high-grade textiles and hardware); $800,000 worth from France (luxury cloth, crafts, and wines); and, surprisingly, some $1.2–2 million worth from North American shippers (flours, plain cottons, and sundries). Imports abated and altered as Peru entered a deep domestic depression, exacerbated by internal war, with little relief in either until 1845. Demand, befitting Peru's stagnant and shattered markets, shifted to more mundane consumer goods (70–80 percent coarse textiles). Yet, continuing import price slides, combined with domestic downturn, apparently contributed to a creeping real growth of the tradables sector.[25] In 1834, import levels reached the $8-million mark again, although 50 percent was now supplied by British firms, expanding in the south. From 1837 to 1841, various reports show a leveling of trade at $8 million, and Britain continued to displace French luxuries and U.S. necessities, even during the war contraction of 1841–45. Imports exploded, this time for good, under the impetus of political stability, guano prosperity, and free trade after 1845. Import value doubled by 1852. British goods dominated markets, while French luxury wares also revived. The import bonanza of the high guano age had begun ($15–20 million annually by the mid-1850s), lasting until Peru's dramatic economic collapse in the late 1870s.

Peru's initial export record is actually less obscure. In the 1820s, mining suffered a devastating decline (likely dating to the teens), and massive capital flight fed into large external deficits. By the early 1830s, however, the mines had vigorously recouped their motor role, producing $3–4 million of silver annually before briefly climbing to colonial-output levels of $5–6 million in the early 1840s. Bullion and coin, then, remained Peru's staple of return (more than 80 percent) throughout the postindependence era. But a significant regional-product shift was also under way. While the import entrepôt of Lima (and the north) funneled virtually nothing but their change back to Europe, by 1839 southern ports had entered modern bulk trades: some $650,000 in wools, $300,000 in nitrates, along with barks, copper, and cotton. Guano exports (from the near south coast) appeared in 1841, became the leading export by 1847, and accounted (with a low base) for Peru's remarkable 1840s annual export growth of 9.2 percent.[26] Guano exports to Britain alone (the major market) averaged $15 million by the mid-1850s. By the early 1850s, guano (and the loans it attracted) supplied 60–75 percent of Peru's foreign exchange, fueling both the import binge and the rapid expansion of the Lima state that owned and managed the nearby trade. These locational trends provide some clues for understanding Peru's insertion into the world economy after 1821. Yet, the lively political reactions of Peruvians to trade proved even more varied than import-export data might suggest.

CONCEPTS, CAVEATS, CHAPTERS

This book attempts to tackle ten problems simultaneously, without nearly the precision or parsimony of the economist. The focus here is overwhelmingly political, even if most historians have not taken the messy politics of this period very seriously. Economic analysis is referred to sparingly, in order to explore some of the motivations of the political actors—who might, in another scenario, be seen as ideal Ricardian interest groups, reacting to their rising and falling *fortuna* in external economic rents. Purposely eschewed, however, are explicitly reductionist macroeconomic explanations for policies that overlook the mediation of social groups and institutions—even though several are quite compelling. An economist might glance at Peru and pretty well predict the global patterns of trade policy. For example, during Peru's export and fratricidal-war depression from 1821 to 1845, the "opportunity cost" for protectionist policies remained quite low. Then, with stability and guano prosperity after 1845, it became very high and liberalization ensued. Under this lens, the shift would appear largely "exogenous," if not decidedly externalist and egoistic.[27] Nevertheless, the task for historians is to unravel how such processes worked their way out within this particular social formation, and thereby contribute to its history and, perhaps, to social theory at large. Sometimes this approach produces counterintuitive findings—even for economics.

Of the ten problems addressed, some are peculiar to the historiography of Peru, while others correspond to more universal social-scientific concerns. First is the simple identification of the elite groups most active in Peruvian trade politics—often not that simple a task. For one thing, there were so many at work: U.S., British, and French diplomats and trading houses, Bolivarians, Chileans, liberal publicists, *arequipeño* free traders, northern landed gentry, slavers, native merchants, shopkeepers and peddlers, millers and master artisans, nationalist and liberal caudillos, rustic military chiefs, rural protoindustrialists and urban factory owners, silver miners, provincial oligarchies, deputies and senators, municipal governments, Lima bureaucrats, national finance cliques, London stockjobbers, and professional nationalists—to name just the major groups encountered. The second empirical aim (but definitional as well) is to capture the early complex of policies subsumed under the rubrics of economic "nationalism" and "liberalism." Again, the field is wide and often surprising.

Two caveats apply here. First, "liberalism" will be approached mainly in its confined sense of "free trade," not as the panoply of European economic and political individualisms often assimilated into liberal programs. Second, "nationalism" is similarly viewed as myriad kinds of protectionism, rather than as a term of national identity or nation-building. (Those broader implications of nationalism will surface in the concluding chapter.) In short, the free traders and protectionists seen here ought not to be taken strictly as the traditional "Liberal/Conservative" antagonists of Peru, even if they are akin to those more complex actors.[28] This heuristic political reductionism is warranted by the facts. In Peru, formal and widely based Liberal and Conservative movements remained relatively unpronounced, and the complications of trade policy help explain why this was so. These categories will also make (preliminary) sense of Peru's hitherto indecipherable regional and political chaos.

The third problem is to explain the contrasting (and changing) political effectiveness of the contending elites and policies. The social, regional, and national constellations of trade politics figure highly in this line of analysis. The fourth theme is the political economy of trade regimes: what moved different elites and the state to embrace their various trade policies? Important variables here include novel postindependence market structures and Peru's special structures of economic and political risk: a pandemic instability, symbiotic with caudillismo, that was actually common to much of the region in this era. Fifth, this book aims for an integrated approach to international political economy. It does not share in the artificial dichotomies between "internal" and "external" causality, "domestic" and "foreign" actors (or "dependency" and "antidependency" positions) that currently pervade much Latin American research.[29] It tries to bridge this methodological dualism by highlighting the critical ground-level interactions between Peruvian and international social forces—interplays naturally pronounced in both trade policy and peripheral state-building. Readers should note, then, that the space required for unearthing (previously unstudied) Peruvian policy configurations in no way abstracts—or detracts—from their international contexts.

The sixth set of concerns has to do with the political impact of economic policy conflict. Do these elite struggles help clarify Peru's main patterns of postindependence politics—the first twenty years of wild civil warfare, the achievement of stability in the late 1840s, the behavior of the guano-age state? The most recent label for this kind of analysis is "state formation"; however, despite renewed interest by students of Latin America, this theme remains virtually untouched for the nineteenth century, when the modern states actually arose.[30] Dependency theory, in a very general way, suggests the hypothesis that trade policy was the formative political issue—or tissue—of the infant republics. It profoundly shaped Latin American elites, their political outlooks, and the states they were constructing. The Peruvian evidence, though not necessarily conclusive for the rest of the continent, will be put to work in order to trace how foreign trade may well have influenced the emergence of lasting states. Through the lens of trade policy, state formation will be observed from a multiplicity of intersecting angles: political, social, ideological, institutional, regional, fiscal, and diplomatic.[31]

A still broader relationship between politics and economics informs the seventh topic: the possible links between economic policies and the emerging forms of political institutions, participation, discourse, and culture. Social scientists of contemporary Latin America devote much needed and timely analysis to these issues, but practically no attention to their historical—and in many ways more enduring—antecedents. These origins of Peruvian authoritarianism and democracy turn out to be, at the same time, both clear and ambiguous.[32] The eighth issue is the transition to liberalism itself. While much of the following text concentrates on the initial protectionist regimes (to draw out their hidden history), this effort will then suggest the critical areas where a transformation would have to—and did—occur for the triumph of free trade and a solid liberal state in the 1850s. A ninth theme is the general political-economic forces that may have prompted shifts to free trade throughout the region. Locational aspects of interest groups are one salient example. Finally, we analyze the most speculative question of all. In the light of new evidence, what does the Peruvian experience tell us about the theoretical interplay among dependency, nationalism, and statehood? Does it, in sum, help clarify that huge dependency counterfactual view concerning the historic role of conservative nationalist regimes? Naturally, along the road to these larger issues, a host of specific historiographic controversies is met as well—for example, the nature of imperialism, regionalism, or fiscality in Peru.

THESE concerns are interwoven in a chapter structure that is both thematic and still largely chronological. Chapter 2 examines the failed first generation of Andean free traders: foreign elites, Bolivarians, liberal intellectuals, and southern interests. Why were they unable to make headway in Peru? Chapter 3 analyzes their chief obstacle to success, the predominance of protectionist elites. What conditions and issues sparked this vibrant nationalist movement in Peru, and how did it evolve? Northern landed elites, the vested interests of Lima, industrial classes, the pro-Chilean alliance, and merchant nationalists are the major actors in this scenario. Together, these two chapters lay out the interests behind the passions, changes, triumphs, and failures to come. Chapter 4 explores political dimensions of trade-policy conflict. Who were the nationalist caudillos, why were they nationalist at all, and how did commercial policy intertwine with and shape political institutions and constituencies? What eventually emerges from this boiling political cauldron is the recipe for the liberal state of the 1850s—and beyond. Chapter 5 unearths the material foundation for competing trade policies and politics: militarist state finance. A permanent fiscal emergency fueled caudillos, functionaries, and the larger protectionist coalitions in Peru—and, ultimately, their knotty conversion into the new liberal alliance with foreigners that would erect the guano-age state. Baffling features of the high guano state stemmed from these primordial fiscal-political struggles.

By way of conclusion, Chapter 6 pieces together some implications of early nationalism and liberalism for the historiography of Peru, for dependency theory, and for analyses of Latin American nationalisms. All said and done, was early Peruvian nationalism that unsung alternative to nineteenth-century elite export liberalism or something of a different order? What lay between silver and guano?

CHAPTER 2

Beleaguered Liberals

WHO WERE the commercial liberals in postindependence Peru? Which groups actually spearheaded the opening drive for free trade between 1820 and 1840? Five distinct liberal currents emerged among the elites: foreign political envoys and their resident merchant houses; the Bolivarians and their ideological orphans, the internationalists; and an incipient southern regional bloc centered in Arequipa. These groups certainly introduced the Andes to the alien ideas of free trade, and each fought as best it could to put these ideas into practice. Yet, as a free trade "movement," these men were to remain divided, isolated, and illegitimate, no match against the majoritarian protectionists who could forge an effective political alliance. The debility of free trade stemmed from the nature of its supportive groups and from the political fallout of their first confrontations with the nationalists in the 1820s. Rather than enjoying a swift and easy hegemony, Peru's first-generation liberals, in the long string of tariff struggles to come, were defeated time after time by the combined weight of upper-crust and popular protectionist foes.

FAILED FREE-TRADE IMPERIALISTS

The initial foreign consuls, chargés, and ministers to Peru—U.S., French and, above all, British—are frequently charged (on the basis of scant direct evidence) with "free-trade imperialism." It is alleged that the new foreign officialdom coerced, cajoled, or successfully persuaded Peruvian elites to adopt liberal trade policies against their own national interests. (Alternatively, foreign historians have used consular reports to exonerate their nationals from the charge of meddling in the name of free trade.) Peru's leading trade partners, the story goes, met particularly easy success here because of the marked weakness of their prey: the chronically unstable, directionless, and bankrupt Peruvian state.[1] The nonstop interference of consuls in local politics, and their proximity to and intense social relationships with well-placed collaborationists, made them in effect members of the political elite, albeit distinct by dint of their foreign allegiance and origin.

Under close scrutiny, the evidence overwhelmingly supports half the imperialism argument: overseas political interests did indeed intervene massively in Peruvian affairs in a push for free trade, far more, in fact, than historians even imagined. However, the second half of the imperialism equation—that they succeeded—is dead wrong. Over time, the isolation and setbacks of ever-active foreign liberals only intensified.

All three sets of diplomats harbored similar objectives: to expand their commerce with Peru through low uniform import tariffs, guarantees of access and safety for their traders, and trade treaties designed to set a liberal system upon an erratic Peruvian state. Part zealous missionaries of the new universalist doctrines of free trade, part cynical defenders of their countries' narrow economic interests, the consuls as a group shared one broad vision. Their ultimate aim, quipped one famed British envoy, was to make Peru's relation to their countries "one of miner to manufacturer."[2]

Only their specific liberal interests and strategies diverged in this difficult mission. The British worked mainly to promote the consignment trade of their large import houses in Lima, their bondholders and their ancillary export-import activities in the south. British interventions in trade politics appear sporadic, yet most approximated a genuine neoimperial strategy. Informed by a "realist" assessment of the antiforeign proclivities of the Peruvian elite (and of the instability endemic to Peruvian politics), the British chose to throw political support to extraregional military forces. These liberal surrogates (e.g., the Bolivian General Santa Cruz) could forcibly impose the full weight of a free-trade regime upon Peru's notoriously recalcitrant elites.[3] Once established, these proxy regimes were to provide a stable institutional framework for massive British investments in exports and state finance, thus transforming Peru into an integral outpost of the expanding British world economy. British efforts climaxed in the mid-1820s (with Consul Ricketts' intimate ties to Bolivarians) and the mid-1830s (with B. H. Wilson's active sponsorship of the Peru-Bolivia Confederation of Santa Cruz). Yet when the British saw their great liberal hopes falter—as inexorably occurred—they rapidly withdrew from Peruvian politics or adopted purely defensive postures against the ensuing attacks by Peruvian nationalists. For the British, it was all or nothing—a sensible attitude indeed, since their overall stake in Peru counted for little in global terms. In any case, British goods and traders were not really the main target of Peruvian protectionists.[4]

The fact is that the scale and persistence of British free-trade campaigns pale beside those of their closest rivals, the impetuous North Americans. Contrary to prevailing historiography, the United States was Peru's most strategic trade partner in the aftermath of independence and, consequently, placed the most aggressive agents in Peruvian trade politics.[5] Yankee shippers dominated the critical flour and coarse-textile trade to the north-central coast (which deflected commerce from the region's coveted Chilean connection), were most conspicuous in coastwise shipping, and included in their realm of influence the key urban, market, and political arena of Lima. Unlike the initially upscale British trade, the staples brought by U.S. merchants posed an immediate challenge to the most commercialized and organized sectors of the Peruvian economy. (This is not surprising, for the two economies shared related market structures and factor endowments, marked by a technologically simple agro-industry geared to mass consumption.) In contrast to European goods, the U.S. exports of the 1820s were competitive with, not complementary to, the Peruvian economy. Consequently, the influential Lima-elite protectionists, merchants, and planters immediately targeted U.S. trade, aiming to eliminate the North American presence altogether, through complete import prohibitions or the galvanizing alternative of a closed market system with Chile.[6]

The United States fought back tooth and nail, in a relentless series of political interventions to maintain this pivotal commercial foothold astride the Pacific basin. North American efforts culminated in a decade-long free-trade drive from 1827 to 1837, orchestrated by their energetic, ubiquitous, and imaginative chargé d'affaires, Samuel Larned. Sometimes, an ersatz Anglo-American rivalry was invoked to excite Washington, but the true stake was the virtually $2 million in trade; the true enemy, Peruvian nationalism. U.S. tactics contrast sharply with British liberal strategy. Rather than remain aloof from Peruvian politics (which the United States could ill afford to do), consuls enthusiastically jumped into the messy ring of local political struggles. They hoped to win over, piecemeal, the hearts and minds of decisive allies among liberal or converted members of the Peruvian political elite. With each new tariff controversy, the United States launched new missionary efforts in an endless quest to sway Peruvian "Publick Opinion," cultivate high-ranking clients, or strong-arm congressional voters. The U.S. approach is exemplified by the fact that North American consuls actually produced (clandestinely) much of the liberal propaganda of the era, defining the terms of early debates. The covert printing press, made ready for each ensuing congressional tariff controversy, might just as well epitomize the frailty of Peru's homegrown liberalism. Washington ordered this special Larned mission to "revoke" Peru's unfriendly trade policies (and made no fuss over the extra printing bills). Yet, despite the daily pitch of multifarious interventionist activity, few Peruvians rallied to the U.S. cause, and the campaign dragged on fruitlessly over the decade.[7]

French diplomats, on the other hand, were at once the least important and most hostile participants in Peruvian trade politics. Out mainly to safeguard the petty luxury trades of the dozens of French retailers based in Lima, French officials adopted a third strategy. Instead of concerted efforts to win allies, change tariff laws, or augment trade, the French

20

relied on intermittent displays of military might aimed at inculcating Peruvian officials with a healthy respect for the property rights of French nationals. The "moral effects" of French gunboats, however, were short-lived, requiring frequent applications, since coercion itself evoked new rounds of anti-French sentiment, particularly among Lima's excitable shopkeepers.[8] The French also conducted a relatively diplomatic campaign to lower the extraordinarily high imposts on French wines, brandies, and crafts—protests diplomatically ignored by Peruvian officials over three decades.

If the campaigns by foreign officialdom fared poorly, overseas private interests (in some ways more closely enmeshed with Peruvian elites) made even less headway against hostile trade policies and practices. Associated with the top-twenty import firms that replaced the *peninsular* import elite after 1821, the four hundred or so new resident foreigners in the Lima of the 1820s were by instinct and profession fervent liberals. Three avenues lay open for Atlantic merchants to spread their free-trade gospel. While often cited as the major ways a free-trade imperialism on private account operated in Peru, in fact each was blocked to foreign merchants until the mid-1840s.

First, free trade could filter into the Peruvian body politic via business clients and contacts near at hand: the scores of leading national merchants dependent on foreign houses for overseas goods, credit, and graces. As will be seen, the embryonic national commercial elite (which was the closest Peru had to a dominant class) staunchly resisted any political blending with their overseas suppliers. Instead, from the earliest days of independence, reliance on foreigners actually had an opposite effect—mounting merchant antipathy to foreign interests—and the national merchant class came to form the wellspring of nationalist ideas among the Peruvian elite.[9] This paradox—indicative of the whole pattern of Peru's risky new entry into the world economy—will be explained shortly.

A second possibility was direct foreign-merchant immersion in liberal trade politics. Given their unusually exposed position in Peru's volatile political scene, no leading merchant dared follow this path. The risks far outweighed possible gains; business survival itself depended entirely on cordial and "neutral" relationships with revolving Peruvian authorities. Otherwise, foreign merchants could easily become the favored targets of nationalist politicians and even, on occasion, mobs, with disastrous results. Foreigners remained foreign to Peruvian political institutions: for example, they were explicitly barred from the influential native-merchant consulado. Only those with nothing to lose—small or itinerant peddlers or "meddlers"—ever gambled in Peruvian politics (and usually lost), and these were the men (like auctioneers) least able or interested

21

in changing trade policy.[10] Similar constraints precluded indirect strategies to undermine high tariffs, such as the often-claimed use of contraband. The clear risks of smuggling were an effective deterrent to established houses, at least in Lima where policy took shape.[11]

The last option for the capital-rich foreign houses lay in their capacity for financial inducement, legal or otherwise. Here, too, the foreign liberals proved to be intelligent risk-averters. Lending to the bankrupt Peruvian state, or bribing officials and caudillos for specific trade concessions, was economically and politically unprofitable—but, above all, fraught with danger.[12] Hard experience with loans during the early 1820s taught foreigners several indelible lessons: loans were rarely repaid, rarely produced reliable tariff reductions (not even better treatment), and invariably exposed merchants to the arbitrary perils of escalating exactions and forced loans, often of a retaliatory stripe. These risks loomed even larger outside Lima and the major ports. (In long-distance finance—the formal bond market of London—Peru proved to be a dead risk upon its summary and indefinite default on more than £1.8 million in independence-era loans.) The local foreign-merchant community thus quickly realized that financial entanglements of any kind were the chief threat to profitability and survival in Peru, far overshadowing the discriminatory trade policies themselves. Their economic resources did not translate into power against predatory caudillos—they made them sitting ducks.

With the concerted help of the consuls—the only realm where coercion proved workable—the core foreign merchants made clear by the late 1820s their principled refusal to fund caudillo regimes and conflicts, no matter what their ideological complexion or promises on trade policy. This enforceable tax exemption amounted to a kind of de facto "extraterritoriality" in Peru's convulsive environment, and these lower risks surely helped foreigners consolidate their primacy in the import trades.[13] Yet, it simultaneously cost foreigners their most promising tool for molding commercial policy. In the fiscal sphere (which by Peruvian norms defined one's basic juridical and political relationship to the local polity), the liberal foreign elite proved inimical to full integration with Peruvian society. Despite the obvious (and growing) economic and social standing of foreign businessmen, they remained outsiders, whose liberal beliefs counted for little in trade politics.[14] In the global perspective, it was the Peruvian state itself, such as it was, that had failed in integration through liberal world finance. When Peruvian politics and finance finally settled in the 1850s, this context for foreign influence would dramatically change.

Merchants and lenders aside, all three cliques of foreign diplomats, whatever their tactics, ultimately failed in their liberalization crusades. If we condense a good deal of intriguing political history, the essential fact is that the 1840s transition to free trade in Peru—when the elites and state first reconsidered their protectionist orthodoxy—occurred in a truly xenophobic context, when foreign political influence had reached its lowest ebb. The British might temporarily press for, and shore up, their surrogate liberal empires, but bereft of any local social base, these quickly collapsed, bringing on anti-British pogroms. Twice Britain withdrew (even its diplomats) from the scene, in 1828–33 and 1839–45, or was forced to devote all energy to the physical defense of its merchants from the discrimination, depredations, and outright attacks their own interventions evoked. This nationalist backlash more than rolled back any British gains in policy.[15]

The United States suffered a more drawn out, and lasting, defeat. None of its local political allies, so assiduously cultivated, proved capable or even willing to overcome the forces of Lima protectionism, targeted so clearly against U.S. interests. North American propaganda failed to enlighten South American opinion. The bald U.S. intervention into Peruvian politics worked only to further taint free trade as a hopelessly "foreign" cause. Each and every tactic (or antic) of the increasingly enervated Mr. Larned spawned its antithesis in nationalist obstructionism, especially in Congress. By the late 1830s, despite some fleeting successes, North American commercial and political stock had plummeted in Peru. By 1840, U.S. officials abandoned all pretense of changing Peruvian commercial policies, devoting their flagging energies to the retrospective task of collecting old damage claims for North American merchants.[16] Ironically, in several ways, this U.S. defeat determined the subsequent age of British supremacy in Peru once the liberal order of the guano age took shape. British economic interests had expanded as U.S. trade suffered its beating. The French, with their sporadic violence and threats, became progressively less safe and popular in Peru, a symbolic affront to growing Peruvian sovereignty and nationalism.[17]

Among a host of specific political circumstances that explain the fiascos of foreign liberalism, two general factors stand out. First, the very "weakness" of the Peruvian state, which at first glance historians assume made a victory by powerful foreigners inevitable, was actually the greatest obstacle to foreign interests. The chronic instability of caudillo-style Peruvian governments, politics, and finance paradoxically protected national economic sovereignty in a larger sense. Each time the consuls managed to make a liberal dent, their favored regime or allies quickly fell from office. In one memorable year alone, for example, consuls had to consult nine different ministers of foreign affairs, absent half of the time. No lasting liberalization was possible by means of free-trade imperialism alone, for no foreign power could ever hope to stabilize, much less capture, Peruvian political institutions.[18] (Nor did Peru exhibit a "statelessness" of the sort that would draw Europeans into direct rule elsewhere in the nineteenth century—Peru possessed a recognizable core of westernized functionaries willing to deal with foreign powers, if on their own terms.) In many ways, foreign interventions complicated the original dilemma, stimulating a perpetual nationalist backlash that translated very readily into trade policy. Antiforeign tirades turned into a war cry of Peru's leading disaffected caudillos, perhaps the easiest way to discredit specific officials and mobilize for revolts.[19] Interventions weakened the position of liberals in the elites, feeding further instability and polarization that ultimately (by the early 1840s) led to total state disintegration. And if intrusions by foreign states proved risky and counterproductive in this clime, their wary merchants stayed completely out of the fray. Peru's main asset against foreign domination, then, was sheer unpredictability.

Second, as a general proposition, the precondition for success of nineteenth-century free-trade imperialism lay in the existence and cooperation of a strong, local "collaborator elite" that, for their own profit, would mediate, construct, and enforce the wishes of North Atlantic traders and nations. Once established, the imperium of free trade was conceived as a relatively costless and self-regulating hegemony of the metropole, diametrically opposed to the inefficient, bureaucratic, and precapitalist Spanish colonialism it replaced.[20] In Peru, however, this critical element was entirely missing: British, U.S., and French free traders found no such willing and dependable collaborators. They discovered instead that their "natural" allies in the elite—practically the entire spectrum of agrarian, commercial, and financial interests—were vehemently antiforeign, loathing the very notion of "free trade." Even efforts to nurture collaborators, exemplified by the secret North American press, had no perceptible impact.[21] In the very long run, the "compradors" would emerge, but primarily from Peruvian processes of change.

How does the Peruvian evidence on foreign elites relate to long-standing general debates on nineteenth-century free-trade imperialism? It affirms and denies aspects of opposing schools, and it shows a more interactive process between external and internal actors. Foreign powers were anything but the withdrawn innocents abroad portrayed in most European historiography. The British, French, and U.S. imperialists tried their best to mold Peruvian trade policy—efforts that in many instances altered the course of local political struggle. But neither were they omnipotent, able to translate their economic prowess into "control," as many Latin Americanists suppose. Strong states could not automatically subdue weak states. The missing variable in both blame-seeking interpretations was the structure of political and economic risk, if not the entire sphere of politics itself.[22] The "excessive" weakness of the early state (and this instability coupled with its excessive bankruptcy) made Peru impenetrable to *direct* external political control or to financial integration into a liberal world economy. This, however, leaves discussion at the level of blunt billiard-ball pressures. *Indirectly*, as becomes apparent, the external actors wielded enormous impact by defining the broadest options available—fiscal, political, regional, entrepreneurial—both for national elites and their incipient state.

Dashed Bolivarian Dreams

The dearth of sturdy collaborators for overseas liberal-trade interests should not be taken to suggest a total absence of liberal groups in the region. Three identifiable sets of liberal elites operated in postindependence Peru: "Bolivarians"; the ideological "internationalist" pressure group of high civil functionaries; and a diffuse regionalist movement led by southern economic elites. Besides weakness in numbers, however, this first generation of Andean free traders shared another disadvantage: they remained isolated from one another and were politically incapable of expanding into a national liberal alliance that could conquer (much less build) the Lima state. Only the southern liberals would survive to affect Peru's actual transition to free trade in the late 1840s; that is, when such an alliance finally became feasible. Like the foreigners without collaborators, Peru's first liberal elites lacked a meaningful social base.

Strictly speaking, Bolivarians were foreigners, too, and foreign invaders at that. Before their liberalism helped trigger "Peruvian" nationalism itself, the prelude to Peru's actual definition as a separate polity, the Bolivarians remained a regional force. (Even after, Peruvian nationalists continued to distinguish their South American brethren from the North Atlantic heathen.) The Bolivarians also bequeathed a few liberal orphans to Peruvian soil: a weak wing of military chiefs, *técnicos*, and *políticos* loyal to Bolívar's vision long after the Liberator's forced exit in 1827.

Both liberators of Peru, San Martín and Bolívar, were free traders by conviction, not out of political expediency alone, which perhaps explains why they played trade politics so poorly in Peru. Their personal visions for an independent South America had coalesced in the two most dynamic commercial territories of Bourbon liberalism, La Plata and Caracas—areas that saw Anglo-Saxon merchants more as allies than rivals. Elsewhere, their free-trade proclamations, and those for de facto liberal alliance with North Atlantic capitalism, helped rally elite support against restrictive Spanish colonialism.[23] In conservative Peru it did not. Both San Martín and Bolívar arrived in Lima eager to transplant free trade by fiat, in 1821 and 1824, in the naive hope that free-trade ideas could survive and wean wary Lima elites from their royalist sympathies. In the case of San Martín, historians now clearly recognize how free trade backfired, mobilizing limeño elites against independence—a key factor in San Martín's 1821–23 Peruvian fiasco.[24] For Bolívar, who marked a generation, the negative consequences were at least as severe.

Opposition to Bolívar's planned trade policies played a critical role in inciting (or inventing) the Peruvian nationalism that ousted the Colombian occupiers from 1826 to 1827. Palpable grievances against the new freedoms and lower tariffs Bolívar promised to foreign traders in 1826, the exile of prominent merchant-dissenters (and their Chilean-Argentine allies), moves to denationalize mines (for debts), and well-publicized plans to make Peru into a liberal British protectorate aroused as much contention as his more flamboyant authoritarian political designs. (The two, Bolivarian liberalism and authoritarianism, moved hand in hand in Peru, on the simplest grounds that free trade remained so unpopular there.) Elite Lima merchants organized this resistance, launching broad appeals to "popular" artisans, miners, and shopkeepers, agitated already by the initial effects of foreign competition. Lima shopkeepers proved most effective as shock troops against Colombian forces during the mob and political confrontations of 1826–27; in fact, the 1820s opening to "free trade" had most directly hurt the native retailing classes.[25]

Apart from the gathering storm of anti-free-trade interests—who deftly combined anti-Colombian invective with economic-nationalist demands—liberals faced internal obstacles to success. The only national stronghold even potentially poised to support free trade in the 1820s, the arequipeño aristocracy, was far from Lima, both geographically and socially. Moreover, disillusioned with Bolívar's centralist political scheme, federalist southern leaders such as Luna Pizarro actually spearheaded the final political challenge to Bolivarians in Congress. Separated by geography and radically different conceptions of the state, early free-trade elites could not act as a unified bloc. Instead, influential southern liberals helped throw Bolivarian troops and collaborators out of Lima, and then watched helplessly as the new Peruvian nationalism became ever more defined in economic (and limeño) terms. This movement climaxed with the "prohibitions" policy of 1828, the fruit of Peru's first genuinely national (and bitterly anti-Bolivarian) Congress.[26] The string of wars against adjoining Bolivarian states would provide even more ammunition to advancing nationalists and northern caudillos. Anti-Colombian camouflage continued to cover economic nationalists well into the 1830s.

Three legacies stemmed from the mid-1820s anti-Bolivarian struggles, political complications that hampered free trade over the next generation. First, free trade became tainted as an irredeemable "foreign" cause, the antithesis of Peruvian nationality (antinationalism was nowhere intrinsic to the concept of free trade). Its connection to North Atlantic interests was only part of the problem. Second, free trade also acquired its antipopular cast. Early liberal elites showed nowhere near the talent or inclination to cater to restless popular groups (e.g., shopkeepers and artisans) as protectionists could and did. Both nationalism and republicanism became, in a sense, protectionist property, increasing the protectionists' mobilization range.[27] The failure of liberalism was, in part, just as some historians suggest, a failure of antiseptic social reactionaries unwilling to consider the plight of Peru's popular classes. Third, free trade was firmly (if paradoxically) associated with authoritarian centralism, blunting the appeal for its sole natural constituency, Peru's federalist liberals of the south. (The Yankee republicans, too, soon abandoned Bolívar out of a parallel political disgust.) This political legacy endured until the mid-1840s, when a new brand of decentralist, regionalist liberal surfaced in Peru, independently, without historical relation to Bolivarian free trade. To some degree, these political handicaps represented the genuine distribution of losses and gains from freer trade. Together they doomed any national liberal alliance.

A more renowned Bolivarian legacy was caudillismo. The Liberator's Andean lieutenants rapidly divided into rival military cliques that would fight over Peru for some two decades after 1825. A few caudillos remained loyal to the Bolivarian ideal of turning greater Peru into an "emporium of free trade," itself an extension of Bourbon policies. The majority read the political signs correctly and defected to the protectionist camp. Andean caudillos, generally portrayed in personalistic terms alone, actually espoused well-defined trade policies; despite fluctuations tuned to the changing fiscal and political climate, their programs also linked up with recognizable regional or social blocs. Generals Nieto, Orbegoso, Vivanco, Vidal, and Santa Cruz emerged as liberal caudillos, mainly associated with the free-trade aspirations of southern regionalism. Until the 1840s, however, such caudillos (along with some civil functionaries brought up in the Bolivarian milieu) were hopelessly outclassed, particularly in the strategic north (and interior), by self-proclaimed nationalist warriors—the gamarristas—their leader Gran Mariscal Agustín Gamarra, and such followers as La Fuente, Salaverry, Torrico, Eléspuru, Iguaín, San Román, and Castilla. For their part, the free-trader Bolivarian caudillos, like Bolívar himself, lacked a secure and broad social base in Peruvian territory. Thus, for example, Santa Cruz's proto-Bolivarian Peru-Bolivia Confederation (1836–38) would remain largely dependent on outside forces, a formula that sealed its overrun by the nationalist caudillo "party," itself helped from Chile.[28] More will be said about the liberal and nationalist caudillos; however messy the alignments and the congeries of issues at play, trade policy became a recurrent theme in the militarist struggles.

27

THE INTERNATIONALISTS, PERU'S WORLDLY PHILOSOPHERS

The second group of would-be national liberals were ideologues and state functionaries best called the "internationalists," including such distinguished members of the political class as Manuel de Vidaurre, José María de Pando, Juan García del Río, and Manuel del Río. Stepsons of the Bolivarian occupation, these men never tired of expounding their liberal plans, frequently from high posts in the finance and foreign ministries, and seemed (at least at first) especially cozy with North American interests. In their origins, these men reflected what one recent historian aptly calls the Atlantic "network of trade and revolution," even in distant Peru. García del Río, Colombian by birth and a frequent socio-tourist in England, had served San Martín and Bolívar on finance missions to London; Vidaurre (a key convert to free trade) wrote from Boston; the ubiquitous Pando enjoyed extensive Continental and Bolivarian contacts.[29] (The foreign liberals were deeply enmeshed, too. B. H. Wilson, the aggressive British consul, had been Bolívar's trusted aide-de-camp in the 1820s, and Larned trained against Chilean protectionists before moving on to tougher foes in Peru.)

Yet they were also internationalist in the deeper sense of what they wanted: an economic transformation far more sweeping than merely lowering the elevated tariffs that mushroomed in the dark cave of Bolivarian defeat. What they envisioned was the development of a full international export economy directly integrated with rising Atlantic commerce. This was a far cry from Peru's timeworn provincial patterns of Pacific commerce and comparative advantage, and even farther from postindependence Lima's regional dependence on costly European transshipments from Chile. Apart from lower tariffs, they advocated lifting all restrictions on bullion production and trade and, as centerpiece, the creation of a *puerto franco* in Callao. The latter had considerable significance, as a veritable "commercial revolution." A free port, with incentives including unlimited storage and transshipment rights, would turn Peru into the leading commercial entrepôt for direct European imports in the eastern Pacific. Moderate taxation of direct overseas commerce, which had bypassed risky Peru for Valparaíso since the eve of independence, and tolerant, even effusive, treatment of foreign importers, would provide revenues and stimulus for a new style of liberal development, enhanced by the nontraditional and tropical exports imagined up and down the coastline of Peru.[30] In this scenario, Chile—rapidly implementing a similar commercial strategy, and playing to the hope of Peruvian protectionists seeking a commercial union of Pacific states—became Peru's natural competitor, if not archenemy. The internationalists were not simple "modernizers": the impending conflict was between men of the Atlantic and the Pacific.

Off and on during the 1830s, the internationalists were catapulted into power by friendly or desperate caudillos, entranced by lavish promises of instant revenue. Yet all their frenetic activism, conspiracies, decrees, and "Political Economy" sermons, as in 1831–33, came to naught. (Pando was the chief player in a political game of musical chairs that took him in and out of the ministries of Finance and Foreign Affairs at least a dozen times.) Their schemes of liberalization from the top were nonetheless blocked by Congress and other disaffected groups. It was they who first spoke of Smith and Say—theorists then invariably lambasted by the public as "slavish," "inappropriate," and "ruinous" for Peru. ("Hypocrisy" was the standard charge. If novices in economic theory, Peruvians scored high on economic history and practice, as they constantly reminded internationalists and foreigners alike of the critical role of restrictions in the North Atlantic's own worldly ascent.) In the end, Pando, usually regarded as the "father" of Peruvian free trade, was, if anything, an impotent one.[31] The reason is simple: the internationalists remained mere philosophers with no palpable support. All their expected elite allies—central to the plan—opposed the grand scheme.

First and foremost, Peruvian merchants would have to comply with the liberal transformation of Callao import structures, when in fact the Lima consulado (as we will learn) viewed internationalist trade strategy as anathema. Merchants, for a range of motives, yearned instead to revive their once lucrative local patterns of trade, especially with Chile; thus sheltered, they might recover from the vacillations of direct foreign commerce, which had taken such a toll in the 1820s.

Second, central-sierran mining interests, the sole functional export sector in the aftermath of independence, would have to rally as well. Instead, silver miners (who, in the decentralized structure of Peruvian mining, barely ranked as "elites") expressed no particular leanings toward free trade. Miners had fought vehemently against Bolivarian attempts to open the sector to international speculators in the 1820s, seemed willing to live with the state's neomercantilist bullion practices, harbored but modest pockets of full-time workers for whom to cut costs, and above all were highly dependent on (if not intertwined with) the persons and credit of the Lima merchant guild, that formidable redoubt of anti-internationalist fervor. The mining guilds, which otherwise might have focused liberal issues, were historically weak in Peru, no match for the centralized consulado. While fecund ground for other sorts of liberal social concerns and, paradoxically, the prop of Peru's export capacity, the central highlands stayed largely within the limeño orbit of trade and politics. Other potential exporters, like the north's influential sugar planters, wishing too upon a Chilean star, were even less enthused.[32] The internationalists' third possible base comprised southern liberals. For a variety of reasons (most notably that internationalists, like others, favored Lima development), little response echoed here. The south coast, and its new Britons, wanted its own free ports, not dependence on a grand Lima entrepôt. In short, like their Bolivarian forefathers, the internationalists operated from within the Lima state, a poor platform indeed from which to spread their Atlantic gospel near and far. Finally, the genuine financial elites of caudillismo—as will be shown—were zealous partisans of nationalist trade and fiscal policies, which went hand in hand with political strife. Fiscal instability, rather than drive officials to the internationalists, would drive a thorn into the liberal side.[33] The internationalist vision could never advance beyond the blueprint stage until the late 1840s— long after these theoretical liberals had vanished from a transformed political scene.

THE LIBERAL WAR OF SOUTHERN SECESSION

Native liberalism had one other potential source of support besides this scattered assortment of post-Bolivarian caudillos and ideologues: southern agriculturalists, exporters, and merchants. From Moquegua to Ica, with Arequipa as its core, lay a vast incipient social ground for Peruvian free traders. Arequipeño liberalism grew from four main roots: a general orientation toward southern markets; distance from the colonial institutional matrix of Lima; "oppression" by monopolistic limeño commercial policies; and incentives from new British-led regional exports such as nitrates, quinine, and wool. Rumblings of differentiation and resistance were first heard by the Bourbon reformers of the 1780s. Yet the promise of true liberal elites exceeded the reality. The movement remained incipient, fraught with contradictions, and proved incapable of merging with other liberals until the 1840s. Instead, the south opted to secede, failed, and rose again.

While northern—and limeño—economic elites collectively gravitated toward Chilean markets and protectionism, southern agriculturalists saw Bolivia as their mecca. "Upper Peru" and the southern sierra had been thriving traditional markets for late-colonial coastal wine and brandy producers, and a ragtag army of southerners earned their livelihood in transport and commercial services (from alfalfa farmers and muleteers up to huge international merchant firms) handling the influx of products into the altiplano. For myriad economic and political reasons (typical of the complications wreaked by Latin America's early nineteenth-century "balkanization"[34]), Bolivia and Chile made wholly incompatible commercial allies for independent Peru, thus effectively dividing the country into two broad zones of commercial interests, north and south.

The larger commercial dynamics at work started with the creation of Bolivia and with Bolivia's creation of a new nationalist import route through its own desert outpost, Cobija, in the mid-1820s. With the help of discriminatory duties, this port diverted traffic from Bolivia's more "natural," closer (and Peruvian) link to the outside, the port of Arica. Chilean interests also favored this new arrangement—transshipments for Cobija traveled through Valparaíso—which meant in turn endorsement by Peru's northern elites, ever anxious to retain their Chilean markets and impress Chilean authorities. Naturally, southern Peruvians, who suffered the brunt of intermittent trade wars with Bolivia across all reaches of the regional economy, were incensed. They needed open frontiers with Bolivia, coveted direct imports through Arica-Islay, and opposed all Chilean pretensions. This meant a southern liberal alliance with Bolivia—or at least with those segments of that (also) divided country who were seeking free trade. Besides sparking a bewildering array of international alliances, tensions, wars, and policies between 1825 and 1845, internally, in ever-clearer fashion, this commercial axis pitted the Peruvian south against the north.[35]

More concretely, emerging southern and northern elites were at loggerheads over a series of critical trade issues. For example, southern grape distillers saw themselves as "ruined" by the postindependence conversion of northern sugarcane into the cheap alcohol that flooded sierran markets; the fertile Arequipa granary appeared mortally threatened by the Chilean wheat imports encouraged by northern pressure groups; the lingering southern wool *obrajes* wanted restored access to Bolivian markets and seemed to blame the free trade in textiles on Lima; and southern desert enclaves (such as Iquique) needed the duty-free food supplies blocked by Lima.[36] Then, too, arequipeño merchants, while dependent upon Lima, desperately hoped to break the closed port system upheld by the Lima consulado, which increased costs through transshipment surcharges and eclipsed all local commercial autonomy (e.g., through costly legal suits that had to be settled in the capital). For the south, lack of free trade for Peru meant little freedom to trade within Peru. Moreover, the relatively rapid initiation of new regional exports— wool, nitrates, and cinchona bark in the 1830s—spurred along by British investment and organization, gave southerners, but not the other Peruvian elites, some hope that a profitable future might indeed lie in changing comparative advantages and free trade. (This contrasts sharply with the north, where many regional economies had lain in unrelieved decay since the early eighteenth century.) And cheap British imports were gradually extending Arequipa's commercial sphere toward Cuzco itself, opening new avenues for those southern elites pushed out of competing activities. Only proud *cuzqueños*, of the old south, might object to Arequipa's growing commercial sway.[37] Finally, institutional and social—even mental—frameworks in the south differed from those of the north; as one example, slavery, still a vigorous institution in northern agrarian and town life, was by 1820 practically extinct south of Cañete. This, too, was reflected in trade disputes.

Despite these classic incentives at play, the southern liberal impulse remained, at least until the 1840s, too weak and isolated to serve as the social pillar of a national free-trade "movement." Regional *hacendados* were still not hard-core liberals; for example, in inconsistent fashion, they fought to ban all foreign wine imports (notably, the French wines savored by Lima aristocrats) and grains (favored by Lima's plebes). Initially, the new British merchant presence stirred little welcome in arequipeño commercial circles, who felt just as beleaguered as other native merchants by the foreigners' rapid inroads into local trade, all the more so because British development was so visible here. In fact, the south produced the sharpest nationalist outbursts (repeated calls to oust foreign merchants, periodic mob attacks on consuls), punctuating its painful transition into the British orbit. While the Confederation might be read as the south's incipient foreign free-trade alliance, the benefits of British expansion into Arequipa's market area remained clouded until the 1840s. The old protectionist strongholds of Cuzco were eroding only gradually, as the austral nitrate regions slowly added new territories to Arequipa's liberal realm.[38] And in the context of this imperfect alignment with Britain, North American trade was just barely perceptible in the south, ensuring that an alliance with Peru's most articulate and active liberals could never develop.

Perhaps most important, in political terms, Arequipa seemed destined to remain a "regional" liberal movement. The south leaned toward liberal secessionism, not hegemony. Its spokesmen, despite other affinities, would have little truck with the centralized liberal state proposed by Bolívar and the internationalists. Federalism, decentralized liberalism, was essential to their cause, as much as reintegration with Bolivia. If trade were not enough, a dozen causes bloomed, intent on keeping political distance between Arequipa and its former colonial satrapy. Yet Peru's geographic reality worked against the south exerting much pull over the "national" Lima state (where trade policies were resolved), a state whose effective influence, even if disposed to consider southern demands, rarely extended beyond the central coast.[39] The south, in short, was neither "integrated" into the initial Peruvian state nor strong enough to conquer it and create anew.

This left rebellion under regionalist caudillos such as Vivanco and

Santa Cruz as the sole avenue for altering commercial policies. By the late 1820s, Arequipa emerged as the legendary "pueblo caudillo" of Peru, a political reunification with Bolivia their utopian aim. The south's peculiar commercial-political aspirations always played a critical role in the smoldering regional revolts of the 1830s and 1840s, revolts whose impact became ever more serious for Peru with the international complications of shifting Bolivian and Chilean allies.[40] Liberal caudillismo acquired a distinct separatist flavor, for a lasting conquest of the protectionist/centralist north soon proved impossible within Peru's prevailing military and political balance. The main legacy of this southern liberal separatism was the chronic instability—political stalemate—of the postindependence era, not free trade.

Paradoxically, southern liberalism established its foothold in Lima in the mid-1840s, following the region's effective pacification (then forced integration) by the expanding Lima state. It was not just a steadier and broader liberal impulse from provincial economic elites. By then, northern protectionism was itself in disarray and, for reasons that will soon become clear, the emerging "Castillan" state proved amenable to the free traders streaming in from the south.[41] By 1850, free trade had finally become an integrative, not divisive, ingredient in the formation of an elite national state.

Free traders were few, far between, foreign, feeble, and factionalized in postindependence Peru. The liberal proclivities of later elites were as yet unknown. The stellar liberals were actually foreign consuls, mainly U.S., who nonetheless failed to win free trade with their multifarious pressures. They could not succeed in the absence of a stable collaborating elite and state. Foreign merchants shied from involvement, knowing all too well the risks. Would-be liberal allies, the Bolivarians and their internationalist orphans, were easily outgunned by nationalist forces, for both groups lacked a credible economic constituency. The only tangible indigenous liberal movement arose in the south, yet was truncated by the very regionalism of its liberal aspirations. In any case, the odds were set against the liberals from the start. For Peru was dominated by powerful protectionist elites.

CHAPTER 3

The Protection of Elites

THE OVERWHELMING majority of Peruvian elites—landed, agro-industrial, commercial, and bureaucratic—were anything but free traders in the postindependence era. These sectors were similar in composition and influence to the commercialized backbone of the traditional viceregal economy, that is, the colonial ruling class. By the mid-1820s, despite declining economic fortunes, they reemerged as a widely based, vociferous, and relatively cohesive republican protectionist movement, well-equipped for defeating the scattered band of liberals who could never manage to form a credible free-trade movement. The protectionist program enveloped a vast range of specific proposals (restrictive practices, state monopolies, and global trade strategies, as well as tariffs) but was held together by a common ideological bond: economic nationalism. At times, protectionists still resorted to prestigious colonial mercantilist thought—which enjoyed a revival in the 1820s as Peru's balance-of-payments crisis drained off currency while barely diminishing the depression in demand. But the galvanizing appeal was to newer and broader slogans of economic independence and national development. The nationalist call won support across a full spectrum of social groups and classes, this in a young nation seemingly imperiled at birth by foreign competitors, imperialists, and a shattering economic decline.[1] Plain-and-simple pledges of protection and privilege for myriad economic interests also attracted a following. Yet, five special factors go a long way toward explaining the political viability of elite economic nationalism: its effective regional concentration in the north-central zones critical to the Lima state; the unifying force of its alternative vision of market integration with Chile; its collective representation by Lima's powerful merchant class; its symbiotic origins in chaotic market and political conditions; and its congruence with the peculiar political and financial dynamics of Peru's caudillo state. The present chapter explores these factors and groups contributing to the vitality of Peru's protectionist movement, as well as the reasons for economic nationalism itself.

AGRARIAN NATIONALISTS OF THE NORTH

The starting point for elite protectionism was Peru's postindependence crisis in agrarian markets—local, regional, and foreign. But it would not

34

end there. Latin American landed elites, acting out of traditional concerns as actual or would-be exporters have most commonly formed the core of liberal regimes, their political weight commensurate with their enormous social power in rural society.[2] The atypical stance of Peru's republican coastal oligarchy, however, should not come as too great a surprise. Not only were export markets far off the horizon and regional markets threatened, their last redoubt—their own local consumers—was suddenly threatened by massive new imports of cheaper foodstuffs, the unwanted by-product of separation from Spain.

An economic and social crisis gripped the estates and *chacras* of the central and northern coast at independence. Indeed, the northern commercial economy had been in continual distress since the mid-eighteenth century. Though still integral to the colonial oligarchy, planters had not fared well during the century's string of environmental mishaps, shifting trade, Jesuit expulsions, and disorienting Bourbon initiatives. Sugar, cotton, wine, and foodstuffs producers, from Cañete to Lambayeque, next suffered incalculable direct damage from Peru's prolonged independence struggle, concentrated in the region, including the hard-to-repair disorganization of scarce slave-labor supply and peasant withdrawal from labor systems. By the 1820s, the unremitting economic risk from political upheaval and capital shortage plagued any attempt to rebuild.[3]

Recovery through reorientation to international markets, enhanced by specialization and free trade, was the least plausible solution. For example, for the sugar estates (Peru's most specialized commercial enterprise), international competitiveness had been a questionable prospect even during late colonial rule, given the constraints of stagnant Peruvian technology, rising labor costs, and relative distance from the new isles of overseas consumers. With the 1820s crisis, any such notion became a dead letter. (The first attempt to place Peruvian sugar in European markets, in 1835, proved to be a dismal failure.) Nor could planters expect foreign capital and assistance in modernizing their estates, with a consequent swing to foreign liberal influence.[4] Foreigners were unwilling to assume the financial and commercial risks of Peru's languishing estates; nor would they until the 1850s.

Instead, planters and farmers turned inward. Their best and last option was to regain lost productivity (and social viability) by supplying basic provisions—mainly sugar, cane liquor, lard, livestock, grains, cotton, rice, and tobacco—to nearby urban markets, inland mine centers and, it was hoped, to a revitalized Pacific interregional trade network. Despite the downturn in domestic markets, these at least promised a way out of autarky or estate disintegration. National merchants could provide the modest capital and expertise for this type of recovery. Yet, in their own backyard, a novel, "unfair," and potentially mortal competition suddenly

35

threatened: Yankee shippers and traders, drawn to Pacific shores by the urban food shortages caused by the wars of independence. By 1825, U.S. suppliers had established a foothold in simple staples of mass consumption, close to $2 million a year in flours, cooking fats, tobacco, rum, coarse cottons, and other mainstays of Peru's economically and socially constrained consumers.[5] These simple concoctions of efficient Yankee technology met the simple but faltering technology of Peru. Peruvian hacendados and U.S. merchants alike had staked their survival on the same product markets. Trade war was inevitable.

Hacendados vigorously responded by writing their needs into the earliest tariff laws of the 1820s. Agrarian power, profoundly weakened in other respects since the republic, became strikingly clear in the sphere of trade policy. Safeguarding national markets may well have been their last economic option, but tariffs also provided the most versatile tool for dealing with declining productivity and a host of other difficulties, such as labor supply, that landed interests could not simply legislate away. Historians—distracted by the quixotic attempts to revive dying colonial textile and artisanal industries—tend to overlook the decisive impact of agrarian pressures on nineteenth-century tariff policies. Yet, it is plain to see from the 1820s tariff debates that protectionism for manufacturers was made possible only by the timely compliance and interventions of landed elites in trade politics. Even in 1827–28, Andean textile magnates were losing the battle for prohibitions until the moment their new coastal allies asserted their supportive sway.[6] And the vast majority of products initially shielded from competitors were actually agrarian: grains, hides, lard, sugar, beverages, olives, noodles—in short, anything that could be raised or processed on coastal *fundos* and estates. When full import prohibitions became policy in June 1828, agricultural products again headed the list; indeed, by 1832 (when that list expanded) Peru's famed prohibitions should be interpreted primarily as an agrarian policy, for in practice most other goods were covered in name alone. Tariff incidence also remained consistently highest on agricultural commodities. Steep specific duties, the main technique, often exceeded 300 percent, lasted longest (well into the 1850s), and provided a considerable edge over ad valorem tariffs, since protective rates increased dramatically as import prices continued their postindependence descent.[7]

The main targets were invariably U.S. merchants and, to the south, French wine dealers. Apart from the more conventional tariff instruments, imaginative and mobilizing tactics were used to harass the enemy. For example, to stifle grain imports, rumors germinated that North American flours contained deadly contaminants (dysentery was the favorite story, typhoid fever if that failed to spread). Dutiful officials had no choice but to confiscate and destroy this clear danger to public health. In this sporadic ritual of destruction, barrel after barrel of fine Yankee flour ended up rotting at the bottom of the River Rimac.[8] These campaigns aptly captured the spirit of agrarian nationalism: foreign food competition was itself a disease in the body politic.

Like southern liberalism, northern protectionism was regionally focused. But here regionalism provided clear strategic advantages, and an almost natural capacity to gather provincial, urban, and political allies. Its force was magnified, by 1830, by strong links with other elites committed to the more comprehensive Chilean market project. Popular cultivators, as well, such as the *chacareros* (truck farmers) of Chancay and Lima's own fertile Rimac Valley, were strongly attracted to the patriarchs' crusade. Agrarian protectionists were active in the south, too (but for different products—liquors, wines, and wheat); indeed, in their drive for cane liquor conversion and wheat imports, northern landed groups collided head-on with their southern counterparts. In the north, though, the vast majority of threatened hacendados and *chacras* were located within market range of Lima. The city's integral rural suburbs were a daily reminder of agricultural decadence and dilemmas. In short, the circumscribed national state could not escape their influence (as they had been able to dodge demands by other far-flung elite groups, such as those of the south). Moreover, agricultural crises were dramatized for politicians by the fact that the north-central coast had also emerged as an area visibly shaken by the new U.S. presence, absent from the rest of Peru. Agricultural staples worried politicians in other ways. They provided sustenance for Lima's volatile population (regularity of supply counted more than price in this respect) and played no small role sustaining the state itself, for duties on inelastic mass necessities at Callao (in the range of 1 million pesos) constituted the most reliable, accessible, and collectible items in customs revenues.[9] Hacendados also made use of their close economic and social ties with the limeño elite at the center of trade-policy ferment. Not only Lima merchants, but the leading urban producers and processers—millers, lard-makers, artisan leather workers, and others—maintained primary links with their country suppliers and, in many cases, cousins. Urban aristocrats, guilds, and hacendados also shared the same outlook on slavery; the same Bolivarians, liberals, and foreigners attacking tariffs were painted as the inveterate enemies of this waning but venerated elite institution.[10] Northern caudillos were happy to comply with the protectionists' wishes, including restoration of the slave trade.

Coastal planters could count on interior elites as allies, too. Protectionism moved inland along the timeworn trade routes that coastal producers hoped to maintain. The *encomenderos* and traveling merchants who plied coastal wares in the interior felt the first rumblings of free trade as an abrupt dislocation of traditional trade routes and fairs, and they did their best to prevent actual foreign-merchant penetration. Their cliental ties with coastal suppliers were still stronger than the pull of price. Even the last Andean obraje operators looked to coastal agriculture. It was U.S. cottons, "tocuyos," that first shook them after independence; and in some areas (e.g., La Libertad and Huamanga) their tariff-induced attempts to modernize were to be fed by ample supplies of coastal cotton, which had, as yet, no other outlets. Such intersectoral cotton, textiles, and wage-goods exchange, proposed the protectionists, would provide more integrated markets, employment, and income to Peruvians than the cheaper products of free trade. (Again, north and south proved incompatible, for the south wanted to support their equally archaic but chiefly woolen-textile industry.) And interior landed groups, of whom little is known, most probably strove to uphold the customary crops and networks of interregional trade (in wool, brandy, and grain for the mining camps) jeopardized in many ways by the new staple imports.[11] It was easy for sierran caudillos such as Gamarra to seal a pact with the power establishment of the north coast and Lima.

In sum, by 1830 a clear regional protectionism had blossomed in Peru, integrating a solid north coast, practically all of Lima's elites, and large zones of the adjacent (and south-central) sierra as well. Northern aspirations were defined not only against the proximate intruders from the United States, but in contrast to the more distant trade-policy orientations of the coastal south. An economically endangered traditional north was poised against a rising south hoping for a future in the emergent world economy. The prohibitions period (1828–40), the most radical phase of Peruvian protectionism, reflected the apogee of the northern elite alliance and its agrarian dictates, not just the autarkic dreams of a handful of sierran textile millowners. It is no accident that as caudillo warfare intensified in the 1830s, it pitted north against south. But to understand these developments, one must look at a wider dimension of northern trade policy: the Chilean market.

NATIONALIST INTEGRATION: CHILE

The gathering of northern elites behind tariffs and import bans in order to defend their local realm was a potent beginning for protectionism; yet it was limited by its defensive nature, as a simple aggregation of negative reactions to the threat of new foreign competition. This was not to be the driving force in Peruvian protectionism. That role fell to the burning issue of Chilean market integration. The Chile strategy offered a comprehensive and positive solution to the endemic competitive difficulties of elites, a strategy far beyond tariffs. It galvanized and held together the

northern protectionist bloc, and it lurked behind much of the trade policy and regional political turmoil of the postindependence decades.

At issue was what modern observers would call "regional integration,"
a kind of nineteenth-century Andean Pact. Proponents wanted a tight
commercial alliance between Peru and Chile, to be established by means
of a trade treaty that would lift all barriers between the two economies,
while discriminating sharply against the goods and shipping of all external
powers. The strategy served multiple ends and interests. All told, instead
of a narrowly autarkic (and easily broken) protection of local markets, a
commercial union explicitly designed to exclude North Atlantic interlopers could provide the groundwork for a prosperous regional economy
based on wider trade complementarities.[12] It was thus an alternative both
to Peruvian autarky and to swift, unimpeded integration into the world
economy.

Essentially, integration meant the trade of Peruvian sugar for Chilean
wheat. Inspired by the dynamic commercial complementarity developed
between northern Peru and central Chile in the late colonial period, it
was also a little-noted response to the crippling market and political balkanization brought on by independence and the centrifugal force of free
trade. Historians have long observed that a major adverse consequence
of independence (for many regions) was the swift breakdown of South
American market integration that had formerly (if inadvertently) been
provided by the Spanish metropole. This integration had actually been
increasing throughout the late Spanish American empire, owing to its
policy of freer and more specialized intercolonial commerce. But the new
Latin American republics, suddenly forced to make do with truncated
national markets in the 1820s (and a decay of overland transport), saw
large hinterlands either regress to self-sufficiency or, where feasible, re-
orient their regional economies in outward fashion to foreign trade. Sac-
rificed as a consequence were potential internal spurs to growth as well
as characteristics that ensured national social integration.[13] Until recently, intra-American trade made up only a minuscule portion of Latin
American commerce, an enduring result of developments from the first
few years after independence. In Peru, however, this trend was hotly
resisted in the earliest protectionist programs.

Trade complementarity between Peru and Chile had actually emerged
quite late in the colonial period (unlike the venerable southern Peru–
Upper Peru nexus). But, for that same reason, the advantages of the
Peru-Chile connection were well known to the entrepreneurs who had
guided and prospered from its development. During the eighteenth century, northern estates gave up domestic grain production in order to specialize in sugar, tobacco, liquors, and other semitropical products for the
burgeoning Chilean market. Chile in turn supplied cheaper wheat, pro-

39

cessed into flour in Lima, long the wheat bread capital of South America. In a sense, this trade was independent of the royal (and royally taxed) international commerce of the Andes, based on silver bullion and coin. Here was a response, indeed, to recent Bourbon fiscal pressures and their attempts to break Lima's traditional spheres of commercial influence. The Pacific specialization intensified with the crown's separation of mining Upper Peru from commercial Lima: by 1791, $458,000 in northern sugar and tobacco were exchanged for $629,000 in Chilean grain (in later years, estimates are even larger). Peruvian merchants and shipping magnates organized and controlled this autonomous trade corridor, and invested heavily themselves in the twenty or so large new mills that centralized (or rather, monopolized) bread production and distribution in Lima. One historian of this elite dubs them Peru's new mercantile "aristocracy."[14] The net gains accrued to Peru, in particular to the limeño merchants, via the shipping services responsible for the late viceroyalty's bountiful surplus balance of trade.

The wars of independence (1810–24) temporarily isolated the two markets, but the aftershocks largely destroyed the corridor. Evading the blockades, North Americans had moved in to supply their flours (not wheat) to Lima. Foreign merchants broke into Chilean markets as well, plying comparatively inexpensive Caribbean sugar and tobacco. The once powerful Peruvian merchant marine lay shattered and decapitalized. According to some accounts, the surviving merchant class would lose 90 percent of their capital through destruction and flight. Meanwhile, Chile itself was swiftly emerging, owing to liberal incentives and the convenience of Valparaíso's port facilities, as the chief Pacific entrepôt for European imports. Now Peru became "dependent" on transshipments from its former "dependency" and began to suffer a chronic trade imbalance (only partially caused by the surfeit of Atlantic imports). The greater dependence this forced on disrupted silver mines (and unprecedented money exports) did little to relieve Peru's postindependence depression.

From the mid-1820s, three important Peruvian elite groups—planters, millers, and merchants—merged in a two-decade crusade to reverse these trends and recuperate from the wars on the basis of reintegration with Chile. The northern sugar planters looked to Chilean markets, insulated from competitors, as salvation, hoping that economies of scale could reverse the cost inefficiencies of their fallen haciendas. More than half a million pesos of sugar alone, they calculated, could be shipped to Chile (although the statistics themselves soon became a tool of the struggle). In the early 1820s, many planters (even in Lambayeque) had placed their initial hopes in state-sponsored self-sufficiency projects: namely, quotas for shipments of national wheat to shortage-plagued Lima. When these schemes floundered by 1828, they turned back to sugar and Chile, neatly exemplifying the protectionist move up from autarky. Planters were a force to be reckoned with in Peru. Along with sheltered trade with Chile, they demanded a renewed "free trade" in their chief imported input for increased sugar production: black human chattel.[15]

Peruvian millers, saddled with large fixed investments in mills designed for Chilean wheat, were equally adamant. The flood of North American flour was "annihilating" a huge enterprise predicated on traditional wheat imports or production. Simultaneously prohibiting U.S. goods and reopening Chilean trade would restore milling to its former glory, with all that much more value added for the Lima economy (or at least for its top echelons, its former aristocracy of wealth). The millers were joined, for many reasons, by their clients, Lima's bakers—another "monopolistic" slaveholding elite guild, most with small grinding mills of their own or dependent on miller-patrons. As in most preindustrial cities, the bread sector and the bread question commanded a special economic, symbolic, and political weight, which these elites assiduously manipulated (drawing on popular pressures) for the Lima state.[16] Again, protectionist elites managed to muster mass support, unlike the antiseptic liberals, even though this was an issue that liberals should have won, for U.S. flours might well have cheapened subsistence for Lima's artisans and workers. Officials were drawn to the plan by notions that wheat duties (on the order of $800,000) provided the most reliable state income; moreover, they harbored hopes that Chile might also join Peru in their larger, geopolitical crusade against the surrounding "Bolivarian" states, Gran Colombia and Bolivia.

Peru's agrarian protectionism excited surprisingly little resistance from urban centers. Little free-trade ferment erupted here as in other cities of the nineteenth-century world. Some liberals, to be sure, tried to raise subsistence issues, but they made no headway. One factor was the overwhelmingly rural context of Peruvian society (Lima—until its swift revival in the 1850s—was actually shrinking, to fewer than 55,000 inhabitants, barely 4 percent of the national population). Inward-looking rural patriarchs faced no true political competition in the European mold. No urban "bourgeoisie" as such existed to play that role—excluding the like-minded protectionist traders of Lima. Indeed, one peculiarity of Peru was that the majority of its commercialized "middle sectors" (retailers, provincial merchants, tradesmen, and the like) identified free trade as their mortal policy foe. Intertwined and cliental city politics also helped. For example, in principle limeño artisans abhorred high-cost grain, but they nonetheless refused to endanger their own protectionist standard; instead, they deflected their subsistence anxieties into other outlets such as popular campaigns ("pan barato") to break Lima's bread monopoly. Finally, the urban benefits of free trade were never so clear-cut. Lima's

41

choice was Chilean versus North American grain (and not the pricey local wheats). Foreign productivity and transport advances, in fact, meant that, even when saddled with tariffs, the costs of flour and food, some 21 and 54.5 percent of workers' budgets respectively, would continue their secular decline from 1825 to 1845.[17] (This state of affairs shifted after 1847, when a wage-goods inflation suddenly struck Lima. Only then could liberals, following the new British paradigm, turn living costs into a political tool to divide and pacify the lingering protectionists of a then expanding metropolis.) Before the late 1840s, however, urban subsistence remained a surprisingly moot issue in the protectionist capital, overshadowed even by elaborate debates over the inalienable right of the rich to imported luxuries.

The prime mover behind the Chilean pact, the group that focused and campaigned for the diverse demands of northern and urban producers, was the merchant consulado of Lima. No enthusiasts of free trade to begin with, as we will soon see, the merchant guild was without question the single most organized and influential interest group for the Lima state. The native merchants embraced the cause immediately after independence, making Chile their central theme in trade policy. In some sense, elite merchants were carrying on here their older struggle against the Bourbon legacy and the dismemberment of their commercial empire. The consulado expounded the pact's statistical virtues to finance ministers, opened negotiations with Chile, and threw their unmistakable weight behind those officials and caudillos who exhibited the greatest zeal for the cause.[18]

The merchants had several immediate interests in mind. Above all, they dreamed of removing the new foreign coastwise shippers (mainly U.S. and British) from along their Pacific shores, the first step in rebuilding their shattered merchant marine. An exclusionist pact with Chile looked far more efficacious in this respect than the string of complex navigation acts that had proved inoperable since 1821, and a revived navy strongly appealed to Peru's militarist chiefs.[19] The merchants hoped to reinvest in Pacific shipping under cover of a simpler, protected sugar-and-wheat corridor. Merchants also rightly sensed that commercial competition would be easier in an indirect transshipment trade from Chile (where they stood a chance), so unlike the new direct North Atlantic import trades that quickly relegated them to risky and subordinate roles as "secondhand dealers" for European houses. No Peruvian merchant could go to Liverpool to acquire cheap inventories, but all could make it to Valparaíso and back. Moreover, merchants were already heavily engaged in wheat shipping, storage, and milling (the encomendero group at their Bellavista warehouses); dozens of mobile Chilean and Argentine traders had just naturalized into their ranks after the war; and merchants looked to future benefits from services to a revived sugar industry based on national capital.[20] Alliance with Chile made more sense than tariffs (which did little directly to aid commercial interests) as a way of restoring the consulado's imperial splendor. All in all, the Chilean strategy reinforced restrictions on foreign traders already in place. Yet it also offered a genuine positive structure of opportunity for commercial growth.

The movement for a Chilean pact, mounting in intensity from 1825 to 1840, and the merchant leadership it spawned were the glue that cemented the northern protectionist alliance, the sometimes hidden yet central core of prohibitions-era protectionism. The pact's political trajectory, once these interests were defined, is too sinuous to relate here. Most of the era's frequent policy shifts signified some change in the local balance of forces for or against Chile, and all occurred within a still wider net of international trade rivalries entangling the United States, Bolivia, and Chile. Gamarra pushed harder and harder for the pact after 1828, but somehow (in this complex diplomatic saga) a sealed agreement continued to elude him. So, despite the political dominance of pro-Chilean elites over the Lima state, an actual treaty was effected only briefly in 1835 (by Salaverry, after his classic Lima oligarchic putsch) before being rescinded by Bolivian invaders under Santa Cruz brought in for expressly that task.[21] In short, the definition of the pro-Chilean bloc brought forth a host of diplomatic, regional, and political conflicts, struggles that underlay the larger crisis of delineating and constructing a viable national state in the postindependence period.

The aggressive machinations of the U.S. chargé (directed wholeheartedly against Peru's merchants and planters) were not the primary obstacle to a treaty, although they helped interfere. Not even wholesale offers of North American sugar markets and industrial technology—Larned's most elaborate ploy of the early 1830s—could sway the Chilenophile protectionists. With sometimes ludicrous regularity (whenever ties soured with Chile) Lima officials scurried to the U.S. envoy for help; Larned would promise copious quantitites of grain, duly thrown into the river the instant relations with Santiago improved. In the end, Larned lay defeated; by 1840, U.S. pressures, merchants, and flours became irrelevant to Peru. The British, who had commercial footholds in both the Peruvian and the Chilean market (Britons even helped outfit the Chilean wheat trade), remained aloof; but they were not displeased, it seems, with the ill-treatment afforded Yankee traders and flours. The French seemed even further removed, although in theory their brisk trade with Bolivia made them partisans of the south.[22]

Nor did the "internationalist" intellectuals, whose mission was actually an elaborate response to the Chile strategy, matter in the outcome. Instead of an illiberal union with Chile, they urged that Peru engage in liberal commercial battle with Chile. But first, wielding statistics and theories, they would have to fight Peru's planters and merchants. In internationalist eyes, the pact promised unequal short-term benefits; worse, it doomed Peru to a costly and perpetual dependence on Chilean reexports from Europe. Peru itself could deflect this profitable international trade directly to Callao, if liberalism prevailed in time, and itself emerge as the "emporium of the Pacific." Several finance ministers noticed, and tried to implement these proposals during moments of diplomatic estrangement from Chile.[23] Yet their argument could not translate into reality so long as Peruvian elites moved in the opposite direction. Meanwhile, a web of diplomatic rivalries and intrigues surrounding Chile, Peru, and Bolivia continued to plague northern protectionist efforts.

The greatest obstacle to implementation was the intensification of regional conflict linked to polarization around trade policy. The north, by 1830, was solidly and aggressively protectionist, aimed toward the Chilean star. This fact, however, forced diffuse southern elites, always skeptical of Lima, to define their own regionalist stance. Their response, as seen, was another form of regional integration: a liberal one with Bolivia. In their general focus (Chile versus Bolivia), and in practically the entire range of specific tariff and trade needs associated with the two master plans, the Peruvian north and south became irreconcilable.

Once these lines were drawn by the north's pugnacious dominant class, the conflict generalized into that byzantine spiral of political instability, caudillo warfare, international tensions, invasions, and counterinvasions that characterized the second decade of Peruvian independence. The international complications sparked by Peru's distinct market zones, and by its liberal successionist and national-statist projects, brought rival Chilean and Bolivian elites (and arms) into the fray, inflaming the already serious civil wars. "Gamarrista" forces, representing the consulado, the north coast, and Gamarra's interior following, won Chilean backing in the protracted struggle against the forces gathered around Santa Cruz, representing the south's liberal courtship of Bolivia. Yet, negotiations between Lima and Chile broke down time and time again as new conflicts or international alignments changed the terms of a possible trade alliance.[24]

By 1840, Gamarra (with his Chilean auxiliaries) had smashed the liberal south, but Peru soon collapsed into another round of internecine warfare, this time, however, in an era of transition away from sharp sectional dichotomies concerning trade policy. For two decades, southern liberals had been a persistent thorn in the side of the seemingly unstoppable northern nationalist forces. Most precisely, for more than twenty years trade-policy fissures had prevented the consolidation of a national state in Peru, thwarting in this sense the protectionist as well as the liberal projects. Both sides ran onto the reefs of instability and conflict.

Ironically, the northern victories of the 1840s came at a time when both the urgency and feasibility of the Chilean solution became obsolete. National consolidation would assume a liberal form despite the defeat in the field of southern liberals. Many factors came into play: the new pull of southern liberals forcibly integrated with Lima; the input of informed officials, such as Manuel de Mendiburu, sympathetic to southern grievances; the state's pressing need for new revenues to defend its hard-won but fragile hegemony; the far-reaching first effects of guano. But as soon as Ramón Castilla and his northern nationalist cohorts consolidated power in 1845 (Castilla, no stranger to commercial issues, actually led the bitter campaigns to extirpate liberal *vivanquistas* from the south), they declared Arica a full port of deposit, on a par with Callao. This was a critical move to defuse the festering issue forever.[25] Mendiburu launched a goodwill tour of the south, extending the conciliatory message of the new northern masters. More inadvertently, the Bolivians helped in this task. When Bolivia entered its own protectionist phase under Ballivián in the 1840s (and on and off blocked its borders with austral Peru) this ruled out southern liberal hopes for a Bolivian remedy. The end of the Bolivian option was actually not a calamity for the south. For over the years a shift from the altiplano to the desert (nitrates) would divert southern commercial attentions. For its future, however, the south had to look to, and accommodate, northern Peru.

The Chilean equation was at work, too, though this time in reverse, helping to liberalize the north. Most important here, by the early 1840s a vibrant new trade had emerged between Peru and Chile. It was not the one hoped for by northern elites. Instead, by 1840 an industrializing Chile had replaced the United States as the major exporter of *flours* to the Lima market, to the dismay of the millers and their allies, who were utterly bewildered by these new developments, thorny complications to an ancient dream. Northern planters now also glimpsed their first prospects of overseas markets, with the sharp drop in the 1840s of world transport prices and with new opportunities for supplying Lima's guano-enriched consumers. Foreign houses, assessing the decreasing risks after 1845, began to contact planters about credit, machinery, and the latest sugar and cotton prices abroad. Lima consumers themselves, rocked by a new inflation after 1847, worried more about food costs than about costly and highly theoretical trade alliances. Meanwhile, direct European trade to Callao began to surge after 1837, despite nationalist intentions, which Chile took as a threat to her own geo-economic schemes.[26] Despite allied official postures from 1839, the negotiations for formalizing a Chilean treaty dragged on fruitlessly throughout the 1840s. By 1845, Lima merchants, eyes opening to wider possibilities, could no longer present Chile as salvation for Peruvian elites.

ARTISANS OF PERU DISUNITE

Even with the sway of agrarian (and merchant) politics over initial protectionism, Peru's sundry manufacturing groups and their motley tariff demands also drew considerable attention, and emotion. In many respects, the vociferous controversy of the 1820s–40s paralleled the concerns of economic historians today. Did indigenous industry somehow hold the key to Peru's future possibilities for technological advance, growth, and employment? How could it survive in the meantime, against the cheaper imports of the Atlantic's novel industrial (and transport) revolutions, in order to provide this groundwork for national diversification and autonomy?[27] Colonial Peru, while hardly an industrial giant (royal import shortages spurred its manufacturing), did bequeath three protoindustrial sectors for republicans to worry over: textile obrajes, rural cottage artisans, and urban craft guilds. A fourth—modern factory import substitution—would briefly hit the scene in the late 1840s. While usually not differentiated at all (despite their marked divergences), all three colonial carryovers shared one distinguishing mark: abysmal technical and cost structures that made open competition in the developing international market virtually unthinkable. What could be done?

Peru's rural obrajes, protofactory complexes specializing in coarse woolen fabrics for the laboring classes, once dotted the large haciendas in highland regions such as Cuzco, Huamanga, and Cajamarca (some former strongholds, notably Quito and Cochabamba, later separated from Peru). Built upon sixteenth-century technologies and natural protection, and run by Indian labor drafts, the obraje network reached its zenith in the late seventeenth century. The Viceroyalty of Peru became the textile capital of South America, employing perhaps 100,000 workers, its obrajes a pillar of rural patrician wealth. However, a severe decline struck in the late eighteenth century: even the mild Bourbon "free trade" had its substitution effects here, as well as reforms in disarrayed *mita* labor systems, viceregal market fragmentation, seeping Atlantic contraband, and new rustic competitors.[28] By independence, it appears that Peru's several hundred substantial sweatshops, some shifting to cottons, had dwindled to no more than a dozen operative plants, many geared to artificial military needs.

Yet even this handful of derelict manufactories proved sufficient to ignite a surprising explosion of proindustrial protectionist fervor in the 1820s. Orchestrated by nostalgic (and connected) regional elites hoping to revive a bygone era, the campaign also drew inspiration from the modern strides taken by the English and New England textile industries. The whole world knew of the Industrial Revolution, especially areas such as Peru where it had already taken its import toll on native producers of cloth. Spurred by forceful cuzqueñan delegates such as Domingo Farfán, backed up by inland caudillos and agrarian magnates, Congress became virtually obsessed with Peru's industrial future, or lack thereof. In 1828, having already hoisted 90-percent tariffs, Peru imposed total import bans on competing coarse cloths, the largest single item in the republican import bill.[29] All, however, recognized the depth of the productivity and competition dilemmas confronting the backward and backwoods obrajes, and some pushed for further subsidies, government contracts and, in a few cases, explicit modernization programs to introduce nineteenth-century technology, training, and organization. Clearly, this coterie of provincial patriarchs banked on the fact that Peru's rural poor would silently shoulder the costs of protection and that the powerful local wool and cotton growers would share in and support the bonanza.

Besides "economic independence" and modernity, Peru's proindustrial prophets talked up the greater "linkage" effects that rural industry would afford to the regions—a mirror image of the disarticulation that import substitution had already revealed. The mass markets for this basic industry seemed clearly in place, visibly carved out by the foreign imports that precipitated Peru's secular decline in the price of cloth. The notion that Peru simply lacked appropriate markets is wrong. (And Peru did hold out against the invectives of North American and British consuls, who clearly wished havoc on all efforts to rehaul an independent textile sector.)[30] Yet, despite Peru's apt conditions and early ideological tour de force, little reinvestment and retooling actually occurred. Civil unrest, risk-capital costs, labor withdrawal, infractions of protective laws, and price slides only deepened in the 1830s. By the mid-thirties, the obrajes' military contracts (farmed out by merchants) seemed to be only a signpost of the local compact with militarism, not a road to recovery. By 1840, no one in Lima, and few elsewhere, still worshiped this chimera of rural factories. Residual protectionism (around 25 percent) now reduced to a symbolic welfare measure (as occurred in the 1845 Congress). Barely an obraje, if any, survived.[31] Thus, one force vanished early from Peru's protectionist lineup.

In part, the obrajes had succumbed to less obvious foes: Peru's diffuse rural artisans. More informal, more appropriate to local costs, labor structures, and tastes, and far less political, the Indian "obrajillos," home-weavers, specialized artisan villages, and peasant craftsmen probably supplied the majority of rough-hewn necessities for Peru's indigenous and *mestizo* majorities from the late eighteenth century. As independent craftspeople, they were the social antithesis of the oppression-steeped,

47

elite obrajes, and no doubt the progressive retreat of labor from the obrajes swelled their ranks. This shift from elite industrialism to a more heterogeneous sector remains little explored by historians. But it seems that, blessed by simple family-labor mobilization, low overhead, and naturally shielded localized markets, these groups proved flexible enough to survive Peru's first wave of industrial imports in the 1820s, even though productivity must have been low.[32] Moreover, the backwoods artisans continued to integrate many regional economies. For example, a surviving mid-1830s census from Huaraz (like the censuses of Puno) graphically illustrates this role: "efectos de la tierra"—the cloth, ponchos, pottery, saddlebags, and blankets woven and exchanged between villages—far exceeded in value the "efectos de Europa" carried in by mule train from Lima. The bustling township of Yungay belonged to its shoemakers in 1836, "exporting" no fewer than 30,000 pairs that year for $11,250 in cash. Some 200 looms operated in the tiny nearby parish of Caraz.[33] With their positive balance of trade, the communities imported mainly coastal foodstuffs to their mountain redoubts. Some of their wares reached as far south as Lima.

Modest regional merchants likely oiled this trade, as seen in such picturesque old regional fairs as the one at Vilque, in the southern altiplano. On occasion, in the Lima Congress, merchants prompted provincial políticos to speak up on behalf of the rural artisans; or rustic caudillos sometimes took note. Rural employment, social stability, and the broader interior depressions were the vaunted concerns, not "industrialization." Yet, it can hardly be said that a policy as such existed for these outcasts, the vast majority of Peru's skilled manufacturing workers. They were aided by continuing prohibitions on "star cloth" (the lowest-grade woolens) or by the putting-out systems of local merchants who filled military contracts, but little more was done.[34] By the 1840s, even these independent workers were shaken by the changing cost structures of overseas trade as, for example, indigent consumers of woolens switched over to substitute cottons such as *tocuyos*. All observers agreed that, year by year, these imports pushed further upland. By 1840, the census takers stopped tabulating the *varas* of *bayetas* exchanged; the fairs, where they remained at all, became emporiums for European imitations. A few protests were heard—notably the stirring scenes of spreading rustic idleness (and unrest) painted by Huamangan delegates in 1845. But this social dislocation was probably quietly absorbed by a return to peasant pursuits, self-consumption, or the untold vagaries of rural underemployment.[35] On some residual level, this sector dragged on (and continues today with the tourist in mind). Lima's trade policies never had clear intentions, or results for the small-scale backwoods craftsmen. In this sense, then, the rural artisans never had to fade from the protectionist scene.

Trade politics actually worked best for Peru's third and least likely manufacturers: the urban craft guilds of Lima. The ostentatious bureaucratic and aristocratic spending of viceregal Lima had left in its wake a rather diverse, but essentially elite-oriented, luxury handicraft market. There were carpenters to finish ornate furniture and carriages; dressmakers and tailors to copy the latest Parisian designs; smiths to furnish their trinkets of silver, tinsel, and gold. In 1830, some 914 fully equipped master-artisan shops still lined the streets of Lima, staffed by several thousand auxiliary workers, apprentices, and skilled slaves. Overall they produced more than a quarter of the city's business revenues.[36] (Peru's provincial town guilds were far less eminent.) Hard hit by the mid-1820s deluge of overseas craft analogues, artisan numbers and incomes had soon stabilized (into prolonged stagnation) as Peru's imports shifted toward more mundane industrial goods, none of which were produced in Lima. In fact, until the late 1840s, the guilds' thorniest problem (apart from their clearly rigid structures of cost and technique) was not cut-rate imports per se, but continued reliance on the evaporating demand of penurious postindependence elites.[37]

Limeño craftsmen exerted a notable impact on tariff policy, one that long outlasted (or even stymied) the struggles of their upper- and lower-class rural peers. A combination of social, geographic, and political factors favored the crafts. Here was a group with utmost visibility to politicians, elites, and the Lima state—used to the hilt—and their outright dependence on aristocratic customers (as well as on merchant and hacendado suppliers) helped to stir warm relations. Moreover, unlike rural weavers, the shopowning artisans were not debased workers, but a kind of entrepreneurial middle class, whose critical function in the urban social order was, if anything, to employ, discipline, and control Lima's unruly and frightening dark-skinned plebes. Exploiting their surviving guild structures, artisans easily turned themselves into the best organized "caste" of Peru, with a literate following readily mobilized for muncipal, social, or political services (from policing runaways and contraband to eradicating Lima's rabid dogs). These roles became enhanced after 1821, as social distances shrank in the republic's chaotic politics and sluggish economy. Above all, the guilds' political stock soared. Their excitable flocks made perfect electors, publicists, or armed mobs for Lima's contending "parties" and putsches.[38] In short, artisans were not only close to elite political networks, but strategic and central to them. And while stridently monomaniacal in their push for tariffs, outspoken artisan spokesmen would rarely transgress their ingrained deference to upper-class patrons.

Peculiarities of craft political economy also magnified the artisans' political assimilation and force; their tariff demands did not blatantly menace any elite interests, whether protectionist, liberal, political, or fiscal. First of all, craftsmen clamored for steep tariffs on only a handful of light finished products, goods with little price elasticity and low demand, particularly during the depression years before 1845. Second, the artisans, who made few popular necessities themselves, pined for lower duties on subsistence products (food and clothing for workers and themselves) and on manufacturing inputs (the foreign cloth, potions, and metals increasingly integral to their polished imitations). The guilds, then, were pursuing what modern economists would call high levels of "effective" protection. Such an orientation hardly endangered any of the goods deemed critical to elites, urban subsistence, or customs revenues. (A progressive loss of monopsonistic guild control over plebian labor intensified this zeal both for dampened wage and input costs of crafts and for compensatory steep tariffs on finished goods.) Moreover, the political economy of crafts remained intrinsically conservative with respect to mass production for mass markets, which might only compound the artisans' own cost dilemmas. Peru's evolving tiered tariff structure (under guild influence, the artisans' tools and raw materials became progressively duty-free) served to institutionalize this wary stance. Finally, while loudly ideological, the crafts rarely took protectionism to exclusionistic extremes. For example, dependent on the imported tastes of a Europeanized elite, they never succumbed to xenophobic outbursts against new immigrant craftsmen, whom natives prized as teachers, partners, and role models after 1821 (foreign numbers and visibility burgeoned by 1840). Thus, neither autarkic nor nativistic, artisan tariff politics were easy to placate from a variety of elite standpoints, from liberal to protectionist.[39] Only in the late 1840s would this artisan condominium with elites come under strain, when guano demand (and new elite fancies for fancier but cheaper luxuries) threatened to displace, for the first time, the traditional urban guilds.

Notwithstanding their eclectic appeal, the guilds quickly emerged as a powerful prop to northern nationalist politics. They were militant, articulate, and successful with the protectionism they wanted. Moreover, in uncanny and colorful ways, artisans claimed to represent the "nation," the flesh-and-blood *hijos del país*, and even Peru's true industrial prospects. As early as 1821, artisans threw San Martín into a militia recruitment crisis because of his refusal to heed warnings against an opening to handicraft imports, and agitation intensified against the Bolivarian group. By 1828, guild leaders were solemnly petitioning the nationalist Congress for prohibitions (above their 90-percent duties on foreign crafts), the first of many expert and victorious interventions with nearby lawmakers. In the following decade, artisans openly attached their fortunes to caudillos such as Salaverry and Gamarra (and to the Lima consulado and *cabildo* as well), who reciprocated with generous favors.[40] In the 1840s, the artisan voice was still strong (notably, in the cigarmaker José María García's eloquent 1849 protectionist memorial before Congress). Only in the 1850s, as we will see, were the guilds radicalized, demoralized, and finally marginalized by the victory of free trade.

Under such relentless pressures, a distinct artisanal slant characterized Peru's trade politics by the late 1830s, as seen in the country's complex tariff structures. A finished piece of locally made clothing, for example, might enjoy tariffs of 50–90 percent; the imported cloth it was sewn from entered at 25 percent; and the tailor's tools came in duty-free. The centralized Lima crafts continued to enjoy such substantial real protection, while others, the obrajes and rural weavers, had gradually lost visibility, force, and appeal. Their protective rates diminished to appease city consumers, fiscal crunches, or even the Lima artisans themselves. Lima guilds' capacity (and sheer talent) for timely protest made them, in effect, the privileged wing of Peru's industrial classes—and pivotal to the north's protectionist bloc.

Mounting Lima bias in manufacturing "policy" must have diluted the divergent manufactory interests of the protectionist cause across Peru. Ultimately, it was the triviality of craft production that favored Lima's artisans, hindering sustained support and survival for Peru's more dispersed, and perhaps more worthy, industrial classes. Guildmasters never insisted that rural factories or labor be protected at any cost—and logically so, since the crafts consumed but did not create their popular goods. Yet, it was informal cottage industry that was the mainstay of Peru's skilled employment. And (as early proponents grasped) it was refurbished factories, entering low-cost, high-volume markets, that might lift Peruvian technology and productivity into the modern age. (In fact, the early nineteenth century was a propitious moment to force infant industrial growth, for internationally competitive economies of scale, as well as capital and skill requirements, had not yet reached prohibitive levels.)[41] Still, the influential Lima artisans remained by nature complacent about, if not adverse to, genuine industrial alternatives.

This contradiction blossomed in full later. After the mid-1840s—moving ahead of our story—an authentic modern factory movement briefly burst onto the Peruvian scene. This fourth sector came on the heels of political stability and the publicity and incentives of the 1845 Congress, which had just pronounced Peru's postmortem on atavistic rural industry. Between 1846 and 1848, well-connected Lima families (including leading merchants) acquired privileges for, and invested large sums in, the latest imported plants for cotton textiles, silks, glass, and paper, and for expanded lighting, distilling, and metallurgical workshops. The movement even produced a compelling "infant industry" ideology, in a bestselling book by the cottons impresario Juan Norberto Casanova, although it was, in reality, an early form of "import substitution" industrialism.[42] These pioneers won immediate and unreserved official and elite backing, as well they might, for these were precisely the appropriate sorts of modern mass industries to root and thrive in the beckoning age of export demand. Guano income could be used to diversify, in markets forged by two decades of industrial imports (exactly what the industrialists proposed), and could provide thousands of jobs for Peru's teeming (and willing) underemployed. Indeed, the owners soon launched a campaign to supply start-up subsidies for the fledgling factories—directly in the form of guano![43] Official ceremonies marked the first products coming on-line in October 1848, when a sheet of cotton, giftwrapped in Lima paper and silk, was presented to an exuberant President Castilla. But sheer enthusiasm was not enough; the factories also needed strong tariff support to ease the difficult transition to full (and thus competitive) levels of output and productivity. Their 40-percent emergency duties were critical for offsetting the temporary cost problems of Peru's import-saturated markets. The supply of labor, capital, and consumers, then, was not the chief obstacle. A supportive trade policy was.

As fate would have it, the presence and outlook of Lima artisans adversely intervened. The cost-wary guilds not only helped fight any new industrial tariffs, but their own desperate actions to escalate craft duties (which for once crossed the bounds of elite tolerance) worked to sink the legitimacy of all manufacturing ventures. These events unfolded during the final liberal backlash of 1849–51, a complex episode that we will explore later in full. The resulting 1852 tariff, with its Manchesterian cost structure, was still in some ways a concession to the traditional artisan class; it also specifically banned the kinds of flexible tariff grants genuinely needed for Lima factories. Rapidly, by 1853, the industry movement and all its factories expired under this sharp reversal of state policy and support.[44] No sensible entrepreneur would again risk his capital in industrial experiments for the duration of the guano age. Thus, the export era, instead of spurring diversification, was to lock Peru into import dependency. The nature and politics of Peru's prior preindustrial base had, in effect, blocked long-run possibilities for industrial advance.

In the early republic, manufactories excited a dramatic and serious controversy around trade policy, yet ultimately could not become its motor force. In large part, this reflected Peru's disarticulated, disparate, and disunited protoindustrial interests, contradictions exacerbated by the pervading political economy and obsequious politics of Lima's craft guilds. All four groups—the tottering provincial obrajes, the dispersed skilled workers of the countryside, the politicized limeño guilds, and the risk-taking elite factory pioneers—could not vie equally, successfully, or together for the political limelight. Not only did their tariff needs diverge, but socially these sectors were worlds apart. Effective ringleaders for Peruvian nationalism would instead have to come from elsewhere, from Peru's most centralized elite.

THE RISE AND FALL OF "MERCHANT NATIONALISM"

The pronounced role of the Lima merchant class in the campaign to capture the Chilean market was, it turns out, but one manifestation of an all-encompassing merchant antipathy to free trade. It was here, in the halls of the consulado, that Peru's lack of a core liberal elite was most keenly felt. On every significant trade issue between 1820 and 1845, Lima's 200–300 leading traders acted as the backbone, organizers, and firebrands for Peruvian economic nationalism, easily drawing the bulk of the regional merchants and countless retailers to the cause. Consulado influence ran deep. Merchants in most historical settings serve as a critical interest group in trade-policy formation, given their strategic position (and specialized knowledge) in commercial activities. They form the classic cohesive "interest" in trade—its grassroots theoreticians as well. Moreover, in postindependence Peru, national merchants were the closest thing the new nation had to a unified dominant class. Despite reduced numbers and relative poverty (relative to their colonial heyday), the cohesive consulado merchants immediately forged a symbiotic relationship with the infant state, a connection unrivaled by any of Peru's scattered and fragmented agro-industrial productive elites. National merchants stood squarely at the interface of the international and domestic economies, keenly aware of the developing tensions. Finally, the rapid rejuvenation of the colonial consulado structure itself, a rarity elsewhere in Latin America, gave Lima merchants the institutional stability and power necessary to advance their trade-policy interests and doctrines with the state. Indeed, the natives-only consulado enjoyed a greater stability than the transient state itself. Illiberal merchants appeared to be active elsewhere in postindependence America, but nowhere with the determination, force, and endurance shown in Peru.[45] It is not surprising that while the Lima merchant class embraced nationalist policies from 1825 to 1845, a protectionism reigned in Peru; nor that when merchants finally converted to liberalism in the mid-1840s, the balance tipped irrevocably to free trade. Explaining Peru's changing trade regimes means understanding the behavior of this merchant class.

The surprise is that merchants were not liberals all along. The historiography paints merchants as born free traders, as just one more republican elite bereft of national consciousness, rapidly surrendering Peru to the liberal foreign interests on whom they depended.[46] Lima merchants were notably dependent on foreign wholesalers for goods and services, which makes the behavior of this intermediary (or "comprador") class seem all the more aberrant. Moreover, Third World commercial elites are typically cosmopolitan liberals, specially placed to profit from opportunities afforded by foreign connections and trade. While certainly citizens of the world in relation to Peru's complex amalgam of precapitalist societies, Lima's merchants were by no means nationless.

Instead, their nearly unanimous vision was the closest expression of a national development project for the new republic: a "merchant nationalism." Merchant ideology stemmed from an explicit rejection of the new classical doctrines of free trade, even as they exalted its theme of the supremacy of commerce. Instead of laissez-faire, the consulado held that the new and expanding currents of foreign commerce and the new powers of an independent state should be strictly channeled toward the forced development of strong Peruvian entrepreneurial groups, the "hijos del país." (In some respects, here was an early call for state intervention to ameliorate what is now dubbed "delayed dependent development," the handicaps Peru inherited from its ancien régime.) Free rein to overseas traders and products would rapidly undermine Peru's traditionally diversified economy, displace aspiring national elites, and leave in their wake foreign command of the country's main assets and dynamic economic sectors. Free trade meant, in effect, the loss of national economic sovereignty. "Unfair" advantages—direct access to goods, cheap capital, and consular protection—explained the foreign menace, not a lack of Peruvian talent, and only concerted state action could right the competitive imbalance. The new foreign merchants invading Peru in the early 1820s, rather than being seen as potential allies, were thus depicted as avaricious parasites on Peruvian development, to be contained as much as possible by the state. For raison d'état itself, Peru had to promote accumulation by "capitalistas nativos."[47] National merchants fit that bill.

The proposed means were varied, often sophisticated, and promised spin-off benefits of protection to a range of ailing national elites, producers, and regional groups. In one sense, merchants frankly opposed "free trade" in its original sense: unencumbered access for foreigners in domestic markets. North Atlantic merchant houses—Peru's new link to the world economy—were to be confined to major ports, forced to consign goods to native middlemen, and prohibited from competition in the local retail market. (More radical merchants simply demanded the expulsion of all foreigners). In this way, "national capitalists" alone would benefit from the internal end of expanding overseas commerce, along with a supporting army of native retailer clients who, given the structures of trade, seemed equally adamant against direct foreign sales. The resulting maze of antiforeign, nontariff barriers formed an essential element of Peruvian protectionism into the 1850s, when genuine "free trade" finally became a reality. These restrictions, and the risks they entailed for foreigners, had upward effects on price levels, to the benefit of sundry commercial and producer groups.[48] In fact, most of the early merchant policies and practices actually translate into resistance to the dominant commercial pressure on Peru's postindependence economy: the dramatic fall in the relative prices of tradables.

Positive steps were needed as well to promote the merchant national capitalists. Throughout the 1820s and 1830s, the merchant guild received in its favor a steady stream of navigation acts, monopolies, contracts, subsidies, differential duties, expanded juridical and commercial powers, and several major mercantile-development projects. Free markets became even rarer in postindependence Peru. In return for these privileges, the merchant class and its allies would serve as the bulwark of a revitalized Peruvian state—in finance, development, administration, and the protection of national rights.

Lima's colonial consulado had once played an analogous role for the viceregal state. It was, indeed, overtly parastatal and constituted the core of an imperial trade zone that once stretched from the shores of the Río de la Plata to the fairs of Panama. However, as is well known, starting in the 1770s imperial bureaucrats systematically sought to dismember Lima's monopolistic commercial hegemony and loosen the merchant grip over the local colonial state. Political and mercantile autonomy for Buenos Aires, Upper Peru, Chile, and New Granada; freer regulation of shipping; administrative reform and strict taxation; and outright political discrimination—all allegedly dealt a mortal blow to limeño merchants. In fact, the consulado compensated by expanding into new fields and by adopting paradoxical political tactics. One of these, after 1810, was to join vigorously in the counterrevolutionary efforts of viceroys such as Pezuela, in the hope that a royalist victory would stem the tide of true "free trade" (embraced by consulado rivals in such rebellious provinces as La Plata). Ultimately, they dreamed of winning back the rewards of traditional privilege. The merchants squarely lost this bet in 1821. Historians assume that the high financial and political costs spelled the demise of the consulado itself.[49]

But the consulado did not end here. After independence, its records clearly reveal merchants at the forefront of every trade-policy struggle of the era, swiftly attempting to implement a transformed nationalist program. A criollo consulado regrouped in time to obstruct the free trade goals of the mid-1820s Bolivarians. From 1827 on, local advocates of liberalism took the brunt of the consulado attack. Sometimes merchants

55

worked through mass mobilization and loud protest (from emergency "juntas generales de comercio" and timely pamphleteering to general strikes); at other times, through the silent and quotidian manipulation of malleable officials, ever more dependent on the rejuvenating traders. This Lima elite was often joined by radical provincial merchants, who pushed antiforeign politics to their exclusionist hilt.[50] (Lima, ambivalently dependent on foreign trade and services, could not wish to emulate Paraguay or China.) And scores of Lima retailers followed the top merchants' lead.

Six major issues fueled republican consulado trade politics. First, the drive for Chilean commercial union, essentially the work of the consulado, aimed at deflecting the harmful direct trade of foreign shippers and forging renewed commercial opportunities in shipping and services for agrarian and urban elites. Second, the consulado sponsored, and then steadfastly tried to enforce, extensive legislation to keep foreign traders out of retailing and the domestic market. These measures ranged from tariff codes prohibiting foreign houses from all but bulk trade in the main ports to ad hoc hounding of straying European peddlers. Conflicts often boiled into international crises, as foreign consuls (notably the French) attempted to uphold their nationals' trade and property rights. Thrice (in 1833, 1835, and 1842) the French took these regulations and ultimatums as a casus belli with Peru. A third merchant issue was foreign dumping, as glimpsed already in the 1834 consulado general strike and the subsequent collapse of the Orbegoso regime. The foreign auction houses that periodically opened in Lima evoked a strident—even apocalyptic—response from merchants terrorized by the martillos' powerful downward effects on prices. No issue contributed more to the definition and polarization of liberal and protectionist ideologies in Peru than the mundane business of auctions; yet, no question dramatized so clearly the implications of free versus constrained markets. After pursuing the Yankee auctioneers for two decades, the consulado was to win its battle for good after 1840, with the exclusive right to run a (limited) service for themselves.[51] Fourth, high tariffs, while not the primary concern, received merchant support for many industries. The consulado played a key role in policing contraband and other infractions of tariff law (as in 1832–34) and spoke forcefully for "national industry" whenever they dominated tariff commissions, at least until the 1840 tariff. Overall, it is unlikely that tariff protection could have emerged at all without merchant backing, as became obvious in the prohibitions victory of 1828.[52] Fifth, national merchants developed and oversaw various projects in state finance, culminating in the 1834 creation of the "Ramo de Arbitrios," a merchant loan bank for penurious caudillos. It was national merchants, not abdicating foreigners, who maintained the Lima militarist cliques. This critical merchant fiscal role (for reasons to be seen in Chapter 5) goes far in explaining the overall form and political viability of nationalist commercial policies. Finally, consulado politics revolved around various state-sponsored projects for merchant development—from navigation acts, to mining banks, to a gamut of revived colonial *estancos* under consulado auspices. The most ambitious plan of all was a monopoly Asian trading company launched in 1839 to propel native merchants from provincial into international markets. A Peruvian rerun of the legendary Manila galleon, the Compañía Asiática carried the Pacific scope of Lima's largest traders to its entrepreneurial extreme. Foreign silk cargoes from Asia were proscribed in order to speed transformation of the Peruvian merchant-shipper into a species of Pacific internationalist. After considerable investment of capital, and protectionist faith, the experiment collapsed in 1843 under the unremitting pressure of renewed civil wars. Its fall brought widespread merchant disillusionment with their own statist models, and thus marks a watershed in merchant nationalism.[53]

Despite the broad appeal of merchant nationalism, all these efforts proved understandably difficult to enforce in Peru's convulsive political and administrative climate. Merchants were not always successful, even as their campaigns around these issues demonstrated a remarkable capacity to gather allies from across Peru and among varied social groups, and even as they became the formative force in the development of trade policy. For lasting success, merchants required (much like their adversaries, the foreign consuls) a state far stronger than the one bequeathed by colonialism and battered by caudillismo. Even the unambiguous support provided by the second Gamarra regime (1839–41)—virtually run by the consulado—was not sufficient, since political upheaval cut short Gamarra's countless merchant projects. Yet, until the multiple economic disasters of this, Peru's deepest round of internecine war in the early 1840s, it appears that these nationalist policies did aid in the consolidation of a national merchant elite, most of whom had begun their careers as decapitalized paupers in the aftermath of independence. In 1829, the consulado encompassed 194 members and 144 wholesale merchants, and its formal 30-man electoral elite enjoyed average annual incomes of $1,200. A decade later, Lima had 208 substantial native importers, their political elite now averaging twice the profits ($2,396), although the number of consulado retailers had declined with another wave of war-induced bankruptcies. All this growth had occurred in unsettled times. By 1839, some of these merchants, such as Quirós, Elías, and Palacios, already fielding newly diversified, extraregional trade empires (with agrarian, mining, and shipping branches), were clearly the leading capitalist "spirits" of the age and would go on to become key entrepreneurial and political figures during the guano age.[54] Not all would forget the nationalist policies that made them what they were.

In part, the intensified political conflict that stalled merchant nationalists in the 1840s was of their own making, as they were a major force eliciting the southern liberal resistance that destabilized the Peruvian state. In the early 1840s, a convergence of adverse economic and militarist pressures—which we will explore later—forced the majority of consulado merchants into deep crisis over their previous reliance on statist restrictive policies, causing many to rethink their previous antipathy to foreign interests. By the mid-1840s, hallowed nationalist doctrines lay largely abandoned, widely decried as failures, and novel cooperative relationships with foreign houses were unfolding on several fronts. Only lowly retailers, left out of the emerging opportunities, clung to a desperate commercial protectionism. By 1850, the liberal conversion of the merchant elite looked nearly complete, and the consulado (which in 1849 finally welcomed foreigners into its ranks) actively espoused free trade.[55] This ended, in effect, Peru's possibilities for nationalist policies in the guano age.

Explaining Merchant Nationalism

Shorn of its nationalist and developmentalist rhetoric—which stands on its own right—what factors help explain this heretical merchant behavior and its favorable reception by the Peruvian state? Our evidence suggests four explanations: merchant ties with producers; a historical proclivity for monopolistic solutions; nationalism as disguised risk-aversion; and nationalism as the consequence of struggles surrounding caudillo state finance. This last perspective, fiscal conflict, provides the roundest understanding of merchant nationalism, for it links the course of merchant trade politics with other key elites, foreign, political, and fiscal (it also requires a full extra chapter to elaborate).

An obvious motive, that merchants were protecting links to local manufacturers, is not convincing. Unlike nineteenth-century merchants elsewhere, elite Peruvian traders played a negligible direct role in the declining manufacturing or artisanal sector. (There were clear links, of course, with agriculturalists, agro-industrialists, and agrarian protectionism.) In some interior zones, notably Cuzco, Ayacucho, and Huaraz, regional commercial elites began the independence era still wedded to surviving circuits of traditional "efectos de la tierra," as dealers in coarse native cloth and other rural artisan products. Provincial merchants often articulated the painful local adjustments to trade expansion in the 1820s and 1830s, and seen in 1830 cuzqueño protests, but these remote protectionist pleas were hardly heard, especially as time wore on, by the Lima consulado.[56] Some centrally located limeño merchants did specialize in inputs, both domestic and foreign, for Lima's diverse craft guilds. Yet these "encomenderos" were losing ground in the Lima import economy and, like the artisans themselves, mainly favored lower duties on imported raw materials, that is, an increased effective protection. Evidence also suggests (as in 1834) that Lima merchants "speculated" against foreigners by amassing stocks of protected goods, whose prices would climb, a pecuniary incentive behind their frequent verbal endorsements of national industry.

In the late 1840s, however, a handful of prominent Lima merchants did begin that portentous drive to implant modern factories. (One merchant, Jorge Moreto, had been toying even earlier with factory privileges.) Impressive investments unfolded in cotton textiles, silks, glassware, paper, candles, and foundries, using the latest imported technology—and the merchants' oldest protectionist pleas. One such investor, Santiago & Sons (owners of the big textile mill), was not only among the oldest of national houses but headed the consulado at the time; Pedro Gonzales Candamo, Lima's wealthiest trader, underwrote several of the projects with soft loans; the leading merchant newspaper, *El Comercio*, itself launched the paper mill and took an early lead in publicizing the drive. It was, however, politically too late, even if Peru's now buoyant economic climate of guano demand (and Peru's consolidating state) clearly favored such experiments in mass-consumption industry. These ventures quickly collapsed, for by then—in the course of the 1851 tariff debates, to be exact—the majority of the merchants' consulado colleagues proved unreceptive even to the modest tariff concessions required by these infant industries.[57] Political forces (to be seen) decided this elite turnabout on industrial protection. In effect, this highly public failure stalled Peru's industrial advance for the remainder of the nineteenth century. Expanding merchant capital quickly shifted back to less risky import/export realms.

The simplest explanation of merchant nationalism regards merchants as classic "monopolists," followers of revered colonial traditions. Merchants were out to translate their political capital into easy economic rents, through restrictions on easy targets (foreigners) and a host of supply-constricting monopolies. As the main suppliers to national retailers, these merchandisers were perfectly placed for building fortunes from monopolistic (technically speaking, oligopolistic) profits. Several historical factors suggest this hypothesis. Their predecessor, Lima's colonial consulado, earned notoriety as the greatest bastion of conservative commercial privilege in eighteenth-century America. Its reactionary merchants fervently resisted even the meek Bourbon attempts at commercial reform. An even weaker republican state then presented a ripe opportunity to reverse liberalization, for the new national political machinery could be used to overcome the new forces (Bolivarians, internationalists, North Americans) that threatened to push Peru into competitive markets.[58] Peru's colonial legacy had left an inefficient imperial economy quite lacking in the types of elites who might benefit from freer trade, and merchants could easily persuade their cohorts of the justice of restrictive practices. Even the structure of commerce heralded by early republican merchants—bulk foreign importers kept at the gates of a closed internal distribution network—looks suspiciously similar to the global design of Spanish mercantilist trade. Furthermore, monopolistic behavior tends to flourish in periods of economic retrenchment and risk, periods such as Peru's deep, three-decade postindependence depression. Restrictions might even compensate for the loss of markets through balkanization and imperial reform—for liberalism historically thrives on a base of expanding and stable markets. Monopoly also makes sense in highly imperfect markets (like Peru's), and in markets where a significant segment of consumers (here, the alleged nonmarket Indian groups) displays little price elasticity of demand. Liberals constantly lambasted merchants as monopolists, and the merchants themselves openly extolled "monopolies"—at least the national ones needed to avert the "monopolistic" stranglehold foreigners would achieve in the absence of market interference.[59]

Although "monopoly" suffices as a fair sociological description—narrow corporate mentalities and interests indeed lived on in the consulado— several factors belie this interpretation. (We will return to its compelling political ramifications, as neocolonial corporatism, in the closing chapter.) In fact, prosopographical data show that few of Lima's activist merchants originated in the colonial consulado; a good many were actually newcomers to the region (from Buenos Aires) and were untainted with colonial practice.[60] Why would the upwardly mobile prefer monopolies? Moreover, mass consumers were responding heartily to declining import prices. Otherwise, why did Peruvian producers and traders alike perceive so readily the menace of new foreign competition? Most important, the personal risks for individuals adhering to monopolistic strategies are far too great—unless they enjoy the backing of a strong state fully committed to strict enforcement of protectionist laws. Peru's feeble postindependence state was patently incapable of fulfilling that role, and wary merchants must have realized this early on. Yet, almost to a man, they persisted in calling for all kinds of market restrictions and price-elevating policies. More specific circumstances must explain the "monopolistic," high-price propensities of Peru's merchant elite and their validation by an infirm state.

This third, more precise diagnosis of "merchant nationalism" stems from a closer analysis of Lima's peculiar commercial structures and of the institutionalized patterns of risk these posed for consulado merchants. To encapsulate a complex model, protectionism was essentially an extreme, yet rational, strategy of "risk-aversion." It reflected the larger pattern of Peru's new 1820s insertion into the world economy, which initially drove merchants to seek largely unworkable monopolistic solutions.[61]

The roots of protectionism lay in the novel economic role assumed by top national merchants when overseas import houses first directly entered the Lima market in the 1820s. The surviving (but decapitalized) natives became "intermediaries," distributors of imports on credit for the new British, U.S., and French wholesalers. These thirty to forty top national merchants passed on the borrowed imports to an army of far-flung petty retailers, a function eschewed by the foreign firms that hoped to avoid the risky (if not futile) task of debt collection from Peru's elusive, unstable, and indigent array of shopkeepers, street vendors, and itinerant provincial peddlers.[62] The large-scale native intermediaries dominated the consulado's political leadership. But would they adopt the liberal politics of their foreign patrons?

As an inventory-laden distribution class, these warehousemen (*almaceneros*) had reason enough to abhor rapid price drops that cut into anticipated profits on borrowed stocks. The foreign importers could always, if they so wished, move directly to undersell these national "secondhand dealers," especially in this era of steady declining import prices. Indeed, this was a sound intrinsic reason to prohibit undercutting foreign retail trades. But wider risks endemic to Peruvian markets, caused by the country's economic and political turmoil, exaggerated these conflicts beyond tolerance for merchants.

Since all imports were dispensed on credit, the top Peruvian merchants sat perilously atop a vast credit pyramid. When rapid price drops occurred or bankruptcies reverberated among lower-level retailers (the typical accompaniment of new civil wars or chronic market-clearing difficulties), national merchants were squeezed in a vicious vise. Collection of full outstanding credits from their dispersed retail clients was all but impossible—even as foreign wholesalers came knocking, with tangible institutional powers (from the consulado court itself), to collect debits due from their Peruvian intermediaries. Thus, all risks from this credit system fell upon Peruvian merchants.[63]

Faced with this quandary, merchants developed their complex of antiliberal and antiforeign policies. (They could hardly turn on unmanageable retailers with tougher debt laws; nor could they realistically believe in an eventual clearing power in Peru's volatile markets.) "Nationalist" restrictions served to stabilize price levels, to prevent foreigners from undercutting already precarious relations with retailers (as had dramatically occurred, for example, with foreign auctions), and, as a long-term solution, to accelerate native capital accumulation and thus ease their credit dependency on foreigners. The merchants often said as much, in the preambles to their protectionist proposals.[64] All these policies substituted, as it were, for efficient economic institutions that might have reduced the risks and costs of debt collection and of Peru's market, political, and social instabilities. Oligopolistic strategies, even if of doubtful practicality given the weak Peruvian state, were desperately pursued by merchants. Survival counted more than mere profit maximization.

In short, a complex web of economic risks prevented Peruvian intermediaries from adopting the liberal path their dependent social status implied—much as the related political instability stopped foreign powers in their tracks. Peru's economic contraction surely contributed to monopolistic mania, for risk-aversion is endemic to bad times. Yet these risks became more specific: economic expansion in and of itself, without political stabilization, would not have been enough to turn these traders into liberals. The role of risk was not, however, unique to Peru; in Europe itself, free trade spread in part as a consequence of the state stability secured after 1815.[65]

This behavior pattern is best confirmed by regions where risks and unstable credit chains emerged most exaggerated. In the regional ports and along the interior trade routes of Peru, provincial traders faced enormous inherent risks from dispersed, shallow, and primitive markets (not to mention the banditry). Regional merchants were also "thirdhand dealers," that is to say, dependent themselves on the Lima intermediaries for their own stocks of borrowed foreign goods. The Lima consulado ensured this condition by pressuring governments to regulate strictly the number and flexibility of regional ports where provincial traders could go to obtain cheaper inventories.[66] Dutiful officials claimed they were only fighting contraband. But rather than protest this artificially centralized port system, a distribution network that dramatically intensified the credit risks for provincials, local merchants turned instead against the handful of foreigners in their midst. To those caught at the far end of the credit chain, it seemed as if cheap foreign direct imports caused their predicament; and so it was, superficially. Thus, from the 1820s through the late 1830s, the merchants of Ica, Lampa, and Cuzco (or most anywhere outside Lima) became Peru's nationalist extremists. Their incessant clamor sought a total ban on foreign traders, whose direct imports appeared responsible for miserably fluctuating prices and waves of bankruptcy and default. Provincial merchants were more than pleased, then, when rustic caudillos and municipal authorities, true to form, took it upon themselves to raid, sack, and shut down foreign shops in their vicinity. (These political risks, more than any law, explain why so few foreigners dared venture outside the major ports before 1840. In that year, still fewer than 200 non-Iberian Europeans, including artisans, plied their trade outside Lima and Arequipa; in all of Cuzco and Ayacucho departments, the census located but 8 new foreigners. The interior belonged to Peruvian nationalists.)[67] Other factors came into play—notably, provincial loyalty to timeworn circuits of local manufactures—but commercial risk structures best account for why these men could not make an earlier transition to liberalism, which was otherwise in their best interests. Only in the 1840s, as we will soon see, would these merchants finally start to blame the limeño policies that compounded their risks. Only then would a new, decentralized liberal movement be born.

A Modeling Reprise

Piecing together the puzzling arguments so far requires the broader perspective of Peru's economy. All these disparate actors in initial Peruvian trade politics, making their debut on the world economic stage of the 1820s, were prompted by a script of revolutionary changes in price structure and profit opportunity. In an impersonal scenario, Peru "should" have been profitably specializing along the lines of its factor endowments—extensive land and mineral resources, and a scarcity of skilled workers and capital. In theory, led by the owners of abundant factors, new benefits should have advanced the march to exports and free trade. Instead, our cast of Peruvian social groups, once they perceived the dramatic dislocations of trade, improvised. Novel competitors, unabsorbable risks, clouded market signals, and political expedience all combined to block acceptance of free international play.

The dramatic change in the offing was the fall in relative import prices, chiefly of mass manufactures or foodstuffs for consumers and workers. Many import prices declined more than 50 percent in the 1820s alone, while the costs of most local goods settled down only slowly from the convulsions of war. Short-term rents should have gone first to commercial arbitrageurs, those forging the more efficient transactions across Peruvian society; later, exporters, service sectors, and consumers of all kinds would gain (including the Peruvian state, an avid consumer of customs duties).[68] The only directly menaced group was Peru's modest and archaic manufacturers, if unable to move into alternative roles. Nevertheless, the actual costs of adjustment spread further and deeper. Artisans and obrajes did perform on cue; but they nonetheless emerged as a mere supporting cast in a sweeping protectionist backlash—upstaged by Peru's commercial, export, and urban elites.

New rivals—those overseas merchants who acquired de facto monopolies in wholesale niches, buttressed by credit and protected from risk—

took much of the immediate windfall from the new import regime. Naturally, these foreign houses (and their farsighted diplomat sponsors) became Peru's free-trade zealots, though constrained by political risk. Yet, to many in Peru, these migrant factors were unexpected, and soon unwelcome, guests. Capital-poor national merchants, for example, discovered overwhelming and imminent dangers in Atlantic imports, coveted monopolies of their own, and calculated as sunken costs their older investments in regional marketing systems. In themselves, Atlantic imports were benign, but not, it seemed, overspecialization and the rival Atlantic importers. Native retailers might have sensed liberal profits through enhanced sales, but wobbly free markets exposed them as well to displacement from their traditionally sheltered roles. Provincial traders felt only a drop in regional demand, and proved most leery of specializing in Atlantic imports in their dilapidated and risky hinterlands. All told, nationality counted. Peruvian commercial interests ended up leading a charge against the downward price trends of laissez-faire—although, over time, resistance was sure to wane.

The embryonic exporters of Peru did not, in the main, receive clearcut liberal cues. They, too, discovered unusual dangers of displacement or incipient markets that required prohibitive retooling to exploit. Incentives from lower labor and capital costs barely registered, for mobile workers and affordable credit were nearly impossible to find in risk-torn Peru. At the same time, new imports did seem to whittle away the profits from planters' and farmers' most established and marketable agrarian pursuits—grains, sugar, and alcohol—and became the motive for opposing staple imports. Only in southern (or Bolivian) export markets could agriculture entertain a switch; elsewhere, survival demanded upholding proven urban, mining, and Pacific markets. Similar were the reactions of native claimants on resources. Southern nitrates and barks brought higher rents, with the help of foreign promoters; but dispersed central-highland miners, Peru's largest suppliers of foreign exchange, feared overseas inroads and ultimate loss of ownership. In short, cost and price changes, such as they were, did not spur the emergence of clear export incentives or lobbies in Peru. The most palpable effects of trade fell instead on consumption structures.

Given the dispersed nature of Peruvian modes of production, a liberal response from consumers carried little counterweight. (Large concentrations of workers and consumers in haciendas, mines, and workshops were a rarity in Peru.) The one region where economizing consumers massed in force was Lima. But here they meshed with, or seemed overwhelmed by, the might of Lima's concentrated protectionist lobbies—merchants, millers, hacendados, artisans—and the officials dependent on their markets of influence and funds. Such social and locational factors often prove essential to trade policy: organized and centralized sectors seize protectionist rents, while scattered buyers (otherwise free riders) remain ineffective at politics.[69] In Peru, the concretion of protectionists proved paramount. Only with concentrated liberal lobbies—an urban bourgeoisie, export factories on the land, or an enfranchised mass market—could the gains of trade translate smoothly into liberal policy. All such groups were lacking in Peru.

A shift to liberalism required perceptible reductions in economic and political risks, new external markets clearly surpassing the old, and a substantial export-based rent accruing to concentrated groups near the apex and center of power. In time, these would come. But for now, Peru's protectionists took center stage.

ONE MIGHT also speculate here about the macroeconomic conditions that allowed such political factors, mentalities, and policies to operate in postindependence Peru. What, in effect, "paid" for Peru's chronic balance-of-trade difficulties and for persisting protectionist responses? What export pattern fueled what was a continuing competition crisis of the north? According to classical theory, embodied at the time in the international price-specie-flow mechanism, Peru's massive early trade deficits should have been rapidly resolved. The gap in returns should have led to an outflow of coin. The reduced money supply should have induced a downward adjustment in domestic price levels and thus market stabilization—through increasingly competitive exports and a slowdown in imports—and substitutions by cheapening home tradables.[70] Overall, monetary and external disturbances, and even risks, should have abated. Faith in free-trade equilibrium (a faith proselytized by local liberals) should have emerged at large.

The problem—apart from the statistical mysteries of the balance of payments—was that Peru fell under multiple external strains at once: structural rigidities, external pressures, and the externalities of civil war. Peru's initial flood of imports was felt mainly in their declining real price (a similar $5-million import bill in 1830 and 1820 brought twice as many goods). It hit at a particularly poor time for locating new (or old) export markets. With limited export capacity, the result was indeed a massive (and, to many, frightful) 1820s export of coin. And, to some extent, the domestic price mechanism did function: preliminary data show a modest (10–15 percent) decline in local food prices from 1830 to 1845. Even some diversification of exports was under way. In 1825, silver shipments accounted for all but 9 percent of returns; by 1840, 18 percent were covered by new bulk products.[71]

Yet, to a larger degree, it seems that price and trade patterns did not adjust to equilibrate the external gap, aggravating Peru's depression.

Aggregate imports continued their rise, though at a slower pace than in the 1820s. Wages (*jornales*) seem to have remained stationary, where commodified labor existed at all, conditions setting a downward rigidity for price adjustments. Peru's national factor and product markets seemed too incipient or fragmented to conduce to an efficient stabilization cycle. In part, the disequilibria were locational, as glimpsed in diverging regional price levels and export responses. While northern exporters (under institutional constraints) could barely respond to the crisis, miners recovered, and southerners began to build up their new bulk export trade in wools, barks, and nitrates. Thus, the liberals corresponded to producers beginning a long-term external adjustment; the protectionists, to those losing income instead. Overall, however, this economy remained sticky in the extreme: in lieu of price changes in relation to the money supply, quantity adjustments ensued; that is, Peru entered its two-decade domestic depression. So the north clung to its protectionism as alternative solutions failed to emerge. Under such circumstances, a true faith in equilibrium markets was hard to come by. Peru exhibited symptoms normally associated with contemporary underdeveloped economies. But none of these rigidities can be abstracted from Peru's traumatic context of perpetual war.

One also wonders about the 1820s surge of bullionist arguments in the protectionist camp. Was this just an ideological atavism, or was there some "rational" core as well? In an economy whose price adjustments appear so tricky, and whose money supply took flight on a shocking scale (exports of coin exceeded $20 million by the mid-1820s alone), protectionists may have insisted on import prohibitions as a primitive but effective kind of stabilization device. Perhaps these "mercantilists" were concerned not only with the foreign-trade crisis, but with maintenance of adequate domestic "effective demand," as economists sometimes suggest, by means of direct controls over money supply and multiplier leakages.[72] Indeed, some early protectionists spoke along these lines.

Whatever the case, Peru itself remained a major currency producer, and this seems to have intensified the welter of controversy between local Smitheans and bullionists during the 1820s. By 1830, Cerro de Pasco mining and Lima minting were in recovery, enough perhaps to cover both the external deficit and maintain stable national money stocks and price levels. In 1830, Pasco production was still only 95,000 marks (less than $1 million); by 1833 it had jumped to 255,000 marks (about $2.5 million); and by the late 1830s national levels had risen to $4–5 million. These advances miraculously continued during the worst of the caudillo tumults, up to 1845, and were bound to calm the mercantilists' worst demonetization nightmares. Yet, cryptic remarks by early finance ministers also suggest another concern—that, as a bullion producer, Peru faced peculiar dilemmas with external adjustments. Mining, it was believed, permitted huge merchandise trade gaps to persist, but with a built-in "overvaluation" (as money supply replenished, too) that might dediversify the economy under open trade.[73] Again, the effects, if any, registered along regional lines. Northern protectionists may have sought either to preserve their best internal linkages as suppliers to the mining sector or to maintain employment in the mine-based service economy of Lima. The south, on the other hand, its exports far less dependent on specie, could more readily embrace free trade. Whatever the case, Peru's adjustments to trade were dislocated, prolonged, confounding, and fraught with shattering political risk.

APART from such speculative models, the hard evidence best supports the economic-risk (and political-concentration) view of Peru's merchant-led protectionism. Its logical correlate—that liberalism required a modicum of economic and political stability to succeed—was, in another sense, just as pertinent to protectionist success. Yet, risk factors still do not clarify why Peru's state actually supported its nationalist merchants, nor why these merchants suddenly abandoned their safety-net strategy in the mid-1840s. To be sure, a somewhat more predictable and efficient import market was then emerging, as foreigners slowly learned the ropes in Peru. And the 1840s expansion of the Peruvian money supply (first with silver, then with guano credits) slowed general price falls and at last dispelled mercantilist anxieties. Still later, after 1845, political and institutional stability (and some critical juridical-commercial reforms) could ease merchants' control of their risky army of retail clients. Nevertheless, a climate of enduring, even intensified, economic turbulence continued to haunt merchant perceptions in the mid-1840s, right when they turned to free trade.[74]

Bald economic forces, then, were not enough to transform the mentalities of men whose deepest attitudes to trade stemmed from the profound shocks of the postindependence era. That would require a full political reconditioning, as well. A rounder explanation for protectionism and the turn to liberalism demands a longer look at the larger political stage on which the Peruvian economy and its actors were planted: the political institutions, class, and dynamics of a "militarist republic."

CHAPTER 4

Nationalist Caudillo Politics and Liberal State-Building

PERU COULD not achieve a stable national state until the 1850s—the liberal guano-age Leviathan erected by Ramón Castilla—whether such consolidation is viewed in its political, social, regional, institutional, diplomatic, or financial dimensions. As the premier "caudillo" regime of postindependence America, the Peruvian state, like most others, has eluded analysis. Historians still assume away structural regularities (or even meaning) in postindependence politics, which is customarily portrayed as a nonsensical merry-go-round of armed, opera buffa executives, frivolous discourse, incoherent policies, fiscal desperation, and stillborn political institutions. Even if such were the case, this sort of view still provides no understanding of the origins and persistence of anarchy itself.[1]

Protectionism, we now know, thrived in a seedbed of endemic instability. In myriad ways, free trade could germinate only in a more settled, less risky business and political climate that might just allow for long-range vistas of liberal development. To appreciate fully the sources of protectionism and liberalism, we must go to the roots of instability and stability.

Trade policy, and the divisions and conflicts it spawned, helps us to decipher patterns out of caudillo politics and state formation in the early republic, just as politics highlights the contours of trade policy. Causality is a multivariate two-way street. Peruvians (as even a glance at political records attests) openly recognized the relevance of trade policy to the wider political struggles of their time.[2] The deeply held regional and social commitments of Peruvian elites with respect to commercial policy (just touched upon) combine with diplomatic pressures to form one piece of the puzzle. Protectionism and liberalism established two broad zones of coastal influence across Peru, north versus south (while sierran regions shifted from one pole to the other), and this elicited overseas and neighboring-state interventions that only exacerbated the geopolitical rifts. If, in addition, the political and fiscal roots of trade-policy conflict are unearthed, a new basis exists for interpreting the evolution of Peru's central state. This hypothesis, however, does not reduce to the obviously wrong picture of rival elites charging into battle under banners of "free trade" and "protection." Trade policy was hardly the sole ingredient in

68

the boiling cauldron of Peruvian politics. Rather, this interpretation isolates the relevant commercial-political factors that fed into caudillo strife and explain its ongoing basis, then demise.[3]

Caudillismo developed a structural affinity with nationalist politics, which helped spark the wider conflicts blocking the formation of a stable national state from 1820 to 1845. In interrelated ways, the consolidating state from 1845 to 1852 had to be a liberal one. Two facets of the caudillo state are analyzed here. First, in this thematic chapter, we examine the nature of the embedded elites, institutions, and struggles that favored protectionism. Commercial policy sheds light onto dimly understood aspects of early Peruvian political structures and political culture, aspects that changed—or had to change—to permit a victory of free trade. These themes include militarism, centralism, federalism, populism, civil politics, plutocracy, and more. Here we also begin to glimpse the genesis of the novel liberal-elite politics of the 1840s. Second, in the next chapter, we uncover the material bedrock of caudillismo, its fiscal base, which allowed for the survival of militarism as a self-perpetuating political system, one with a pronounced protectionist slant. (That chapter also integrates the full chronology of the new liberals' triumph of 1840–52.) Together, these political and fiscal dynamics reveal why the ingrained economic nationalism of Peruvian elites found such resonance in the state. When nationalist political and tax structures altered in the mid-1840s, the path was finally clear for Castilla's construction of the relatively stable, liberal, and national state of the guano age.[4]

A Nationalist Caudillo "State"

Identification of the political interests of the caudillo state best begins with its mercurial elite, the caudillos themselves. When projecting themselves into the national political arena (the local basis for caudillismo, "gamonalismo," remains very obscure), most caudillos openly asserted themselves as partisans of specific trade policies. In Peru, other issues of national import, such as church/state or open federalist/centralist conflicts, provided comparatively little fuel for caudillo struggles, and the question of military versus civilian rule was a foregone conclusion. The peculiarity of Peru's caudillo trade politics stemmed in part from a striking geopolitical feature: the major port, central state, principal elites, and central artisan sector were all located in one city, Lima. To a large degree, caudillos adopted trade policies because these best expressed powerful regionalist aspirations, and because these military chiefs correctly sensed the importance of such policies for the economic viability of the Lima state, their ultimate prize. Mobilization tactics—ideological, social, and financial—prior to *pronunciamientos*, barracks revolts, or civil war, set forth the trade-policy positions and favors the victor would implement and dispense. These promises were generally respected, if unstable in the long run. Changes of government, which sometimes reached a dizzying velocity, usually marked deep changes in trade regimes: complete overhaul of tariff law, turnover in key personnel, and basic new attitudes toward foreign interests. In some cases, convictions even came into play, although the caudillos as a group appear less ideologically inclined than their civil-elite supporters. To be sure, caudillos sometimes fell into "opportunistic" or contradictory trade politics, abandoning their programs midstream for the lures of short-term (mainly fiscal) gains. But such turnabouts (e.g., those of La Fuente and Gamarra in 1829 and 1832) were usually contained by client-group pressures, especially the de facto veto exercised by Lima's protectionists and political bodies. It was, then, the seriousness, not the frivolity, with which caudillos played trade politics that best explains the chaotic succession of tariff legislation and economic projects in postindependence Peru.[5]

Illustrating a typical sequence of nationalist and liberal caudillo alliances—who they united and excluded, their consequences for trade policy and the state—will help us pinpoint some core dynamics of Peruvian caudillismo. The two examples here, the gamarrista "Restoration" of 1838–41 and the vivanquista "Regeneration" of 1841–44, were variants of caudillo scenarios played out time after time in the postindependence era.

The gamarrista triumph in late 1838 followed a prolonged military campaign by a motley union of close to a dozen major nationalist caudillos, aided by Chile and amply oiled by strident nationalist politics. Their political title, "Restoration"—all caudillo alliances assumed symbolic nicknames—meant in reality restoring Lima's commercial and political hegemony and placing northern agrarian and sierran economic interests back in power. The southerners and foreign consuls who had backed Santa Cruz and Orbegoso from 1836 to 1838 (in the Peru-Bolivia Confederation) knew exactly what was coming their way. They especially sensed the retributive mood of the enflamed conquerers. Warned one British envoy: "Hostility to Foreigners and to Foreign Commerce and Industry (in contradistinction to their Protection so wisely accorded by H. E. Gen. Santa-Cruz), will, I have no doubt, henceforth be the Fundamental Principle of Peruvian Policy; as Jealousy and Hatred of Foreigners are undoubtably the two most powerful characteristic passions of the Peruvian Nation."[6] European reasoning aside, they were at least right to predict now a Peruvian policy for a Peruvian nation.

This particular gamarrista coalition, so many diverse military chiefs with so many interests in tow, proved remarkably cohesive over the next three years, held together by antiforeign rage and the charismatic figure of Agustín Gamarra himself. Gamarra, after all, had been the chief military organizer of nationalist blocs since the mid-1820s. The gamarristas also had at their disposal the full powers, resources, and administrative personnel of the Lima state, and these could be deployed without danger of collapse from within. In the year or so following victory, Gamarra ordered these major policy changes: annulment of Santa Cruz's liberal pro-Bolivian tariff, new commercial code, and trade treaties with the United States and Britain; one week for foreigners to close all illegal retail establishments; rearrangement of tariffs to promote northern exchange of sugar for Chilean wheats; a total ban on foreign auctions (and exile or jail for their pariah owners); unheard-of new institutional powers for the Lima consulado, countless official monopolies (salt, tin, tobacco, auctions, snow, etc.), and the traders' exclusive right to devise the new protectionist tariff; charter of the quasi-statal Compañía Asiática for a national merchant monopoly on Asian trade; lucrative new incentives and guarantees for native merchants lending to the state; innumerable private prebends to Peruvian merchants (including one rather special new privilege for the export of "huano" to Europe); a prohibition on coarse-woolen textile imports while jacking up duties on a multitude of agricultural and artisanal goods; closure of most regional ports (especially those toward the south) and reservation of coastal shipping and fishing for nationals; an end to payments on the external debt and foreign claims (while diverting public funds to the internal debt held by Lima merchants and bondholders); the minting of debased currency against the interests and objections of foreign exporters; expulsion of overseas investors from mercury mines; and, last but hardly least, a draconian new "forced naturalization" campaign against foreigners.[7] The latter drive, compelling all foreign nationals to adopt Peruvian citizenship, or else, was magically to deprive them of consular protection and thereby make overseas merchants vulnerable at last to forced loans.[8]

This (nonexhaustive) list lends only the official flavor of a new trade regime. Behind the scenes, where a new administrative team took over, inveterate radicals such as Herrera, Iguaín, and Ferreyros (the hand-picked foreign minister) manipulated xenophobic politics to the limit. This politics combined simple revenge, personal advancement, and the need to widen the regime's political base—in addition to a well-calculated campaign to instill a fearful climate in which liberal foreign politics, property, and persons would be perpetually insecure.[9] The Huancayo Congress—purposely held in the Andean core of the coalition's base, so far from foreigners—solemnly discussed the most efficacious means for formally expelling all foreign traders and consuls from Peru. Rumors spread of an impending official debt moratorium: Peruvian merchants could default en masse on the millions owed to their foreign creditors.

Provincial military prefects across the country stepped up their routine raids on foreign shops and consulates, arresting merchants or instigating mobs against them. No foreigner was safe from these efforts to placate enraged provincial interests. Several died; a few others were hideously tortured (one English merchant woke up to discover a corpse carefully planted in his cell). Lima officials abetted xenophobic newspaper campaigns (with headlines such as "Death to Foreigners") and, in 1841, helped plot an actual assassination attempt against the despised British consul-general, B. H. Wilson, who sensibly fled Peru in time (not to be confused with his namesake, H. Wilson, expelled from his post at Tacna that same year). All attempts to shield foreigners from persecution were ably deflected by the hard-line Ferreyros. The new minister of war and finance (one Ramón Castilla) challenged the French chargé to a duel (using lances, Castilla's forte) for Saillard's insistence that Peru honor some tiny French loans to the defunct liberal regime.[10] (Cooler officials placed the consul in protective custody to avert his potentially embarrassing defeat.) A change in trade regimes, it becomes apparent, involved much more than simply raising or lowering tariff schedules.

Southerners as a whole took this calculated blow as well. All knew they had supported Santa Cruz, and would again if given half a chance. Lima levied special punitive taxes (e.g., those on the south's major products, wines and wheat) as well as monthly forced loans of $10,000. The rebellious province of Arequipa was split in two, its border with Bolivia closed. Gamarra downgraded Arica to secondary import status and threatened to shut down all other southern ports. Just in case liberal malcontents missed the point, the new military prefects stationed in the south were men especially renowned for their capricious nationalist zeal.[11]

One such malcontent was the southern caudillo Colonel Manuel Ignacio de Vivanco, one-time Arequipa prefect and old aristocratic associate of Pando, who launched his first counterattack there in January 1841. Vivanco received a local hero's welcome (despite the fact that this Lima-born officer had only adopted the south). Street crowds volunteered to man his army of "Regeneración," and the area's merchant class liberally signed up for the war bonds Vivanco issued from the Arica customshouse. (Cuzqueño elites wavered, then stuck to their gamarrista traditions, giving Gamarra a crucial military foothold in the south.) Southerners were especially cheered upon hearing Vivanco's first campaign pledge: to overturn the new protectionist tariff for the prosouthern 1836 Santa Cruz code.[12] Vivanco also increased his following by manifold promises to use his links with Bolivian rulers to gain open altiplano markets; to reopen Arica as a full-fledged entrepôt; to develop southern agriculture by restricting (Chilean and Argentine) grain and cattle imports into Moquegua, Arequipa, and Puno; and to lift all internal customs and cumbersome taxes on wine commerce, ban the sale of northern cane liquors, and find new outlets for southern vineyards, the area's leading industry. These were promises that could be redeemed only with a complete triumph over Lima. The Gamarra government vigorously condemned this "demagogic" exploitation of trade politics (the same politics they, of course, had used to seize power) and declared all loans to the rebels non-refundable, before sending their crack forces south to defend the nation and the national tariff.[13]

Vivanco was also eager to disclose his plans to British and French officials at Tacna and Arica (typically, the North Americans in Lima had barely heard of Vivanco). Foreigners were duly impressed, but unduly optimistic about Vivanco's chances: "Vivanco is well-disposed towards H.M.'s subjects and will not countenance the scandalous monopolies, nor cramp commerce in the way the *late* [*sic*] government did. . . . It is but justice to him to say that he listened with the greatest attention to all Mr. Wilson's suggestions in the favour of British interests."[14] From the field, Vivanco annulled the entire set of "forced naturalization" decrees. To the French, Vivanco offered a far sweeter plum: cancellation of the gamarristas' monopoly guano contract—to the national merchant Quirós—so that French merchants (such as Allier) could share in this bonanza. These gambles, though reflective of Vivanco's liberal thinking, failed to produce results. The foreign powers knew that intervention on this scale again could only mean their complete and violent finale in Peru. (For good measure, Gamarra expelled Hugh Wilson, the Tacna consul, merely for chatting with Vivanco. English merchants expressed relief that the punishments stopped there.)[15] Nor would Bolivia come to his aid this time; for, in 1841, the gamarrista analogue General Ballivián had just seized control.

Within a few months—as long as it took for troops to reach the blockaded south—Gamarra vanquished the vivanquistas. The ragtag southern militias were no match for Lima's superior generals (San Román and Castilla), endowed with the full resources of a central state (perhaps for the first time utilizing the trickle of funds from Lima's new guano monopoly). Characteristically, this did not mark any final Lima conquest. Vivanco revolted again in December of the same year (but then defected to Lima upon Gamarra's death at Ingavi later that month). Again, in 1843, the south rebelled under Vivanco's sponsorship and the same set of trade-policy pledges. This time (with northern caudillos in disarray) Vivanco managed to enter Lima and began to decree his full liberal program. The "Directorate," as this was called, in many ways reflected an old Bolivarian model of illustrious despotism and drew leadership from the last survivors of Pando's personal "tertulia," or entourage. Yet, unlike the northerners in power, Vivanco's regime remained unstable at its core. It could not go far in Lima's antisouthern climate, and the episode ended with the 1844 civilian revolt of Lima (led by prominent merchants such as Elías) against Echenique, Vivanco's *puneño* colleague.[16] This time, Castilla's new alliance, army, and guano reserves could make their victory stick, and southern revolts became, if never extinct, less threatening affairs.

These two polarities, northern protectionist caudillo alliances and southern liberal responses, dominated Peru's caudillo struggles for the twenty years between 1825 and 1845. After that, with the advent of the guano age, a new breed of centralized caudillo—liberal-nationalists within an institutionalizing state—took charge, before a final transition to civilian plutocratic rule in the 1870s. In some respects, Peru was following the modal pattern of nineteenth-century Latin American politics: the postindependence decades of militaristic regionalism, the midcentury centralizing caudillos of "order and progress," and the final coalescence of "oligarchic republics." But trade policy stamped Peruvian developments in special ways. What, to begin with, were the main elements in Peruvian politics that, at the outset of this process, so favored the northern protectionists?

Against the backdrop of ubiquitous protectionist sentiments in Peru—the endless clamoring for redress against foreign competition—protectionism rapidly emerged as the predominant caudillo ideology, and protectionists constituted a major prop and clientele. This makes sense "structurally" in the patrimonial ethos of caudillo politics. Protectionism was paternalism—the colonial conviction that the state existed to protect the jurisdictions, rights, and interests of vying corporate groups. For caudillos, paternalism was protectionism, especially in its ample capacity for proffering privileges and bonuses to potential client groups (no matter how this cluttered the ensuing protectionist programs). In this way, protectionism played into the vacuum and legacy left by the hierarchical colonial state. In contrast, the hallmark of liberalism—its uniformity or absence of particularist privileges—was its chief political liability for the caudillos. It would take very special conditions for liberal uniformity to become a "public good" for Peruvian elites. At first, the only tangible reward for distribution seemed to go to foreigners, an off-limits (or, at best, self-defeating) clientele in caudillo politics.[17]

By 1830, propelled by the anti-Bolivarian struggles, "gamarrismo," under such military leaders as Gamarra, La Fuente, San Román, Torrico, Salaverry, Castilla, Bermúdez, Eléspuru, and lesser notables, formed a fairly cohesive antiforeign, antiliberal "party." As the writer Flora Tristán noted, they heartily identified themselves with the protectionist "system of Gamarra." Despite recurrent rivalries, they continued to think and coalesce as the nationalist "gamarrista party," the same party blasted as the scourge of foreign consuls for more than twenty years. The regional base of the nationalist caudillos was often obvious: Lima, the north coast, and various interior provinces that could be carried into alliance. Place of birth was not the chief influence; rather, political prospects were the paramount concern for mobile caudillos. As prefect in the mid-1820s, Gamarra courted his first clientele among natal Cuzco groups, a following he maintained into the late 1830s (with lavish promises of textile protection and restrictions on foreigners) while wedding himself more and more to the emerging Lima and northern pro-Chilean and statist groups. Political power derived from gamarrista "authoritarianism" as well as from the campaigns against older "foreign" officers (Colombians) and for an expansive native military caste. Beneath everything, however, lay Lima's special resources for maintaining warrior cliques, as well as a strong appeal to concentrated Lima groups, at the hyperactive capital of protectionist politics. Capture and retention (and expansion) of Lima was, after all, the foremost prize in the caudillo struggles. Once there, Lima's vociferous protectionist groups, particularly the consulado, landed elites, and artisans, kept the caudillos on a steady protectionist path. The merchants repeatedly showed their preference for gamarrista "candidates" (indeed, the consulado's institutional stability often surpassed the state's itself). This pact is wonderfully glimpsed in the ways limeño aristocrats, political lights, and sugar barons led the core and cabinet of Salaverry's militarist machine of 1835.[18] (It also helped that, in sheer numbers, the vast majority of the early caudillos were scions of Lima and the coast.) But the existence of a state in Lima, however flimsy, was the nationalist bottom line. For, unlike the southern liberals, nationalist caudillos automatically found a rather elaborate administrative, financial, and military apparatus at their disposal. This allowed them far greater strategic flexibility and control.

Caudillos also found in Lima an amenable, well-defined, and notoriously nationalist bureaucratic elite, a group whose presence (though not ideas) overshadowed the more celebrated internationalist ideologues ready to aid liberal chiefs. Caudillos rarely stayed at the helm in Lima (their regimes were largely absentee, as they marched off to crush new rebellions, riding back to the city to collect fresh funds). This governing group, then, attained considerable informal power—men such as Manuel Ferreyros (in and out as foreign minister, whenever the hard line was demanded against foreign liberals) or Campo-Redondo, Larrea y Loredo, and Martínez, favorites for running that central institution for caudillos and trade policy alike, the Ministry of Finance. At times, the latter was appropriately renamed the Ministerio de Guerra y Hacienda; foreigners in turn dubbed gamarrista protectionism the "Ferreyros system," after their ubiquitous nemesis.[19] Functionaries such as Ferreyros and Eléspuru (frequent Lima prefect) effectively sealed the centralist bonds be-

75

tween limeño and militarist elites. And, against the foreign consuls, these men proved indispensable for safeguarding Peru's beleaguered economic sovereignty, if not statehood itself, in the postindependence era.

Outside Lima, a powerful centrifugal force acted on the core gamarrista generals, as well. This was a veritable army of minor rustic lieutenants and prefects whose main claim to fame was their unabashed xenophobia. A colorful and important example was Colonel José Félix Iguaín, a provincial chief who managed to complicate every antiliberal affair of the postindependence era, and from Piura to Tacna at that. "One of the most daring and dangerous Revolutionary Characters that has appeared in Spanish America," warned one British consul.[20] Their basically uncontrollable "outrages" against foreign interests (forced loans, closed shops, arbitrary expulsions, and assorted assassination plots against consuls) seemed to foretell, at least to foreigners, a Chinese path for Peru. In reality, their terroristic politics served to placate antiforeign provincial merchants and, in the larger game of national politics, to discredit their superiors and gain prominence by exposing a supposed laxity toward foreign incursions. These forces were at work beneath the 1839–41 gamarrista episode just described. Usually, however, such efforts only drove the leading Lima caudillos into a further spiral of protectionist radicalism. In this realm, Peruvian caudillos were akin to the Rosas-type "Americanist" parties found elsewhere on the continent, something foreigners recognized (and loathed). At heart, Lima cliques and caudillos desired some form of accommodation to the new foreign presence: namely, normal state-to-state relations and (protected) trade. Instead, the mavericks continuously brought Peru to the brink of war with foreign powers (as in 1830, 1839, and 1845—when they provoked the British bombing of Arica). Their pacification by General Castilla (himself no proxy for foreign interests) in 1845–46 was essential if Peru was to establish conventional overseas diplomatic ties, a prerequisite to guano-age stability and liberalism.[21]

Another, more social ingredient initially strengthened the hand of nationalist caudillos: the loosening of colonial social hierarchies, the blurring of social distinctions in the cauldron of embryonic republicanism, civil unrest, and prolonged depression. Nonelites could also participate in the informal or rustic arenas of caudillo showdowns, albeit on unequal terms. Protectionism was a decidedly "popular" cause, if any existed; at the very least, nationalists quickly showed that they were eager to dirty their hands in search of support. One example was how Lima's predominantly mestizo and black artisan guilds (and peddlers) curried favor with *militares* as well as with parliamentary politicians in exchange for tariff favors. With the institutional fluidity of the state (which precluded other methods of social control) and the absence of formal political parties, craftsmen came to exert their new pull in republican politics and were valued for their ability to mobilize forces for the paramilitary or electoral exploits so crucial to caudillos. Whether such factors operated in the interior remains unknown: did the new bands of destitute rural artisans flock to caudillo armies and color their politics? Gamarra's men at least acted like they did. Even congressional delegates recognized some relationship between unemployment and instability, as they voted for tariffs in the wider hope of establishing social peace and eclipsing caudillo rule.[22] And the frequent foreign denunciations of the gamarristas, especially provincial ones, as "rude Indians" or "Incas" (most, like Gamarra himself, were mestizos) suggest cultural or racial affinities at play in the struggle between free trade and protectionism. The nationalists were, after all, up against the Europeanization of Peru.

Against these forces and factors, the isolated liberal caudillos and políticos hardly stood a chance in national politics. Waves of nationalist backlash could always drown or fatally obstruct the programs of such free traders as Orbegoso, La Mar, Vidal, Nieto, Vivanco, and Santa Cruz, more loyal descendants of Bolívar. Liberals, to begin with, suffered a grave geopolitical disadvantage. The endgame in caudillo struggles was the capture and pilferage of the Lima state and, ultimately, the transformation of its policies. The south's customshouse at Arica or the recruitment of Arequipa's popular classes was sufficient only for sparking a rebellion. Granted, this was enough to keep the south in turmoil for most of the era. But the liberals based in the south were essentially "stateless" relative to their northern rivals. As one critical example, the Peruvian navy could effectively blockade the south, and it did at every given opportunity.[23] If temporarily victorious, moreover, liberals soon operated in hostile territory, for virtually all of Lima's organized groups, elite and popular alike, were nationalist, with the notable exception of their target, the local foreign community.

Under these conditions, liberal conquests followed a monotonous pattern: a dictatorial free trade by decree, repression against Lima elites, a resurgence of Lima protectionists, and on to the final defection of garrisons and finance ministers. Neither side seemed much committed to civil or democratic process. Still, the professional liberal collaborators (the Pandos and Vidaurres) failed time after time to realize their top-down projects from the Ministry of Finance; they were stopped in their tracks by the noncooperation or uncivil disobedience of limeño interests, usually the consulado, as in 1830, 1832–34, and 1836–38. The Peru-Bolivia Confederation (1836–38) epitomized this regional and political debility of free-trade caudillos. Its southern component, the "Estado sur-peruano," could approximate a form of representative government, and even foreshadowed the weakening mid-1830s appeal of gamarristas in Cuzco. (Perhaps it was, as some now suggest, an embryonic southern-state ideal, though linked to the early southern expansion of British trade.) But its northern half, the "Estado nor-peruano," was bogus, being little more than a bald dictatorship of the south over the north. Even its principal functionaries (e.g., arequipeño Pío Tristán and Colombian García del Río) had to be imported, for Lima's aristocracy declined to cooperate.[24] The consulado resisted these aliens from start to finish. Without external support, the northern state was doomed to fail.

A second factor gave protectionist caudillos their edge over liberals: the dramatic effects that nationalist (or xenophobic) politics could produce in the midst of specific tariff struggles. Liberals were always tainted by close association with foreigners, real or imagined. Indeed, with few other groups to court in Peru, the link with foreign merchants, powers, and doctrines was often real enough, even as it discredited the liberal cause. But the easily discernible concessions to foreigners spelled political suicide, constituting a perfect issue for rallying protectionists under the selfless cover of "national sovereignty." The weakness of Peruvian political institutions facilitated the multifarious guises the backlash could assume, from endless stalling in Congress to all-out caudillo war. Thus, for example, when La Mar and Orbegoso placed foreign merchants on tariff commissions (in 1827 and 1834) they doomed the chances for congressional reform and, indeed, furthered protectionism. When Orbegoso conceded auction rights to two small U.S. merchants in 1834, as seen, the nationalist outrage of the consulado ended only with the president's ouster.[25] "Han vendido la patria a Extranjeros"—usually "ingleses," as Anglos were hard to distinguish—became the most potent protectionist refrain, capable of unifying the most disparate forces. Even Peru's best committed liberals found it impossible to concede too much to foreigners, knowing these political costs. In this way, they internalized the constraints of nationalist politics, disappointing their foreign mentors time and time again. For example, although everyone knew where he stood, Pando could never simply follow foreigners' whims, even under prodding. Santa Cruz himself dressed up Confederation liberalism in a "national" cloak (to the dismay of London), but to no avail. And gamarristas, when forced onto a liberalizing path, had to compensate by placating their nationalist constituents in other fields. In one astonishing December 1832 episode, Gamarra, hoping to ease some import prohibitions (for access to customs) and finding not a single high-level official publicly willing to renounce them, decided it prudent to outlaw foreign retailing in the same liberal package. He ended up destroying his entire liberalization drive instead.[26] In sum, Peru's political dynamics always led to further protectionism, never to free trade.

Liberal caudillos and functionaries, in the third place, also worked under a fatal assumption: that foreign powers might truly substitute for domestic support. Yet, by nature (and nurtured by Peruvian experience), free-trade imperialists were out to minimize messy political, financial, or military entanglements in Peru, as were the risk-avoiding overseas merchant houses. Liberals, while placing their political careers and stability itself at extreme risk, gained few concrete benefits from liberalization. Foreign consuls and merchants offered some technical advice on tariffs and gave moral support (in 1837, Santa Cruz received a stirring letter of commendation from the young Queen Victoria!) but little more. Financial rewards, desperately needed for regime consolidation and defense, were paltry. Foreign houses avoided lending even to liberals, while formal overseas credit on the London exchange remained paralyzed by Peru's 1820s default and perpetual instability. Any wider spin-offs of liberalization—the upsurge in commerce, investment, and customs revenues a treaty alliance might bring—were so long-term as to be of no practical use. The brief lifespan of liberal caudillos, made even briefer by the instantaneous mobilization of nationalists their announced policies provoked, meant in effect no harvest of liberal benefits. These were Orbegoso's fatal dilemmas in 1834. And when the crunch came, foreign military support was out of the question. Foreign gunboats would not intervene to save their surrogates (much less promote liberal tariffs), but only for limited police actions to safeguard their merchants from actual physical assaults, as during the banditry that accompanied turmoil in 1830, 1835, 1836, and 1840. As Santa Cruz watched his financial and military base crumble in 1838, for example, he worked frantically to lure his overseas mentors into a military defense of his regime, sending off long lists to London of all he had done in the name of liberal foreigners. He screamed betrayal loud and clear, for the British, French, and North Americans knew precisely when to cut their losses.[27] Liberal caudillos were basically on their own in the framework established by free-trade imperialism.

An institutionalized relationship among foreign diplomacy, free-trade finance, and liberal state building, therefore, first required the consolidation of political stability in Peru. Foreign interests would not and could not help create that stability; and continuing instability intrinsically favored nationalism on more than one score.[28] Turmoil spawned risks and protectionist responses, fed into caudillo backlash, and kept foreign influence at bay. The very real process of political and economic integration with foreign states—treaty negotiations, credit restoration, liberal concessions, export expansion—could begin in earnest only after 1845 when, largely for regional reasons, the abatement of caudillo turmoil finally became feasible. Even then, foreign interests faced serious roadblocks from die-hard Peruvian nationalists that lasted well into the 1850s.

Congress blocked treaties and expelled consuls, debt negotiations stalled, and resurgent nationalist demands flourished. Peru would, however, finally make it into the international state system, with all the discipline this implied for Peruvian politics and policies. The financial aspects of this story will soon become clear.

The two-decade politico-military stalemate of the caudillos, which fueled the spiraling instability of the central state between 1825 and 1845, boils down to two political factors. First, liberal chiefs, based mainly in the south, were incapable of subduing Lima; or, when they were, policy implementation was thwarted, and no one came to their rescue. But their failure to conquer Lima or even to exact liberal concessions only hardened southern-separatist resolve during the 1830s. Second, the nationalist Lima state was hamstrung as well. Owing to a chronic dearth of resources (for an efficient military and transport apparatus), effective control rarely extended beyond the north, thus allowing southern rebellion to seethe. Until the mid-1840s, the central state, while able to decree an endless stream of protectionist measures, could not pacify the rest of Peru, and thus make good on its nationalist promises.

As will soon become obvious, the protectionist elites, by their affinity with and dependence on nationalist caudillos, had actually made an unfortunate long-term political choice, for the fratricidal caudillos made inherently unstable allies. It was not really a "choice" at all, but a natural symbiosis, for protectionism itself stemmed from and thrived on tumult. And when, after years of deadlocked and ineffectual policies, the caudillos turned on the protectionists during the horrific phase of state disintegration in the early 1840s, northern elites had seen enough.[29] They were ready to defect to liberalism and to a more minimalist but reliable, state.

PACIFICATION, GUANO, AND
LIBERAL PLUTOCRACY

The unmaking of interminable caudillismo, Peru's 1840s pacification process, was filled with paradox, particularly for trade policy. Lima was helped by technical-military innovations (the steamboat) and a favorable international conjuncture (Chilean support and Bolivian nationalist regimes that stymied southern separatism), but especially by access to the new riches of guano. Early guano revenues were channeled almost exclusively into military projects: the consolidation of the state was brought about by the transmutation of silver into guano, and of guano into power. But neither the stabilizing nor the liberalizing effects of guano were all that obvious, as this preview will show.

Lima's singular and profitable form of statist control over the new export, monopoly and consignment, was hardly fortuitous, but was modeled on the time-honored nationalist merchant formulas at their apogee when guano was "discovered" in late 1840. Nor were the forms taken by Peruvian state consolidation coincidental. The two fortunate and fundamental accidents in the process were that guano, which required few local inputs (simply birds, shovels, and conscript labor), was an island export uniquely amenable to rapid development during protracted instability and that it fell into the lap of the Lima state. The Chincha Islands were close at hand and easy to control, exploit, and monopolize from Lima. Moreover, foreign shippers and investors did not seem to mind that the caudillos whom they paid for export rights were busily destroying themselves in a frenzied fratricidal contest from 1841 to 1845—a contest that finally produced a clear set of victors, northern victors who had strong notions of what to do with the state this time. That Ramón Castilla, the stepson of gamarrista nationalism (Gamarra's last minister of finance in 1841), led the consolidation process from 1845 actually makes perfect sense. Besides their recent military debacle, liberal caudillos had little chance of success with either political pacification or development of the guano trade, particularly as negotiating the delicate new relations with foreign powers would have left them exposed to the usual destabilizing nationalist fury. Castilla even resurrected ultranationalist Ferreyros to contain the inevitable foreign pressures during this sensitive transformation while, on the home flank, the last aging internationalist, Manuel del Río, was charged with implementing economic reforms.[30] The triumph of centralized caudillismo under Castilla and Echenique after 1845—with their increasingly professionalized and nationalized army—moved apace with the availability of guano funds, although the process of repression/co-optation is far from documented. (For one thing, monies were available to buy off, or integrate, restless southern militias and their commanders.) Yet, among other paradoxes, a continuing guano trade required a rapprochement with the foreign powers Lima had always opposed, not to speak of overt concessions and guarantees for the foreign guano consignees themselves—particularly if Lima was to maintain its fragile new hegemony over Peru.

The *pax castillana* thus involved, in rapid succession during 1845–46, the stamping out of radical nationalist "caudillitos" (notably, exile for Iguaín, who would later die in prison); co-optation of the south (the opening of Arica as an independent port of deposit); a halt to the antiforeign merchant campaigns ("forced naturalization" decrees, especially, and the calculated insecurity of foreign property rights in general); and a rapid start to negotiations on foreign claims, loans, and trade treaties. Like trade-policy conflict before it, guano became the fulcrum for interacting external and internal pressures on the state, and Peru's new leaders seized the critical moment in 1845.[31] In this way, guano helped establish the modicum of stability needed to make liberalism a viable (or even desirable) alternative for the first time in the republic. Once secured, Lima's monopoly over guano ensured a quite literal monopoly of violence, put to good work.

Nationalist consolidation thus quickly turned into a broad liberalizing front, and continued stability in the late 1840s only reinforced these hesitant first steps. For the first time since 1821, a shaky peace allowed external pressures and incentives to work incrementally on the Peruvian state. Finally, Peru's legendary export potential (that begger atop a mountain of "gold") could freely exercise its more obvious and direct liberalizing effects on the economic consciousness of Peruvian elites, although the forms of liberal conversion were, as will be shown, quite specific. Liberalization by guano was no simple handmaiden of opportunity cost—nor of greed: nationalism and guano bequeathed stability, which in turn helped give birth to liberalism, the reverse of Peru's old instability-disequilibrium trap. Guano's consolidating and liberalizing impact was mediated by a host of related and necessary political, diplomatic, military, commercial, and financial transformations in the state. Dramatic changes within the Lima nationalists were also at work.

The legacy of early nationalism on the guano enterprise itself ran deep, especially that of the merchant radicals. It explains that singular paradox so central to Peru's guano-age state: an extreme import liberalism fueled by a statist—and in some ways still highly nationalist—export monopoly. The foreign powers attracted by Peruvian dunghills in 1841 initially interpreted the exclusive contracts and absurd claims of state ownership as just the latest instances of an endless string of discriminatory gamarrista monopolies. They were right. The guano monopoly was patterned after the consulado's traditional monopolies, meant to protect and enrich national entrepreneurs while providing the state with a decent income.[32] Only once established did the Peruvian caudillos realize that this estanco was of a different order: not only were they suddenly solvent, but they were potentially the richest military clan on the planet! The rapid transfer of export quotas from national merchants to the better-endowed and more capable foreign houses, starting in 1841, was the natural next step. Adroit management and strict control of the opportunity was essential, and Castilla, from inception to full bloom, saw to that. Had guano been discovered and developed at a later liberal date, by a different Peruvian regime—or had Castilla lost his challenge to a French consul—its history and Peru's would have been very different.

So too with the long-term evolution of the guano monopoly and its impact on Peruvian society. Britain, France, and the United States never ceased to oppose the monopoly, and little Peru never ceased to defend its curious sovereignty over bird excrement, against the concerted efforts of the nineteenth century's liberal superpowers.[33] How could this be without Peru's previous training on the battlegrounds of postindependence trade policy? This time, however, Peruvian resistance occurred within the framework of normalized and conventional diplomatic channels.

Despite the (clearly necessary) early concessions to foreign houses such as Gibbs and Montané to cultivate the monopoly's overseas markets and trade, Peruvian export policy actually became even more nationalist over time. Starting in 1849, Peru adopted an incremental nationalization program for the trade. Surprisingly modern in tone, the aptly named "hijos del país" laws aimed at placing management and profits directly into the hands of private national entrepreneurs, working in concert with the state. By the 1860s, this program (which again enraged foreign potentates) proved eminently successful. Peruvian traders became respected men in the markets of Liverpool, Baltimore, and Bordeaux. At home, the enriched guano barons went on to build Peru's modern finance structures, to design and expand its state, to diversify the country's export base, and quite literally to become the modern plutocracy that would run Peru, not just the guano enterprise, for decades to come.[34] (The fiscal dimensions of this policy and state-building push will be analyzed shortly.)

One overlooked angle of this familiar story is its origins. The merchant "hijos del país" who, starting in 1849, forced Peru to nationalize the trade fully were, to a man, none other than the seasoned merchant nationalists of the 1830s. They had not only come of age in the prior nationalist era. Their "anti-imperialist" entrepreneurial rhetoric, which worked so well in the sons-of-the-country debates, was simply a vintage nationalism specially rebottled for the occasion—and it still carried great resonance for Peruvian opinion and state-makers. Peru still needed, so they claimed, "national capitalists"; the state still belonged to Peruvians.[35] Literally, the board of directors of Gamarra's failed Asian Trade Company, traders such as Barreda, Quirós, and Rodrigo, resurfaced as the successful directors of a worldwide guano-export concern, the first national consignees in 1851. The old merchants reincarnated as "internationalist" liberals. And so at last the old "hijos del país" came of age as the new "dueños del país," as well.[36]

There are two ways to interpret this process. On the one hand, the liberalism of the late nineteenth century was deeply marked by the nationalism from which it came. That is true. Alternatively, it underscores that the new liberalism of elites and the state remained ever ambiguous, never straying too far beyond their pocketbooks. The costs of liberalism—of unimpeded free trade—would be borne by other sectors of

Peruvian society, those have-nots shut out of the new statism. The plutocratic elite continued to enjoy a plethora of pecuniary contracts,
giveaways, sinecures, policy favors, and sheer venality based on a symbiotic relation with the Peruvian state—this time, however, one fed by
liberalism and guano. In new ways, then, that old compact between the
high Lima elite and their state seemed to persist or even deepen during
the allegedly liberal guano age.[37]

Incontrovertible, though, is one striking feature of Peru's nineteenth-
century export experience: the unique national-statist and entrepreneurial control which meant that an astonishing share of the final returns—
some estimate more than 70 percent—remained at home. This record
would not be approached again by other export nations until the mid-
twentieth century.[38] The elites' radical new import liberalism and new
statism may have helped squander the long-term benefits of these riches
for nineteenth-century Peru at large, but their old nationalism had made
this proverbial "lost opportunity" available in the first place.

Economic liberalism after 1845 also brought about the twilight of the
caudillos, as one might expect. The old Lima-militarist pact was slowly
transcended by a compact with liberal civil elites, with fiscal transformations at the heart of the story. Domingo Elías, Santiago Távara, and Francisco Quirós, three of the earliest, wealthiest, and most nationally based
of the merchant converts to free trade (they exempted their own vineyards, sugar mills, and guano deposits, of course), launched in 1845 the
first concerted drive for a civilian elite politics in Peru.[39] Along with such
thinkers as Gálvez, and such financiers as Candamo, they were also
among the closest of Castilla's civilian entourage when he began to build
the stable central state of the guano age. Clearly, the equation of unpredictable militarism with antiforeign primitivism, predation, protectionism, and no-growthism figured in the merchants' calculation. By
1850, this voice rang loud in their newspaper (and political club), *El Progreso*—as the name suggests, virtually a bourgeois platform for free
trade, alignment with new regional liberals, capitalist reform of the state,
national guano contracts, and civil control over politics. The year 1851,
by happenstance, saw both Peru's first peaceful transfer of power (albeit,
between two military men) and the victory of free trade. The liberal-elite
efforts to replace and succeed the vintage caudillos moved slowly,
though. As throughout Latin America, the transitional 1850s and 1860s
in Peru marked, in effect, a liberal alliance with the stable centralized
caudillos—who richly rewarded their liberal kin with handouts as well as
with increased political clout within the strengthening state. Castilla and
his ilk were the closest Peru had to nineteenth-centry caudillos of "order
and progress," but it was enough. By 1872, this liberal-praetorian state
had bequeathed a Peruvian plutocracy potent enough to manage directly,

on their own, their own state.[40] "Civilismo" was born and, with it, for better or worse, Peru's modern saga of elite party politics.

A CONGRESS OF PROTECTIONISTS

Apart from the maze of militarist politics, three civilian elite institutions wielded significant political pull in republican trade policy: national congresses, local federalist councils, and bureaucratic interests within and around the Ministry of Finance. Liberal civilismo had its civil antecedents. Yet, until the late 1840s, all three bodies had built-in biases toward protectionism. Their transformation after 1845 heralded the victory of free trade. It is best to begin with the congresses.

The capricious meddling of caudillos in legislative processes has led historians to underestimate the legitimate role of civilian republican forums after independence; consequently, no study of the development or impact of Peruvian congresses exists. This, despite the fact that congresses, the bastions of elite political pretension, were frequent (suspended only during prolonged bouts of internecine strife), courted and respected by many political factions, and the scene of continual and sophisticated policy debates, particularly over commercial policy. Moreover, each episode of parliamentary government, or the fact of legalistic republicanism itself, worked to bolster protectionist causes. So much so, that by the late 1840s, after Peru's surviving caudillos had generally turned liberal, free traders recognized Congress as the last obstacle to free trade.

A comprehensive litany of congressional trade-policy initiatives could encompass a whole book. National assemblies in 1823 and 1825–26 began the assertion of local nationalist economic grievances against Bolivarian occupiers. After involved and passionate studies and debates, the 1827–28 Congress culminated in the prohibitions policy and a host of ultranationalist legislation. The congressional nature of prohibitions (all constitutions vested tariff-making in legislators) meant that revocation would come only after a decade of counterattacks.[41] From 1831 to 1833, congresses deliberately and successfully obstructed the refinement and implementation of the internationalist liberalization package. Significantly, the Confederation enacted its liberal tariff and overseas trade treaties without convoking a Peruvian Congress; this made their repeal a heated defense of legalism by nationalists. The 1839 Huancayo Congress was the most nationalist body in Peruvian history. It came close to severing Peruvian relationships with the external world, while allowing protectionist groups (e.g., the consulado) a direct voice in its proceedings. Pent-up protectionist demands flooded the little-known 1845 Congress with complex debates around a new industrialization policy to help Peru maintain its precarious new internal peace.[42] The 1847 and 1848–49 congresses elicited a widespread protectionist backlash against the initial effects of guano prosperity. Politicians heartily endorsed it (allowing, once again, old guild leaders and new industrialists to plead successfully before the chambers) and resisted the government's plans of tariff reductions and financial and trade accords with overseas powers. Only with the 1850–52 Congress, and a rapid wave of liberal conversions that swept reluctant deputies and senators, did free trade stand a chance.[43] Thereafter, congresses could handily ignore the die-hard protests of protectionist groups in their halls, as they proved in the aftermath of the 1858 Lima-Callao artisan riots. Other elite political bodies, such as the Napoleonic watchdog Consejo de Estado, appear equally nationalist in policy until their role, too, reversed in the late 1840s.

As such, congresses represented the central forums for the ventilation, collection, and escalation of protectionist pressures. Delegates, unlike the caudillos, were well versed in the latest European controversies over "Political Economy" yet, like Peru's merchants, usually manipulated these to resist free trade. Foreigners often noted, with chagrin, that the políticos appeared far more antiforeign than the Peruvian people at large. The protectionist propensity of Congress was so notorious to contemporaries that the greatest nightmare of foreign consuls and liberals was a simple constitutional prerogative: the one requiring legislators to ratify each and every article of new tariff codes. Followed to the letter, which it usually was, this meant that each trade-policy project, painstakingly devised by small, handpicked executive or congressional committees, faced an agonizing but certain death in congressional debate.[44] (The United States, for example, sapped all its energies between 1827 and 1835 trying to sway the congresses, which invariably turned against them.) Apart from the inventing of new constitutions, commercial issues probably ranked as the leading item discussed in Peru's congressional agendas from 1825 to 1852.

Many factors account for this congressional passion for protectionism, and for the close correlation of protectionist campaigns with the meeting of congresses. First is the simple clarification that, despite known obstacles, representatives seemed to take their jobs seriously. They tried to represent faithfully their constituencies (rather elite ones, given the strict voter qualifications), and economic grievances ranked first. These were usually protectionist, and many a congressional record is punctuated, as in 1828 and 1845, by emotive speeches decrying the deleterious effects of foreign trade on this or that province.[45] Deputies and senators also duly represented themselves; the fact that most were "propietarios," for example, hardly hurt agrarian protectionism, that motive force of the nationalist movement. Second, national congresses served as the only proportional meeting ground for provincial interests in the Peruvian political system. By simple arithmetic, easily discernible in surviving vote counts, the regions (sierra and north, at least) together made an overwhelming protectionist majority.[46] Other policy-making bodies (e.g., the Finance Ministry) did not have to give serious consideration to regional concerns, and rarely did. It is no accident that the 1830s, when successive civil wars scuttled most congresses, show the most distinctly Lima-oriented economic policies.

Third, and most important, the holding of congresses itself excited a contagious protectionist mobilization, one that was rarely restrained once it reentered the chambers. Lively debates in Congress, instantly disseminated in newspapers, were public knowledge and controversy, especially in such a compact world as literate Lima. (As with other matters, such open debate recedes perceptibly during the peaks of caudillo campaigns or repression.) Nationalist arguments swiftly gained ground, goaded along by spirited pressures of lobbies such as Lima merchants, hacendados, and guilds—all within walking distance of Congress. Just in case, artisans would enthusiastically pack the galleries, providing catcalls or cheers on each político's move. Trade politics thus acquired a kind of escalating "demonstration and pork-barrel" effect. As one group or region won protectionist concessions, all other groups unleashed their demands, which were, each argued, just as "worthy." Congress heeded all. This phenomenon erupted most dramatically during the 1828, 1845, and 1849 debates. Its spontaneity had little to do with a planned program of balanced protectionism.[47] It also reflected a curious and overlooked side of the caudillo period: this was surely one of the most politically open eras in Peruvian history, a time when institutions (and the class structure) had yet to assume their stifling formality.

Fourth, congresses were also nationalist arenas in the broadest sense: delegates considered themselves to be "nation-builders" (and, as time wore on, as opposed to the disruptive caudillos). Economic nationalism came as second nature in this milieu. Peru's need for an "economic independence" to match its political sovereignty was one stirring ideal linked to protectionism. Other representatives argued that the state needed national capitalists to guarantee its existence or that protected industries would alleviate the social rot (e.g., unemployment) weakening the fabric of Peruvian society and government. Only in the late 1840s would "nationalist" free-trade arguments come forth; for example, those vaunting Peru's need for freedom from Chile or touting liberalism as a national policy to bring the regions into Peru. Finally, as good politicians, the members of the Peruvian Congress were politically astute. They understood clearly what "electors" (urban elites, master artisans, merchants, hacendados) expected, not to mention the expectations of restless or allied military officers. They were highly attuned to the political costs of appearing too liberal and to the rewards, electoral or otherwise, of nationalist rhetoric.[48]

There was, then, a built-in protectionist slant to Congress, that salon of the rich, cosmopolitan, and educated. Liberals (and foreigners) quickly grasped the dynamic: that congressional sessions on tariffs, and the wider controversy they aroused, invariably harmed their cause. Thus, most liberalization schemes went hand in hand with conscious efforts to stifle debate. In some circumstances, liberals defended the integrity of national political institutions (such was Pando's reaction to obtuse foreign pressures); in most cases, they and desperate caudillos resorted to a combination of secretive, exclusionist, or autocratic politics. Semiclandestine tariff commissions served this purpose (e.g., in 1827 and 1834), as did free trade by fiat in 1836 and systematic admonitions to keep the public uninformed on tariff revisions (strikingly so in 1840).[49] Since protectionism thrived on "democratic" process, free trade (so unlike its coeval popular movements in Europe) became antidemocratic. More was at work here than the Bolivarian legacy.

THIS PROCESS culminated, and reversed, during the 1849–52 tariff struggle, the final conflict to usher in the radical free trade of the guano age. It would seem a landmark in the narrowing of Peruvian democracy as well. By 1850, as we will review later in full, key Peruvian elites already embraced liberalism: the national merchants, regional oligarchies, ex-caudillos, fiscal functionaries, native bondholders, urban consumers, and others experiencing renewed pleasures of imports or new visions for national development. Moreover, the novel income of guano was increasing social distances as never before in the republic. Only Congress still seemed to ignore the liberal imperative.

Most important, liberals, ever more vocal, had realized the essentially political nature of Peru's lingering protectionism. The problem was not the absence of protectionism, as normally assumed, but its ubiquity. The open congressional tariff debates in 1848–50 (exacerbated by the heated presidential contest between Echenique and Vivanco) had once again unleashed the frustrations of myriad groups, this time those left out of the first stage of guano recovery. The usual contagion of tariff demands erupted as deputies and political "clubs" bowed to each group: first to Peru's hopeful new factory pioneers, then to lowly artisans (squeezed between revived craft imports and an unsettling inflationary spiral), followed by a welter of agrarian and regional interests.[50] Prohibitive tariffs appeared to be on the rebound, before Peru could even savor the first fruits of its newfound stability and export bonanza.

Soon enough, young liberal ideologues (led by Peru's first student class in "Political Economy") counterattacked with untried but remarkably effective political solutions and tactics. They stressed the open incompatibility of chaotic protectionist demands, and deftly used it to divide their bickering foe. Above all, for the first time, in 1850–51, they advocated minimal and uniform ad valorem tariffs—with no exceptions granted for any group, no matter how worthy their cause. A single-standard radical free trade, these "cursantes de economía política" argued, was the only way to arrest the endless debates and populist concessions that invariably drove Peru to a closed economy. Their case for Manchesterian uniformity rang true, not as an imported and trendy ideology (for Peruvians had never swallowed imports, not even corn laws, whole). For now, even sympathetic politicians grasped the irrational results of ad hoc favoritism. This system privileged a few groups, yet no longer seemed to jell into a coherent alternative to liberal development.

But who were Manchester's uniformity (and goods) aimed at? What rooted the new politics of trade in local terrain? Old-style trade politics, stressed the *cursantes*, had delivered excessive political might to groups such as Lima's artisans. Who were this riffraff—"populacho"—to dictate now the sybaritic lifestyles of an emerging plutocracy? As trivial as it sounds, this argument now resounded in a high society where consumption increasingly legitimized class status as well as welfare. The protectionist "threat" symbolized concerns beyond the economic. In any case, free traders added, the "nationalism" of artisans was bogus. It was utterly dependent on Peru's most Europeanized and elite consumers, and increasingly serviced by Lima's foreign-immigrant craftsmen to boot. Moreover, in this liberal crusade, even eminently respectable protectionism (such as that for Lima's promising factory experiments) had to go in order to contain protectionist epidemics. This meant no special tariff favors, a sacrificial demand that even some of the class-conscious factory pioneers swiftly embraced.[51] For there was no safe middle ground, in contrast to what some politicians still believed, of prudent, selective protectionism. In short, if economic policy had to be depoliticized, low uniform tariffs could do the job.

For most elites, whose investments spanned several spheres, the switch now to liberal political economy could be had at minimal cost, if not personal benefit. Not so for those others in Peruvian society who were wedded to traditional skills; no funds would help them retool for the guano age. Sensing the tide against them in 1850, and the betrayal of their old politician-allies, Lima artisans launched a series of bitter attacks against liberals, the Congress, and guano elites ("aristocrats" all). This was Peru's delayed and miniature "1848." In the early months of 1850, Lima's popular Jacobins stridently demanded even more protectionism and an independent political mobilization to get it. (Indeed, some even hoped to replace unresponsive políticos with craftsmen.)[52] In fact, this unusual radical outcry was a sign of artisan weakness, not strength. Outnumbered in the emerging liberal economy, they were losing their privileged political ground as well.

In this sense, the victory of free trade in Peru emerged from "class struggle." Even this slight exposure to pugnacious artisan-democrats and other petite bourgeoisie in 1850 persuaded fearful elites, with prodding from their neoliberal ideologues, to mend their ways and redefine their interests separately. They were not only to be import-consuming plutocrats (endowed with guano wealth to ease their transition). They were Peru's true guardians of social order, rational political process, and economic development. Elite liberal pretensions were defined in reaction against the rabble below and, equally significant, against any political attempts, even their own, at manufacturing. (Their self-sacrificed and soon abandoned factories were to become, ironically, Lima's most striking mausoleums of nationalist "failure.") In the years 1848–52, Peru's liberal economic norms and policies were set for the remainder of the nineteenth century, and with them was born Peru's modern oligarchic consciousness. Artisans and other popular elements (while temporarily soothed by the liberals' low-cost food and cloth imports) proved remarkably conscious themselves of this historic shift in elite politics, and despaired. The "artisan voice" was to become, as one craftsman later bewailed, "like the prophet in the desert, with no one to hear them or make fruit from such burning desires."[53] The radical free-trade standard in Congress was integral to all these developments.

Brandishing this simple argument in the final debates of September 1851, liberals rapidly won congressional support. Peru's deputies and senators had exhausted themselves by the ritual of following the snowballing whims of every protectionist lobby. Their conversion was dramatic and swift: the same body that had unanimously voted 90-percent craft duties in November 1849 approved, almost to a man, tariffs of 15–25 percent two years later, including the rollback of special industrial tariffs. Not only did this mark Peru's first genuine free-trade code, but the new law also explicitly prohibited any and all political tampering with tariff rates, privileged specific duties, and executive amendment.[54] In this way, liberalism—and this fight was posed explicitly against the politicized corporate handouts of the caudillo era—finally became a palpable "public good" for Peruvian elites. By finally conquering Peru's intractable political system, free trade could at least endure. Thus closed Peru's long era of open trade politics.

This conflictive episode in midcentury political culture deserves highlight because, besides the welter of key issues resolved here, Peru's other arenas of class strife were remarkably quiet. Peru had no rebelling peasants, recalcitrant nobles, or striking workers to speak of. What differentiated Peru's little "1848" from the real, European kind (besides the one-year lag) was precisely the role of free trade. In Europe, nineteenth-century free trade was less critical (freedom of industry more so). But free trade acquired distinctly "popular" overtones, argued, in the main, against the "feudal" privileges of rural landed gentry, who starved urban groups (middle classes, laborers, the bourgeoisie) with their exorbitant grain. And when some artisans (like those in Paris and in German towns) added protectionism to their revolutionary agendas, liberals, libertarians, and socialists alike joined in strenuous efforts to purge these popular errors. In Peru—and most of Latin America for that matter—there were few democratic attempts to persuade artisans, who by 1850 were the last major protectionist lobby. In Santiago, Bogotá, La Paz—and Lima—more political energies went toward excluding them; and free trade, rather than being aimed against rural oligarchs, seemed to be a major issue conjoining urban and rural magnates.[55] National social structures were that different from those of Europe, and even small differences could visibly affect emerging political structures. In Latin America, by 1850, the expendable groups were mainly popular and (besides the otherwise excludable peasant masses) few in numbers. At one pole of world economy, trade policy contributed to democratization; in places like Peru, it helped detract.

Like all questions of democracy, this was one of "politics for whom?" For some, mainly regional groups, as we will next see, elite liberal state-building meant greater, not less, representation in the state. To be sure, other pressures and other arguments also propelled the liberal juggernaut. But in the political forums, and for a majority of Peruvians of limited mobility and incomes, exclusionist liberalism had indeed begun its long career in Peru.

NEIGHBORHOOD NATIONALISTS

When economic nationalism had thrived at the apex of the Peruvian political system, it also received impetus from below. In the mid-1820s, Peru's first national (i.e., anti-Bolivarian) constitution embraced short-lived decentralist experiments, in a country renowned for its centralist traditions. Apart from autonomous municipalities, major tasks of local representative government fell to the *juntas departamentales*. The juntas, essentially federalist councils of provincial notables, were charged among other things with the "promotion of local industry" through designated commissions of industry, commerce, and agriculture. Their efforts deserve study.[56] How otherwise to understand the failure of federalism?

The juntas enthusiastically embraced their new economic role. They rapidly emerged as focal points for elite economic grievances, as regional pressure groups against the central government, and as nodes of autonomous policy-making (along with, of course, those most freewheeling of policy-makers, the rustic caudillos à la Iguaín). As one example, the Cuzco junta devoted session after session in the late 1820s and early 1830s to protests to Lima for prohibitions on foreign cloth and retail merchants; devised its own plan for regional reindustrialization (imports of foreign teachers, instead of goods, for the area's artisans and obrajes); and even took independent steps to stem the flow of competing manufactures into the sierra. In these concerns, they followed the lead of their recent prefect Agustín Gamarra, and gamarristas were undoubtedly aware of, and supported, continuing regional activities. Cuzco was not alone. The same process unfolded across Peru; for, if anything, republicanism meant new freedom to express the regional aspirations increasingly suppressed under the centripetal late colonial regime.[57] Many regions had resented in particular the Bourbon "free-trade" policies imposed by alien bureaucrats. At the least, backwoods officials everywhere promoted the pogroms and putsches against the risky price swings of foreign intruders.

The Lima junta, working closely with the municipality and prefects, coalesced as the principal coastal-elite protectionist lobby. Its organizing culminated in the most dramatic instance of open protectionist rebellion in the period. From the department's agricultural commission came the first known proposals for the exclusionist Chile treaty, designed to save Lima's hacendados from inevitable "ruin." Area merchants (e.g., those of Ica) funneled their complaints over illegal foreign retailers to the same junta. Contraband, the scourge of tariffs, was closely monitored. With the passage of prohibitions, the junta became the zealous watchdog against the central state's possible vacillations in trade policy. Together the local governments in 1830 launched their deadly propaganda against "diseased" U.S. grain shipments, which city officials then obligingly confiscated and destroyed.[58]

Their campaigns climaxed with an abortive rebellion of the junta in September and October 1830, an attempt to force errant government officials to comply with prohibitions laws. With Gamarra absent from Lima on yet another military adventure, his erstwhile lieutenant, La Fuente, seized advantage of the death of the nationalist finance minister Larrea y Loredo to decree a series of entry concessions for U.S. flours—in exchange for quick infusions of cash. The junta not only declared the exemptions illegal, it declared itself in a state of open rebellion. La Fuente acted quickly enough, ordering troops to surround the junta and municipal offices, exile the ringleaders, and censor the agitating Lima press.

The ferment continued well into 1831, as La Fuente tried to translate his extemporized power into an extensive and formalized liberalization drive, with the enthusiastic help of his new finance minister, Pando, and, behind the scenes, Mr. Samuel Larned. Lima watched not in vain. For Gamarra, with family interests tied to the junta (and with the aid of his loyal protectionist prefect, Eléspuru), eventually returned. Gamarra, in his first acts in April 1831, banished his own vice-president (along with Pando), restored the Lima junta to power, and reaffirmed prohibitions. Local interests won this round; another liberal conspiracy crushed, liberalization reversed.[59] Clearly, gamarristas regarded the juntas as pillars for their nationalist policies.

In 1834 the federalist councils were abolished, soon followed by the replacement of even the traditionally elected cabildos by government-appointed police commissioners. Until the 1860s, Peru repressed all autonomous local government, which only weakly returned. The central paradox of these complex developments is that a liberal constitution (1834) and liberal presidents (Orbegoso and Santa Cruz) actually decreed their destruction, an unusual centralist record for nineteenth-century liberals.[60] One factor must have been the equation of strong local interest groups with protectionist activities and gamarrista caudillos in particular; although in one important region—the south—it was the nationalist camp that smothered federalist aspirations. Whatever the case, Peru's much-deplored republican centralism was a legacy of the early republic, which had witnessed this brief florescence of local nationalist politics. Partly offsetting this dismal record, the next generation of liberals would turn out to be fairer to the regions, at least to those with nothing left to lose.

The Rise of Grassroots Liberalism

In the 1840s, regional elites across the Andes turned in their old slogans and began to hoist a new banner for free trade. This novel movement generated many foci of protest encircling the protectionists of Lima (especially its merchants), finally overcame the crippling Bolivarian legacy of liberalism (the conflation of centralism with liberalism), and in this way became a main ingredient in the triumph of free trade and the making of the more integrative liberal nation-state of the 1850s. It was a ground swell for open ports, cheaper transport, new exports, and genuine free trade—a grassroots liberalism.

From one angle, the new country liberals were desperate refugees from a shattered world of regional protectionism. Given the disproportionate weight of northern, littoral, and limeño interests in early Peruvian nationalism, Lima had never served them well, neither in its centralism nor its protectionism. First of all, the Lima consulado had imposed a monopolistic centralized commercial system upon Peru—as unitary as the Bolivarian schemes it opposed. Only two (or at most four) ports could enjoy direct overseas connections and a full array of commercial services. The rest, every inlet up and down Peru's elongated coastline, the gateways into sierran arteries, markets, and societies, had to depend upon costly Lima transshipments (and on price-gouging merchants). This was an outright denial of "free trade" and administrative autonomy, although the initial reaction of rural commercial elites, as seen, was the paradoxical one of blaming the closest foreign intruder for the exaggerated risks this framework entailed.[61] Price drops were terrifying, not terrific bargains. Provincials became the antiforeign extremists of Peruvian nationalism—the expurgators of alien peddlers—and exerted pressure throughout the 1820s and 1830s against the more cautious nationalists of Lima.

It was only a matter of time before the illusions sustaining this system wore thin. Provincial elites first tasted brief freedom with Santa Cruz, between 1836 and 1838; for the Confederation (with its internationalist advisers) opened port after port in a purposeful effort to lure direct foreign trade to Peru and to spur on new exports. Even if they opposed Santa Cruz and liberalism per se, a new consciousness was born that could not be erased with the closing of these regional ports in 1839. Why should every province have to rely solely upon Lima? It became most rational to press for direct access to imports, new ports, and improved roads. By 1840, the regions stopped blaming a handful of conspicuous foreigners and started criticizing Lima instead. The sharp drop in coastal transport costs (and risks) in the 1840s—heralded by the dependable steamboat in Peru—provided more steam to these first inklings of liberalism. In contrast, Peru's difficult overland transport had suffered cost (and risk) rises with the loss of imperial upkeep, mass diversions of mules, and other wounds of war. Therefore, as the relative price of tradables fell over time, it made ever more economic sense to break any institutional barriers to trade. That meant more direct routes to the coast and free ports.[62] By the early 1840s, this incipient movement had become particularly pronounced in the south, merging there with the classic strains of arequipeño liberalism.

The free-port movement necessarily coincided with a deeper economic and sociological transformation shaping Peru: the painful abandonment of traditional rural manufacturing for export roles. Regional oligarchies had to believe that more foreign trade was better, rather than calamity itself. In this thought-change they were helped by the second failure of Lima's centralized protectionism. Regional efforts to revive dying (and by now grossly inefficient) colonial artisanries initially fueled the tariff crusades of the late 1820s, when the sierran influence on policy peaked. Provincial

94

merchant elites, tied into rural industries as suppliers of inputs or peddlers of cloth, often led these movements, as in Cuzco. Although the topic is too broad for digression here, it is clear now that erratic postindependence protectionism actually did little to save archaic manufactories. Under pressure of continuing price declines and substitution of woolens by cottons (or by dint of the usual catastrophes of war), the last substantial obrajes went under one by one in the 1830s. Rural underemployment spread, even among the independent peasant-weavers, and broader regional depressions threatened to drag down the provincial elites as well. The strains on manufacturers converged from all sides. Internal costs, imports, risks, market fragmentation, and primary export prices all rose together. Critical choices confronted the rural oligarchies: should they invest more in protectionism and, say, continue to sell their wool or cotton to the stagnant local spinning markets, or should they change direction and more profitably market their fibers abroad? Others have begun to trace out this transformation (particularly in wools), its timing and effects. In the early 1830s, some regional handicraft centers (such as Huaraz and Puno) managed to hold on; by the early 1840s, statistics and witnesses alike show them to be nearly gone.[63] Regional blocs attached to the northern alliance drifted away.

This failure of Lima protectionism was political as well as practical. In the long run, Lima's tariffs favored Lima's industries and interests over all others. In the 1830s, capital policy-makers, increasingly isolated from the interior (by warfare, stalled congresses, decayed transport, or default), decided that regional manufacturing was either dead or irrelevant in the calculus, including fiscal calculations; tariffs on textiles and other goods of popular consumption were lowered, thus hastening the fall. Sometimes these decisions catered to lower consumer costs in Lima, or to lower costs of imported inputs for urban craft guilds, essentially at odds with the needs of sierran producers of crude, mass-consumption goods. Lima's sumptuous tailors (an important example), with their hundreds of helpers, and mounting use of imports, benefited from the effective protection gained from cheaper (and more prestigious) European textiles. (Lima guilds would continue to confect a wide range of luxury crafts under continuing moderate tariffs, even into the 1850s, and never suffered as drastic a fate as their faraway rural kin. Although sheer economic geography—proximity to the port—seemed to disfavor their survival, political geography—proximity to the Lima state and elite consumers—favored their persistence.)[64] Whatever the roots of failure, the accelerating decline of rural industry progressively eroded its political legitimacy and role—leaving Peru with one less protectionist prop.

By 1840, conventional wisdom in Peru, based on observation or premise, agreed that provincial manufacturers had entered their final throes,

long past resuscitation by tariffs or other means. So argued a leading gamarrista—Gamarra himself—who pronounced them dead, "relics without remedy," in his presidential address of 1839. This long-passionate
advocate of regional protectionism spoke highly of the victims but, this
time, offered little aid.[65] (This switch may have reflected Gamarra's own
long-term shift of political gravity, too, from the highlands to the coastal
commercial nationalists.) The 1845 Congress, when regional delegates
swarmed on Lima for the first time in a decade, produced the last (but
very sharp) debates over interior manufactures. By then, even the vociferous deputies from Ayacucho, Puno, and Cuzco couched their pleas in
fatalistic terms. Their economies were "agonizing," "ruined," "extermi-
nated" from freer trade; where could they turn next? (Littoral delegates
retorted that if Peru needed industries, the modern ones, as happened,
should be on the coast, nearer consumers.) The last special military contract for sierran textiles expired without great protest the following year;
Castilla's model army would be clothed and armed from abroad. Here
was a sure sign of the drift of the new state. Never again would this lost
cause of rural industry erupt in tariff debates. At the same time, open
resentment exploded against Lima. Lima alone, interior elites exclaimed
by 1845, had captured all the benefits of increased trade after independence, whereas the provinces had suffered all its displacement costs.
Now they would demand their share of the benefits, too. Delegates
started by demanding direct trade.[66]

The threatened regional oligarchies felt themselves to be painfully on
their own, in dire need of a new foundation for social power or, in some
cases, survival. Finally, in the 1840s, they began an archetypical nineteenth-century search for exports, and the hunt intensified as political
stability endured after 1845. The urge to export hit desolate elites hard,
as if they had to make up for lost time. In this, the old resentment of
foreigners rapidly became obsolete.[67] Also typical of nineteenth-century
Latin America, the elites involved had little left to lose (while those who
might suffer were the abandoned workers or others without the means to
move with ease to a full export economy). Instead, the left-behind rural
populace would enter the pages of Peru's folk literature.

The port question loomed large for the newly export-conscious. Lower
internal transport (a mighty problem in Andean Peru), closer entrepôts,
rapid communications, and freer transshipments could make all the difference in the new world markets beckoning in wools, copper, quinine,
sugar, cotton, nitrates, and other local specialties. Each interior oligarchy
demanded its own outlet to the sea, each coastal valley a port, in a race
that soon acquired a competitive edge. Cuzqueños stopped demanding
tariffs, as they had always done, and instead insisted on central-govern-
ment funds for an improved road system.[68] Also crucial was an end to

discriminatory or inappropriate Lima-based tariffs. For example, a handful of Lima artisans built heavy carts, so for their profit alone the price of overland transport throughout Peru was artificially exorbitant. Arid enclaves, such as the nitrate-rich southern deserts, needed to import all food (sometimes even water) if they were to export; therefore, Iquique pressed for duty-free staples, something Lima's outspoken chacareros opposed. Precious little is known about these broad regional transitions to decentralized export liberalism. What, for instance, was the role of foreign merchants in the new local coalitions? Obviously, as foreigners spread out in the safer conditions of the mid-1840s (when provincials quickly ceased demanding their ouster), they became valuable local sources of information about outside markets, and maybe more.[69] (In the south, Britons clearly helped organize and capitalize the new traffic in wool and nitrates.)

Not all areas participated equally in the race for cheaper imports and exports. Yet, by 1845, all signs pointed to a brewing rebellion of the regions against limeño centralism and protectionism (represented so well by Gamarra's unitary constitutionalism of 1839). The extreme nationalists had become Peru's most extreme free traders. This was not a strategic threat to Lima—as battle-scarred southern liberalism had been—for these free traders were dispersed and intracompetitive; but it did pose a clear political challenge for anyone contemplating a broader national politics.

CASTILLA and the post-1845 Lima liberals understood these dangers (and opportunities) for the new Lima state. Mendiburu, for example, one of Castilla's closest aides, carefully laid out the dilemmas of regional commercial autonomy absorbed from his years as military prefect of Tacna; and his postwar interior and southern tour of 1846 combined more fact-finding with conciliation. For many reasons—including, no doubt, the regionalist revolts witnessed when he was Gamarra's finance minister in 1841—Castilla was keenly interested in tying the regions into a Peruvian nation-state. IIis was not simply a militarist pacification program for the vanquished south. Throughout the 1840s, accelerating after 1845, the concessions to open new ports multiplied, along with expanded rights to export bullion and other products. Lambayeque got San José, Ancash its very own port, too; Ayacucho won Chala, and Tumbes came away with flexible rules for coastal trade; Ilo was created; and Arica emerged as a full port of deposit with free facilities for its burgeoning Cuzco trade.[70] But discriminatory and cumbersome nationalist commercial legislation persisted, mainly owing to the weight and inertia of the Lima consulado. For example, as late as 1848, Congress awarded Lima's merchants a new set of self-serving navigation acts.

In contrast to their Bolivarian ancestors, whose indifference failed to win greater Peru, the new Lima liberals of the late 1840s embraced this regional challenge. Indeed, regionalism became a central tenet of the new arguments for free trade. In part, this reflected the new libertarian currents of the latest imported trade theory (whether French radicalism or the late-1840s British repudiation of the Navigation Acts and Corn Laws); but, to a larger degree, it reflected these very Peruvian experiences and pressures. In the late 1840s, liberal ideologues, such as Elías (who himself, along with Quirós and Távara, was more of a wide-ranging regional merchant), went out of their way to present free trade as attractive for other regional elites. These new liberals were not mere arequipeños. A sign of the times was the regionalist stance of the influential "cursantes" political-economy group, superseding the vanished internationalists. In effect, the contradiction between federalist political impulses and economic needs ceased plaguing the liberal cause outside Lima. Moreover, free trade was suddenly becoming a "nationalist" cause, too. Only decentralized liberalism, "free trade" up and down the coast, offered a coherent, consistent, and egalitarian development project for the nation's scattered elites.[71] Thus, free trade made the only genuine national policy (just as liberals now openly attacked the venerable protectionist call—for interdependence with Chile—as the most dependent, antinational, and outmoded policy imaginable). Moreover, the spontaneous regional cry for local direct trade amounted to a mass repudiation of the indirect patterns embedded in the old Chilean formula. In a sense, the new liberals of the 1840s proved more effective because they were right: a modern national state could not privilege Lima elites over the rest of Peru.

These new ideologies, actors, and developments came together in the tariff struggle of 1849–52, the last great barrier to a liberal state. "Equality of Rights for the Ports" became a potent commercial slogan against recalcitrant Lima protectionists. During the debates, national-liberal pressures closed in upon the isolated commercial centralists. Liberal government bodies, such as a converted Consejo de Estado, scurried to publicize the latest regional studies, such as the one from Arequipa's merchants that condemned protectionism as a deleterious, retrograde, and Lima-biased development program. Ministers' reports echoed these themes. This was intended to sway the still-wavering Congress and merchant guild, and so it did (in part, as we will see, because merchants were acquiring new interests themselves now). In short, the decentralist liberal victory was complete in 1852. The new tariff regime swept away all vestiges of navigation acts and radically amplified or simplified Peru's port systems, paperwork, and interregional trade.[72] Merchants won equal trade rights in six "major ports"; eight other flexible regional centers rounded out the new commercial constellation.

Over time, the new liberal state did little to revive the protodemo-cratic representative institutions lost in the early republic or, for that matter, during the final tariff debates themselves. Democracy was not the point, for this was a consciously praetorian state. Nor did the liberal guano-age state magically stop favoring Lima's predominance—which ex-panded in new ways, using its largely autonomous resource and rapidly displacing and co-opting the early breed of provincial caudillos. (No longer exclusively men of Lima, the majority of Peru's military *jefes* dur-ing the 1850s–70s age of "order and progress" flowed from all parts, lured in and integrated by the capital's wealth and power.) Nor would region-alist discontent suddenly leave the map. Provincial elites, for example, spearheaded the series of revolts against the guano-dispensing Eche-nique regime in 1854, although Elías and Castilla deftly managed to channel the benefits of those revolts for themselves.[73] Guano would still belong to Lima, but much less so its wider commercial policies. Politi-cally, a broader national-elite alliance made the liberal state tick. Once the bane of Peru's curiously centralist liberals, the regions now served as outposts of support.

Peruvian caudillos have yet to receive their empirical or analytic due. We now see their rise and fall to be deeply mired in the politics of trade; caudillismo and political struggle, in turn, infected trade policies to the core. In other regions, the caudillos have already met their theorists.[74] Some see in Latin America's rustic and regional military chiefs the em-bodiment of an early patrimonial and patriotic "inorganic democracy"; in Peru, these traits are discernible, although it was protectionism that made these three adjectives fit. As always, democracy proves to be an ambiguous noun, for nationalist and liberal caudillos alike did their share of weakening and bolstering representation in the state. "Disorganic democrats" is perhaps the better term. Others have rescued the chaotic caudillos from traditional scorn as "barbarians"; they necessarily filled the vacuum left by colonial despotism, and messily came up with nation-states instead. Peruvian nationalists did fill the political void, although they had to shed much nationalism before the havoc could end. Still others grasp caudillos as consummate predatory creatures, whose sys-tematized plunder would cease only when redirected by a healthier ap-petite for exports and order. To what extent did these material needs and processes lurk behind Peru's transition to free trade and a liberal state? Who fed Peru's caudillos? What made them progress from their meager protectionist menu to a rich liberal fare?

CHAPTER 5

Fiscal Politics: From National to
Liberal Finance

A CORE DIFFICULTY with all political analysis of caudillo regimes, including the attempt just offered, is identification of any stable political
elite or vested interest in a revolving state. The bewildering turnover of
executives, policies, and personnel; the hamstrung development of civil
institutions—all leave the impression that no political continuity could
have existed. Yet, some underpinning must have existed to permit the
very survival (for nearly three decades in Peru's case) of a system based on
permanently militarized politics and rapid succession of rulers. In Peru,
civil war was indeed the extension of politics by other means.

Key realms in which to seek out regularities are fiscal policy and the
bureaucracy responsible for, and living off, state finance. In a war economy, a significant sector of urban elites looked to state employment as its
preferred option (Peru's proverbial "empleomanía"). So did the caudillos,
their finance ministers, armies, and grasping civil clients. Yet the fiscal
apparatus supporting a perennially bankrupt state must have been strikingly different from that which is optimal, or possible, in more tranquil,
institutionalized regimes and economies. These issues remain clouded
for all of Latin America's caudillo period.[1] Equally mysterious (and
global) is the related question of how young peripheral states became
integrated into international fiscal circuits over the course of the nineteenth century. When, and how, were states brought into the liberal
world?

In Peru, militarist modes of finance were intricately developed, provoked a specific set of fiscal interest groups and struggles, and played a
pivotal role in trade policies.[2] The initial impact on trade policy, however, was not the liberal one deducible from logic alone: namely, that
tariffs fell to enhance revenues and appease moneyed foreigners. Instead,
Peru's peculiar emergency means of mobilizing finance for penurious
militarists accounts for the dominant dynamic in commercial policy from
1820 to 1840, the state's leanings to economic nationalism. This state did
not simply bow to the incessant pressures of its nationalist elites; it had
its own reasons for acting. Conversely, deep 1840s alterations in caudillo
revenue structures explain the first transformations toward liberalism,
how the liberal regime took hold, and enduring, central, and baffling features of the stabilizing and mature guano-age state. The hidden history

100

of finance also reveals a hidden chapter in elite formation: how propertied classes survived the war years and how they came to infiltrate a consolidating state. But through all these mutations, the modus operandi in Peru remained the special one of emergency finance: networks of funding both highly coordinated and supremely ad hoc. The solution to the fiscal puzzle is as bewildering as a "militarist republic" itself.

A NATIONALIST FINANCE REGIME
(1821–41)

The general problems of caudillo finance are well known, its solutions are not. Peru's caudillo regimes between 1825 and 1845, like those across the region, were systematically bankrupt, fiscal desperation a constant. Military expenses ran high (more than 70 percent in primitive budgets), unforeseeable outlays remained the norm (mobilization for and against new revolts), and concrete rewards on short demand were critical to maintain bloated cadres of officers, clients, and bureaucrats; or else, the logic went, risk another rapid revolt and disintegration of the central state. On the supply side, bleak prospects for ordinary revenues spiraled ever downward. The devastation (and extraordinary risks) of perpetual unrest contributed to deepening economic depression and capital flight, while administrative capacities for internal tax collection languished beyond hope. Instability and default thwarted any attempts to obtain new overseas financing in order to save Peru from this vicious cycle.[3] In short, postindependence conditions contrast sharply with the solidity and diversity of the colonial fiscal regime and were clearly a fundamental problem in republican state-building. Permanent bankruptcy led in circular fashion to renewed warfare, even worse fiscal conditions, and on again to more wars. Only the miracle of guano—deftly managed by Castilla's generation—could lift Peru out of this slide after 1845.

A wishful budget for the central state in 1831 provides the statistical flavor of the caudillo fiscal crisis. Ex ante, Peru hoped for $3,309,000 in revenues, more than a third to come from Indian tribute (which rarely reached the capital, as with other decrepit colonial-era taxes) and another 42 percent from customs (which also remained largely unavailable). Foreseeable expenditures reached $4,973,550, with 59 percent already pledged to warfare. That is to say, the *anticipated* deficit was 35.5 percent! The ex post reality of 1831 proved far worse: emergency military needs soared, tax collections lagged or never arrived, and the pressuring defaults of external and internal debt already weighed in above $15 million. No wonder the caudillo's ministers of "war and finance" stopped counting their sorrows over the next decade—by forgetting to publish budgets. No surprise that huge structural deficits—roughly 30 percent—

remained the distinguishing feature of the Lima treasury during the caudillo era.[4] These were hardly Keynesian deficits, to be papered over (no banks or paper money could exist); they were simple invitations to political disintegration. For Peru's provincial caudillos, fiscal mobilization may have been a relatively simple affair: live off the land (plundering estates) or its people (the Indian head tax diverted from Lima coffers). But how could a central state—with its extensive full-time staff—survive deficit after deficit? Under such conditions, how could states consolidate, much less expand?

Public finance in caudillo regimes, as in any other, is usually taken as the crux of trade policy as well as survival. The theory about Peru's unstable fisc is particularly clear. Bankrupt regimes such as Peru's, many argue, were swiftly forced into a radical dependence on taxation of foreign trade, the only reliable (or even collectible) revenue base for a central state. This addiction to customs duties led in turn to an intrinsic state interest in tariff liberalization. At the very least, the argument goes, this weak state could hardly resist compounding liberal fiscal pressures. The adoption of low "revenue" tariffs would minimize irrepressible contraband; with given elasticities, the moderate levies on increased legal commerce could resolve militarist deficits. In the long run, this turn to a fiscal free trade might foster new taxable exports and open new possibilities for overseas credit. Another variable that historians highlight was the incentive for liberal policies offered by the well-capitalized foreign houses, keenly aware of the Achilles' heel of protectionism at the treasury.[5] Foreigners could supply rescue loans to caudillos, timely bribes in exchange for coveted liberal concessions.

In either scenario, the belief here is that the fiscal interests of a weak caudillo state leaned structurally toward free trade and the emergence of a "liberal fiscal regime"; in other words, the state would become oriented to the external sector. This constitutes our major interpretation for Peru's adoption of free trade in the nineteenth century. The argument appears persuasive, as well, for such developments would be expected in any economy having difficulties in taxing internal trade or production. And, on paper at least, duties on bulk imports did come to account for more than half of Lima's revenues, a marked change from colonial fiscal structures.

Such liberal outcomes did not, however, occur in Peru—or, at best, arrived thirty years past predictions. Although early finance ministers frequently invoked the theory of low-revenue tariffs (imbibed from weekly tutorials with foreign consuls), this was a case of wishful thinking. In practice, this liberal strategy simply would not work under the chronic instability of a caudillo state. From 1821 to 1841 the opposite occurred: fiscal exigency bred deepening protectionism.

First and foremost, liberalization could not produce the needed revenues at the needed times. Perpetual warfare kept foreign trade uncertain
or depressed, no matter what the incentives; often, imports could not be
disposed of at any price. At Lima/Callao—the only port effectively integrated into Peru's central treasury—contraband was not a crippling fiscal
problem, crying for solution, for smuggling posed grave risks to exposed
importers. And Peru's impressive statistics on customs revenues appear
to be largely fictitious, as most were long mortgaged to importers for past
obligations. Cash flows from imports were slow and risky, if not impossible, to obtain within the deadlines imposed on desperate caudillos.
Customs, in short, could rarely be a pressing concern on the funding of
Lima. Often, officials read elasticities to mean that high tariffs (or even
import prohibitions!) would actually bolster revenues through higher
prices. Most important, liberal solutions, at the customs house or in the
economy at large, required long-term and stable vistas to develop—the
one luxury not available to harried finance ministers and caudillos under
the gun. Santa Cruz, for example, energetically strove to implant a full
liberal finance regime in 1836–38, but his explicit fiscal tariffs could not
increase income fast enough to save him from ignominious fiscal and thus
military defeat.[6] All told, the opportunity costs remained quite low for
ignoring the illusory fiscal benefits of liberalization.

Second, while it may have seemed alluring, direct foreign aid as a stopgap solution was unavailable to Peru. Caudillos were often willing
enough to offer last-ditch liberal concessions for loans, but Lima's credit-
rich foreign houses refused this bait. By the mid-1820s, foreign interests
grasped the inherent perils of feeding the erratic, endlessly predatory
caudillo appetite and, with the help of consuls (and visiting gunboats),
firmly established their full exemption from all emergency taxation.[7] To
foreigners in Lima, the ideological complexion of Peruvian caudillos,
whether liberal or nationalist, did not matter, nor even the forced or voluntary nature of loans—only their risks. And in London, where Peru de-
faulted (by 1825) on long-term portfolio investments worth more than $8
million, no banker in his right mind would throw good money after bad
to underwrite, in their eyes, a mere clique of distant bandits. In short,
with customs, short-term loans, and overseas credit, Peru's pandemic instability blocked the development of a liberal fiscal regime. For postindependence Peru, no form of financial integration into the liberal world
economy looked feasible.

How, then, could the central state, its employees, caudillos, armed
flocks, and finance ministers survive? If not through customs or foreign
aid, where was Peru's strategic realm of finance? This query touches on
more general mysteries of Latin American finance in the decades after

independence—a period when integration with world capital and product markets reached historic lows, and risk reached its highest point.

Unpublished Peruvian treasury accounts reveal the answer: the development of elaborate systems of emergency finance—short-term loans, customs, and tax bonds—supplied primarily from Peru's national merchant elite. For caudillos, ordinary revenues such as tariffs and direct taxes were not the immediate and dire concern. Instead, the relevant fiscal vistas were those resolved on a month-by-month, or weekly, basis—deficits bridged with multiple forms of extraordinary merchant credit.[8] The state looked inward to national capital, not outward, for its strategic needs. As a result, a clear set of protectionist fiscal and policy interests arose, producing the inverse of a liberal finance regime.

Three forms of short-term finance dominated the Lima treasury from 1825 to 1845: mortgage of customs revenue through marketable bonds on duties (the "abonos" system); similar bond advances guaranteed on mint profits and taxes; and institutionalized "forced loans." Peru's true struggles over finance, hidden in a labyrinth of obscure decrees, statistics, and debates over caudillo "credit," took place in this subterranean world of perpetual emergency finance.[9] And each form of credit, strategic as it was, labored under grave limitations, amid the complicating political and monetary machinations of competing cliques of national and foreign interests.

The customs bonds provided the largest share of this finance in the caudillo era, and since the collateral was both firm and impersonal, some foreigners could willingly contribute here. From 1827 to 1830 (an abonos boom that allows calculation) the state released more than $2.1 million in customs bonds, an average of $70,000 each month. Only 60 percent of these loans actually produced hard cash, but they still required fully half of Lima customs to liquidate. Foreign merchants, often with astonishing profits, bought 57 percent of the bonds, national importers the rest.[10] In this era, abonos dominated the treasury, although other kinds of credit would soon catch up.

The fatal drawback of abonos, with respect to the medium-range maintenance of the state, was that in complex fashion they actually aggravated deficit crises. The rapid accumulation of outstanding bonds—ranging anywhere from $200,000 to $500,000—effectively dried up all current funds from customs, pledged to liquidation in advance. And, as the bargaining power of bondholding merchants grew, so grew the costs of borrowing, as measured in terms of the growing discounts granted to merchants in nominal import duties. At times, finance officials had to tender up to 90-percent reductions in tariff rates as an incentive for emergency bond sales. Bond values could also float, which only exacerbated the unpredictability of revenues and the possibilities for merchant pressures against the state—a rivalrous "abonos politics." Thus, each and every new regime, whether liberal or protectionist, vigorously condemned this "ruinous system." Each piously pledged to stamp out customs bonds altogether as Peru's sole avenue to restored fiscal rationality and stability. Nevertheless, sheer fiscal starvation kept abonos basically uncontrollable until 1836, and they would return again in force in the early 1840s. With the visible foreign activity in abonos, one might surmise that this system encouraged liberalization (apart from its de facto devaluation of tariff rates). Instead, for a variety of reasons, abonos actually intensified public, private, and official hostility to foreign liberal interests: foreign competitors were increasingly resented as parasitic "speculators" destroying the fiscal fabric of Peruvian society.[11] On a lesser scale, similar problems and politics plagued the Lima mint, whose limited but sturdier fees and export levies were always in hock.

Given the flaws of abonos, the truly optimal solution for the caudillos was direct forced loans, a hallmark of militarist societies everywhere. Such loans possessed a strategic value even beyond the volume of cash delivered. Unlike bonds, loans could be precisely timed and, if correctly managed, would not fatally undermine other revenues. Loans, for example, became especially urgent at the outbreak of every war; and, indeed, forced levies of every kind erupted at the height of the fighting. The chief difficulty with loans—apart from the fact that foreigners refused to provide them—lay in their "institutionalization." Even when pressured, lenders paradoxically required ironclad guarantees that predation would not reach decapitalizing levels. Lenders needed assurance of political neutrality and continuity in credit (lest the next caudillo capriciously cancel the debts of his predecessors and foes), and they demanded autonomous sources for steady amortization of scarce capital, protected from the pillage and risks of an erratic state.[12]

By necessity, all responsibility for such loans fell on the national merchant elite, notoriously capital-poor relative to the exempt foreign houses. Nonetheless, consulado merchants, endowed with less than $1 million in working capital in the 1820s, were able to generate impressive volumes of short-term finance. At a minimum, Lima's top traders lent some 2.7 million pesos between 1821 and 1845, far more than any comparable group in Peru. This fund became caudillismo's war chest. (This is also the best aggregate figure that can be spliced together from motley archival data.)[13] Loan capital stemmed from the merchants' pivotal role in Peru's concentrated commercial networks, from links to miners and the mint, and, in the worst of times, from drawdowns on past obligations and balances. The early and complex 1820s history of these loans meshed with shifting crises around foreign lending, arcane political-fiscal struggles, and the manifold reactions of national merchants caught in the middle. During and after the wars of independence, one huge exaction after another nearly annihilated Peru's penurious merchant elite, just as foreigners won their invaluable fiscal exceptionalism. By 1828, with all other tax systems defunct or deemed insufficient, the nationalist caudillos in Lima began to look exclusively upon the national merchants for aid—by then their political (and, it was dreamed, fiscal) allies. This recalled colonial practice, the merchant financiers who once courted viceroys, and the consulado's desperate bid after 1810 to prop up royalist regimes. Congress restored suppressed consulado powers, many related to fiscal tasks, and all officials and politicians expected the pauperized merchants to handle, if not wholly direct, national state finance.[14] Peru's merchants, unlike the foreigners, had little choice; but they turned their risky ordeal into a political and economic opportunity.

A brilliant institutional adaptation to instability accompanied and enabled this rise of national finance. Formalized by 1834, the Ramo de Arbitrios was an autonomous, quasi-state merchant loan bank. Run by the consulado, the bank (Peru's only feasible finance institution, public or private, in this turbulent era) maintained lenders' confidence throughout a wild flux of caudillos, policies, and fiscal crises.[15] With its own administration and revenue pools, it could recycle scarce capital for moments of greatest need and, in theory, help rather than impoverish the native elite. In the initial years, the Arbitrios system performed remarkably well, given the perils inherent in its very conception—institutionalized forced loans. In less than a year, the enterprise funneled more than $300,000 to needy caudillos; by 1836, the figure exceeded half a million pesos, and a stable core of professional *prestamistas* had formed around the venture.[16] Its success bonded the limeño marriage of caudillos, officials, and merchants.

A typical operation of the Ramo de Arbitrios can be glimpsed in early 1835, during an interlude of nonstop war between Orbegoso and Salaverry. On the final day of 1834, Minister of Finance Zavala publishes a memo to the executive in the official press: "Our government is enveloped by its immense weariness with meeting current expenditures." With taxes in arrears, October's salaries still unmet, and a new monthly shortfall of 20–30 percent expected, he requests a "voluntary loan over the Ramo de Arbitrios administered by the consulado." In fact, as the consulado's own "acta" reveals, this $20,200 loan is easy enough to collect at one sitting. A hefty charge of 2 percent monthly (guaranteed with a special customs surcharge) is sufficient to override the merchants' political aversion to the disintegrating regime.[17] By March 1835, under Salaverry, explicit war loans loom larger, and hints of resistance abound. The new government gazette issues a veiled threat of force to the merchants (but also notes the prefect's "scrupulous" security for the loan). Alvarez

Calderón and Izcue, respected "priors" of the consulado–Ramo de Arbitrios, call an emergency junta of merchants, to distribute the "quotas" to sixty-four members. Their grand total this time is $69,688 (and 7.5 reales). Despite their grumblings, twenty-six natives provide more than $1,000 each, punctually recorded. One smaller band (with Blanco, Candamo, and Santiago & Sons, Lima's strongest and oldest firms) registers loans of $4,000 to $8,000 apiece. By year's end, lending reaches $242,156. Yet, the merchants seem satisfied all year with the faithful payments of interest (and some principal) by the Arbitrios board, by the fact that the task of coercion has stayed within their ranks, or by the sympathetic policies of Salaverry himself.[18] This scenario of major native levies would be recorded at least thirty more times over the next decade.

National finance—caudillo finance—had clear policy implications for Peru. In the first place, it provided national merchants, already the leading protectionists in other fields, with added political clout in the caudillo state. Peruvian merchants (like Mexico's infamous *agiotistas*) were, after all, keeping warriors as well as bureaucrats afloat—even more reason to shun liberal aliens. High points in nationalist policy (e.g., the Salaverry and two Gamarra regimes) correlate with peaks in merchant lending, and even Peru's liberal chiefs came to placate these merchants. Furthermore, merchant finance directly fueled antiforeign policies. Nationalists, for example, invariably justified exclusionist bans on foreign activity in the domestic market on the grounds that foreigners refused to participate in what was, notwithstanding its peculiarities, still national taxation. National merchants required—and demanded—all kinds of special privileges, favors, and rewards to compensate for the onerous risks and costs they alone suffered.[19] Caudillos and their ministers listened to and acted on these cues, for their survival hinged on appeasing national merchants. Alternatively, lending and its favors may have become a critical survival mechanism for Peru's most capitalist elite, adrift in a war-torn and contracting economy. (If foreigners wanted benefits, they too could integrate with national finance; few jumped at this risky proposition, embodied in such doomed schemes as "forced nationalization.") Finally, on a more abstract plane—beyond the day-to-day mutual blackmail between merchants and caudillos—nationalist policies represented that classic institutional motif whereby a state promotes the economic development of the class on which it depends. This theory saw light in such large-scale promotional projects as the Asian Trading Company, and in countless other monopolies and franchises.[20] In the absence of political stability and foreign finance, it was just as the merchants claimed: Peru needed a group of wealthy capitalists as the bedrock of a national state.

In sum, it is the peculiar structure of caudillo strategic finance after independence that best explains the success of Peru's civil elite in capturing the endorsement of the political class for their nationalist crusade. From the 1820s to the 1840s, a militarist-merchant symbiosis produced a Peruvian protectionism that could withstand all countervailing pressures, especially the fiscal and foreign ones thought so irresistible. Peru's perpetual postindependence crisis led paradoxically to a "nationalist" rather than to a liberal finance regime. Liberalism was but a phantasm in the nightmare of Peruvian chaos.

"Amortization Politics" (1839–41): Liberalized Exclusionism

The subterranean history of fiscal politics was far more complex than has been sketched herein and, if extended over time, truly earns its explanatory keep. Fiscal struggles unveil the precise processes and alliances beneath the liberalization of national merchants and the state in the 1840s. We are witnessing nothing less than the excruciating birth of the liberal finance regime that indeed would characterize guano-age Peru. Essentially, the process ran in reverse: breakdown of the national fiscal system followed by a broad wave of accommodations with foreigners integrating into Peruvian state finance. Three stages marked this emergency-finance road to a liberal state: the rise of "amortization politics" (1839–41), its fall (1841–45), and "consolidation politics" (1845–52). By 1852, the liberal elites and state that were to dominate the guano age were fully in place—and, with them, free trade. Extraordinary finance paved the way to free trade, just as it had prevented it for three decades.

Amortization politics marks the apogee of exclusionist merchant finance during the nationalist Gamarra Restoration, with one vital twist. It led to a tariff liberalization, even as antiforeign politics reached their climax in Peru. The fiscal strategies of consulado merchants and the militarist state explain this paradox—from their shared desperate need to amortize past debts.

Merchants took the political helm in 1839 during their bleakest economic crisis (so far) of the republican era. Five unbroken years of warfare since 1834 had left a trail of merchant bankruptcies (which by 1837 alone had felled seventy-six Lima traders worth $1.1 million). The Confederation struggles, marked by unbridled military extortion on both sides, strained the resources of their lending bank to the breaking point. By 1839, the Ramo de Arbitrios' principal—its unpaid bills to merchants— reached $666,000, more than twice that in 1835.[21] Most ominously for the merchants, the final round of conflict shook the very foundations of the Arbitrios system, the key to its and their own survival. Desperate caudillos in 1838 had raided the bank's autonomous tax base; payments stopped, sapping the hard-won confidence needed to attract and recycle new loans.[22] In any case, few funds remained in the hands of Peru's de-capitalized merchants.

When Gamarra assumed power in 1839, he prepared to offer the consulado everything they had hoped for since 1821, and then some. His was to be the purest nationalist-finance regime yet, something his systematic persecution of foreign traders ensured. To the consulado, however, the gamarrista opportunity—the dozens of monopolies, projects, and privileges proffered by the Huancayo nationalists—meant nothing if merchants lacked the capital and security to profit from (and support) their state. Theirs was an unparalleled liquidity crisis. As one example, the much-vaunted Compañía Asiática began on a sour note. Eighteen months passed before merchants could muster sufficient funds to launch the enterprise (even as the state cut the minimum private investment from $500,000 to $100,000), and the company was to remain pitifully undersubscribed, despite merchant enthusiasm.[23] Each new loan order produced new anxieties for the merchant leadership, forced to squeeze more and more out of their shrinking pool of resistant and demoralized colleagues. In 1839 the consulado saw little ground for hope.

Against this backdrop, "amortization" became the obsessive merchant standard and a source for renewed optimism. Prompt recognition and repayment by the state of overdue loans—virtually all their working capital—was the only way to place the national merchant class back on its feet. To this end, the consulado, with unreserved official backing, completely overhauled the Ramo de Arbitrios in 1839, thus entering, they believed, a new era of nationalist affluence.[24] Administrative reform, restructured debts, new tax powers, and autonomy guarantees were part of the package. The other half was finding expanded and dependable revenues so that past debts could be honored rapidly, and the continuing higher demands of public finance met—obligations which now rested wholly on the backs of native elites. The solution, worked out by the consulado itself in 1840, was lower tariffs.

Moderate—30–45 percent—duties on textiles (and other goods of mass consumption) had nothing to do with a liberal awakening of merchants and the state. These tariffs were designed solely to speed the amortization of Peru's internal debt. Nor were they "revenue" tariffs—a direct bolstering of state finance—in any meaningful sense of the term. The revenue was for merchants, who could then relend to the state.[25] If anything, the political climate produced by gamarrista finance only intensified the illiberal doctrines and pressures against foreigners. (Then, as today, foreign diplomats were incensed that Peru wished to divert to nationals funds that "rightfully" belonged to their awaiting bondholders.) Foreign powers had but a negative impact on Peruvian policy, especially on tariffs, in this period of retrenchment and defeat by Peru's staunchest nationalists.[26] Understanding the fiscal politics of this era solves that major riddle—how Peru's first steps toward a lasting liberalization occurred under the auspices of its most nationalist regime on record.

Yet, there was a sharp difference from past trade politics. Before, in every setting since 1825, an array of Peruvian interests had converged in tariff-making. Artisans, retailers, rural cloth-makers, landed gentry, and others were brought into alliance around the consulado. In 1840, trade politics belonged to a reduced clan of Lima merchants and their state, and now only amortization, not "protection," mattered. (The recent bankruptcies had concentrated even further this national-finance clique.) In one sense, the new outlook of the consulado was made possible by the changing economic configurations of protectionist lobbies: for example, the secular erosion of rural manufacturers, now largely out of mind to these Lima-centric merchants and militarists. But the consulado had also secretly prepared the new tariff expressly to deflect the inevitable protests of such other, still potent groups as urban artisans. Borrowing this old liberal tactic seemed to work, and merchants were handily able to ignore the typically well-crafted protectionist proposals of the guilds.[27] Their ambitions rose, too, along with a foreseen rise in Callao customs duties from 1 million to 1.5 million pesos. A permanent flow at customs, lucratively and securely parlayed through the state, would create a solid base for continued commercial capitalization, not just recovery from this single crisis. Now merchants even planned to extinguish the colonial consulado debt—worth more than $7 million—the fantasy of many an old family of Lima.[28] Here was a formula that Lima's leading aristocrats, bureaucrats, and traders could agree on.

In one sense, these developments were the logical outcome of Peru's merchant-class dominance, and of the symbiotic relationship between nationalist caudillos and merchants that had fueled protectionism over the years. Once their elite state was firmly established, as seemed to be happening under Gamarra in 1840, their older phalanx of allies could be readily forgotten. The state was fully captured by its merchant elite. Their dual policy—antiforeign yet procommercial—faithfully reflected that narrowing yet quintessential alliance. Failure of this scheme, however, could bode far worse for Peru's assorted protectionists.

Amortization got off to an auspicious start. With relative calm, fewer new loans to carry, a recovery of trade, the merchant tariff, official graces, and a reconstituted Ramo de Arbitrios, 1840 became a banner year for the consulado. "Confidence" was restored to a functioning national-finance system—thanks, in no small part, to more than $300,000 dispensed to merchants for interest and principal. In their year-end report, the consulado waxed eloquent over their rapid success and future prospects: "The Ramo de Arbitrios, as the principal source of credit, will be the faithful thermometer marking the degree of Illustration of our government."[29] If so, illustration would find new lows.

WOUNDS OF WAR (1841–45),
LIBERAL MEDICINES

In January 1841, Peru suddenly exploded into new civil and border wars, the deepest, most byzantine round in its turbulent history, lasting four torturous years. The gamarrista caudillos fell into bitter disarray. With Gamarra himself felled in the battle of Ingavi at year's end, Peru's state disintegrated (at one high point, in 1844, four warring caudillo "governments" simultaneously claimed legitimacy). The loss of charismatic Gamarra no doubt contributed to losses of nationalist resolve and unity. Yet, something deeper and different was also at play: the fall of the national-finance system itself. When Peru awoke from its anarchic nightmare in 1845, neither merchants nor the state could ever return to nationalist finance. The early brand of Peruvian economic nationalism lay shattered beyond repair.

The Ramo de Arbitrios swiftly collapsed at the outbreak of war. Still nursing old wounds, Lima's merchants could not possibly meet the massive wave of new war depredations ordered in 1841—six in all, for more than $325,000. Instead, they demanded customs bond guarantees, a return to the safer but "ruinous" system of abonos. (Nor could natives supply these funds alone; by year's end, overtures went out to despised foreign traders for help with the customs bonds.)[30] The intense pressures of renewed warfare doomed the merchants' fantasized amortization; tolerable emergency taxation reached its intolerable level. And, aware of the paralysis of the Arbitrios fund, the revolving caudillos of 1841–44 simply decreed its death. Death by predation, for the military chiefs moved in one after another to siphon—pillage—its last protected funds, promptly halting all payments of interest and capital. Merchant pleas were repeatedly ignored, and the deadlocked capital soared to more than $1 million by late 1844.[31] Most of the bank's smallholders simply sold out their worthless debt bonds to interested buyers. This time, confidence expired for good.

For the merchants, multitudinous other disasters befell this dark period of change. Gamarrista promotional projects fell one by one, taking leading national merchants with them. The worst blow was the sabotage of the Compañía Asiática in June 1842. A new round of army officers, hoping to appease potential foreign abonos lenders, broke the fragile new company's import monopoly, allowing in ship after ship of competing Asian cargoes. Merchant warnings were ignored, the company crushed.[32] After that, and a string of similar "betrayals," the nationalist caudillos

111

could never be trusted again. Peru's merchants as a class would barely hold on during this protracted spree of predation and war depression from 1841 to 1845. By 1844, membership of the core *almacenero* group (those enhanced by previous nationalist drives) was halved from forty to twenty; that year alone, merchants declared another $150,000 in bankruptcies.[33] This catastrophic outcome should have surprised no one. The notion of institutionalizing predation—the heart of the Ramo de Arbitrios system and of caudillo nationalist policies—was utopian. Merchants learned the hard way that an inherently predatory state would sooner or later consume its own.

During these dismal war years, the outlooks of the elite merchants and the caudillos—toward each other, toward foreigners—began to shift. The merchants' class crisis bequeathed a broad ideological crisis. Peruvian merchants had invested more than their cash in nationalist projects; they had invested a worldview. Yet, even in the best of times, the nationalist regime had ultimately failed to deliver, had failed to reduce the risks. Now, in the worst of times, dependence on the weak caudillo state had magnified their perils beyond endurance. Lost faith in this state became, by extension, disillusionment with all the merchants' prior statist conceptions. One option remained for survival: reduced reliance on the state; recovery through less risky private arrangements, if these could be found. This meant, by default, embracing the merchants' oldest twin foes: foreigners and liberalism.

It was, however, no accident that individual and group accommodation to foreigners constituted this last option. Officially shielded from plunder, partnerships with foreigners naturally appealed now to beleaguered nationals. Moreover, in the Peruvian commercial economy, foreign merchants, while abdicating their political power, had in the long run enhanced their economic sway. Despite nationalist discrimination, they were freed from many of the worst calamities that afflicted native merchants. This proved the greater advantage. Over two decades, the foreign interest had slowly grown in numbers, scale, and diversity—remarkably, even during the intensified turmoil of the 1840s. British surveys indicate about thirty branch houses operating across Peru in the 1820s, exactly forty in 1842, and fifty after the wars.[34] Possible arenas for profitable and safe collaboration with foreigners had expanded commensurately. (This also helps explain why foreign houses were especially well placed in the early 1840s to exploit the new commercial opportunities of the guano boom—and, hence, their leap to predominance in Peru after 1845.) This foreign presence, through its promise of lower risks, became a source of Peruvian economic liberalism.

This embrace of a protected foreign enclave had wider political implications, a story familiar to those who have studied emerging capitalism elsewhere. The relative security of foreign commercial property and finance (an "interest" that could be liberally augmented) might, the merchants proposed, put a brake on the unbridled "passions" of Peru's capricious, despoiling leaders. The coerced respect for foreigners, if supported and extended, might somehow generalize into a hallowed and calculated protection for all business and wealth. All entrepreneurs in Peru, they hoped, would benefit over time from this eclipse of arbitrary caudillismo, from an enhanced security and sanctity of property rights.[35] (Postfiasco thinking moved in other directions, too—for example, into the merchant-led "civilista" politics of 1845–50). The merchants, then, did not simply look to liberalism and foreigners with greed, but as props to help restructure Peru's unruly relations of state to society. Trade expansion, once the bane of social conflict, took its place as a classic and wishful *doux commerce*. Into a few years' time, Peru's elites had, in effect, telescoped a few centuries of the history of liberal capitalist thought.

The most prominent native merchants (those survivors who could) thus began unprecedented moves to cultivate close business, social, and political ties with foreigners. This was a movement from state investments and broad, national affiliations to investments and narrower alliances with the private, external, and foreign sectors. Finally, then, after twenty years, a trickle-down of liberal ideas began to flow from overseas houses to their best customers. Accommodation took many forms.

In April 1842, for example, the consulado elite abruptly withdrew all support from their own draconian retail restrictions devised just two years earlier (to the chagrin of concerned officials and retailers). This way, the consulado could collect taxes from foreign retailers and become their knowledgeable accomplices in the domestic market. As usual, merchant preference bore policy, and restrictive laws henceforth became a dead letter, despite the pleas of other groups.[36] In the same debate, the leading merchant newspaper, *El Comercio* (until then staunchly nationalist), launched editorials lambasting caudillismo and demanding a wider protection of foreign property and commerce. Moreover, the merchants' shift impinged on another facet of relations with retailers: a new 1840s push for repressive debt laws in order to strong-arm shopkeepers into taking responsibility for their credits. Instead of the old and failed nationalist solutions to credit risks, coercion against the unruly "little man" might alleviate merchant worries. Appropriately enough, foreign and national merchants also began working in tandem on military-supply contracts (that symbolic arena of Peru's economy which thrived in war). Nationals enjoyed the best local political connections, while foreigners had the best and most economical imported uniforms and munitions. Predictably, these new compacts enraged the beleaguered local-artisan war profiteers. Similar shared arrangements worked splendidly with abonos and, at first, in the new contracts for guano. When foreign merchants clashed with officials over new tax quotas, veritable tax strikes of the day, top national merchants rallied to their side, reversing the terms of time-worn fiscal conflicts. Spurning the risky Arbitrios fund, nationals joined the new Bolsa—a sort of foreign stock exchange—and took out shares in the new English steamship line, shielded of course from official interventions. An ambitious plan for a consulado-financed railroad (a Lima–Callao line) was soon scrapped for one using foreign contractors.[37] In 1843, the consulado voted to permit foreigners to operate as private loan sharks; this outraged the Peruvian retail *prestamista* guild, yet the merchants clearly grasped the possibilities for cheaper credit. By 1845, the consulado went on record to the state against punitive taxes for foreigners or, for that matter, any form of official discrimination: "The country needs Foreign Capital, because we lack our own. . . . [T]he widest interest of the State would facilitate and protect the entry of Foreign Capital and industry; instead of persecution, help it."[38] Smaller traders hardly welcomed this message either.

THREE ASPECTS of this sea change in merchant ideas and practice deserve a closer look here, even though they lead us ahead of our story. For one thing, the merchant rapprochement with foreign importers promised further disengagement from the host of petty Peruvian clients once sheltered under the umbrella of elite nationalism—the process first glimpsed in 1840 with the amortizing tariff. Without consulado allies, retailers and artisans in particular could no longer hope for successful political redress in the 1840s, though redress they did. Their denunciations of elite merchants became ever more targeted and bitter (much like the merchants' own charges of caudillo treachery); and worrisome officials and políticos still listened, at least, anxious about the social consequences of untrammeled trade expansion.[39]

There were real economic consequences, too, most notably in Lima. With peace and guano, imports flooded into Peruvian markets again in the late 1840s (a twofold increase), led this time by luxury wares. Yet, most small businessmen did not share in Lima's rapid economic rejuvenation. The structure of commerce, not just politics, had irrevocably changed in the 1840s. Now, foreign houses, in conjunction with their consulado auxiliaries (and often tapping connected immigrant "artisans" as outlets), moved quickly into retail sales. Their stiff competition deprived many nationals of their best opportunities for recovery, and Lima retailers felt especially pressed competing under the new import regime. Nor could local craftsmen expand in tandem with demand if their elite market was captured from abroad, owing often to considerations of taste and prestige rather than cost alone. The shift back to upper-class demand did not bring their long-awaited prosperity. New economic evidence, beyond the ubiquitous cries of small business, bears this out.[40]

Contrary to what might be expected from economic theory, service sectors in this export economy did not burgeon, but actually declined in the early guano age. Much of this decay represented the displacement of native retailers. In 1839, these firms enjoyed on average $278 in annual taxed revenues (down, like the rest of the Lima economy, from 1830 levels). In 1844, that figure was $218; in 1850, it fell to $195; and, by 1857, it had slid to $183. The number of businesses, their real incomes, and employment dropped as well. All this occurred amid a booming elite economy.[41] *Desempleomanía*, not the elites' *empleomanía*, was to be their fate. Artisans on the whole would fare somewhat better, for into the 1850s they enjoyed some residual tariff protection, the cost-saving concessions of Manchesterian tariffs, plus greater agility to specialize in servicing imports and the nontradable building industry. Their income and numbers held stable. But prospering immigrant craftsmen—often the disguised retail partners of foreign houses—owned a fifth of the workshops and earned three times the nationals' average by 1848. Overall, the artisan dependence on elite society, and their welcoming of foreign migrants, had borne bitter fruit. Contemporaries and historians long suspected skewed distributional benefits from the guano boom, a common enough pattern during rapid, export/import-led growth. Indeed, for many in Peru, this recovery was no less than disastrous. A thriving and nationalist "middle sector" that had once dominated Lima was largely pushed aside during the 1840s as its commercial economy rapidly internationalized. This economic shift helps explain the further erosion of artisan/retailer political power, as seen already in their climactic defeat during the tariff battles of 1849–52.

The incessant shopkeeper and artisan protests against merchants and foreigners over the next two decades rang true. Loss of their political patrons in the early 1840s, followed by economic displacement and political deprivation, contributed directly to the plight of these *menu peuple* (in these niches, many women worked, too). For them, protectionism had proved a failure as well, although it would also offer their only escape. Increasingly, they decried effete merchants as well as free trade, for the top merchants had become in their eyes an uncaring and oppressive "guano-eating" aristocracy. Déclassé, they became the "social problem" of Lima in the 1850s—an army of the excluded, left-behinds, destitute, and underemployed, the feared tinderbox for crime and antimerchant mobs (and, though to no avail, occasional mass protest).[42] They exploded, for example, in the artisan/retailers' protectionist riots of December 1858 (repulsed by Castilla's crack cavalry after three days of rampage against merchant property and the liberal state). To those with a conscience, their mere existence belied the glossy elite prosperity of the export age.

Secondly, for themselves, the select national merchants had made the right move in the early 1840s. Foreigners coveted their superior local-market knowledge (and their political networks), and the informal covenant paid off. The profits of foreign houses jumped precipitously in the mid-1840s—enhanced by their entry into retail networks—but this still left handsome opportunities for the largest Peruvian traders, as well as an efficient division of labor. By 1848, when credible figures can be computed from tax records, the foreigners engaged in Lima grand commerce averaged profits 65 percent greater than their native counterparts. Yet, in large part this was an illusion: if the wealthiest overseas-consignment houses are excluded, a typical Peruvian entrepreneur enjoyed 34 percent higher revenues. In the market spheres below warehousing, Peruvian merchants came out ahead by fully 49 percent.[43] In sum, in the wholesale and large-scale retail trades, knowledgeable natives fared even better than their foreign partners.

There was, then, an economic sense (or basis) to the compact formed between national and foreign elites in the early 1840s. Peruvian merchants could prosper as the local middlemen, salesmen, and political agents for the international traders handling imports. A small national commercial elite thrived in the guano age (although top foreign merchants would thrive even more, especially during the 1850s). In retrospect, this shift in national merchant postures seems fated. From 1821, state policies to forge a new national intermediary class out of the ashes of independence gradually worked. But once that class had formed, it would eventually act—even if prompted by this deep crisis of the early 1840s—just like the dependent intermediaries they were.[44] In the mid-1840s, foreigners finally met their willing and able liberal collaborators in Peru.

The third point worth stressing is that whatever rewards this future may have held, merchants did not become liberals out of conversion to a promising new doctrine of progress. They were still refugees, reluctant and hesitant, the only ones who could flee from Peru's shattering economic nationalism. (This Lima metamorphosis paralleled, under different pressures, the 1840s transformation of regional elites already seen.) Elite liberalism was born from defeat and failure in Peru. Survival, not maximized greed, was its primary motif in this inversion of old forms of risk aversion. "Accommodation," then, is the right word. Nowhere in the records, at least until the late 1840s, does one find exuberant ideological support for free trade, at least not from Lima. That step—the product of an active social alliance with foreign liberals—required another impetus, which would come into play after 1845.

Yet, the specific failures afflicting nationalism in the 1840s concealed specific meanings, which deeply affected the free trade, elite mentalities, and liberal state-building to come. This was no simple failure of protected industries (and traders) to flourish, although the fact that protectionism was fruitlessly tried emerged as an ubiquitous, convenient, and often exaggerated argument against all further attempts during the nineteenth century. More important is liberalism's reactive birth—as the antithesis of unbridled caudillismo, social breakdown, economic decay, state pillage, and nationalism, all compressed into one bitter class memory by the climactic events of 1841–44.

Peru's long and painful apprenticeship in caudillo-nationalism lent a special emotive staying power to its free trade. For the alternative, forever brandished, embellished, and distorted by subsequent liberals, was regress to Hobbesian anarchy itself. Furthermore, rather than as a libertarian ideology, liberalism arose here tied to the consolidation of a stronger, reliable, and effective state—a state less arbitrary and more pacific in its interventions but, above all, the strict guarantor of elite order and progress. In this sense, the Peruvian road to free trade paralleled the liberalisms that emerged across postcaudillo Latin America. Mexico's autocratic liberals of 1857, responding to a similar social crisis, were one well-known analogue.[45] That Latin American liberalism followed caudillismo, and not independence itself, seems essential to its lasting and dogmatic appeal. The tailored positivist ideologies that arrived later in the century were more a reflection than a cause of these developments. In short, a negative demonstration effect was the critical legacy of the region's early nationalist experiments.

In Peru, the authoritarian bent of liberalism was further accentuated by its roots in this wholesale conversion of desperate statist elites, in search of survival and order. Few novel voices (or new social groups) entered into the final liberal triumph. Libertarians filled a minor function in playing up the peaceful role of commerce, which now rapidly overcame its threatening guise of the 1820s. For Peru's elites, the accommodation to foreigners and free trade seemed to offer salvation from self-destruction itself.

NOTHING better illustrates—or contributed to—this accommodation to foreigners than the realm of state finance, where the most portentous change occurred during the caudillo standoffs of 1841–45. Instead of bashing foreigners as a punishment for failing to lend, by 1842 the consulado and others began to encourage foreign houses to assist. Their new philosophy was simple, expressed during all new requisitions for loans.[46] If foreigners joined in, lured by positive liberal guarantees, then perhaps the national merchants could finally be spared, relieved of this destructive and horrible burden. Thus began the liberal finance regime.

The state—although this dizzy merry-go-round of warlords between 1841 and 1845 barely warrants the name—was also changing beneath the chaos. For the most part, officials did not mourn the loss of merchant support for nationalist policies. Save as a social palliative for urban unrest, nationalism had proven unworkable for them as a system, as clearly shown by the abrupt 1841 demise of the Ramo de Arbitrios. Some caudillos (perhaps) even grasped the self-defeating nature of their predatory habits; other officials openly celebrated a coming age of national-foreign collaboration, particularly if it rubbed off in finance.[47] Most important, the pressures for a liberal finance regime finally began to operate on an unstable and, by now, notoriously weak state. For the state, as well, once caudillos had annihilated their esteemed national intermediaries, there was no one left to turn to for credit, except foreigners.

In this sense, the wars forced an end to Peruvian ideology, and for once it became difficult to distinguish the tactics of unruly "nationalist" caudillos from those of "liberal" caudillos. Pragmatism rather than despair marked the state's march to liberalism (although its newfound guano could also raise hopes). If foreigners were to participate in Peruvian finance—and now they had to—the only workable strategy left was liberal inducements and securities. Attempted coercion had clearly failed, as shown by the superb economic protection afforded by consuls to their merchants during the severe gamarrista backlash of 1839–41. Then, even the extremist "forced naturalization" program had failed to exact a single peso from the foreign islets of capital.[48]

An explosive round of abonos finance—the first since 1835—made finance officials hyperaware of the largesse of foreign investors, even as it ate into customs futures. The first came in January 1841, a $37,500 joint, native-foreign voluntary subscription under customs guarantees. By year's end, abonos emissions surpassed $250,000, of which 44 percent was taken out by foreigners. By late 1844, when this spiral was stopped, caudillos had mortgaged customs in the amount of $1,089,352, for some $600,000 in hard cash. Here, and with the mint, the novel cooperation between nationals and foreigners bore tangible fruit for the state. The 105 contracts involved thirty-nine natives and twenty-six foreigners, the latter now supplying 62.6 percent of total funds.[49] Here was sterling evidence of what benevolence and security might coax from the capital-surplus foreign houses. Coercion was out, suasion was in; the transition seemed to work. To foster the trend, officials by 1843 had lifted the most noxious tenets of forced naturalization, broken several key monopolies, let foreigners win several critical tax struggles, and stopped worrying about such petty matters as retail laws, just as the merchants had done.

Then there was guano, the extraordinary future of finance. The early guano trade instantly transformed into a tool of emergency finance in 1841; it would never truly escape this condition of its birth. As noted earlier, its capture and change into a Lima state monopoly, together with a remarkable political characteristic—its literal insularity from chronic instability—made guano the finance of choice for the northern caudillos in their pacification of Peru, even if that task required some three years to accomplish. At this point, Peru would doubtless have disintegrated for good without its salubrious new monopoly of wealth, power, and violence.

Others have done a good job of tracking the early record and evolution of the guano monopoly, for this was no small fish in the world history of nineteenth-century exports.[50] Three immediate fiscal-political consequences bear repeating, as we begin to explore that controversial theme of why the Peruvian state became largely dependent on foreign agents, then massive overseas finance, in the Age of Guano. First, Peruvian officials rapidly—by 1842—adopted the much-maligned "consignment" system, which came directly from guano's militarist finance role. The state rarely sold its bird dung by the ton, which might have provided greater initial control over final prices and profits. Instead, gross export rights were in effect auctioned off for loans, very quick loans, to whichever merchants could supply the largest "adelantos" on profits. This knocked Peruvian merchants (e.g., Quirós, who fleetingly enjoyed the first contract) out of the picture. Only foreigners such as Gibbs and Montané had much liquid credit on hand, and they quickly came to dominate both the trade and caudillo finance.[51] In fact, the denationalization of the early 1840s proved to be a blessing in disguise; for, as others have pointed out, only large international firms had the capacity to develop a broad market for fertilizer on such far-off lands as England, France, and Australia. (Once these markets were created, Peru could in fact gain greater leverage in the trade, and did so, since it was a world monopolist as well as the local monopoly.) Until the late 1840s, these consignment contracts remained exceedingly ad hoc, an unpredictable game of push and pull between the state and the contractors over loan conditions. Yet, even under such uncertainty, the advances certainly dwarfed all previous short-term finance instruments. A typical early-1840s adelanto exceeded $200,000; by 1846, Peru had received more than $1.3 million in guano advances, virtually all of its initial profits from the trade.[52] It is not hard to imagine the effects on the imaginations of Lima's treasury officials.

Second, guano naturally produced an immediate new appreciation for foreigners among Peruvian military chiefs, and perhaps even a better appreciation for liberalism. The caudillos were more than willing to extend the negligible liberal concessions necessary to get the venture moving.

119

No caudillo was about to bite the hand that fed him, especially when the portions were so generous. The primitive exclusionism of the 1830s was by 1845 fully bankrupt.

This transformation was one of increased self-discipline; direct foreign pressures played little or no part, although all the interested foreign powers abhorred the monopoly from beginning to end. Essentially, Peru began to shed its old protective unpredictability. Foreign diplomats, intensely concerned, took cognizance of their new potential for influence over Peru in the 1840s—for example, a simple blockade or expropriation of the Chincha Islands—but generally chose not to act. (One attempt, the 1852 "Lobos Islands" affair, resulted in a Peruvian rather than a U.S. triumph.)[53] But why not dismember in a free-trade era that saw a French war over the price of pastries in Mexico and gunboats at the gates of China? Foreigners were also aware of the erstwhile quagmire in Peru over such seemingly simple issues as duties on flour and bleached cottons: tiny Peru's early intransigence paid off. Imperialism in Peru had always been a dialectical imperialism, letting neither side off the hook. Europeans and North Americans preferred, then, that guano freely work its own liberalizing effects on Peruvian elite consciousness and on their incipient state. The north and Peru liberalized on their own volition, at their own pace. In this sense, the "exogenous" appearance of guano accelerated a process already under way. The potential integration with foreign finance was one local, if pressing, consideration.

Third, guano provided the state, however disarrayed, with autonomy vis-à-vis the national finance cliques that had previously captured and constrained it with their lending. In a sense, the national-finance system had already expired before the first shipload of guano reached Liverpool; and the surviving merchants heartily endorsed, if not suggested, the dual guano policy of monopoly and milking foreign finance. The Peruvian state might still favor national elites—and did—but it was no longer obligated to do so.[54] While providing Peru the flexibility needed to erect new finance structures, much of this novel political autonomy of the 1840s would be lost as the guano age unfolded.

The final actors in the early-1840s scenario were the foreign houses themselves. Why did they put aside their historical (and astute) antipathy to defraying the costs of caudillos—now, at the height of Peruvian instability? The evidence here is surprisingly nebulous. First of all, foreign merchants correctly perceived that, without the prop of merchant nationalism, the chances for a severe nationalist backlash had subsided. No viable elite social base remained to sustain a regress to a regime such as Gamarra's. Conversations with their new friends at the consulado must also have persuaded them. It was apparent, too, that the broader shift in the social balance of Peru—the crisis of national merchants combined with their own steady expansion—now moved steadily in favor of foreign houses. Second, the abonos on customs had always made a relatively secure investment for foreigners—all the more so now, since guano exports propelled a robust demand for imports and customs revenues, and since official benevolence had become explicit policy. As for those few dealing in guano loans, they were either mesmerized by the prospects or certain that Peru knew the severe costs that reneging on such deals would entail. Now it was Peru's turn to inspire "confidence" in foreigners.[55] Lastly, every foreign merchant in Peru must have recognized (clearer than anyone) the revolutionary potential of guano. While only a handful of merchants received contracts, all might be similarly blessed if they ingratiated themselves with the right caudillos and officials. A loan became a profitable, politic investment, if still never a way to change disagreeable policies. With the help of God and guano, fiscal stability, perhaps even governability, lay on the horizon. Lending was one way to get in on the ground floor. Thus, for example, in the early 1840s, shrewd foreign houses busily began to buy up the (then) worthless government debt certificates (including those of the defunct Ramo de Arbitrios), sensing that their day would come.

"CONSOLIDATION POLITICS" (1845–52) AND THE CONSOLIDATING STATE

The debacles of the early 1840s marked a break with age-old beliefs and the breakdown of the prior protectionist dynamics among merchants, fiscal authorities, and the caudillo state. The new order, however, was not yet determined. That called for an institutionalized solution to Peru's ongoing fiscal emergency and, in that quest, more institutional relationships with the external sector and overseas powers. Above all, the triumph of a stable "liberal finance regime" required the formation of a new elite social alliance, at the center, to push through free trade against the recalcitrants still permeating Peruvian society. "Consolidation politics," the movement formed around Peru's internal-debt resolution from 1845 to 1852, hammered out, if inadvertently, this winning concentric alliance of merchants, foreigners, and the state. Yet Peru's final push to free trade was again mediated by the force and filters of emergency finance. This irregular birth left its scars even on the operations of the mature guano-age state.

When Ramón Castilla assumed command in 1845, the direction in which the new central state would turn was still barely discernible. Despite the growing bounty of guano, Peru's permanent fiscal emergency remained a severe constraint on state-building. In his first moves in 1845–46, Castilla clung to his basically nationalist training and instincts:

he looked to the consulado for material and political support. They refused all offers. This time, distrustful of risky public finance and perfidious caudillos, the merchants, along with others, simply demanded their money back.[56] Officials had to turn elsewhere—in part, to satisfy this demand—and soon enough did.

Despite the abatement of fratricidal war, the 1845–52 period was, from the perspective of Lima's bureaucratic stewards, still one of chronic crisis. Many factors abetted continuing fiscal instability. On the demand side, military and other (less coercive) pacification projects remained at nearly pre-1845 levels. Peru's precarious new social peace cost dearly to build and maintain. The pent-up demands of a generation—for back salaries, new infrastructure, overhauled bureaucracies, and expensive reforms—increased when the fighting subsided. To remain intact, Peru also had to make peace with an army of foreign and national creditors, clamoring for more than $40 million for defaults and damages incurred, or supposedly incurred, by caudillos.[57] Clearly Peru's new statesmen wanted to expand the capacities (and spending) of the state, as one example, to augment and secure its territorial range. But where would the new funds come from?

On the supply side, peace in and of itself hardly ensured adequate and reliable resources. Two decades of caudillismo had shattered beyond repair most of Peru's ordinary tax systems; and the Castillan "tax reforms" of 1845–55 would consist of a politic, step-by-step dismantling of surviving direct taxes. This pleased artisans, Indians, and capitalists far more than it did budget-makers. The 1841–44 orgy of abonos to satisfy caudillos had paralyzed current revenues; in 1845, officials inherited a customs and a mint whose overhead mortgage exceeded $700,000. Nor did a few lower duties on necessities automatically produce a boom at customs, and officials continued to discount the imported theory of liberal revenue tariffs. (Congress, for example, repeatedly surcharged tariffs until 1852, under the conviction or pretext of resolving deficits.)[58] Not even guano magically revolutionized state finance. Between 1841 and 1849, the state collected $5.5 million in fertilizer profits—nearly all in the form of extraordinary advances and loans—meeting only one-tenth of Peru's budgetary requirements. The profit rate on the monopoly was discouragingly low, and Peruvians knew it. Most important, the early guano markets, prices, and contracts remained dangerously volatile. On several occasions, deals fell through at the last minute, leaving desperate officials scurrying around Lima for makeshift funds.[59] Peru's London default kept overseas finance markets out of reach; resolution of these claims (and those of individual foreigners) called for a determination and fortune that Peru still lacked in 1845. Finally, while not in and of itself producing prosperity, peace did intensify the sheer perception of fiscal crisis. Republican Peru's first formal statistical and political deliberations around budgets, starting in 1845, immediately unmasked the structural deficits obscured by decades of impromptu finance. The longer policy vistas that peace allowed created only wider gaps between foreseeable incomes and expenses. Civilian politicians could note, dramatize, and lay blame for the shortfalls.

The consequences were threefold. First, the insurmountable deficits in ordinary revenues—those needed just to meet current salaries—remained, or even rose, in the late 1840s. In 1847, the gap reached $1 million (one-fifth of the budget); the 1848 budget introduced more precision with its deficit of $904,938; and in 1851, Peru's ordinary income of $4,269,600 suffered a 25 percent shortfall.[60] Second, the stopgap solution was still short-term loans, although the burden was shifting ever more to the guano consignees. In 1847, for example, seven loans were tendered by Gibbs, Montané, Cotesworth, Powell, and Canevaro, for a grand total exceeding $2 million. With the Arbitrios gone and abonos newly banned, guano unambiguously emerged as the state's prime tool of emergency finance. Finally, fiscal politics, now in the open, became far more acrimonious. It seemed as if the bygone battles of the caudillos had been replaced by legalistic skirmishes over budgets. As political institutions jelled, Peru entered its first (and exceedingly lively) era of "legislative politics." Political crisis and combat erupted with each government request for a budgetary supplement, raising fears of greater politicization and destabilization. Campaigns raged against unpopular ministers (such as that by Elías in 1847). In one July 1849 scandal, Congress sacked Castilla's favorite finance minister, Manuel del Río, for bearing bad news—a civil first, it seems, in the annals of Peruvian democracy.[61]

To farsighted officials and elites (and only peace cleared their vision) something had to be done. Guano could not remain an ad hoc fluctuating revenue rationed in costly and uncertain deals. A permanent basis had to be found for an expanding and vigorous state. In short, Peru needed to enlist a new set of fiscal intermediaries. Yet, national elites staunchly refused, pleading their sheer penury after a decade of uninterrupted wars, and the new civil aspirations of Castilla's court (no more forced levies) meant that these agents, by necessity, would be foreigners—at least to begin with. Peru now faced the opposite fiscal dilemma from that of the caudillo era: how to involve foreign over national support. Foresight blurred at this point, however, for the aim was still the paradoxical one of stabilizing emergency finance, albeit on a scale hitherto unimagined. This program required anchoring the guano trade (Peru's mortgage for fiscal solvency); normalizing diplomatic and commercial relations with foreign powers (through trade treaties); creating substantive liberal incentives for foreign entrepreneurs (other forms of inducement had clearly flopped); and resolving the external debt (a $22 million downpayment for access to overseas capital markets). All these reforms required the broader institutional and mental frameworks of free trade. Peru's state-building was again subject to intersecting and competing external and internal lures. But the struggle to implant this liberal fiscal regime would not come so easily.[62]

Initial moves in this direction, from 1845 to 1849, mainly from the executive, were largely reactive, short-term, ineffective, or blocked by nationalists. At base, most Peruvian elites remained indifferent about the urgency and virtues of fully integrating Peru into world economic and fiscal currents. Sweeping away the petty vestiges of caudillo-era exclusionism—Castilla's first steps in 1845–46—did not spark controversy. Forced naturalization, retail prohibitions, and studied intimidation in regard to foreign property rights were no longer tactical necessities, at least for elites, and were clearly antithetical to extending the cooperation and finance of resident foreigners.[63] Castilla's modest aim here was to invite more loans from foreign houses in Lima. Once the consulado had declined to aid, this goal was agreeable to all. But the larger issues, such as treaty rights, massive foreign-debt transfers, unhindered free trade, and the ultimate control and form of the guano enterprise were another matter. On these questions—which made explicit Peru's evolving relations with the outside world—Congress (and others) broke ranks. Sharp political debates augured the wholesale return of protectionism, as nearly happened during the volatile 1845 Congress. Against Castilla's wishes, reacting nationalists raised tariffs in 1848 and 1849, blocked loans, and then threw out the first British, North American, and French treaties and claims conventions, which had been worked out in painstaking detail.[64] Domestic support lagged. More open policies seemed thinkable, but they still lacked a firm liberal-state coalition. Foreign fancies and financiers were not pleased with Peru.

"CONSOLIDATION POLITICS" would fuel the needed Lima elite conversion to a liberal finance regime. The "Consolidation" refers to Peru's complex process of recognizing, restructuring, and reimbursing domestic and external debts in the 1846–53 period. At the external end, historians rarely miss its meaning: the settlement necessary to restore London credit after the twenty-year hiatus of Peru's 1820s default. Only the degree of foreign pressure applied remains in dispute. As for the internal debt, historians have long assigned special significance to the consolidation—as a mammoth and resolute swindle. Recognized claims jumped from around $1 million in 1845 to some $4 million in 1849, and then skyrocketed to more than $23 million by 1853—a venal government transfer plan to revive a viable oligarchy. Peru's modern ruling class, in this view, was born from corruption itself. Recent research questions this intentionality and outcome, stressing, for example, how combined national and foreign commercial speculation on the debt actually deprived Peru's traditional, provincial, or landed families of their rightful share of spoils.[65] And rather than an unbridled orgy of class greed, the consolidation might be described as a typical and necessary Latin American liberal reform, intended to divest the state of colonial-style property prerogatives while incorporating private enterprise under the aegis of a national state. A full restitution of state-plundered property would sanctify the strict new norms of a liberal capitalist state. Whichever the case, the "consolidados," those members of the high elite who cashed in on the (unquestionably) exaggerated and concentrated internal-debt bonanza, emerged by 1850 as Peru's decisive domestic constituency for liberalism. Their unfolding alliance with foreigners and the state drove the triumph of a liberal finance regime.

Consolidation politics, the fervent underground networks and public machinations to retrieve past debts, at first sight appears to parallel amortization politics—or even the oldest cries to endow a national capitalist class. In fact, its roots lay firmly in the amortization period. The original and core group of national-debt beneficiaries were precisely the survivors of the ill-fated Ramo de Arbitrios, Peru's traditional and tottering national-finance clique. For them, consolidation began in 1845 as a growing demand, upon first inklings of receding warfare and state solvency, to reclaim the $1 million in defunct loans to caudillos that had been filtered through the bank. Recovery through redemption of state debts embodied the same dream: rapid infusion of capital to save merchants from a lingering death. In this, guano was manna; had it not dropped from the sky? For the state—and it was still their state—an efficient and generous amortization of the Arbitrios debt would serve as a trial run for the generalized and inflated reimbursements to follow.[66] Given the exertions and interests on both sides, it makes perfect sense that the consolidation was born from Peru's established commercial elite.

The second continuity was institutional. Amortization of the internal debt (which passed through a complex series of legislation, strategies, and stages) actually employed for its first decade the good offices of the merchant consulado and Ramo de Arbitrios. (The consulado had performed such services before, in the 1820s.) From 1846 to 1850, the state reorganized the Arbitrios fund as a vast amortization machine for busily stamping, multiplying, and paying off the claims on all loans and property lost during the independence and caudillo upheavals, and then some.[67] This, in effect, became the consulado's main line of business by the late 1840s.

Finally, past amortization politics, while following a nationalist logic, also had ties with the external sector: namely, the doomed scheme to turn lower tariffs into a capital pool for top merchants. These same men fully grasped in the late 1840s that the brilliant success of the endeavor this time around—more than $2 million in bonds redeemed for cash via customs—depended entirely on the continuing health of foreign trade. The revenue for capitalizing bonds (whose value rose felicitously) came directly from import surcharges and, furthermore, starting in 1850, from guano reserves specially earmarked for the expanding internal debt. Who were they to tamper with a good thing, this liberalization that was making them solvent? The conclusion of this external logic to an internal debt came in 1853, with its "conversion." In a move that sent tremors across the capitals of international finance (and prompted a revolution in Peru), President Echenique "secretly" converted some 45 percent of the by then $23 million of internal debt into claims on Peru's foreign debt. This extraordinary act was to ensure a value, credibility, and guarantee for Peruvian domestic public bonds, which had become shaky, to say the least, amid the explosion of speculation and peculation during Echenique's reign. The operation was funded by enormous overseas loans, backed by guano.[68] (This gamble worked, too; even the revolutionaries who overthrew Echenique in 1854, in part over this scandal, ended up recognizing the ironclad and enforceable external guarantees.) Consolidation politics made, then, an eminently successful rerun of failed amortization politics. It was progressively to wed a close-knit and recovering Lima elite to the prosperity of the external sector.

Discontinuities with amortization politics were just as pronounced, and just as vital for understanding how the "consolidados" became the prop for a liberal fiscal regime. Amortization politics had sought to build a permanent class of state fiscal intermediaries. The consolidation merchants, on the other hand, certainly were not hoping for a regression to the perilous finance role that had nearly destroyed them in the early 1840s. Their objective now was the simpler one of taking back the capital kidnapped by the caudillo state, for good use in the safer and more lucrative opportunities beckoning in "private" enterprise. (The political corollary was scorn for crude military despotism and hopes for its speedy removal by trustworthy civilian elites.) Peru's new commercial possibilities, made all the more appealing by progressively expanding business ties with foreign houses, made consolidation politics a consummate liberal movement. The merchant liquidity crisis seemed analogous, but this time merchants coveted deadlocked capital for alternative liberal investments, not militarist monopolies. Even Lima's new tariff-sheltered factories struck consolidation elites as a risky aberration. (And the funds and flexibility provided by debt rebates would eventually help those already involved, after failing to win direct guano subsidies, to switch out by

1852.) Finally, it mattered not one iota that the pandering state had actually revived the Ramo de Arbitrios in 1845 as a possible source for renewed, short-term public finance.[69] The consulado turned down these loan requests one after another (until 1849), insistent that liberal foreigners perform that hazardous duty.

The second difference lay in the scale of transfers. Based on future returns from guano, consolidation dwarfed all previous attempts to capitalize Peruvian elites. By 1850, even a part of the colonial consulado debt won recognition, and most prominent members of the Lima elite—functionaries, urban rentiers, retired caudillos, coastal planters, and especially its merchants—shared some stake in the bonds. The nominal value approached $25 million in 1853. This massive giveaway of state property (comparable to the disentailment of church and public lands elsewhere in Latin America) can be seen as nineteenth-century laissez-faire enshrined, as the dispersal of colonial public functions and patrimonies to private individuals. In Peru, neither land nor freed Indians, but guano profits and bonds were distributed to a liberal clientele. By accident or design, Castilla and Echenique had spawned here a sturdy elite political base for the emerging regime, an elite increasingly dependent upon the liberal definition and policies of that state itself.[70] Finally, Peru achieved that Lima-centric liberal lobby missing since the 1820s. It proved critical to an effective limeño politics of free trade that was to gather the scattered liberal pulse of the provinces.

Consolidation was not greed alone. It directly embodied classic liberal designs and, indirectly, forged the concentration of liberal interests historically needed for free trade and a liberal state. However, the sheer scale of the transfer, and the growing stability of the dispensary state itself, would bring contradictory results. The initial impulse of elites after 1845—their resolve to distance themselves from the state for private economic allies—would weaken.

Third, the modus operandi of amortization politics—as in the backlog of Peruvian capitalization schemes—had been commercial exclusionism. This stemmed, as we have seen, from the state's disinclination or incapacity to integrate foreign capital into volatile caudillo finance, although this was changing by 1845. With consolidation politics, not a trace of commercial protectionism remained. Perhaps as a pure subsidy for Peruvian elites—rather than a discriminatory policy—the consolidation was, in effect, the more efficient solution. But certainly by the late 1840s, exclusionist politics became the exclusive domain of petty shopkeepers and artisans, those increasingly excluded from the guano bonanza and disenfranchised by the emergent elitist culture of the liberal state. In late 1849, as if to celebrate the end of antiforeign politics, Peru's merchants officially opened the consulado's doors to foreigners, a fitting end to colonial norms—and an unthinkable act just a decade before.[71] Profound shifts of policy ensued.

Finally, the politics of internal debt was not just open to liberal foreigners: it became a joint venture. It was here, if such processes can ever be traced with precision, that Peru's new political and social alliances between foreign and national capital were forged. Foreign houses, recent work shows, became major beneficiaries of the final internal-debt settlement in the 1850s, a paradox having roots in the early 1840s. Then, overseas merchants, with capital to spare (and the correct hunch about guano), had speculated heavily in sunken government paper—for example, buying out bonds at discount from the smaller and bankrupt lenders to the Arbitrios fund. By the late 1840s, this venerable source of Peruvian nationalism had become, in effect, a foreign property as well. This explains, once consolidation pressures erupted, how a reduced clan of national merchants moved beyond their mere accommodation with foreigners, in the early 1840s, into an active alliance. Working together, they would claim more than 40 percent of the final consolidation benefits. This joint speculation of commercial cliques dramatically concentrated their share of debts originally dispersed among myriad native groups.[72] National and foreign speculators on the Peruvian state would mesh in a common pursuit: a solvent state, whose viability was ever more synonymous with its export capacity and overseas credit rating, to use the modern terms. (Moreover, top foreign houses played indispensable roles managing the consolidation program; for instance, in negotiating the loans that underwrote the 1853 conversion.) Within a few short years, the consulado itself seemed swamped by foreign members, bond agents, and voters. By 1850, then, it was no longer possible to distinguish an "internal" and "external" debt in Peru—nor, for that matter, discrete "national" and "foreign" elite interests.

THE LIBERAL FINANCE REGIME
(1849–52)

All these trends converged with the agenda of fiscal elites in the late 1840s to erect a reliable and externally oriented fiscal regime for Peru. Events and process here become immensely complicated. For they were caught up not only in the vicissitudes of Peru's last major tariff battle of the nineteenth century but, ironically, in a new drive by Peruvian merchants to distinguish themselves from foreigners as renewed fiscal agents for a guano-age state. Historians have separately chronicled most of these events before.[73] Yet Peru's struggle over free trade, consolidation fever, civil elections, revolution in finance, overseas-debt settlements and treaties, the burning question of the Gibbs contract and guano, and the "hijos del país" debate—all formed a historical and fiscal unity. The result, between 1849 and 1852, was a resounding consensus, and victory, for elite liberalism.

In July 1849, Castilla's finance minister discovered yet another crisis in ordinary revenues, more than $800,000, and implored Congress for yet another stopgap loan from Peru's foreign guano consignees. Congress roundly rejected this first request (firing Minister Río instead). But this only brought into the open a wider and dramatic controversy concerning Peru's emerging relationships to the world economy. Several issues converged in the heated press, congressional, and ministerial debates of 1849–50. All knew that the Gibbs contract would come up for renewal later that year, and that Peru's government was most anxious to establish its guano lifeline on a solid, long-term, and expanded basis.[74] Negotiations for trade treaties with the major Atlantic powers, as with Peru's foreign bondholders, had reached a tense stalemate. The consolidation emissions had just entered their frenetic expansionary stage, with all the uncertainties this posed for speculating elites. Free elections approached—an attempt to bring about the first peaceful change of executives—adding more uncertainty to foreign and local perceptions of Peru's evolving state. And Peru's protectionist holdouts, from artisans to nouveaux industrialists, mounted their spectacular campaign to reverse the movement toward free trade, with frightening initial success in Congress.

In September 1849, Peru's merchant "hijos del país," emboldened by their new promised capital and the nationalist pyrotechnics around them, suddenly entered the fray. This merchant turnabout followed their realization that the state would need permanent fiscal intermediaries in the Age of Guano and that the prospects for gain now outweighed the decreasing risks. Herein lay the disguised essence of the famed September hijos del país debate: future fiscal mediation, not control of the guano trade per se. Instead of mortgaging Peru's guano to Gibbs in perpetuity, merchants such as Rodrigo, Delgado, and Canevaro proposed, Why not let the "national capitalists" do the job? Like Gibbs himself, all they needed was a steady share of Peru's guano patrimony for collateral. On this basis, the consulado then advanced a program of huge alternative national loans instead, in order to lift Peru from its continuing fiscal malaise.[75] (But the nationalist polemics of September 1849—the outright and vitriolic attacks on the European "finance oppressors" of Peru—were as contrived as they were effective. These were the men closest to leading foreign houses, and they certainly did not figure to manage guano and the treasury on their own.)

Out of these conflicts (and behind the scenes) emerged the final 1850–52 push to a liberal finance regime. Their rhetoric aside, Peruvian elites and finance officials knew perfectly well the real and enduring stakes at

129

hand. They were not simply the costs of one national versus international loan. The show of nationalist resistance provided the last shove. In early 1850, Gibbs won his coveted, long-term extension of guano control, which would last over the entire next decade. The contract paid off immediately for Peru, too, by essentially making Gibbs the short-term banker for the rapidly growing guano state. In 1850 alone, Gibbs supplied more than $1.4 million in emergency loans to the Lima treasury. His contract (and half his guano profits) were explicitly pledged to settlements for British bondholders, thus restoring international credit to Peru; another $120,000 went directly into payments on Echenique's skyrocketing internal debt.[76] And, in 1852 alone, Peru's net profits on guano reached $3.3 million. Over the next few years, Gibbs arranged the $2-million covert loan for converting the internal debt (allaying elite anxieties) and began dispensing to the Peruvian state a regular monthly allowance worth close to $1.5 million annually.

State profits from the guano trade would leap from levels of 33 percent in the 1840s to 65 percent during the following decade. Emergency finance—with this ability to elicit loans, guano never became an ordinary budget item—revolutionized and institutionalized at once. By 1855, guano covered more than half of Peru's $10 million in expenses (in 1847, the numbers had been a mere 6 percent in a budget of $5 million), a proportion that vigorously expanded along with state spending over the next two decades. In fact, in these four short years, 1850–54, Peruvian budgets had doubled.[77] This was Peru's heady "afluencia fiscal."

Lima signed the pending treaties with Great Britain, France, and the United States, which finally, after thirty years and many false starts, committed Peru to orderly and "reciprocal" conduct in the liberal world economy. This time the incentives were mutual, instead of the one-sided foreign pressures of the past. The elections seemed to work, too, for Peru's first pacific political succession since the republic was announced in 1821. This bode well for state stability and for the civilian elites pining for power. The new president, General Echenique (a son of the south who had adopted the north), would lay to rest Castilla's ambivalent nationalist-liberal legacy and vigorously campaign for free trade alone. Nor were Peru's growing hijos del país displeased. In October 1850, they won a valuable consolation prize for their immediate loss to Gibbs: future rights to export guano and, in due time, to compete as alternative agents in state finance. In the meantime, they could bask in the secured wealth of the consolidation, put to good use in tandem with foreign houses in the booming import economy of the early 1850s (Peruvian imports also doubled between 1847 and 1851, to nearly $10 million). Other Lima guanocrats were just as delirious over the buoyancy this meant for their treasured *vales de consolidación*.[78] In 1851, the government fully amortized $537,000 in internal-debt bonds; the following year, that figure rocketed to $944,000.

Not surprisingly, free traders smashed Peru's obdurate artisan and industrial protectionists during the tariff debates of 1850–52. This was the final touch in the making of a durable fiscal regime. Liberals won, in part, by stressing that Peru could no longer "afford" protectionism—at a time, of course, when Peru seemed to be able to afford everything else. Apart from the sparks of class struggle, and clamors for regional integration with a national policy, the long-range concerns of the budget weighed heavily on the minds of Congress. In 1852, the vague notion that higher tariffs could actually help the treasury was finally extirpated from the official imagination. For the first time, classical revenue-tariff arguments swayed Congress, as liberal spokesmen and treasury officials whipped up a specter of continuing fiscal emergencies. So did the combined weight of liberal national and foreign merchants, working together at last in trade, the consulado office, and debt operations. No doubt all the "consolidados," eager to convert their newfound wealth into freely imported lifestyles, influenced deputies as well: "rights" to luxury emerged for the first time as a serious issue in Peruvian tariff ideology and as a plague on Peru's embattled light craftsmen. At the close of the debates, the Senate passed the new tariff on to the merchants, allowing them to rewrite any sections they pleased before final passage.[79] The 1852 tariff was aptly dubbed "in protection of commerce"; it could just as well have been "in protection of fiscality" (or debt bonds). For these worries propelled Peru's elites to embrace free trade as never before.

The fiscal theory seemed to work, too: customs revenues expanded by nearly one-third in 1851/52 alone to more than $3 million. In truth, though, liberal customs would serve only as an adjunct fund to guano, apportioned in loans, for the duration of the export age.[80] Peru's revolution at the treasury, and the buildup of the state, occurred mainly by dint of direct emergency finance. Yet the symbolism was fitting enough. In the same year that Peru adopted free trade, 1852, officials proudly announced Peru's first balanced budget.

BY 1850, then, a genuine liberal fiscal regime was finally possible in Peru. The triumph of free trade was but the crowning achievement of this new liberal alliance among merchants, foreigners, and the state. It celebrated the incorporation of Peru's stabilizing state and elites into the international economic order. A new chapter had opened in the history of the Peruvian state—marked by protection for the external sector and the beginning of Lima's peculiar symbiotic relations with finance cliques, of collaborating nationals and foreigners. This new order arose, in one sense, from dynamics begun in 1821, from the original clash of merchants, foreigners, and the state. The conflicts of internal and external actors had intensified ever since. Now they would converge in an institutionalized dependence.

All other liberalizing trends met these fiscal developments in the Lima of the early 1850s. A broad but concentrated social alliance of free-trade elites, infeasible for a third of a century, became a pressing reality in Peru, especially around its internal debt. The Chilean and the Bolivian market alternatives had both faded, superseded by incipient regional exports and the incorporation of vanquished southern liberals into an expansive national state enriched by guano. Provincials, now without industries, clamored for more foreign trade, not the closed door, and finally found allies in the capital willing to disavow commercial privilege. By 1850, the risks that drove men to protection were clearly in retreat, and elites had had enough of the risk-making caudillos who pledged to protect them but consumed them instead. Myriad partnerships prospered with the foreign houses, who broke into domestic markets and politics itself via the consulado. Merchants no longer sheltered a collective of anxious retailers, nor coveted industry. There was the clampdown on protectionist outbursts in republican forums, thus increasing social distances, elite self-consciousness, a liberal public good, and economic and political marginality for die-hard artisan and popular nationalists. The forced retirement of xenophobic caudillos and heightened concern for the fragile hegemony of the central state allowed new forms of foreign-power influence over a stabilizing state, and that predictability was enshrined in the new trade and claims treaties. There was the hard-won sovereignty over guano and the long list of promises and fantasies it might realize for hopeful elites. But all these export-economy alliances, and the new liberal state they enveloped, emerged directly from the previous political economy—that of Peru's overlooked nationalist era.

A GUANO-AGE LEVIATHAN?

The outcome of this history was the guano-age state, with its legendary proclivities and debilities. Historians have long pondered, with morbid fascination, why nineteenth-century Peru, endowed with a seemingly endless state income (nearly $500 million), never managed to control its wealth and translate guano's "fictitious prosperity" into a real and enduring development. Peru became the textbook case of boom-and-bust export dependence.[81] Economic historians are still not sure whether Peru experienced any net productivity gain during the guano age! And despite its respectable income and stability, the guano-age state could not become a "strong" or even a lasting liberal state. A few new clues to these riddles emerge from the conditions surrounding the birth of the guano state in the late 1840s, from its inherited and transmutable characteristics.

At face value, the guano-age state was an astonishing success, if measured in terms of its capacity to mobilize finance, the chief concern of its architects at conception. In the 1850s, Peru jumped from last to first place as the world's largest borrower on the London market. By the 1870s, among nonindustrial nations, only Peru's old nationalist analogue, the Ottoman empire, earned the dubious distinction of a greater external debt. Peru owed some £35 million. This edifice had to crash; and when it did, in the late 1870s, so did the Peruvian economy jerry-built around the guano state. Countless warnings about uninhibited dependence on fluctuating and depletable monoexports and foreign finance were ignored for three decades. One high point of this fiscal folly occurred in 1855. A blue-ribbon panel, which had been convened to reform Peru's fiscal structures, deliberated and then announced its sterling plan: abolish all surviving domestic taxation. Peru's shaky reliance on guano and guano-induced loans only grew, so that by the 1860s seabirds supplied more than 75 percent of government revenues.[82] The 1870s export crisis became an unabsorbable shock.

There are many possible reasons for an exaggerated propensity to borrow. Clearly, this pattern was historically ingrained in the very way the guano-age state emerged, as a funnel for extraordinary finance—funds largely consumed in refinancing past debits. Genuine fiscal stability and rationality were never achieved in this compulsive cycle of emergency borrowing, and in this way Peru's "productive" investment in the guano age remained minimal. In some sense, had Peru's curious nationalist legacy not led to state ownership of the guano fortune, Peru's institutional development might have taken a steadier and, one presumes, healthier course.

Radical free trade was another legacy. Economic historians have now convincingly shown that the conformist uniformity of Peru's import liberalism after 1852 caused severe cost-price dislocations and impeded the emergence of a more diverse and diversified Peruvian entrepreneurial class. A compelling enough domestic market was there, forged by the powerful demand effects of guano itself. But Peru was catching a "Dutch disease" and sought no cure. With chronically overvalued exchange rates—presumably aggravated by Peru's profligate borrowing—any differential tariff preference to industry might have favored diversification and growth.[83] Instead, we saw that a small elite, terrified by prospects of political and class struggles around tariffs, and justified by the "failures" of 1830s-style protectionism, chose to bury the problem, resorting to dogmatic and blanket liberalism. History produced here a scorched-earth variety of free trade: elites even destroyed their own factories in the process. The new attachment to liberalism ran so deep that two decades later, when the guano bonanza began to wane, Peru's leaders still would not deviate from radical free trade, even though it became wholly rational to change course in the 1870s. Repentant radicals such as these are generally their own best enemies. At some level, one is also speculating here about the nebulous theme of the "rentier" psychologies that matured hand in hand with the rentier economy of guano.[84] If anything, that outlook was rooted in the central rentier relationship of the era: that of elites to their state, the by-product of developments in the 1840s. Whatever the case, some effort at diversification—in part, diversification from the state—might have cushioned the fall from Peru's abject reliance on the world economy. Instead, when the export crisis hit in 1877, Peru had little to show for its three decades of guano development, and nothing to fall back on.

Trade policy even tainted the political complexion of the consolidating state—perhaps for some time to come. Shutting out small traders and manufacturers from the new elite state certainly hurt their economic prospects, perhaps Peru's, too, by turning potential entrepreneurs into Peru's festering "social problem" of the guano age. It may have also harmed political development. The politics of the guano age became the exclusive domain of small but wealthy urban elites, who habitually resorted to coercion whenever their privileges were questioned from below. In 1858, for example, Castilla's crack cavalry and artillery brigades squelched the latest protests of artisans and the unemployed against free trade.[85]

A civil-elite politics began to flourish after 1860, but its relationship to popular participation remained, at best, top-down. If we are to believe the grandiose sociological schemes that purport to trace modern forms of authoritarianism to nineteenth-century patterns of "modernization," the consequences were severe. Indeed, we ought to add an early authoritarian-liberalism to the historical typologies.[86] The return of elites and an exclusive state fed by foreign commerce was, in some sense, a revival of colonial despotism. In Peru, the lively and novel basis for postindependence politics lay in its relative inclusion of nonelite groups. When these urban middle sectors expired (politically and economically) with the triumph of free trade, so did some wider possibilities in Peruvian political culture. The appeasement of free-trading provincials did not offset these urban losses and, in time, only helped fasten Peru to its patriarchal past. The narrowly elite social mooring of the guano-age state has never been taken as a sign of its inherent strength.

The liberal sociology of the guano-age elite was also double-edged. In one sense, the guano plutocracy was not liberal at all, despite their conversion to free trade. This ambiguity was striking in their continuing penchant for statist privilege, contracts, and largesse, and in their protection (denied to the rest of Peruvian society during the guano age) from bald market forces. As a capitalist elite, a very curious one, they remained dependent, obsequious, and "weak" in relation to the state—dangerously so. The state generated their original wealth, and over the next three decades the state continued as their prime field of investment.

The movement toward private enterprise in the mid-1840s proved slight and short-lived, as soon as the opportunities from renewed symbiosis with an export state became readily apparent. After having been "consolidated" by guano in the 1840s, recast as official guano traders in the 1850s, and again as public fiscal intermediaries in the new national banking network of the 1860s, these "hijos del país"—*hijos del estado* is the better term—had essentially returned full circle to their niche of the 1830s. No doubt the lures overwhelmed them: for example, in 1865–66 alone, elite bank loans of 35 million soles for public finance netted a straight 30-percent profit. Their banks proliferated on a speculative scale, in tune with expanding state budgets.[87] Yet, despite the fancier institutional apparatus of their guano and banking empires, and new investments in services and export agriculture, Lima elites remained largely sycophantic creatures of the state.

The early returns notwithstanding, the state turned out again to be a poor and risky investment, indeed. When Peru entered its fiscal crisis of the 1870s—just as had occurred four decades before—the state turned capriciously against its elite. With the famed Dreyfus contract of 1869, for example, officials pulled the rug out from under national entrepreneurs by suddenly canceling their guano contracts and handing guano and banking back over to foreign financiers—a rerun of the topsy-turvy fiscal struggles of an earlier epoch. The worst was yet to come. Starting in 1873, increasingly desperate treasury officials began to intervene arbitrarily in the oligarchy's banks in a hungry scramble for emergency funds. These levies were no less forced loans than were the extortions of plundering caudillos a generation earlier, and the bank panic spread. With more than 10 million soles impounded by the state by 1876, the new finance system collapsed, bringing most branches of the oligarchy down with it.[88] Official predation triumphed again, and in the wake of this fiasco (and the devastation wrought by the related War of the Pacific), Peruvian elites again had to start over from scratch in the 1880s. The affluence of the guano age had changed nothing.

One can not help but wonder. During the formative period 1845–52, if a cleaner separation had been cut between liberal civil society and the state, would fewer disasters have occurred? The heights of the Peruvian economy remained, so to speak, "politically embedded." Again, the fact that the state owned, mediated, and distributed the returns from foreign trade did not help. This was the central and most profitable commercial investment in Peru, albeit oiled by political favors; little incentive existed for a vigorous, competitive, and diversified "private" economy. Indeed, such a paradoxically successful free trade produced few of the classic pressures for further liberal and structural reforms, of the sort that defined and strengthened entrepreneurs (and states) in other parts of the capitalist world.[89] At best, the new Peruvian plutocracy remained a weak bourgeoisie, liberalism a weak façade.

Greater autonomy might have helped the state as well. Clearly, from the moment the guano monopoly was pronounced in 1841, Peruvian development in the nineteenth century was going to take some sort of statist path. And at first, the peculiarities of guano production and ownership seemed to promise a state with a large measure of freedom from short-term contending forces and pressures, local and foreign. In this way, the early guano state was able to enact important social reforms (abolition of slavery and the like) and create some semblance of modern capitalist institutions, despite the inertia or resistance of Peruvian elites. In a comparative vein, few states have equaled such an independent fiscal base (the resemblance here to contemporary petroleum emirates extends beyond the rentier economy to the core of politics itself). But this structural autonomy was never fulfilled in later practice. Instead, the guano-age state quickly fell victim (as did its captors) to the oscillating machinations of finance cliques and foreign creditors and to the truncated vistas of its manufactured plutocratic elite. Along with the systemic proclivity to borrow, these developments help explain this state's bizarre lack of control over its own income as well as the deep and harmful policy instability of the guano age. It was, to be sure, an instability of different degree and kind from that of the caudillo age. Yet, despite their best intentions and efforts, Peruvian policy-makers failed to come up with a coherent or workable "development plan" for the use of guano—although several compelling ones were suggested at the time.[90] In large part, the erratic flux of policies reflected the incessant push and pull of Peruvian elites (e.g., the huge transfers of the early years), of unmanageable overseas finance, the built-in antipathy toward protectionism, or a typical nineteenth-century exporter mania for imitative models. In some ways, this state made an even weaker target for imperialism, broadly conceived. All these factors decreased the state's potential flexibility, effectiveness, and power, and each was rooted in the developments of the late 1840s. Long-term visions were difficult to sustain; nor could the state then act as freely as its fount of funding implied. When one scheme finally won out in the late 1860s—massive investment in railroads—it was much too much, much too late. Under the combined weight of manic activity, unrestrained borrowing, dismal choice of projects, the evaporation of guano, and gross fiscal mismanagement, Peru's state finally collapsed in the late 1870s.[91] From there, the frenzied plans for replacing guano with the new miracle solvent of nitrates dragged Peru into war with Chile, for which, understandably, Lima was ill-prepared. The War of the Pacific was but the coup de grace to an already prostrate state. From the promise of autonomy in the 1840s, Peru's first attempt at liberal state-building expired from its cogenital weakness.

The guano-age Leviathan, then, was more apparent than real. The state and society that emerged from the resolution of 1840s conflicts remained fiscally unsound, hamstrung by its dogmatic trade policies, predicated on a shaky social and economic base, destructive to its own elites, and undermined by vacillating outside pressures. It was, in short, disaster-prone from the start.

CHAPTER 6

Conclusions: Nationalism, Dependency, and the Peruvian Nation-State

AT THE START of this study, we saw that a central tenet in the historiography of Peru is the dearth of nationalist elites in the early republic. This forms the cornerstone for influential new conceptions that purport to explain Peru's subsequent "underdevelopment" under nineteenth-century free trade. The implied relationship here, among elite protectionism, Peruvian nationalism, and national development, will remain controversial. However, this book argues that the republic was actually founded by highly nationalist elites whose influence spanned three decades of republican rule. Peru, historically one of the most liberal of Latin American economies, experienced one of the most vigorous interludes of nationalist politics in the postindependence era. The country most dominated by later liberal elites, Peru entered its national existence guided by entrenched, nationalist dominant classes—agrarian, commercial, and political. Historians should focus now on the nature of this early economic "nationalism" and on the factors that explain its later inversion into the radical liberalism of the guano age.

NATIONALIST AND LIBERAL STATE-BUILDING

Given our conceptions of the behavior of Latin American elites, the nationalism of early Peruvian elites is surprising. Yet this was an explicable response to the initial shocks of integration into the world economy and to the specific domestic conditions—above all, chronic political and economic instability—that Peru shared with most postindependence states. The value of recognizing and analyzing elite nationalism is that previously incomprehensible developments can be understood in trade policy, politics, and the formation of the Peruvian state. In complex fashion, Peru's political trajectory reflected its new patterns of entry into the world economy.

Early free-trade interests were mainly confined to the isolated, unpopular, and unsuccessful imperialists from the United States, Britain, Gran Colombia, and France, as seen in Chapter 2. These foreigners failed because they lacked significant collaborators within Peru itself. Their pressures were as unmistakable as their ineffectual liberal tactics. The pivotal local elite rejected an overseas liberal alliance, so long as unstable mar-

138

kets and politics obscured the potential benefits. The few Peruvian liberals were either wishful-thinking post-Bolivarian ideologues, with no social following, or incipient and contradictory southern free traders, more prone to caudillistic separatism than to hegemony over the Lima state. Only with a second wave of liberals in the 1840s, and a vastly altered social context, were these handicaps of first-generation liberals overcome.

Peru's dominant elites all proved to be decidedly protectionist, as demonstrated in Chapter 3. Their ability to unite, to attract the support of popular groups, and to capture the nearby Lima state produced a viable protectionist movement. Northern planters and regional merchants, bereft of overseas market opportunities, opposed foreign penetration of their traditional heartlands. They hoped to lead Peru into an illiberal commercial union with Chile rather than with North Atlantic capitalism. Pugnacious artisans, millers, shopkeepers, and provincials found solace in exclusionism and also sponsors among the elites. The Lima merchant class organized the protectionist forces, even as it erected its own barriers against foreign commerce with the aim of creating a state-sponsored national capitalist class. As Chapter 4 shows, the informal nature of Peru's political system made military and civilian leaders alike highly susceptible to these pervasive protectionist pressures and to a nationalist style of politics. Caudillos and bureaucrats, far from succumbing to liberal fiscal pressures and strategies, became dependent on the national financial intermediaries explored in Chapter 5. This forged the final structural link pulling together the initial nationalist state. However, the same conditions of economic and political instability that encouraged protectionist responses also hampered Lima's ability to consolidate national power, implement consistent policies, and bring lasting benefits to its nationalist constituency. This was a viable nationalist movement but, ultimately, not a viable nationalist state. Two decades passed before Peruvian elites fully realized this dilemma. With the political and fiscal changes generated by stability and new guano exports, they began their 1840s trek to free trade. Still, much had to change before the liberalism of the guano age became a feasible historical option. Even then, the new liberalism of Peru would show the sure signs of its nationalist birth.

THE TRANSITION from protectionism to free trade was, at the same time, part and parcel of a larger and dynamic contest around Peruvian "state-building." This conception best clarifies Peru's shifting welter of interest groups and trade politics in the postindependence era.[1] The Peruvian state passed through four phases between 1820 and 1860. First, in the decade after 1820, Peru achieved its external sovereignty, coeval with the northern elites' assumption of internal control over the capital left by colonialism. Despite their initial resistance to independence, Lima's role became solidly "nationalist"—with the assertion of homespun protectionist interests, a widening social base, the consciousness-forming expulsion of Bolivarian invaders, and the witting (and unwitting) victory over attempted Atlantic policy domination. An array of neighboring social groups and political bodies converged around this restitution of Lima's power, as did the caudillo-commercial fiscal nexus that kept the primitive state apparatus autarkic and afloat. By 1830, nationalists had quashed all proximate liberal alternatives.

Second, the 1830s marked the first attempt to generalize and implement the limeño statist project on a national scale. External pressures remained at bay, but the national state as well suffered severe setbacks. Resistance by southern forces paralyzed consolidation of the state, whose external dimension now revolved around the sharply polarizing Chilean-Bolivian market axis. The global stalemate of sectional/caudillo conflict in the 1830s may have favored Lima's political pretensions, but its unsettling effect was to forestall in practice all commercial (and state-making) options. Yet, militarism as a mode of governance could intensify indefinitely, or so it seemed, in symbiosis with the fiscal cliques of the Lima area and with their undaunted protectionism.

Third, the 1840s ultimately ushered in a dramatic new state coalition based on liberal models. Paradoxically, this change emerged in the wake of the limeño triumphs over the south and in the absence of (and defeat of) direct pressures from abroad. By 1845, the Chilean-Bolivian antipodes ceased to rip at the Lima state, opening a novel possibility for a stable national polity. This occurred just as the spread of a new regional liberalism placed new pressures on the traditional protectionist-centralist formulas of Lima. Nor could the original Lima coalition hold its own. The unbridled militarist crisis of the early 1840s shattered the narrowing alliance between limeño elites and nationalist caudillos, as well as the ties between elites and their petty protectionist clientele. These developments spawned a new antimilitarist and antistatist civil bloc, one for unfettered elite social pretensions and for reconciliation with southern and overseas interests. All of these prerequisites to a national state required liberalism to work. The order-and-progress Castillan army spearheaded late-1840s national state construction, a process still managed by and for Lima elites. Between 1845 and 1852, Lima officials co-opted southern aspirations and integrated other regional liberals, stamped out the old provincial militarists, externalized and stabilized Peruvian finance, bolstered civil-elite forums, overcame their abject predation of elites, excluded the urban masses, normalized foreign diplomacy, and carved out a solid liberal-elite constituency (via debt consolidation) from the former nationalist stronghold of Lima. Guano exports and a precarious peace helped accelerate the liberal incentives and conversions behind each of these shifts. But this time it was nationals who sought out foreigners as their local collaborators—the precise opposite of the pattern during the 1820s. Free trade in 1852 capped and institutionalized this victory of a viable, expanding, and peripheral elite state.

In the fourth stage, Peru's guano-age state would embody the 1840s transformations. These also defined many of its limits. The liberalism of the state remained almost uniquely commercial and fiscal. Peru's new bureaucracy and plutocracy were externally financed, more broadly spaced, and well integrated into the main currents of nineteenth-century world culture and economy. Both the guano elites and the state grew precipitously and in tandem, even as elitist political forms slowly infiltrated and overcame Peru's stabilizing army of the transition. From the extremes of tumultuous, limeño, and autarkic state formation in the 1820s, external dependency had become the linchpin of a more stable, modern, and national polity. It remained, however, fragile at the core and swiftly collapsed with the withdrawal of external markets, finance, and support in the late 1870s.

Historians have yet to explore other facets of early Peruvian state formation; surely we see now that commercial factors left a deep and enduring mark. Two points stand out in the general relationship here between trade policy and state-building. First was the need for a hegemonic national center for liberalism to take hold. Political economists have long stressed the emergence of a stable world center—a "hegemon"—as the cornerstone for any viable, international free-trade order. An analogous process works at the national level, if for no other reason than to concentrate liberal lobbies under an umbrella of growth-inducing stability. In Peru's case, the hegemon was an effective national state. That state developed from early nationalist pressures, yet the concept also clarifies why its hegemony would paradoxically transform into a liberal one. Second, historians ought to explore further the ties between liberalism and state-building. Relationships between economic nationalism and state formation have been an obvious concern, from the mercantilism of the seventeenth-century core to the top-down, delayed development of peripheries in the twentieth century.[2] We also recognize the many links between political liberalism and political nationalism. But economic liberalism as a mode of state-building, of the sort that developed in Peru, merits more attention in our typology of states.

DEPENDENCY AND NATIONAL ELITES

What significance should be assigned to Peru's original—in both senses of the word—nationalism of elites? What was its contribution to Peruvian history? Above all, was this nationalism the type of "autonomous" and "progressive" alternative to elite export liberalism that recent historians seek for nineteenth-century Latin America? What do historians really mean by invoking that counterfactual nationalism? These questions were broached at the start of this book, as we reviewed the recent perspectives of dependency historiography. By way of conclusion, these last sections will attempt to assess the nature and implications of Peru's turbid early brand of conservative nationalism. A host of interpretations seem to fit it, whose ambiguities are defined, then refined in order to reach a closing analysis. This task also requires that we move through the surprisingly uncharted territory of the relationship of nationalism (in abstraction and history) to dependency theory. The nationalism of Peruvian elites, it turns out, was at once forward-looking and reactionary, far-reaching and limited in scope, and both inconsequential and crucial for subsequent Peruvian development.

New dependency interpretations of Peru's era of independence have sparked recent debates over nationalism. The controversy became a revisionist challenge to the traditional—and official—version of Peruvian independence. Historians used to celebrate liberation from Spain as the product of profound nationalist struggles by heroic elites, who were then able to define the groundwork for a legitimate national state in Peru. The revisionists came closer to the mark: in Peru, independence did occur largely by default, and the caudillismo that followed was hardly convincing evidence for the legitimate state. Moreover, mere separation from Spain barely disturbed Peru's web of archaic colonial social relations, and republican elites did little else to change them. Dependency historians were also right to regard independence itself as a minor subplot in the larger drama at play, Peru's transformation into a subaltern member of the world economy.[3] (Hence their term "neocolonialism," a switch of one colonial master for another, or the survival of colonial norms under republican and liberal guise.)

Notwithstanding these novel insights, the *dependentistas* were still arguing, at base, on a terrain similar to that of their traditionalist foes: whether or not an elite nationalism existed. The new historians simply chose to deny its possibility. It was the dearth of nationalism that ordained Peru's republican predicament. Perhaps lost in this negation was another, more interesting question: what sort of nationalism was feasible in the postindependence era, and what did it mean for Peru?

The dependency approach actually stems from an older, broader, and overtly political controversy about republican societies; a common analysis from the Latin American Left since the 1920s, Peru's Mariátegui and Haya de la Torre became its celebrated spokesmen. Latin America lacked—in some cases, still lacks—an authentic "national bourgeoisie."

The reactionary elites inherited from Iberia were nationless appendages of world economic currents, unfit for nation-building. Without a genuine bourgeoisie—and its revolutionary nationalism—economic backwardness, foreign domination, and authoritarian politics inevitably disfigured the region's social development. Latin America never experienced true capitalist development, for its elites had never stood up for themselves. The dependency school further specified the problem: it was the region's peculiar "colonial" role in the world economy—as purveyors of exports— that truncated the historic role played by nationalist entrepreneurial elites elsewhere.[4] To be saddled with this free-trade "lumpenbourgeoisie" was not very heroic.

Sometimes this unfulfilled nationalist ideal was construed in its widest possible sense (a renovative movement to integrate disparate social, ethnic, and regional groups, mobilized by a national consciousness and cutting social reforms). At other times, it reduced to a simple propensity for high tariffs (a vibrant, progressive, and autonomous bourgeoisie is, after all, industrial). In extreme cases, a vulgar dependency analysis turned this indictment of elites into a catchall explanation for all forms of Latin American underdevelopment—economic, social, political, cultural. Out of this analysis, and its intellectual roots in Peruvian experience, emerged today's dependency counterfactual view: if only the republics had enjoyed nationalist elites and nationalist policies in the nineteenth century, their development would have moved on a par with the North Atlantic world, rather than under its thumb.

Ample reasons exist to question this approach on analytical or comparative grounds alone, and skeptics of dependency theory abound.[5] Should the evolution of one social formation be framed in terms of the supposed formation of this other, Atlantic capitalism? At best, the version of bour geois nationalism invoked here seems to be an idealization of European experience. Dependency theory was born as a trenchant critique of Western modernization theory. Has it simply degenerated into another form, importing a hypothetical bourgeoisie to replace the rejected "middle sectors"? Dependency also suffers by overlooking new scholarship on nationalism and state-building. Among the new questions posed is whether "nationalism" has been a precondition to development anywhere, or whether the construction of states and territorial economies usually precedes the invention of nations and national consciousness.[6] Historians may also wonder whether a counterfactual nationalism provides genuine historical insight or, instead, obfuscates with a voluntaristic (or teleological) reading of the actual choices historically available to elites. After the past forty years of economic experience (and long past Mariátegui's), is it still useful to conflate protectionism, nationalism, and national development? Elsewhere, intellectuals—especially those of the

Left—have rarely regarded nationalism as a necessarily progressive force. Perhaps liberalism, with its own vision of national modernization and of an autonomous economic citizenry, should count as nationalist ideology, too. We are also confronted with the fact that, historically, any number of social groups have appropriated nationalist symbols, with vastly different meanings in their various contexts. With these types of questions in mind, what can "nationalism," or economic nationalism, actually mean?

In this book, our critique has built from fresh evidence and has centered on the historiographic accuracy and analytical capacity of dependency theory. Both are wanting. The point of this effort, however, is not to banish, but to draw on, the enduring conceptual advances of the dependentistas. The current dependency view of the nineteenth century, when Peru acquired its modern underdevelopment, is just too simple. Some of its assertions are factually untrue. According to that account, Peru lacked coherent dominant classes with a coherent national project: they fell into senseless fighting among themselves—caudillismo—while capitulating without a fight to free trade; liberalism, in turn, brought the multiple fiascos of the guano age, then even greater humiliation with Chile (and beyond).[7] Nothing but dependent underdevelopment showed for this disastrous century of elite mismanagement.

In fact, dominant groups did exist in postindependence Peru, as did strong nationalist currents among the elites, who directly obstructed foreign liberal domination. More important, these new data can advance our analysis of the birth of dependency itself. Trade policy loomed larger than even dependency theory supposed. Caudillistic struggle ceases to be utter chaos but, in complex fashion, followed the patterns of Peru's insertion into the world economy. Both shaped Peru's initial attempts at state-building, and the consolidation of a liberal state involved much more than sheer surrender to foreigners. Peruvians were actors, not just spectators in the transformation to a dependent economy.

ANALYSIS should not err in the opposite direction when setting this record straight. These men were not the heroic bourgeois nationalists sought for in the dependentistas' counterfactual case; nor can we regress to the traditionalist hagiography of elites. What sort of appraisal, then, best fits this Peruvian nationalism? Can it address the broadest historiographic question posed earlier in this book? That is to say, was this nationalism a viable alternative to the elite liberal models that ultimately triumphed in the nineteenth century?[8] With the uncertainties affecting all historical conjecture, the answer seems negative: this nationalism was a flawed and fleeting failure. But the dependency criteria for judging it appear to be just as flawed—and even hapless failures leave a historical mark.

First of all, this was a nationalism that failed. Just as the activity of belligerent imperialists did not guarantee their successful domination over Peru, the rise of aggressive protonationalist ideologies and ruling groups did not ensure Peru a viable nationalist project. Despite the pull of northern protectionists over the Lima state, they faltered in their professed aims: to wield power effectively, to erect a lasting nationalist state, or even to mold consistent policies. Judged by absolutist perspectives, Peru's nationalist experiment seems to be an absolute and irrelevant failure. The nationalist miscarriage, however, is more interesting than that—it left lasting legacies, and the conditions behind its fall reveal much about the nature of this (and other) nationalisms.

One legacy worth restating is the impetus that the nationalist failure provided to liberalism itself. Without the three-decade nationalist interregnum, free trade could not have acquired its remarkable hold over Peruvian elites: export liberalism, despite ups and downs in its economy, would endure uncontested for more than a century after 1850. This was, to begin with, simply a negative demonstration effect. Protectionist policies (e.g., as those for manufacturing) had been fruitlessly tried. Peru's stock liberal leitmotif became the lack of workable alternatives to an unbridled export economy. Nationalism, free traders would insist, had proved "impractical," "inappropriate," and "disastrous" for Peru.[9]

More lasting still were social lessons imprinted from the form of the nationalist debacle during the early 1840s. In this collective memory of disillusion, nationalism became synonymous with intense social conflict, caudillistic disintegration, and state predation—the long postindependence nightmare of the elites. It was not an entirely unfounded association (for the time) and even found echo in universal liberal tracts against militant mercantilist-absolutism. In contrast, liberalism and commercial expansion, in mind and in fact, were coterminous with the 1840s arrival of political order and the revived basis of elite rule. Liberalism became embodied in Peru's consolidating state and elites. No one wished to lead Peru back from civilization to barbarism.[10] (In effect, this is the story of how the life-saving *doux commerce* of the 1840s overcame the life-threatening cruel commerce of the 1820s.)

Put another way, nationalist failures produced a charged lens with which to magnify the benefits and costs of trade policies, protectionism being indistinguishable from its early traumatic context. And Peru was not alone in its initial republican cycle of stagnant nationalist disorder followed by liberal "order and progress." These are the consequences that make the examination of Latin America's overlooked nationalist-caudillo episodes relevant, more so than any putative value as genuine nationalist alternatives. For without this brief but immunizing dose of nationalist failure, liberalism as reactive ideology and practice might never have captured so fully the Latin American imagination. (After all, South

Americans had widely dismissed free trade as the "impractical," "inappropriate," and "disastrous" option of the 1820s.) Nevertheless, the nationalist legacy was not simply negative.

Second, this nationalism fell largely because it was flawed, especially in its relation to political and regional instability. Peru's traditional and beleaguered northern elites could not easily accommodate the aspirations of rising southern and, later, most other provincial elites. The resulting political instability played no small part in their failure. (This is a paradox, too, in that underlying conditions of political and economic turmoil helped motivate the nationalist movement in the first place.) Moreover, the nationalists' political reliance on inherently unstable and predatory militarist representation ultimately hurt their chances for survival, notwithstanding caudillismo's role as the dominant political mode of the new "republic." Caudillismo could not form the basis for any successful national project, much less one based on statist requirements. Thus, nationalism was consumed by its own creation and creators in the early 1840s. Liberalism, in various ways, held a greater affinity with civilian rule (despite its initial, self-defeating centralism), and it was liberal elites who inaugurated Peru's slow trek toward stable civilian rule after 1845.

Overall, one suspects that, had the Peruvian state consolidated earlier, liberalism would have, too.[11] We saw these conundrums at work after 1845: when tranquillity and national outlooks prevailed, it was northern protectionists (such as Castilla) who actually wound up constructing the liberal, guano-age state. With its wider national scope and its stronger links to civil society, moreover, this liberal state appears no less "nationalist" than those revolving, protectionist ones which were based on vested Lima interests and militarist cliques.

Third, with hindsight, this Peruvian nationalism also appears to be an ephemeral movement with limited autonomy. Responding to chaotic and depressed conditions during Peru's first stage of open encounter with the world economy, nationalism might well have receded in any case with economic prosperity. In this sense, world economic cycles governed its rise and fall. Even self-styled nationalists remained at the mercy of the international economy.

Latin American nationalism, as a general rule, is plagued by a long-run and built-in countercyclical bias. Economic nationalism has flourished during bouts of depression (when opportunity costs for protectionism are low), only to evaporate with each upswing in the external sector. This means that nationalist policies have rarely enjoyed the heady and sustained conditions for growth that liberalism naturally exploits. Nationalist regimes thus prove difficult to legitimate economically, engender few perpetual interest groups, and thus remain isolated "experiments." Some economists regard this reactive cycle as the root cause for the region's secular inability to overcome orthodox liberal dependency. (They high-light, for example, the fluctuating and episodic record of nationalism during the twentieth century.)[12] Early Peruvian nationalism was similarly blocked. This was evident in the chief geographic locus of trade conflict: the stagnant north versus the expanding south. The dynamic later came into play in the curious way that Peruvian free trade arose not out of conflictive victories of new groups over old, but mainly from mass defections within a disaffected nationalist camp at the start of the export upturn. That Peru's nationalism was spearheaded by highly mobile merchants, who could easily switch their investments and political loyalties elsewhere, made this a particularly vulnerable nationalism. The only obvious continuity from Peru's initial policy phase was the statist guano monopoly—a nationalist monument of sorts, but not the kind of ongoing interest group or technological or ideological fixture needed if Peru were to offset a deepening liberal bias in its very social structure.

This weakness of postindependence nationalism is best seen in comparative light. Unearthing these rich political struggles over the terms of Peru's entry into the world economy could tempt one into facile, historicist errors: that such lively nationalist alternatives reveal the power of human agency, that they could have prevailed and would have made a difference.[13] Nevertheless, we should not exaggerate what are basically new details in a regional process of incorporation. Across postindependence America, analogous nationalist episodes broke out, with monotonous timing and—most important—outcomes. By 1860, the age of protectionism was over; free trade was ascendant everywhere. Wider contexts gave life, then death, to events in Mexico, Bolivia, Chile, Argentina, and Colombia, as well as Peru. In short, even the much-sought "autonomous" regimes lacked historical autonomy. Only in one peculiar case, Francia's Paraguay, have historians ventured to say that early nationalism left a lasting material imprint, and even there the experiment eventually went down to ignominious defeat.[14] On some level, dependentista fatalism—that the region was destined for a subaltern role in the world economy—is warranted, even when we better understand how it got there.

IF ULTIMATELY transient and weak, Peru still experienced a nationalist episode. But where does it fall within the wider conception of nationalism? Imagine a continuum of nationalisms with two extremes: "hegemonic" and "corporatist." Hegemonic refers to movements of broad national incorporation. Nationalists of this sort build nations by addressing the social aspirations of largely unintegrated masses of society. The nation is legitimized as it is modernized in myriad realms—participation, education, civic equality, effective government, the overthrow of old exploitations—no matter who happens to lead the movement. (Capitalists and communists, ranchers and librarians have all played this historical role.) At the other extreme, corporatist-nationalism, a private economic interest is elevated to a national concern. Characteristically the interests of already privileged groups have been jeopardized in novel ways by new developments. These groups move to capture the state (or, sometimes, the state captures them). Thus, the status quo of traditional forms of power becomes embodied in the state itself, disguised amid national symbols.[15] Hegemonic-nationalism breaks down the institutional, caste, or class divisions of a society; corporatist-nationalism strives to maintain them.

Several implications are possible here for early nationalism. These relate to the social conservatism of protectionist movements which, in a sense, weakens the dependency notion of the nationalist alternative itself. When protectionism serves as the driving force for nationalism, it generally approaches a corporatist mold. The verb form "to protect" gives this away. Economic nationalism usually coalesces as a defensive reaction to new competitors, on the part of previously organized and advantaged groups and those closest to the existing state. (The ideological fury of the liberal critique of statism should not blind us to its grain of analytical truth.) Consequently, most economic nationalisms remain clearly limited in their nationalist aims, capacities, and mobilization. They pale beside, say, actual social revolutions, foreign invasions, and colonial occupations, which profoundly disrupt the daily lives and livelihoods (social relations) of masses of people, and which indelibly alter the consciousness of the peoples under duress. These events have been the wellsprings for most hegemonic-nationalisms. Conversely, most Latin American nationalisms have lacked this punch.[16] This is the conventional view of Latin American independence movements as incomplete, aborted, or even reactionary social revolutions; or, of the myriad corporatist "revolutions" of the twentieth-century status quo. (The telling exceptions have been those revolutions in zones closest to imperial influence.) Historically, Peruvian nationalism, so removed from real invaders and upwelling revolutions, has retained a corporatist structure; the economic nationalism of the Velasco regime is just the most recent example.[17] In short, economic nationalism per se creates a poor substrate for hegemonic-nationalism.

Even so, dependency theory routinely projects an image of the requisite and viable "nationalist project," with three interlocking elements. To begin with, its central feature is precisely economic nationalism, for the overarching goal is autonomy from the debilitating world system. Protectionism is the minimum requirement; autarky, almost ideal. Second, the nationalist vanguard must possess substantive class cohesion and economic stature; otherwise, the movement lacks the coherent power and program to effect lasting change. Third, cosmetic reforms and the rhetoric of nationalism are not sufficient; radical social reform and incorporating drives are the only means for uprooting the internally grounded structures of dependency. Most dependentistas regard this prescription—filled by a "hegemonic" class—as some form of socially progressive nationalism.

This type of hypothetical movement seems an unlikely combination; for elite economic nationalism, in and of itself, produces the least ground-shaking implications for society. Its initial external spark, in effect, limits how far it can go internally; and the social implications it does generate are generally captured by corporate and, in many cases, overtly conservative elites. (In the historical extremes, socialist nationalism became its obverse, national socialism—clearly not what dependency had in mind.) Paradoxically, dependency thought in Latin America actually emerged in the 1960s as a rejection of the disappointing political potential of a "progressive bourgeoisie." Yet, even as its quixotic search for viable replacements widened, the theory itself still hinged on the need for a progressive dominant class.[18] One political implication here is that the ambiguous economic nationalism of that presumed class rarely substitutes for other kinds of hegemonic-nationalism. (The newest brand of dependency analysis—"world systems" theory—purports to dissolve the messy praxis of dealing with particular nationalisms and classes; but it merely displaces it onto a utopian plane, for the only meaningful social change remaining is its impending global, world-historical revolution!) For a regional historiography steeped in dependency frameworks, it seems high time to rethink the basic notion of an unfulfilled need for a national bourgeoisie.[19]

No conceivable nationalist movement, existing or past, could pass the political and social litmus tests posed by dependency theory in its present form. Instead, such movements should be approached for what they are, with all their built-in flaws. What kind of nationalism was this one?

LIMITS AND REACH OF
CORPORATIST-NATIONALISM

Early Peruvian nationalism came closest to a "corporatist" movement, distinct from the merely "conservative" movements described for other parts of Latin America. This is revealed by the limited social implications of its program, from its defensive and reactive definition of nationalism, in the colonial-corporate institutional roots of its statism, and by its peculiar geographic and class origins. Nonetheless, recognizing the limited scope of this economic nationalism hardly invalidates its historical role. Its profound impacts on the national consciousness of Peruvian elites essentially defined the new republic. Without this timely dose of nationalism, the Peruvian nation-state might well have perished at birth. What made this both a crucial and a corporatist movement?

The restricted social reach of protectionism was conspicuous from what was left out of its program: concern for the 80 percent or more of Peruvians who were rural, peasant, or Indian. Nationalists lent no sustained attention to the notion (voiced only by foreign intruders such as Bolívar) that the new "nation" had to encompass, actively incorporate, or relieve the burdens of these masses. In practice, to be sure, early protectionists did display some flexibility (greater than liberals did) in catering to popular economic aspirations—of largely urban shopkeepers, chacareros, and artisans—and, indeed, the enthusiastic response of these groups did bolster the nationalist cause. Yet, in the surrounding universe that was Peru's deeply divided, dual colonial society, these urban *menu peuple* were eons closer to the literate milieu of criollo aristocracy than to any submerged nation of Quechua-speaking comuneros outside Lima. Even these urban plebians stretched the limits of elitist nationalism. When craftsmen and retailers (marginalized by the first shocks of the guano trade) moved to act on their own after 1845, Peru's political elite was the first to clamp down. They redefined their nation as an exclusively liberal one, for protectionism and class conflict now menaced the revival of oligarchic values and interests.[20] At no time, then, did Peru's nationalism break the confines of a constricted criollo class.

Four interpretations might explain this missing nationalist effort to widen the scope of Peruvian citizenship and national consciousness: nationalism as socially reactionary; as the expression of an apathetic, dualist elite; as a defensive economic interest; and as atavistic colonial corporatism. The first (which permeates recent historiography) simply accentuates the social-reactionary anxieties common to all Peruvian elites, a minuscule stratum that actively oppressed the "Perú profundo."[21] Which was it, after all, that posed the greater threat to elites: imported flour at a few pesos less the barrel or a peasant rebellion? To some extent, such fears may have been a relevant concern to, say, slaveholding planters or millers (and slavery was indeed tied to their protectionist crusade) or to those with the longest memories of Túpac Amaru. Yet, as seen, Peru's first free traders suffered the greater handicap as social reactionaries, for the world of greater Peru posed a more direct complication to their supposedly libertarian worldview. In itself, protectionism implied little about democracy; nor did the nationalists embrace actively antipopular causes. Moreover, the triumphant liberal state proved no better on the score of political representation, freedoms, and centralism, even though in its rise some democratic claims were made. "Reactionary," then, is too vague a notion for understanding Peru's lack of hegemonic-nationalism.

More to the point was the remarkable inattention of Peru's dominant classes to all matters of political incorporation and social relations.

This second interpretation stresses that all elites belonged to a very thin and isolated, modern commercialized sector in Peru (this would even include urban popular groups). All other would-be Peruvians stood wholly outside the web of North Atlantic commercial competition, if not alien to capitalism itself. Elevating their consciousness simply could not matter in Peru's intra-elite squabbles over trade policies and state-building. Only deluded foreign liberals (as in the apocryphal story about San Martín) could think to decree the masses instant "Piruvians." Geographically, the role of this small commercial vanguard was neatly reflected in the active battlegrounds of protectionist and free-trade elites: Lima, the north coast, and the non-Indian south. A social cohesiveness, formed by a privileged minority status in colonial society, may even have added to the national sense of Peruvian elites (most likely, they knew one another by name) and then perhaps to the nervous afterthought that, if they did succumb to foreign competitors (those strangers), they might lose their only true edge over the indigenous poor. Dualism, and not class consciousness, therefore shaded corporate and national loyalties. These remain but educated guesses, for historical records rarely articulate such fundamental concerns and structures.

The difficulty with this dualist view of elites—it is an accurate description of Peru's commercial and social structures—lies in how historians extend it into a teleological injunction. To have had a true nationalism, this influential argument runs, Peruvian elites must have spearheaded explicit social reforms to overcome dualism. This, however, presupposes a revolutionary consciousness not available until the twentieth century, and thus does little to explain why elites acted as they did in the past.[22] (More broadly, the implicit comparison here of Latin American to "classic" nineteenth-century European nationalisms is overdone: these, too, were mainly thin and reactive political movements, led by and for tiny educated elites.) The kernel of truth to dualist arguments stems from largely contemporary concerns: a century and a half later (as in the ineffective, "revolutionary" Velasco reforms) the unyielding dualism of Peruvian society and politics would still pose a serious barrier to nationalist experiments.[23] We will return to the dualist issue. But a clearer appreciation of postindependence nationalism must unravel its roots rather than its presentist branches.

A third possible interpretation for Peru's economic nationalism would highlight its eminently defensive nature. Although it may have been nationalism's original stimulus and strength, a reactive birth could also impede the development of a deeper national consciousness. New, cosmopolitan interests and doctrines mortally threatened the position of

Peru's traditional elites in the 1820s. The reaction was a closing of ranks, drawing together in defense of their "patrimony," even if one had to be invented for the occasion. The increased foreign presence and pressures correlated with the rapid spread of national feeling among the Peruvian "hijos del país." Each foreign intervention intensified protectionist resolve; each tested the boundaries of what national sovereignty really meant. Harangues against foreigners, and exclusionism as such, were not just convenient political devices: they faithfully represented the beleaguered spirit of early Peruvian elites. The anti-Colombian surge of protectionism—the separation from the foreign occupiers willing to collaborate with Atlantic merchants—was, as we have seen, a vital component in the definition of who was a Peruvian and who was not. (In this view, the real declaration of Peruvian independence occurs not in 1821 but in 1827.) This reactive nationalist movement was even able to extend beyond stark xenophobia and autarky. Its Chilean vision testifies to that.

All told, could such a defensive conception of nationality positively define who the Peruvians genuinely were, especially when most Peruvians lived a world apart from this drama of traditional elites versus foreign interlopers? Nationalist propaganda, it seems, voiced an ever-sharpening sense of who the "others" were, a diabolical "anti-nation," but only the most elementary notions of who the Peruvians were (all the hijos del país put together?) or, more important, of who they should become. This brand of nationalism meant sovereignty against foreigners—not popular, political, or societal sovereignty. Its negative spark stopped far short of the civic sensibility and destiny that infused other nineteenth-century republicanisms. In some fashion, the defensive limits of Peruvian nationalism afflicted even the nuts and bolts of the protectionist platform.[24] Restriction of foreigners was easy to agree on, but what kind of workable or convincing model could point toward how the new Peruvian economy and society should develop? Despite frequent speeches about forging a complementary economic independence, the model (by default) was the backward-looking one of colonial statism and corporatism. It failed to work.

This argument seems persuasive, particularly given the general dilemmas of reactive economic nationalism. But it also severely underestimates the critical achievements and implications of a Peruvian elite nationality that so rapidly developed from this crucible of confrontation with foreigners. The Andes, as so many historians have shown, were no hotbed of embryonic nationalism in the late-colonial period (criollo-consciousness movements like those of Mexico were virtually unknown in Peru). If anything, Peruvian elites completely lacked an extraregional common identity when independence, which they had not actively striven for, fell into their laps in 1821. Peruvian nationality was a tabula rasa.[25] How, then, do we explain the survival over the next three decades of the new Peruvian state, which faced very real risks of disintegration from within, of foreign annexation (the Peru-Bolivia Confederation is just one example), and of North Atlantic policy dominion? All these dangers were successfully resisted.

By the late 1820s, as this book has shown, an active nationalist party dominated the Peruvian state and dictated its economic policies, against the grain of powerful external interests. While poor in other aspects of national consciousness, this novel Peruvian nationality was defined by the (underrecognized) nationalist economic ideas and interests of elites, a defensive definition rapidly accelerated by the force of direct confrontation with foreigners. Even a failed free-trade imperialism became a dialectical imperialism, spawning its antithesis in a nationalist drive. The movement for independence was not nationalist, but postindependence Peru was increasingly so. This ensured the survival of an artificially created, extremely fragile state, one that otherwise might have quickly shared the fate of Gran Colombia or of the countless federations of Central America. This state was highly unstable, to be sure, torn by regionalist and political pressures; but it was also increasingly "legitimate," for it directly served the interests and ideology of a recognizable ruling elite. That "Peru" existed in 1850 was no accident.

Dependency historiography first placed Peruvian independence itself into proper historical perspective, underscored the negligible national consciousness of its founders, and stressed the powerful external and centrifugal forces operating against Peru. It can now add this fundamental accomplishment of the early republican elites: a nationality and a state with enduring historical presence (recognizing, of course, as in most state-building experiences, that the submerged "nation" would be last to arrive). Another achievement, we will see, fell within the realm of ideas: the elaboration of a distinctive Peruvian ideology of self-interest and self-respect.

WHILE ensuring the birth of the Peruvian republic, early nationalism still retained its corporatist stamp. The corporatist face of Peru's economic nationalism, my final interpretation, is readily analyzed from its geographic concentration, institutional forms, social bases, and direct roots in colonial corporate practice. Peruvian nationalism—in sharp contrast to what might have been expected—emerged in the coastal trade region most integrated into the Atlantic economy, usually the locus of liberal ferment in Latin America. Unlike Peru's, most of the other conservative nationalisms of the postindependence era flourished in the interiors of America. The pattern of Spanish colonialism explains the Peruvian enigma.[26] Lima was not only a noncompetitive economy, it was also the core region of the viceregal, colonial-institutional matrix. (These two facts appear related.) In Lima, colonial norms, organizations, and privileges had taken deepest root: the entire elite of the region, Peru's ruling group, had evolved in close symbiosis with a colonial corporatist state, replete with "lords" and "feudal courts." A competitive, individualistic, market-oriented social order—less alien to the marginalized south, so far from colonial authority—was anathema to Lima's monopoly-laden, late-colonial elite.[27] Merchants, millers, planters, and bureaucrats were hardly the revolutionary scions of Peruvian society, if any existed in this profoundly conservative country. In Peru, a "revolutionary" meant any unabashed capitalist and liberal.

After independence—in some sense, freedom from the Bourbon reformers who threatened Lima trade privileges—a reversion to older colonial social models paralleled the rise of economic nationalism. The reconstitution of the institutional functions of the consulado—that corporate relic par excellence, closely followed the commercial favoritism awarded Peruvian merchants by the new state. By the close of Gamarra's second regime in 1841, the consulado had won a gamut of privileges and exclusive spheres unknown even in the late colony: their *fuero* was completely restored.[28] For Peru's hobbled state, unable to govern on its own, the object was administrative ease and a replication of the financial nexus that had served the viceregal regime so well.

Liberal propaganda aside, these merchants and kindred Lima elites were out to defend a monopolistic position in Peruvian society, in concert with a malleable and cooperative state. The model was distinctly patrimonial—Lima against all extremes of market competition, with the rights and status of each economic sphere enforced from above. The threats to corporate order were internal as well as external, regional as much as foreign, and newly impersonal (market forces) as well as personal (foreigners). Before this neocorporatist state fell apart in the early 1840s, it had busily managed to regulate the Peruvian economy from top to bottom, from its strict usury laws to ordinances governing the habits of street hawkers.[29] Historically, such a social pattern thrives in provincial economies; in an area like Lima, it had to be shielded artificially from outside economic pressures. Hence the association with protectionism.

In other republics, historians depict protectionism as an outgrowth of conservative nationalism. For Peru, the severest analysis of early nationalism would go to its deepest roots: a seventeenth-century "Hapsburg," practically feudal, mode of structuring the relationship between the state and civil society. Nationalism was inherently conservative, statist, even reactionary. A parasitic intertwining of the state and elite spheres was meant to preserve colonial venality and stifle social change. The nationalist face was mere neomercantilism—the elite belief that a new, local state would be easier to capture for their sole benefit than the stronger, more impartial, and alien late-colonial state had ever been. The liberals, for their part, from Simón Bolívar to Samuel Larned, were simply extending the program initiated by Bourbon reformers in the late eighteenth century; they wanted to open Peru to competitive winds and cleanly separate out an autonomous, impersonal, and truly modern capitalist state. The postindependence conflict, then, was the same one seen when the Bourbon crown first attacked Lima privileges in the 1780s, a trend ferociously resisted by Lima merchants and officials up to 1821 and, now it appears, even beyond. Protectionists were disguised Hapsburgs; free traders were latter-day Bourbons, revolutionary modernizers hopelessly outgunned in Peru.[30] In this view, Peruvian nationalism actually retarded the development of a modern state and its economic institutions, which arrived long overdue in the 1850s.

If this last interpretation of nationalism fits—and these elements were surely at play—it at least turns the confusing vocabulary of dependency theory on its head. For rather than resisting neocolonialism in their efforts to fend off foreigners and liberals, Peruvian nationalists were actually resuscitating the oldest and most venerable version of colonial society. (In any case, "neocolonialism" was always a confusing misnomer. The origins of modern Latin American dependency lie as much in nineteenth-century strategies for superseding colonial legacies as with the colonial legacy itself.)[31]

But was the collective greed of Peruvian elites—i.e., their "class interest"—ultimately different from any spirited movement to mold a state responsive to local interests? The global difficulty with corporatist views is that "corporatism" is such a broad and metamorphic concept. Latin Americans have been re-creating it and creatively merging it with new ideologies for half a millennium now. It need not carry atavistic connotations; in other contexts, corporatism simply means a "harmonious" social structure with built-in checks on contending interest groups. Chameleonlike, corporatist ideology constantly blends in with other elements, modern nationalism included.[32] Thus, to specify its meaning, and the limits of this Peruvian corporatist-nationalism, we need to grasp the specific social relations behind the merger.

The nature of the social alliance driving Peruvian nationalism best explains why its program lacked social depth. Reduced to its quintessential elements, nationalism reflected the symbiotic relationship between Lima's commercial and political elites. Other Peruvian elites—productive groups such as agrarian capitalists, miners, or rural manufacturers—were too weak and scattered to exert a steady pull on the state (much less to form any class basis for liberalism). But was nationalist Peru's commercial-political nexus a meaningful class relationship? The distinctive feature of these groups (commercial capitalists and bureaucrats) was that neither held but the most remote or indirect relationship with the social and productive arrangements of the larger society in which they operated. (Lima wholesalers or officials would themselves have felt like foreigners in the precapitalist backlands of Peru.) Nor did they have to form close ties with the broader society: for, historically, both groups have been able to live off and with virtually any kind of social structure. Peru had a most peculiar ruling class in the aftermath of independence.[33] These traders and functionaries were the least likely to imagine an active program to involve the submerged nation in their nationalist call, much less to think about overhauling Peru's colonial (and sometimes precolonial) social relations. They sat too ethereally above them.

Left alone, a commercial-political nexus was "corporatism" enshrined. It was the state. The interlocking, merchant-bureaucrat embrace—financial, political, administrative—could develop in almost any direction, except "hegemonically." Moreover, the strange sociology of this ruling class slowed Peru's march to capitalist reform. At best, they left most of Peru's precapitalist obstacles to growth intact. At worst, the merchants' own privileges, fiscal pressures, and example actually tightened the grip of colonial institutions, practice, and mentalities. For merchants, the embrace with functionaries was ultimately deadly; the state proved too unstable to fulfill even their minimal nationalist program. Once fully convinced of this fact in the early 1840s, their transition to liberalism—a relatively private approach to gain—came swiftly. Once there, however, Peru's elites soon regressed to their reflexive and profitable statism. Intertwined now with the guano-age state, nationalism's liberal progeny would still do little to promote social change. In this abstract sense, dependency theory is right: merchants plus bureaucrats never equaled a proper "bourgeois" class for Peru.[34] Divorced as they were from the country's social reality, perhaps they were not even a "class" at all.

IN SUMMARY, early Peruvian nationalism hardly fits the prescription for the bona fide or progressive nationalist movement found in dependency theory. The defects and failures of this corporatist-nationalism are easy to list: it was ephemeral, governed by external cycles, elitist, blind to the larger problems of integrating a nation, defensive in scope, backward-looking, predicated on a foolhardy statism, and anything but the work of a revolutionary bourgeoisie. Nor does lumping it in with Latin American "conservatism" solve the analytic problem; if comparable, Peru's nationalism drew on specific social roots. Yet, as we have also seen, the criteria for a viable nationalist project in dependency theory are either unrealistic or openly contradictory. It makes sense to focus instead on the unusual strengths and contributions of this movement to form a new nation. Peruvian elites proved unable to create a stable nationalism. In trying, however, they helped define from scratch the objectives and national consciousness needed to construct and preserve their young and imperiled state, a task continued by their liberal heirs. They made history, if not just as they pleased.

A REALM OF IDEAS

Apart from the modern Peruvian state itself, the elites left another profound, but less evident, legacy: an original weltanschauung of forgotten, economic-nationalist ideologies. Whatever the nature of their class project, the thought of the Peruvian elites was a remarkable achievement, perhaps unique in postindependence America. Few could hold their own against the mighty intellectual force of imported dogmas and cultures.

Even the keenest accounts of economic thought in Latin America overlook the postindependence era. Most historians will argue that economic nationalism played no part whatsoever in the initial repertoire of indigenous ideas and political nationalism. The nineteenth century became the age of positivist "self-incrimination." Latin Americans thought they had no one but themselves to blame for economic backwardness. Everything homegrown was second-rate: inferior products, labor, styles, ideas, and race. To remake themselves for modern development, Latin American elites had to import liberal doctrines wholesale (as well as foreign capital and machines) and imitate wholesale, at breakneck speed, all the trappings of North Atlantic culture and economy.[35] Modern dependency stems from these manic imitative efforts. Only in the twentieth century, the story goes, did Latin Americans become confident enough to respect themselves, and to blame others as well.

On the contrary, the first stage of Peruvian nationalism in the 1820s is distinctive precisely for its conscious rejection of imitation and self-reproach. The fashionable, new free-trade doctrines, pushed down their throats by zealous foreign consuls, were widely dismissed as "inappropriate" for Peru. Peru's political freedom had to be joined by economic independence, and Peru had to chart its own course in the world of nations. Early nationalists did not make invidious comparisons with the outside world: they neither disparaged native entrepreneurs (just as savvy as the foreigners with their unfair advantages), belittled native products and styles (superior quality was the frequent boast), nor downgraded the reliable and strong native labor. Within itself, Peru found the elements for progress.

From these basic, self-respectful beliefs sprang other notions, surprisingly modern in tone: the need to promote national accumulation over entangling foreign capital; employment, skill, and technological advance as the prime objects of policy; awareness of unequal benefits of unfettered trade between industrial and preindustrial countries; priority of domestic economic reactivation over foreign transfers; the integration of Peru's national economy through cultivation of industries and trades with far-reaching linkages; the social ill-effects of unchecked markets and greed; the necessity for an alliance of Latin American nations and markets against the power of price-setting foreigners; and, with great passion, a distaste for the rank hypocrisy of advanced, industrial trading nations who did not practice the free trade they preached.

In Peru, economic-nationalist thought was not just around after independence; it was primordial to the conception of nationalism itself. Without protectionism, Peruvian nationality itself would have been unimaginable. The force of these ideas, weighing on the larger events of Peruvian statehood, was a decisive factor in the survival of the Peruvian state. Even to initiate nationalist policies, Peruvian officials ran up against the strongest ideological currents of the day; and, in their countless replies to consuls, these men passionately defended Peru's sovereign right (if not duty) to pursue its independent course.[36] On no occasion, until the late 1840s, did Peruvians cave in to the incessant foreign harangues of "impolicy" and "interest." Even then, they followed their own path with regard to the country's most precious resource, guano. Such strength flowed from the well of self-respect found in their economic nationalism.

In this sense, the persistence of protectionism in Peru was a highly ideological affair. Peruvian elites were slow to accept the incontestable prestige of European theory, and thus continued to interpret their experience in a very different light.[37] Perhaps these ideas, once retrieved from oblivion, will constitute the early economic nationalists' gift to Peruvian posterity. Only when free trade was accepted, imported, and imitated in the 1850s did the age of wholesale self-incrimination begin. And only in recent decades has Latin America again stopped blaming itself.

STATISTICAL APPENDIXES

APPENDIX 1

External Economy

TABLE 1.1. Peruvian Export Quantum Indices, 1830–55
(all products, 1900 = 1,000)

	All Products	All Except Guano and Nitrates	Guano	Nitrates	Silver	Sugar[a]	Wools
1830	100	100	0	1	54	4	—
1831	110	110	0	3	64	4	0
1832	140	140	0	3	91	4	—
1833	140	130	0	6	87	4	—
1834	150	140	0	10	87	4	4
1835	160	150	0	9	99	4	0
1836	180	170	0	10	91	4	13
1837	190	180	0	11	90	4	26
1838	200	190	0	8	94	4	31
1839	220	210	0	10	101	4	30
1840	230	210	0	15	109	4	38
1841	280	250	9	18	122	4	43
1042	260	230	28	23	131	4	21
1843	250	220	3	24	116	4	34
1844	230	170	30	25	103	3	3
1845	260	210	27	24	98	4	36
1846	300	230	41	26	106	6	34
1847	380	240	107	24	104	6	49
1848	390	240	119	31	101	7	51
1849	490	290	168	28	115	4	43
1850	420	180	211	33	78	4	33
1851	560	220	291	45	106	6	38
1852	390	190	162	38	89	4	38
1853	620	210	351	57	93	4	40
1854	800	160	590	47	83	4	30
1855	820	190	571	61	96	3	33

SOURCE: Hunt, "Price and Quantum Exports," table 24.
[a] Until 1844, Chile is excluded.

TABLE 1.2. Peruvian Silver Production and Guano Exports, 1800–55

	Silver		Guano	
	Production (marks)	Value (pesos)	Exports (metric tons)	Value (pesos)
1800	569,111	—	0	—
1810	464,509	—	0	—
1820	476,508	—	0	—
1821	118,781	—	0	—
1822	104,181	—	0	—
1823	35,022	—	0	—
1824	68,467	—	0	—
1825	110,068	—	0	—
1826	232,236	—	0	—
1827	293,573	—	0	—
1828	250,535	—	0	—
1829	156,764	—	0	—
1830	213,687	—	0	—
1831	250,155	—	0	—
1832	342,692	—	0	—
1833	334,033	3,273,523	0	—
1834	336,372	3,330,087	0	—
1835	418,490	4,143,055	0	—
1836	369,586	3,695,862	0	—
1837	356,660	3,530,937	0	—
1838	380,970	3,771,604	0	—
1839	422,840	4,228,404	0	—
1840	464,566	4,465,665	0	—
1841	538,519	5,385,195	8,085	103,000
1842	586,609	5,807,433	23,441	711,500
1843	492,156	4,823,132	2,617	79,500
1844	415,252	4,110,994	27,189	823,500
1845	379,615	3,720,229	24,701	734,000
1846	424,943	4,164,444	36,914	1,120,500
1847	407,460	4,033,854	96,724	2,936,500
1848	397,992	3,940,120	107,356	3,222,500
1849	382,365	3,785,413	151,621	3,830,500
1850	305,415	3,054,150	185,724	4,822,500
1851	416,972	—	262,739	11,138,000
1852	349,199	—	145,968	4,783,500
1853	365,503	—	316,116	6,428,500
1854	326,194	—	533,280	12,724,500
1855	377,856	—	514,957	14,715,500

SOURCES: Hunt, "Price and Quantum Exports," tables 19 and 21; Deustua, *Minería peruana*, tables 2 and 4; Bonilla, "Coyuntura comercial del siglo XIX," tables 5 and 7.
NOTE: Few reliable figures exist for silver exports (the data frequently include circulating coin). Guano export values are estimated from peso conversion of Bonilla's British/ French sales at "constant prices."

TABLE 1.3. Peruvian Import Estimates, 1820–60

Index of British and French Import Values (1840–44 = 100)

	Total	French Share (%)
1830–34	60.9	26.5
1835–39	73.7	10.2
1840–44	100.0	14.0
1845–50	137.7	24.6
1851–54	216.7	37.3
1855–59	276.4	48.5

Imports from Britain

	Value (£1,000s)	Textile Share (%)		Value (£1,000s)	Textile Share (%)
1820	39	—	1840	799	93
1821	86	—	1841	536	91
1822	111	—	1842	684	88
1823	226	—	1843	659	84
1824	373	—	1844	658	52
1825	559	—	1845	878	90
1826	199	—	1846	825	90
1827	228	—	1847	623	88
1828	374	—	1848	853	86
1829	300	—	1849	878	45
1830	368	—	1850	845	82
1831	400	96	1851	1,208	87
1832	275	92	1852	1,204	83
1833	387	88	1853	1,246	84
1834	299	85	1854	949	73
1835	441	91	1855	1,285	79
1836	606	94	1856	1,046	76
1837	472	93	1857	1,171	77
1838	412	91	1858	1,163	77
1839	635	92	1859	857	73

SOURCES: Hunt, "Growth and Guano" (1973), 97; Bonilla, "Expansión comercial británica," tables 1 and 3.

NOTE: French share is proxy for luxuries. £1 = 5 pesos. Reliable aggregate import figures do not exist; approximate values are 4.5 million pesos for 1826, 7.3 million pesos for 1837, 4.9 million pesos for 1847, and 9.4 million pesos for 1852 (BRT 1827; Macera, "Plantaciones azucareras," table 6; Piérola, *Memoria que presenta al Congreso de 1853 el Ministro encargado del Despacho de Hacienda* [Lima, pam., 1853]).

TABLE 1.4. Estimated Composition of Peruvian Trade, 1826 and 1837

Imports		Exports	
1826			
United States (including $200,000 in Asian goods)[a]	$1,250,000	Precious metals (including coin)	$3,000,000
France	800,000	Cotton, wools, hides, bark (cinchona)	500,000
Netherlands, Bremen, etc.	400,000	Debt payments by mine sales, etc.	500,000
Great Britain	1,550,000		
Chile and Guayaquil	525,000	Sugar, tobacco (to Chile)	474,600
TOTAL	$4,525,000		$4,474,600
1837[b]			
United States (includes $270,000 in Asian goods)	$1,370,000	Bullion and specie	$5,752,433
		Bark (cinchona)	291,943
France	650,000	Copper	76,966
Netherlands, Germany, etc.	350,000	Tin	81,780
Italy and Spain	450,000	Nitrates	372,080
Great Britain	4,500,000	Cotton	235,766
		Sugar	52,653
		Hides and skins	59,926
		Wools (vicuña, sheep)	345,000
		Alpaca wool	60,000
TOTAL	$7,320,000[c]		$7,327,548

SOURCES: For 1826, BRT 1827 (FO61/8, Ricketts to Canning, 27 Dec. 1826); for 1837, BRT 1837 (FO61/53, Wilson to Palmerston, 29 Sept. 1838).

NOTE: Until the 1850s, 1 Peruvian peso (8 reales) equaled 1 U.S. dollar, and both used the same $ sign; $5 equaled £1. In 1862, Peru converted to the sol of 10 reales.

[a] Estimates of U.S. trade in 1825 exceed $1.5 million.

[b] Excluded figures for trade with Chile vary widely—from $754,700 in exports and $235,840 in imports to $289,717 in exports and $275,550 in imports (1835/36) (*El Redactor Peruano* [Lima], 25 May 1836).

[c] "North Peru" = $5,145,000; "South Peru" = $2,175,000.

APPENDIX 2

Lima Economy

TABLE 2.1. Sectoral Development of the Lima Economy, 1830–61

| | Total Number | Number of Businesses (Index: 1830 = 100) | | | |
		All Sectors (3,396)[b]	Manufacturing (914)	Commerce[a] (342)	Services (2,140)
1830	3,396	100.0	100.0	100.0	100.0
1833	3,320	97.8	88.6	98.5	100.4
1834	3,266	96.2	96.5	100.3	94.3
1837	2,766	81.7	76.5	97.1	80.6
1838	2,587	76.2	78.4	102.6	70.2
1839	2,814	82.9	75.2	102.1	81.9
1842/43	2,681	78.9	75.7	97.7	76.5
1844	2,730	80.4	75.9	121.3	74.6
1846/47	3,261	96.0	83.3	143.0	92.9
1850	3,048	89.0	84.6	131.3	84.2
1852	2,958	87.1	83.8	134.2	80.1
1857	3,180	93.7	92.1	131.9	86.8
1859	3,410	100.4	95.2	174.9	89.7
1861	3,550	104.5	99.9	184.8	92.5

TABLE 2.1. (cont.)

Real Business Revenues
(Index: 1830 = 100, constant 1830 prices)

	Nominal Gross Revenues (1,000s of pesos)	Price Index	All Sectors (1,246)[b]	Manufacturing (270)	Commerce[a] (316)	Services (660)
1830	1,246	100.0	100.0	100.0	100.0	100.0
1833	1,351	100.4	108.0	98.9	113.5	109.0
1834	1,309	96.7	108.6 [94.7][c]	109.4	167.3 [107.0][c]	80.1
1838	934	103.2	72.6	84.4	88.6	60.1
1839	1,144	102.8	89.3	86.2	118.2	76.8
1842/43	875	82.0	85.5	84.9	117.0	70.7
1844	889	82.2	86.7	83.7	123.2	70.0
1846/47	1,434	81.5	141.1	104.9	248.1	104.7
1850	1,226	82.1	119.7	95.4	229.4	76.7
1852	1,489	85.6	139.5	130.7	261.8	84.6
1857	1,740	108.4	128.8	113.5	267.8	68.4
1859	1,850	104.1	142.6	122.3	303.7	73.9
1861	1,938	121.7	127.7	111.3	264.1	69.1

SOURCE: AGN H-4 and H-1, "Matrículas de Patentes de Lima," in Gootenberg, "Artisans and Merchants," app. I; price index from Gootenberg, "Price Levels in Peru," tables 8, 9.
[a] Includes almaceneros, consignatorios, encomenderos, pulperos, prestamistas, repartadores de plata y de ropa, and tenderos de ropa.
[b] Figures in parentheses are 1830-base-year totals.
[c] Figure in brackets excludes foreign auction houses.

TABLE 2.2. Sectoral Composition of the Lima Economy, 1830–61

	1830	1834	1839	1844	1850	1857	1861
Establishments (%)							
Manufacturing	26.9	27.6	24.4	25.4	25.4	26.5	25.7
Commerce	10.1	10.5	12.4	15.2	14.7	14.2	17.8
Services	63.7	62.5	63.0	59.2	59.8	59.0	56.4
Revenues (%)							
Manufacturing	26.7	21.8	21.0	21.3	17.5	18.1	18.9
Commerce	25.4	39.1[a]	33.5	36.0	48.6	52.7	52.4
Services	53.0	39.1	45.5	42.7	33.9	28.1	28.7
Real Revenue per Firm (constant 1830 pesos)							
All Sectors	367	414	396	397	490	505	448
Manufacturing	296	335	340	328	335	365	330
Commerce	924	1,543	1,069	939	1,616	1,877	1,321
Services	325	259	285	286	278	240	229

SOURCE: AGN H-4 and H-1, "Matrículas de Patentes de Lima," in Gootenberg, "Artisans and Merchants," app. I; 1830 price deflator from Gootenberg, "Price Levels in Peru," tables 8, 9.
[a] If auction houses are excluded, 1834 composition is Manufacturing, 25.0%; Commerce, 30.1%; Services, 44.8%.

TABLE 2.3. Foreigners in the Lima Economy, 1847/48

Total Economy	Number of Businesses (2,328)	% Share by Sector	Revenue in current pesos[a] (1,375,000)	% Share by Sector
Total Foreign	598	21.1	626,000	45.5
Manufacturing	122	17.5	86,000	38.7
Commerce	272	55.6	431,000	67.4
Services	204	12.4	108,000	21.2

Revenue per Firm, Foreign and Native Businesses[a]
(current pesos)

Total Economy	Average (486)	Foreign (1,047)	Peruvian (336)	Foreign as % of Peruvian (312)
Manufacturing	320	707	238	297
Commerce	1,307	1,585	960	165
Services	312	534	281	190
Commerce, Excluding Foreign Consignment Houses	797	654	878	74 (134)[b]
Substantive Middlemen[c]	643	548	814	67 (149)[b]

SOURCE: AGN H-4 2184, "Lima, Matrícula de Patentes," 1846/47, and AGN H-1 342/1339, "Razón de los extranjeros que pagan patentes de industria," 1848, in Gootenberg, "Artisans and Merchants," tables 8, 12, 13 and app. v.

[a] In current and unadjusted taxed revenues.
[b] Figure in parentheses is Peruvian as percentage of foreign revenue.
[c] Includes all commercial groups (see Table 2.1, n. a) except consignatorios, almaceneros, and encomenderos.

APPENDIX 3

Emergency Public Finance

TABLE 3.1. "Abonos" on Customs, 1827–30 and 1838–45

	Bonds Released	% Paid in Cash	Monthly Average	% Share of Callao Customs	% Share by Foreigners
1827–30					
Aug. 1827–					
Mar. 1828	$615,521	58.3	$76,940	55.0	58.8
Apr. 1828–					
Sept. 1828	353,129	60.9	58,854	42.0	49.6
July 1828–					
Jan. 1830	1,135,019	66.4	63,056	45.0	59.0
TOTAL	$2,103,669	59.2	$70,120	50.0	57.4
1838–45					
Sept. 1838–					
Jan. 1840	$200,000 (approx.)	—	$12,500	9.1	0
Jan. 1841	74,600	—	74,600	71.5	50.0
July 1841–					
Oct. 1844	1,089,352	55.7	27,234	23.7	62.6
July 1841–					
Apr. 1842	269,262	—	29,918	28.6	40.0
Apr. 1842–					
Nov. 1842	67,691	—	11,281	9.8	100.0
Oct. 1842–					
Mar. 1843	494,072	63.5	82,345	85.0	88.0
July 1844–					
Aug. 1844	222,000	48.6	111,000	83.9	77.9
Feb. 1845	120,000	52.5	120,000	102.6	95.0
TOTAL	$1,483,952	55.3	$19,272	17.9	56.1

SOURCE: *La Prensa Peruana* (Lima), 12 Apr., 30 Oct. 1828; AGN H-1 175/770, Jan. 1829; AGN H-4 1638, Jan. 1830; *El Comercio* (Lima), 25 Jan. 1841, 1 Dec. 1844; *El Peruano* (Lima), 25 Mar. 1843; AGN H-1 285/287, Jan. 1841; AGN H-1 295/597–598, 18 Aug., 2 Nov. 1842; AGN H-1 326/708, 27 Apr. 1846. Customs data are from *Comercio*, 17 Jan. 1852.

TABLE 3.2. Merchant "Loans to the Lima State, 1821–45

Period/ Regime	Date	National Merchants	Foreign Merchants	
		Lower to Upper Estimate[a]	Single Estimate	Known Guarantee
1821–23	Aug./Sept. 1821	$133,776–150,000	–	–
Various	Sept. 1822	150,000–240,000	$73,400	–
	Mar. 1823	40,947–100,000	7,000	–
	Aug. 1823	72,976–150,000	–	–
	Oct. 1823	135,000	65,000	–
SUBTOTAL		$532,699–775,000	$145,400	–
1824–27	—	—	—	—
1828–29	June 1828	$71,500	–	abonos
	Oct. 1828	11,432	$87,898	–
Gamarra/La Fuente	Dec. 1828	5,405 (monthly)	–	–
	Jan.–Sept. 1829	3,000 (monthly)	85,000	mint
	July 1829	–	60,000	abonos
SUBTOTAL		$90,905 +	$232,898	–
1830–33	—	—	—	—
1834	Mar.	–	$37,500	–
	Feb./Mar.	$79,763	–	–
Orbegoso	May	3,700	–	–
	June/July	75,000–100,000	–	–
SUBTOTAL		$158,463–183,463	$37,500	–
		($184,482)[b]		

TABLE 3.2. (cont.)

Period/Regime	Date	National Merchants Lower to Upper Estimate[a]	Foreign Merchants Single Estimate	Known Guarantee
1835	Jan.	$20,200	—	—
	Mar./Apr.	97,619	—	—
Salaverry "	Aug./Sept.	76,500	$28,500	abonos
SUBTOTAL		$194,519	$28,500	
		($153,346–242,156)[b]		
1836–38	Jan. 1836	$100,000	—	—
	May 1836	71,385–100,000	—	—
Santa Cruz	Nov. 1836	200,000	—	—
	June 1837	14,688–107,600	$102,000	—
	Mar. 1838	—	12,500	—
	May 1838	150,000	—	—
SUBTOTAL		$436,073–657,600	$114,500	
1838–41	Sept. 1838	$11,600–50,000	—	—
	Dec. 1838	100,000	—	—
Gamarra	Mar.–June 1839	93,700–188,162	—	—
	Sept. 1839	88,614–100,000	—	—
	Mar./Apr. 1840	13,000–14,508	—	—
		($260,631)[c]		
	Jan. 1841	135,000–149,450	$37,000	abonos
	Mar. 1841	60,000	—	—
	Aug. 1841	40,000	—	—
SUBTOTAL:		$455,631–702,120	$37,000	

1842–45		National Finance	Foreign Finance	Total Finance
Various	Dec. 1841	$75,000	—	—
	Feb. 1842	25,000	—	—
	Dec. 1842	14,900	—	—
	Apr. 1843	43,600	$42,200	abonos
	July 1843	39,734	28,500	abonos
	Aug. 1843	45,734	—	—
	Sept. 1843	—	20,000	abonos
	Oct. 1843	70,000	—	—
	Dec. 1843	60,000	—	[c]
	July/Aug. 1843	35,750	70,250	abonos
	Oct. 1844	22,540–62,000	—	—
	Jan. 1845	20,000	—	—
	Feb. 1845	—	80,000	abonos
SUBTOTAL		$452,808–492,286	$240,950	

Summary

		National Finance	Foreign Finance	Total Finance
All 1821–45	Minimum:	$2,282,000	$837,000	$3,119,000
	Maximum:	$3,152,000	—	$3,989,000
	Mean:	$2,717,000	—	$3,554,000
Subperiods				
Postindependence wars (1828–45)	Minimum:	$1,749,000	$691,000	$2,441,000
	Maximum:	$2,337,000	—	$3,069,000
	Mean:	$2,063,000	—	$2,755,000
Post–Ramo de Arbitrios (1834–45)	Minimum:	$1,658,000	$458,000	$2,117,000
	Maximum:	$2,286,000	—	$2,745,000
	Mean:	$1,972,000	—	$2,431,000

SOURCES: These estimates were calculated from more than seventy archival (mainly AGN) sources. For a complete listing and methodology, see Gootenberg, "Merchants, Foreigners, and the State," app.

[a] The lower bound is from actual treasury receipts, and the upper bound reflects realistic loan quotas; all foreign-loan figures appear to be precise.

[b] Reliable archival estimates for these subperiods.

[c] Reliable archival estimate for this subperiod, Sept. 1838–May 1840.

TABLE 3.3. Recognized Debts of the Ramo de Arbitrios, 1834–53

Date	Principal	Date	Principal
Mar. 1834	$134,946	May 1840	$680,197
Dec. 1834	211,920	Jan. 1841	632,699
Nov. 1835	397,253	June 1841	679,859
July 1836	482,996	Nov. 1841	701,528
Dec. 1836	337,051	Mar. 1842	727,745
Dec. 1837	445,023	Mar. 1843	789,104
May 1838	609,528	July 1844	974,778
Dec. 1838	506,007	June 1846[a]	974,193
July 1839	572,316	July 1847[a]	912,797
Nov. 1839	666,519	July 1851[a]	1,338,045
		Jan. 1853[a]	990,050

SOURCES: *El Conciliador* (Lima), Mar. 1834; *El Redactor* (Lima), Dec. 1834; *El Eco del Protectorado* (Lima), Dec. 1836; *El Peruano* (Lima), Dec. 1838, July, Nov. 1839, May 1840, Jan., June, Nov. 1841, Mar. 1842, Mar. 1843, July 1844, June 1846; AGN H-1 241/717, Nov. 1835; AGN H-1 248/495, July 1836; AGN H-1 264/714, May 1838; AGN H-1 367/546, July 1851; M. del Río, *Memoria que presenta el Ministro de Hacienda del Perú al Congreso de 1847* (Lima, pam., 1847); Quiroz, "La consolidación," table 15.

[a] During amortization.

TABLE 3.4. Guano Advances and Loans, 1840–55

Gibbs		Other Reported Advances		
Date	Amount	Date	Firm	Amount
		Nov. 1840	Quirós	$40,000[a]
		Dec. 1841	Quirós-Allier	287,000[a]
Feb. 1842	$487,000 (with Poumarroux, Quirós-Allier)			
		Oct. 1845	Gibbs	200,000
Feb. 1846	300,000			
		Feb. 1847	Canevaro	72,000
		Mar. 1847	Cotesworth, Powell, Prior, Schneider	100,000 (orig. 500,000)
		June 1847	Blanco	57,516
July 1847	700,000			
		Oct. 1847	Gibbs-Montané	850,000
Dec. 1847	700,000	Dec. 1847	Gibbs-Montané	850,000[a]

TABLE 3.4. (*cont.*)

			1848	Gibbs-Montané	24,000
1849	360,000	Aug.	1849	Gibbs-Montané	400,000[a]
	472,000		1849	Lequerica	30,000
1850	800,000		1850	Soutter?	384,000
			1850	Alsop	800,000
May 1850	384,000	Oct.	1850	Barreda, Rodrigo,	
Aug. 1850	95,000			Alsop, Soutter,	
Oct. 1850	34,000			Zaracondegui	200,000
Dec. 1850	93,000				
Jan. 1851	60,000				
Feb. 1851	30,000				
Apr. 1851	80,000				
		Oct.	1851	Gibbs-Montané	80,000
		Mar.	1852	Murrieta	50,000
		Nov.	1852	Kendall	50,000
		Jan.	1853	Sevilla	100,000
Mar. 1853	1,460,000[b]				
1853	2,000,000[c]				
1854	500,000				
	200,000[b]				
1855	500,000				

SOURCES: For Gibbs, Mathew, "Gibbs and the Peruvian Government," 351–353. For the others, Basadre, *Historia* II:798–806; Tantaleán, *Política económico-financiera*, table 9; Dancuart, *Anales*, vols. III–V.

NOTE: This is not an exhaustive list. The figures for Gibbs are reliable; those for the others are less so, having been drawn from fragmentary, overlapping secondary accounts.

[a] Loans probably not implemented.

[b] In monthly advances.

[c] "Secret loan."

NOTES

ABBREVIATIONS

AGN   Archivo General de la Nación (Lima)

AGN H-1   AGN, Section H-1, Archivo Histórico de Hacienda, Comunicaciones (cartas/oficios)

AGN H-4   AGN, Section H-4, Libros Manuscritos Republicanos de la Sección Hacienda

AGN H-8   AGN, Section H-8, Tribunal del Consulado (Republicano)

AML   Archivo Municipal de Lima

AML PS   AML, Papeles Sueltos

ARE   Archivo General del Ministerio de Relaciones Exteriores del Perú

BN MS   Biblioteca Nacional del Perú, Colección de Manuscritos

BRT   British reports on the trade of Peru

CCC   French commercial and consular correspondence from Peru

FO61   British Foreign Office, correspondence with Peru

M154   Dispatches from U.S. consuls in Lima

pam.   Pamphlet

T52   Dispatches from U.S. ministers to Peru

For more information on archives, see Bibliography.

PREFACE

1. Gootenberg, "Artisans and Merchants" and "Merchants, Foreigners, and the State." To conserve space, reference will be made to these works in the notes, particularly to their statistical material.
2. Economic policy issues have not stimulated as much fruitful research and debate as did, for example, the dependency school's initial characterization of Latin American rural relations; see Duncan and Rutledge, *Land and Labour in Latin America*. For analogous advances around commercial history, see Abel and Lewis, *Latin America, Economic Imperialism, and the State*, or Love and Jacobsen, *Guiding the Invisible Hand*.
3. This imagery is not entirely new: "It is interesting that in the story of the republic such coarse and humble substances as guano and nitrates should have taken over the role that had been reserved to gold and silver in a more romantic and less positivist era" (Mariátegui, *Seven Essays*, 10).

CHAPTER 1

1. "Lo que se dice," *El Telégrafo de Lima* (Lima), 24 Aug. 1834; "Movimiento mercantil," *Telégrafo*, 25–26 Aug. 1834; J. T. Roldan, "Representación hecha

al Tribunal del Consulado por el apoderado del gremio," *El Genio del Rimac* (Lima), 26 Aug. 1834; *Genio*, 25–28 Aug. 1834.

2. "Movimiento mercantil," *Telégrafo*, 25 Aug. 1834; "A los anti-martilleros," *Telégrafo*, 26 Aug. 1834. For early 1834, "Un ruego al señor Ministro de Hacienda," *Telégrafo*, 29 Mar. 1834; "Comercio," *El Limeño* (Lima), 27 Mar.–3 Apr. 1834; *El Conciliador* (Lima), 14 Mar. 1834. For a sample of the enormous pamphlet and polemical literature on auctions, see "¡El Comercio!" *Los Clamores del Perú* (Lima), 17 Mar. 1827; [M. Pérez de Tudela], *Martillos o utilidad pública de estos establecimientos* (Lima, pam., 1832); "Un comerciante de la sierra," *Telégrafo*, all Sept. 1828. For a summary of the entire martillo struggle (1821–50), consult Gootenberg, "Merchants, Foreigners, and the State," 93–101.

3. "Ministerio de Hacienda," *Conciliador*, 11, 14, 22 Mar. 1834; *El Redactor Peruano* (Lima), 5, 30, Apr., 17 May, 26 July 1834 (some of these decrees and reports from official gazettes are reproduced in Quirós, *Colección*, vols. I–VI. FO61/27, Wilson to Palmerston, 20 May 1834; AGN H-4 1707, Consulado, Actas, "Indagaciones del Consulado de Lima sobre un tratado con Chile," 10 May 1834; "Clamor de los hacendados, *Telégrafo*, 4 June 1834; *Genio*, 17 June 1834. *Note*: Until the 1850s, 1 Peruvian peso (8 reales) equaled 1 U.S. dollar, and both used the same $ sign; $5 equaled £1. In 1862, Peru converted to the sol of 10 reales.

4. "Informe que dio el Tribunal del Consulado," *Genio*, 10–16 July 1834 (published as *Razones poderosas que da el Comercio de esta Capital por las cuales no deben permitirse los establecimientos de martillo* [Lima, pam., 1834]; *Telégrafo*, 9 July 1834; *Genio*, Aug. 1834.

5. Orbegoso, "Mensaje del Presidente a la Convención Nacional," *El Redactor* (Lima), 13 Aug. 1834 (or *Genio*, 16 Aug. 1834).

6. *Redactor*, 16 Aug. 1834; *Genio*, 22, 25 Aug. 1834; AGN H-1 233/587, Consulado, 13 Aug. 1834; AGN H-4 1707, Consulado, Actas, 18 July 1834; T52/2, Larned to Lane, 20 Aug. 1834 (selected print versions of U.S. reports are in Manning, *Diplomatic Correspondence*, vols. III and X).

7. *Genio*, 22, 25 Aug. 1834; *Telégrafo*, 23 Aug., 30 Sept. 1834.

8. "Informe del Consejo de Estado . . . sobre la representación que ha hecha el comercio de esta capital solicitando la abolición de las casas de martillo," *Genio*, 10 Sept. 1834; *Telégrafo*, 6–12 Sept. 1834; "Análisis de informe del Consejo sobre martillos," *Genio*, 14–15 Sept. 1834; "Martillos," *Telégrafo*, 11–13, 17 Oct. 1834; *Redactor*, 27 Sept., 22 Nov. 1834.

9. "Los mercachifles," *Telégrafo*, 15 Oct. 1834; M. Rivera, "A los monopolistas de la Calle de Bodegones," 10 Oct. 1834; *Telégrafo*, 10 Sept.–Oct. 1834 (Rivera's own pamphlets are too prolific to cite). See also poetry: "Martillos," *Genio*, 4 Oct. 1834, and esp. 7, 16 Oct. 1834; AGN H-1 233/577–583, Consulado, 11 Oct.–15 Nov. 1834.

10. Basadre, *Historia* I:359–363; even our best histories miss the consulado role in these political events.

11. "Patriotismo," *Telégrafo*, 30 Jan. 1835; Roldan, *Telégrafo*, 4 Feb. 1835. For an overview of Salaverry promerchant reaction, see *La Gaceta del Gobierno* (Lima), all Feb.–Mar. 1835; or see T52/3, Larned to Forsyth, Jan.–Aug. 1835.

12. Thorp and Bertram, *Peru*; Cotler, *Clases, estado y nación*; Bonilla, *Guano y burguesía*; Levin, *Export Economies*, ch. 2; Gilbert, *Oligarquía peruana*.

13. The dominant theme of Thorp and Bertram, *Peru*.

14. Many (contrasting) tariff periodizations exist for nineteenth-century Peru; for

my analysis, see "Merchants, Foreigners, and the State," 44–52, with stress on nontariff trade barriers and policy instability. See also Boloña, "Tariff Policies in Peru," ch. 2; Rodríguez, *Estudios económicos*, 361–403, 456–466; Dancuart, *Anales*, vols. I–VI; and Hunt, "Growth and Guano in Nineteenth-Century Peru," table 16, in Cortés Conde and Hunt, *Latin American Economies, 1880–1930* (I will cite the original and extended 1973 Princeton version of Hunt's critical essay as "Growth and Guano").

15. Cortés Conde and Stein, *Guide to Economic History*, 12, 567–569; Halperín-Donghi, *Historia contemporánea*, chs. 3–5; Lynch, *Spanish-American Revolutions*. An update of issues is provided by Abel and Lewis, *Latin America, Economic Imperialism, and the State*, 95–100, and the essays therein by Thompson (Mexico), MacFarlane (Colombia), and Ortega (Chile); or see the older sweep in C. Griffin, "Economic and Social Aspects of Independence." For general debates, see Platt, "Dependency: An Historian Objects" (with the Steins' reply, 131–148).

16. For example, see Bonilla, "Perú entre Independencia y Guerra"; Bonilla, "Peru and Bolivia from Independence"; Tantaleán, *Política económico-financiera*; Yepes, *Desarrollo capitalista*; Flores, "Militarismo y dominación británica"; Macera, "Algodón y comercio exterior"; Piel, "Place of the Peasantry in Peru"; or, from different angles, Bollinger, "Bourgeois Revolution," and Pike, *U.S. and the Andean Republics*, 50–72.

17. Assumptions codified in Véliz, "Mesa de tres patas"; Véliz's later *Centralist Tradition*, ch. 6, relates a more complex view of elite trade proclivities. For criticism in precisely this generalized Chilean case, see Palma, "Growth of Chilean Industry," chs. 1–2.

18. See Potash, *Mexican Government and Industrial Development*; Burgin, *Economic Aspects of Argentine Federalism*; Ospina Vásquez, *Industria y protección en Colombia*, chs. 1–4. For colonial holdovers in general, see Stein and Stein, *Colonial Heritage*, chs. 5–6; Lynch, *Spanish-American Revolutions*, chs. 8, 10. On Peru, see Anna, *Fall of Royal Government*; Bonilla and Spalding, "Independencia en el Perú."

19. The two striking dependency revisions were Frank, *Capitalism and Underdevelopment*, 51–85, 162–166, and *Lumpenbourgeoisie*, ch. 4 ("Civil War: Nationalism versus Free Trade"). Burns, *Poverty of Progress*, completes the reversal. Critique by Mallon, "Economic Liberalism," 178–179; dependency death in Platt, "Dependency: An Historian Objects"; and living on in such textbooks as Skidmore and Smith, *Modern Latin America*, 39–45, and Keen and Wasserman, *History of Latin America*, chs. 9–10.

20. Attempts to treat dependency theory as a counterfactual problem appear in Burns, *Poverty of Progress*; Albert, *South America and World Economy*, chs. 1, 7; and Zeitlin, *Civil Wars in Chile*; or, as an economic test, in Thorp and Bertram, *Peru*. Nineteenth-century lag is shown in Coatsworth, "Obstacles to Growth"; Hunt, "Growth and Guano" (1973); and McGreevy, "Recent Research."

21. Elsewhere, other questions overshadowed commercial policy: e.g., church-state relations in Mexico or federalism in Argentina. For doubts regarding trade policy as the divisive issue imputed in dependency views, see Safford, "Post-Independence Spanish America." For Peru, specific conditions help explain the predominance of trade conflict: viz., the location in one city, Lima, of the country's capital, main port, and manufacturing groups.

22. Bonilla, "Continuidad y cambio en el Estado independiente," 481–498, and

"Perú entre Independencia y Guerra"; Cotler, *Clases, estado y nación*, ch. 2; Pike, *Modern History*, chs. 3–4 ("good" vs. "bad" caudillos). See analysis of caudillo politics in V. Villanueva, *Ejército peruano*, chs. 1–2.

23. For surveys of political developments, see Basadre's (interpretive) *La multitud y el campo*, or Cleven's (descriptive) "Dictators."

24. A thorough description of 1820s shifts is Ricketts, "Report on the Commerce of Peru" (BRT 1827), printed in Humphreys, *British Consular Reports*, 107–207. Also see Bonilla, "Expansión comercial británica." For price pressures, Gootenberg, "Merchants, Foreigners, and the State," 53–58.

25. See Appendix Tables 1.3 and 1.4, above. Key sources include BRT 1827, BRT 1834, BRT 1837, BRT 1840; Hunt, "Growth and Guano" (1973), 97–100; Bonilla, "Coyuntura comercial del siglo xix."

26. See Appendix Tables 1.1 and 1.2, above; BRT 1840; Hunt, "Price and Quantum Exports," table 24; Deustua, *Minería peruana*, chs. 1–2.

27. For broad economic models, see Boloña, "Tariff Policies in Peru," ch. 2; Hunt, "Growth and Guano" (1973), 105–106. Hirschman, "Against Parsimony," suggests the uses of nonreductionist reasoning for economists; Kindleberger, "Rise of Free Trade in Europe," suggests that, for historical trade-policy analysis, such complexity is inevitable. The political and institutional approach used here owes much to P. Anderson, *Lineages of the Absolutist State*.

28. Basadre's *La multitud y el campo* remains our classic analysis of Liberals and Conservatives; Gleason, "Ideological Cleavages in Republican Peru," covers most issues (except trade); Gootenberg, "Beleaguered Liberals," attempts to place trade conflict in the wider context of nineteenth-century liberalism.

29. For empiricist "internalists" and dependency "externalists," see Platt, "Dependency: An Historian Objects"; Staniland, *What Is Political Economy?* ch. 5; Albert, *South America and World Economy*, ch. 1; and Cardoso, "Consumption of Dependency Theory." This methodological dualism is the major theme of Gootenberg, "Merchants, Foreigners, and the State," 11–21.

30. Oszlak, "Historical Formation of the State in Latin America"; Schmitter et al., "Historical Perspectives on State, Civil Society, Economy"; Arnaud, *Estado y capitalismo en América Latina*. Renewed general interest in "state formation" reflects European studies: see Tilly, *Formation of National States*; Breuilly, *Nationalism and the State*; or Evans et al., "Toward Adequate Understanding of the State."

31. Efforts to analyze Peruvian state-building include Tantaleán, *Política económico-financiera*; Friedman, *The State and Underdevelopment*, chs. 5–7; Berg and Weaver, "Reinterpretation of Political Change"; and Gorman, "State, Elite, and Export."

32. See Collier, *New Authoritarianism in Latin America*. One long-range, regional perspective is Véliz, *Centralist Tradition*; Moore's global view in *Social Origins of Dictatorship* is applied to Latin America by Coatsworth, "Orígenes del autoritarianismo." See Palmer, *Peru: The Authoritarian Tradition*, for a "political culture" approach.

CHAPTER 2

1. Bonilla, *Bretaña y el Perú*, vol. v: *Un control económico*, 76–77, and "Perú entre Independencia y Guerra," 418–422; Flores, "Militarismo y dominación británica"; Macera, "Algodón y comercio exterior," 287–288; Yepes, *Desa-*

rrollo capitalista, 43–44—views informed by Gallagher and Robinson's famous "Imperialism of Free Trade." Obverse views are Mathew, "Imperialism of Free Trade: Peru"; Platt, "Imperialism of Free Trade: Reservations"; or, more generally, Platt, *Latin America and British Trade*, pt. I.

2. FO61/8, Ricketts to Canning, "Report on the Commerce of Peru," 17 Dec. 1826 (BRT 1827). The following section condenses British and U.S. consular evidence found in ch. 4 of my "Merchants, Foreigners, and the State," as well as newer evidence from French reports.

3. FO61/vols. 1–187, 1823–60. See esp. BRT 1827; FO61/11, Ricketts to Canning, all 1827; and FO61/37–53, Wilson to Palmerston, 1836–38, for major interventionist campaigns. Summaries in FO61/53, 29 Sept. 1838 (BRT 1837), and FO61/82, 15 Apr. 1841 (BRT 1840).

4. FO61/11, Ricketts to Canning, 11 May 1827, "A Few Remarks Connected with the Commerce of Peru . . ."; FO61/12, 20 Dec. 1827; FO61/vols. 13–21 (various), 1827–32; FO61/62, Wilson to Palmerston, 4 Sept. 1839, "Report upon the Trade of Peru for 1838" (BRT 1838); BRT 1840; defensive posture after 1839 documented throughout FO61/vols. 58–100 (various), 1839–43.

5. Full treatment of this episode in Gootenberg, "Fabricks and Flours, Hearts and Minds" (based on M154/vols. 1–6, U.S. Consuls, 1823–54, and T52/vols. 1–6, U.S. Ministers, 1826–61).

6. See esp. T52/1–3, Larned to Van Buren and Forsyth, 1829–35; BRT 1827; or X.Y.Z., *Reflexiones sobre la ley de prohibiciones reimpresas y aumentadas con notas* (Lima, pam., 1831). Most works overlook initial U.S. roles in Peru (e.g., Bonilla, "Emergencia del control norteamericano"); exceptions are Bollinger, "Evolution of Dependence," and Clayton, "Private Matters."

7. For interests and strategy, see esp. T52/1, Larned to Van Buren, 5, 8 Mar. 1830, and "Conference on the Subject of Prohibitory Duties," 20 Apr. 1830. Also see M154/1, Tudor to Pando, 2 Nov. 1826; Tudor to Clay, 15 Jan. 1827; ARE 6-3, Diplomático, E.U., 13 Oct. 1830; Anon., *Observaciones sobre el proyecto de Reglamento de Comercio presentado al Congreso por la Comisión de Hacienda* (Lima, pam., 1828), 6–18; and [S. Távara], *Análisis y amplificación del manifiesto presentado al Congreso del Perú por el honorable Señor Ministro Don J. M. Pando* (Lima, pam., 1831), 1:42–53.

   For overall campaigns, see T52/1–4, Larned to Van Buren, Livingston, Lane, and Forsyth, all 1829–36. Also see T52/1, Larned to Van Buren, 5 Mar. 1830 (instructions); for secret propaganda efforts, M154/2, Tudor to Clay, 1 Mar. 1828; M154/2, Prevost, 26 Apr., 17 May, 6 June 1828 (with large set of samples); and T52/1, Larned to Van Buren, 25 Oct. 1830, 4 July, 1 Aug., 5 Sept. 1831.

8. Based on CCC/vols. 1–12 (Correspondance Consulaire et Commerciales, Lima), 1821–62, and Correspondance Politique (Pérou), vols. 1–16, 1798–1847. See esp. CCC/1, Chaumette, 8 June 1827, and Barrère, 14 Oct. 1829, 29 July 1830, 26 Aug. 1831; CCC/2, 17 Dec. 1832, 3 Jan. 1833; CCC/3, 18 July 1833. Also see ARE 6–14, Legación de Francia, 1829–44. For typical anti-French reactions, FO61/33, Wilson to Palmerston, 7 Aug. 1835, or BRT 1837.

9. British awareness of merchant role in FO61/8, FO61/11, Ricketts to Canning, 15 Sept. 1826 and 11 May 1827, or BRT 1837. Also see CCC/2, Barrère, "Tableau general du commerce," 6 June 1833. Chapter 3, below, explores the merchant paradox.

10. For example: T52/5, Pickett to Forsyth, 4 Dec. 1840; T52/6, 31 May 1842;

FO61/26, Wilson to Palmerston, 5 Feb., 27 Apr., 5 May 1834. For this reason, consuls throughout the period insisted on merchants' strict "neutrality"; see "Notice: Legation of the U.S. in Lima," *El Comercio* (Lima), 16 Apr. 1842, and *El Peruano* (Lima), 25, 29 Oct., 6 Dec. 1845.

11. T52/3, Larned to Forsyth, 12 Jan. 1835; M154/5, Bartlett to Forsyth, 11 Jan. 1839; FO61/13, Ricketts to Canning, 9 Aug. 1827; CCC/1, Barrère, 14 Oct. 1829; S. Távara, *Informe sobre contrabando* (Lima, pam., 1832); "Medidas para evitar el contrabando," *Comercio*, 7 July 1845.

12. Bonilla et al., "Comercio libre y crisis andina," 9–11, or Tantaleán, *Política económico-financiera*, 61, 223–224, for other views. See Gootenberg, "Merchants, Foreigners, and the State," 289–308, for loan issues; good illustrations in FO61/35, Humphreys to Palmerston, 16 Apr. 1835; FO61/47, H. Wilson to Palmerston, 17 July 1837; CCC/3, Barrère, 10 Apr. 1835; and "Respuesta del Cuerpo Diplomático relativo a la lei sobre empréstitos estrangeros," *Peruano*, 6 Dec. 1845. (*Note*: Archaic spellings have been followed where appropriate.)

13. FO61/1, Rowcroft to Canning, 9 Aug. 1823, and "Memorial from British Merchants in Lima," 17 Mar. 1823; AGN H-1 185/1207, Prefecturas, Dec. 1828–Jan. 1829; AGN H-1 241/622–640, Consulado, Apr. 1835; speech by Dep. Alegre, *Comercio* 8 Aug. 1845; "El art. 61 del Reglamento de Comercio," *Comercio*, 26 Apr. 1842.

14. "Informe del Consulado," *Comercio*, 10–30 Jan. 1840; "Los zeladores del Congreso, *El Telégrafo de Lima* (Lima), 21 Mar. 1828. Pressures most evident in Peru's "forced naturalization" campaigns: *Peruano*, Aug., Sept. 1840; FO61/70, Wilson to Palmerston, 27 Sept., 4 Oct. 1840; CCC/5, Le Moyne, Apr.–July 1842.

15. FO61/8, Ricketts to Canning, 15 Sept. 1826; FO61/11, "Secret," 6 Feb. and 11 May 1827; FO61/17, Willimott to Palmerston, June–July 1830; FO61/51–60, Wilson to Palmerston, all 1838–40. Also BRT 1839, BRT 1840, BRT 1841.

16. See statistics in Nolan, "Diplomatic and Commercial Relations," 103–105; Bollinger, "Evolution of Dependence," 1–22. Also see T52/4, Larned to Forsyth, 1836–37; FO61/63, Wilson to Palmerston, 7 Aug. 1835.

17. For France, CCC/4, Barrère, Aug. 1835; CCC/5, Saillard, 16 July 1839; CCC/7, Le Moyne, 15 May 1843; CCC/8, "Rapport por l'Etat y la Condition des Etrangèrs au Pérou," 1 Nov. 1846. Also see BRT 1837; FO61/88, Sealy to Canning, 26 Mar. 1842; and *Comercio*, 13 May 1842.

18. Bonilla, "Perú entre Independencia y Guerra," 418–422; Flores, "Militarismo y dominación británica," 119–120; Tantaleán, *Política económico-financiera*; 223–224 (weak-state arguments). Recognition as obstacle: FO61/12, Ricketts to Canning, 20 Dec. 1827; FO61/45, "Petition of British Merchants in Lima," 28 June 1837; FO61/108, Adams to Palmerston, 8 Feb. 1845; CCC/3, Barrère, 21 May 1834; T52/1, Larned to Van Buren, 1 Aug. 1831.

19. Examples seem endless: T52/1, Larned to Van Buren, 8 Mar. 1830, 4 July 1831; BRT 1837; FO61/58, Wilson to Palmerston, 27 Mar., 2 Apr. 1839; *El Tribunal del Pueblo* (Lima), Sept.–Dec. 1839; *El Rebeñique* (Lima), Aug.–Oct. 1841.

20. Robinson, "Non-European Foundations of Imperialism," 117–143; applied to Peru in Bonilla, *Guano y burguesía*, 44–45, 63–64.

21. As examples, the repeated "betrayal" of British and U.S. aims by collaborators Pando, Llosa, and Santa Cruz: FO61/11, Ricketts to Canning, 11 May 1827; T52/1, Larned to Van Buren, 12, 16 Apr. 1830, 10 Sept. 1832; M154/1,

Tudor to Clay, 2 Nov., 24 Dec. 1826, 6 Jan., 3 Feb., 23 Mar. 1827; M154/2, Prevost and Radcliff, 7 Nov. 1827, 6 Feb., 17 May, 30 Aug. 1828.

22. Louis, *Robinson and Gallagher Controversy*; T. Smith, *Imperialism*, chs. 1–2. Views here seem most compatible with the analysis of intrastate relations in Doyle, *Empires*, pt. II, esp. 222–226 ("Dependency in Latin America").

23. Graham, *Independence in Latin America*, chs. 2–3; Jaramillo, *Bolívar y Canning*, 228–235; Temperley, *Foreign Policy of Canning*, app. IV ("Bolívar's Overtures to Canning, 1825–26"), 555–561.

24. Anna, *Fall of Royal Government*, chs. 6–8; and esp. Melzer, "Kingdom to Republic in Peru," chs. 5–8, focusing on the consulado.

25. FO61/8, Ricketts to Canning, 15 Sept. 1826; FO61/11, "Secret," 6 Feb. 1827 (also 3 Mar., 11, 16 May 1827); *Los Clamores del Perú* (Lima), 5–12 Mar. 1827; F. L., *Manifiesto que se presenta a la Nación sobre reformar la aduana y comercio por el ciudadano F.L.* (Lima, pam., 1827); AGN H-4 1584, Consulado, "Copias de oficios y informes" (Actas), 18 Mar., Nov. 1825, June–July 1826; AGN H-8-1 (Tribunal del Consulado Republicano), 30 Mar., 1 Sept. 1825.

26. See debates in *El Mercurio Peruano* (Lima), Aug. 1827, 5–25 June 1828; "Comercio" and "Nuestra Patria y el bien de nuestra Patria," *Telégrafo*, Feb.–Mar., June 1828; "Comercio y fábricas," *Telégrafo*, May 1828; *Observaciones sobre el proyecto de Reglamento de Comercio (1828)*; [Távara], *Análisis y amplificación*; X.Y.Z., *Reflexiones sobre la ley de prohibiciones* (Lima, pam., 1829).

27. Popular memory lasted: "Reglamento de Comercio: los artesanos," *Comercio*, 1 Aug. 1850. See FO61/11, Ricketts to Canning, 11 May 1827, for British revulsion at this marriage of "mob" republicanism and protectionism.

28. Gootenberg, "North-South," explores links among regionalism, trade policy, and caudillos; see Chapter 4, below. For a liberal example (Vivanco), see *Peruano* decrees, 6 Feb., 24 Mar., 5 May 1841 and 10 May, 22 Apr., 3 July 1843. For protectionist chiefs, see Tristán, *Peregrinaciones de una paria*, 350–351 (novelistic account of "party of Gamarra" caudillos), or ubiquitous foreign perceptions (e.g., T51/1, Larned to Van Buren, 8 Mar. 1830; FO61/24, Wilson to Palmerston, 18 Dec. 1833).

29. Liss, *Atlantic Empires*; Baltes, "Pando: colaborador de Gamarra"; Palacios, *Deuda anglo-peruana*, ch. 1; Pike, *Modern History*, 42. Also FO61/91, Foreign and Domestic, Palmerston, 17 June 1842; CCC/4, Barrère, 1 June 1836.

30. "Exposición del proyecto de Reglamento de Comercio," *El Conciliador* (Lima), Nov.–Dec. 1832; "Economía Política," *Conciliador*, May–Oct. 1831, esp. 8 Oct. 1831; M. Vidaurre, *Discurso sobre la acta de navegación pronunciada por el Diputado Manuel Vidaurre* (Boston, pam., 1828), reprint in *Conciliador*, 18 Feb. 1832; J. M. Pando, *Memoria sobre el estado de la Hacienda de la República Peruana en fin de 1830 presentado al Congreso por José María Pando* (Lima, pam., 1831); [Távara], *Análisis y amplificación*; Anon., *Apuntes relativos a la operación práctica del Tratado de Comercio llamado de Salaverry concluido entre las Repúblicas de Chile y del Perú* (Guayaquil, pam., 1836).

31. E. Romero, *Historia económica*, 268–271; Bonilla et al., "Comercio libre y crisis andina," 12. Their efforts and defeat are graphically illustrated in FO61/21–23, Wilson to Palmerston, 1832–33; T52/2, Larned to Livingston, 1832–34; CCC/2, Barrère, 4 Feb., 1 July, 26 Aug., 10 Oct. 1831; *Telégrafo*, Jan.–Aug. 1833.

32. "Tratado de Comercio entre Chile y el Perú," *El Redactor Peruano* (Lima), 25 May 1836; AGN H-1 248/485–493, Consulado, May–June 1836; "Análisis de las proposiciones del Sr. Vidaurre," *El Eco de la Opinión del Perú* (Lima), Aug.–Sept. 1827; P. de Rojas y Briones, *Proyectos de Economía Política en favor de la República Peruana* (Lima, pam., 1828), 6–8, 25–28; *Clamores*, 13 Mar. 1827. *La Prensa Peruana* (Lima), 15 Mar. 1828; *Telégrafo*, 1 Apr. 1828 (miners); general portrait of miner class in Deustua, *Minería peruana*.
33. See Chapter 5, below.
34. "Balkanization" should properly be termed "Latin Americanization," as the process unfolded prior to the fragmentation of the Balkan states.
35. CCC/8, Le Moyne, "Rapport sur le commerce d'Arica et Tacna (Pérou) 1845," 16 Mar. 1845; CCC/1 (Arequipa/Arica), Villamués, "Mémoire sur le Départment d'Arequipa," Apr. 1846; CCC/2 (Lima), Barrère, "Histoire de la Contestation Existante entre le Pérou et le Chile," 12 Oct. 1832 (and 24 July 1830); FO61/71, "Report on the Trade of Peru," Wilson to Palmerston, 30 Apr. 1840 (BRT 1839); "Breves reflexiones sobre el tratado de comercio concluido en Arequipa a 8 de nov. de 1831 entre Bolivia y el Perú," *Conciliador*, 9–20 June 1832.
36. Dávila, *Medios para salvar Moquegua*, 1–85; Rivero, *Memoria sobre industria agrícola*, 7–38; *Conciliador*, 25 Aug. 1830; *Comercio*, 9 Jan.–15 Aug. 1841, 10 June 1842; *Peruano*, 30 Jan. 1841, 10, 20 May 1843; *La Bolsa* (Lima), 9 Sept. 1841.
37. Flores, *Arequipa y el sur*, 45–93; Ponce, "Social Structure of Arequipa," ch. 3; Jacobsen, "Landtenure and Society in Azángaro," ch. 2. See esp. "Memorias del Gen. Manuel de Mendiburu" (MS, Biblioteca Denegri Luna), 3 vols., 1829–54, I:115–118, 131–146, or "Representación del Comercio de Arequipa al gobierno," *Comercio*, 14–15 Aug. 1850.
38. For insight into strains, see P. J. Gamio, *Representación que el Comercio del Arequipa ha dirigido al Supremo Gobierno* (Arequipa, pam., 1832). Also see M. de Loayza, *Refutación a las observaciones de S.M.B. D.B.H. Wilson en el Correo n. 47* (Lima, pam., 1840); CCC/2, Barrère, 14 Feb.–1 Mar. 1833; FO61/58–90, all 1839–45.
39. A compelling analysis in this vein is Wibel, "Evolution of Arequipa," esp. chs. 9–12 (and prior chapters for regional trade orientation and policies).
40. Carpio, "Rebeliones arequipeñas del siglo XIX"; Herrera, *Rebeliones*. For trade issues in southern revolts, see *El Regenerador* (Arequipa), 12 Jan. 1841; *Peruano*, 12 Jan., 24 Mar. 1841, 2–22 Apr., 10–20 May 1843; FO61/29, Crompton, 2 Aug., 14 Sept. 1834; FO61/64, H. Wilson to Palmerston, 3 Oct. 1839; BRT 1839; FO61/83, H. Wilson to Palmerston, 16 Jan., 3 Feb., 20 Apr., 15 May 1841; FO61/100, Wilson to Earl of Aberdeen, 8 Apr. 1843; and examples in Chapter 4, below.
41. "Memorias del Gen. Mendiburu," I:136–146, III:527–528 (1842–52); "Representación del Consejo de Estado sobre el proyecto presentado por el Ministerio de Hacienda," *Comercio*, 14 July 1850; "Comercio de Arica," *Comercio*, 7 Aug. 1851; "Política económica," *El Progreso* (Lima), 10 Aug. 1850. Regional integration processes are examined in Chapter 4, below.

CHAPTER 3

1. See, for example, *Los Clamores del Perú* (Lima), Feb.–Mar. 1827; "Nuestra Patria y el bien de nuestra Patria," *El Telégrafo de Lima* (Lima), Feb. 1828;

"Comercio y fábricas," *Telégrafo*, May 1828; Consulado, *Razones poderosas* (see Chapter 1, n. 4, above). On mercantilist issues, see [M. E. de Rivera], *Busca-pique a la piña o observaciones sobre las ventajas de la libre circula-ción de las pastas de oro y plata* (Lima, pam., 1830), or *Principios que siguió el ciudadano José de Larrea y Loredo en el Ministerio de Hacienda de que estuve encargado* (Lima, pam., 1827).

2. Véliz, "Mesa de tres patas"; Burns, *Poverty of Progress*, 7–10; Graham, *Independence in Latin America*, ch. 2; Skidmore and Smith, *Modern Latin America*, 44; Cardoso and Faletto, *Dependency and Development*, ch. 3. For Peru, see Bollinger, "Bourgeois Revolution," 27–34.

3. Engelsen, "Social Aspects of Agricultural Expansion," chs. 1–2; Macera, "Plantaciones azucareras," 39–91; Burga, *Encomienda a hacienda*, chs. 4–5.

4. Engelsen, "Social Aspects of Agricultural Expansion," chs. 1–5; Ramírez, *Provincial Patriarchs*, ch. 7 (which would date the region's crisis even earlier). Once, the U.S. consul offered export market assistance (on a grand scale) for policy concessions: T52/1, Larned to Van Buren, 25 Oct. 1830; to Pedemonte, 13 Oct. 1830.

5. BRT 1827; Alsop, "Statement of the American Trade in Peru" (1826–31) in FO61/33, Wilson to Palmerston, 4 Aug. 1835; T52/1, Larned to Van Buren, 5 Mar. 1830; CCC/1, Barrère, 14 Aug. 1829; CCC/2, Barrère, 10 Feb., 26 Apr. 1832; X.Y.Z., *Reflexiones sobre la ley de prohibiciones* (Lima, pam., 1829).

6. See different analysis of prohibitions in Bonilla et al., "Comercio libre y crisis andina," 1–25. On agrarian pressures, AML PS, "Comisión de agricultura a la junta departamental," 16 Sept. 1829; AGN H-1 164/1714–1727, "Proyecto del Reglamento de Comercio," 5 June 1827; "Observaciones sobre el Tratado de Comercio que se piensa hacer entre el Perú y Chile," *El Mercurio Peruano* (Lima), 16 Feb. 1828; Anon., *Observaciones sobre el proyecto de Reglamento de Comercio* (see Chapter 2, n. 7, above); speech by Dep. Cuadros, *La Prensa Peruana* (Lima), 18 June 1828, "Comercio," *Telégrafo*, all Feb.–Mar., 10–18 June 1828; *Mercurio*, 10–18 June 1828, 14 July 1830.

7. Rodríguez, *Estudios económicos*, 456–464; [Távara], *Análisis y amplificación* (see Chapter 2, n. 7, above), I:51–53; "Conciliador extraordinaria," 9 Oct. 1830; *El Conciliador* (Lima), 25 Aug. 1830, 6 July, 8 Oct. 1831, 22 Feb. 1832; *La Gaceta del Gobierno* (Lima), 6 June 1835; Rivero, *Memoria sobre la industria agrícola*, 2–8, 24–28, 34–39; Ledos, *Sobre la agricultura*, 12–13, 167; *El Comercio* (Lima), 23, 29–30 Nov. 1849. French consuls were most attuned to agrarian protectionism: CCC/1, Barrère, 15 Nov. 1830, 26 Aug. 1831; CCC/2, 10 Feb. 1832; CCC/6, Saillard, 18 June 1840; CCC/8, Le Moyne, 17 July 1847.

8. "Harinas podridas," *La Miscelánea* (Lima), 3–9 July 1830; AGN II-1 197/2578–2634, Prefectura a la Junta Municipal, June–July 1830; AML, Libros de Cabildo, nos. 46–47, 1827–32; ARE, sec. 6-3, E.U., all 1830; T52/1, Larned to Van Buren, 5 Mar., 23 July, 10 Aug., 13 Oct. 1830, 4 July, 1 Aug., 5 Sept. 1831.

9. "Notable," *Telégrafo*, 10 Aug. 1829; M. Vidaurre, *Sobre la nueva ley del Perú prohibiendo la internación de muchas mercancías estrangeras* (Boston, pam., 1828); AML PS, "Comisión de agricultura," 16 Sept. 1829; AML PS, Paquete 47, "Informe," 1 July 1830; AGN H-1 179/1–10, "Actas de la Municipalidad de Lima," 1827–28; *La Bolsa* (Lima), 9 Sept. 1841.

10. Consulado, "Informe presentado sobre las bases del tratado de amistad, comercio, y navegación, y sobre lo que demanda la protección de los intereses

nacionales," *Telégrafo*, 21 May–6 June 1836; AGN H-4 1707, Consulado, Actas, 3 Apr. 1832; AGN H-4 1838, Consulado, Actas, 22 July 1845; J. M. Pando, *Reclamación de los vulnerados derechos de los hacendados de las provincias litorales del Departamento de Lima* (Lima, pam., 1833); S. Távara, *La abolición de la esclavitud en el Perú* (Lima, pam., 1855).

11. T52/1, Larned to Van Buren, 5 Mar. 1830; "Comercio y fábricas," *Telégrafo*, May 1828; *Observaciones sobre el proyecto de Reglamento de Comercio* (1828), 7–16; *Mensaje del Prefecto del Cuzco V. León a la Muy Honorable Junta Departamental instalada el día 1 de junio de 1829* (Cuzco, pam., 1829); *La Minerva del Cuzco* (Cuzco), 4 June 1831, 16 June 1832. Regional trade patterns and interests seen in AGN H-8, Tribunal del Consulado Republicano, legs. 9–15, "Contenciosos/Concursos," 1822–43; or see García, "Aduanas y comerciantes: Trujillo," for northern entrepreneurial networks.

12. Overviews of the proposed pact include "Observaciones sobre el Tratado de Comercio que se piensa hacer entre el Perú y Chile," *Mercurio*, 16 Feb. 1828; *Apuntes relativos al Tratado de Comercio* (see Chapter 2, n. 30, above); [Távara] "Paralelo entre los tratados denominados Salaverry y Santa Cruz," *Comercio*, Nov. 1846 (orig. Sept. 1840); [Távara], *Análisis y amplificación* I:50–53. The issue receives little attention in secondary sources.

13. Furtado, *Economic Development of Latin America*, chs. 3–4; Halperín-Donghi, *Historia contemporánea*, ch. 3; Macera, "Plantaciones azucareras," 41–51.

14. Flores, *Aristocracia y plebe*, chs. 1–3; Helmer, "Commerce et industrie au Pérou," 519–526; Hunt, "Growth and Guano" (1973), 19–26; BRT 1827 (excellent source on postindependence trade shifts and crises).

15. AML PS, "Comisión de agricultura a la junta departamental," 16 Sept. 1829; AML, Cabildos, no. 46, 23, 28 Mar., 22 June 1827; AML PS, "Proyecto de agricultura," 18 July 1831; Consulado, "Informe presentado sobre las bases del tratado de amistad, comercio, y navegación," *Telégrafo*, 21 May–6 June 1836; *Telégrafo*, 1 Mar. 1828; *Conciliador*, all Sept. 1832, all Dec. 1834; [Alzamora], "Proyecto," *Comercio*, 13 Jan. 1843 (history of wheat projects); Pando, *Reclamación de derechos de los hacendados*.

16. "Notable," *Telégrafo*, 10 Aug. 1829; *Observaciones sobre el proyecto de Reglamento de Comercio* (1828), 13–14; *Miscelánea*, July–Oct. 1830; AML, Cabildos, nos. 46–47, 1827–32; much data in T52/1, Larned to Livingston, 10 Aug.–Dec. 1830 and July–Sept. 1831.

17. For urban population and price trends, see Gootenberg, "Artisans and Merchants," app. III, and "Price Levels in Peru" (research from military hospital accounts in AGN H-1 and Archivo de la Beneficencia Pública de Lima). See, too, "Pan libre quiere el pobre," *Comercio*, 27 June 1840 (anti–bread monopoly struggles); *Conciliador*, 8 Feb. 1832 (liberal arguments on living costs and luxury rights); Senate debates in *Comercio*, Aug. 1851 (final triumphant subsistence issues).

18. Consulado, "Informe presentado sobre las bases del tratado de amistad, comercio, y navegación," *Telégrafo*, 21 May–6 June 1836; AGN H-4 1707, Consulado, Actas, "Indagaciones del Consulado de Lima sobre un tratado con Chile," 20 May 1834; AGN H-1 248/485–493, Consulado, May–June 1836; *Telégrafo*, 4 Feb. 1835; CCC/2, Barrère, "Tableau general du commerce," 6 June 1832; CCC/4, 24 Mar., 1 June 1836.

19. See Denegri, *Historia marítima* VI:334–345 ("Legislación Proteccionista") for survey of navigation acts. For a sample of pressures, see AGN H-4 1584, Con-

sulado, Actas, 5, 18, 20, 22 Nov. 1825 and esp. 6 June, 5 Aug. 1826; AGN
H-4 1707, Consulado, Actas, "Los propietarios de buques nacionales de la
República," 10 July, 10 Dec. 1830.

20. AGN H-8-1, Consulado Republicano, Administrativo/Juntas de Comercio
(Actas, 1821–27): 11 Aug., 11 Nov. 1825 (role of Chileans) and 28 Mar. 1825,
17 July 1826 (commercial protection pressures). Also CCC/3, Barrère, "Examen raisonné du régime commercial du Pérou," 4 Apr. 1834.

21. "Tratado de Comercio entre el Perú y Chile," El Redactor Peruano (Lima),
15 May 1836; FO61/38, Wilson to Palmerston, 4 Oct. 1836; BRT 1839; BRT
1840. Regional repercussions are discussed in Burr, By Reason or Force, chs.
1–4.

22. T52/1–3, Larned to Van Buren, Livingston, Lane, and Forsyth, 1829–36, details U.S. campaign and Chile treaty pressures; analyzed in Gootenberg, "Fabricks and Flours, Hearts and Minds." Also see T52/1, Larned to Pedemonte,
13 Oct. 1830 (market offers); FO61/29, Wilson to Palmerston, 14 July 1835
(fifty-page "Memo" of British opinion); CCC/4, Barrère, no. 11, 24 Mar. 1836
(detailed report of French positions).

23. See esp. Pando, Memoria de Hacienda 1830 (see Chapter 2, n. 30, above); [Távara], Análisis y amplificación; M. Vidaurre, "Discurso sobre la acta de navegación," Conciliador, 18 Feb. 1832; "Economía Política," Conciliador, May
1831–Feb. 1832; M. Río, "Tratado de Comercio entre Chile y el Perú," Redactor Peruano, 25 May 1836; Apuntes relativos al Tratado de Comercio, 1–14.

24. Suggestive sources are T52/2, Larned to Livingston, all Jan. 1832–Dec.
1834—esp. 20 Sept., 13 Nov., 11–13 Dec. 1832, 6 Mar., 30 Aug., 2 Dec.
1833, and 3 July 1834. Also see BRT 1838; BRT 1839; BRT 1840; FO61/25,
Passmore to Palmerston, Jan., Mar., July 1833; FO61/29, Passmore and
Crompton (Tacna), 29 Apr., 21 May, July–Dec. 1834; and CCC/8, Le Moyne,
"Rapport sur le commerce d'Arica et Tacna (Pérou) 1845," Mar. 1846.

25. "Memorias del Gen. Mendiburu" (see Chapter 2, n. 37, above), I:115–146
(1840–41); BRT 1840; El Peruano (Lima), 30 Jan. 1841, 10 May 1843; "Ministerio de Hacienda," Peruano, 12 Feb. 1845, 26 Feb., 15 Nov. 1846; Comercio,
15 Sept. 1845; AGN H-1 326/286–300, "Actas de los comerciantes de Tacna,"
30 July 1846; CCC/7, Le Moyne, 15, 22 Sept. 1845; Basadre, Historia II:740.

26. For changing perceptions of Chilean commerce, consult AGN H-1 279/884–
918, Consulado, "Proyectos y otros documentos del Reglamento de Comercio," Oct. 1840; informe of Río, Redactor Peruano, 25 May 1836; "Memoria
del Ministro de Relaciones Exteriores del Perú," Comercio, 22 Aug. 1849;
"Paralelo entre el tratado denominado Salaverry y Santa Cruz," Comercio,
Nov. 1846; "Política económica," El Progreso (Lima), 27 July 1850; and Ledos,
Sobre la agricultura, 167–170.

27. Hunt, "Growth and Guano" (1973), 97–107; Bonilla et al., "Comercio libre y
crisis andina"; Tantaleán, Política económico-financiera, ch. 8. A precursor of
contemporary debates was E. Pasquel Castañón, "Esquema de nuestra historia económica en el siglo XIX," Comercio, 28 July 1957. For general controversies on nineteenth-century industry, consult Weaver, Class, State, and Industrial Structure, ch. 3.

28. Silva, Obrajes en el Virreinato; Moscoso, "La industria textil en el Cuzco,"
67–94; and esp. Salas, "Los obrajes huamanguinos," 203–233.

29. Telégrafo, 14 Aug., 22 Dec. 1827; "Comercio," Telégrafo, Mar. 1828; "Comercio y fábricas," Telégrafo, May 1828; Prensa, 11 Oct. 1828, 23 Sept. 1829;
Mercurio, 16 Aug. 1827, June 1828; "Política económica," El Acento de la

NOTES TO CHAPTER 3

Justicia (Cuzco), Sept. 1829; *Minerva*, 4, 23 June 1831, 16 June 1832; *Observaciones sobre el proyecto de Reglamento de Comercio* (1828); Vidaurre, *Sobre la nueva ley del Perú*. Bonilla, "Perú entre Independencia y Guerra," 424–425, has a revealing depiction of interior merchant links.

30. See esp. "Comercio y fábricas," *Telégrafo*, all May 1828; M154/2, Tudor to Clay, 6 Feb., 6 Mar. 1828; T52/1, Larned to Van Buren, 5 Mar., 16 Apr. 1830; FO61/24, Wilson to Palmerston, 18 Dec. 1833; BRT 1837. Debates over market potential include Bonilla, *Guano y burguesía*, ch. 3, and Tantaleán, *Política económico-financiera*, ch. 8.

31. "Industria," *Conciliador*, 21 July 1831, 30 June 1832; BRT 1837; "Mensaje del Presidente provisorio de la República al Congreso" (Gamarra), *Peruano*, 14 Sept. 1839; "Reglamento de Comercio," *Peruano*, 16 Dec. 1840; *Comercio*, 17 June 1840; Congress debates in *Comercio*, 8 July, 8–9, 23–27 Aug. 1845; "Seis mil camisas de tocuyo," *Comercio*, 19–25 Nov. 1846; *Comercio*, 28 July, 30 Oct. 1848.

32. See, for example, descriptions in Choquehuanca, *Estadística de Azángaro*, and Stevenson, *Historical Narrative of South America* II:51–52, 78–79, 162, 182; also, nostalgic descriptions of Dep. Cabero to Congress, *Comercio*, 25 Aug. 1845. An excellent indicator of survivals is the overlooked national census of 1827 ("Cuadros estadísticas . . . ," *Prensa*, Aug. 1828–Nov. 1829; some duplicated in *Telégrafo*): 23 of 34 reporting provinces, mostly sierran, note rural artisan sectors of economic importance. Peru's informal craftsmen share many features of Mexico's as analyzed by Salvucci, *Textiles and Capitalism*, ch. 2.

33. "Estadística de Huaraz," *Comercio*, 14 Dec. 1839–16 Jan. 1840, esp. 16, 20, 24 Dec. 1839.

34. Promising as a source on rural artisans are early military-supply contracts in the Archivo Histórico-Militar del Perú (in AGN H-1 after 1840). For regional merchant ties, AGN H-8, vols. 9–15 (Concursos, 1821–45) contains many examples. Also see letter from N. García, *Comercio*, 16 June 1840; FO61/24, Wilson to Palmerston, 18 Dec. 1833; Urrutia, "De las rutas en Huamanga"; and *Allpanchis* 18/21 (1983), which is devoted largely to Andean traders.

35. "Estadística de Puno," *Comercio*, 1 July 1840; "Mensaje," *Peruano*, 14 Sept. 1839; Congress debates (Deps. Cabero and Ponce), *Comercio*, 9, 23, 25 Aug. 1845; "Un patriota verdadero," *Comercio*, 12 July 1845; reflection by Sen. Ugarte, *Comercio*, 20 Aug. 1851. See Hunt, "Growth and Guano" (1973), 116, for later peasant artisans.

36. See Appendix Tables 2.1 and 2.2, above, for long-term artisan (manufacturing) trends. For an economic and political study of Lima guilds, see Gootenberg, "Artisans and Merchants," chs. 3–5; for the colonial period, Harth-Terré and Márquez, "Las artes en el Virreinato," 352–446. Calculation for 1830 from AGN H-1 198/1066–1078, Contribuciones, Comisión Fiscal de Patentes de Lima, 1830.

37. [Távara], *Análisis y amplificación* I:51–52. See descriptions of economic woes in AGN H-4 1517, Lima, Matrícula de Patentes, 1834, 230–236 (*botoneros*) and AGN H-4 0277, Lima, Matrícula de Patentes, 1842/43, 348–349 (*sayeros*). For analysis of cost, market, and tariff dilemmas, see Gootenberg, "Artisans and Merchants," ch. 5.

38. Aspects of craft political participation are revealed in "Elecciones," *Telégrafo*, 30 July 1828; *Comercio*, 10 June, 7, 13, Aug., 1840, 5 July 1844, 16

July 1845, 17, 20 Oct., 1, 8, 15 Nov., 22, 28 Dec. 1849, Jan. 1850; *Peruano*, 19–26 Nov. 1845; "Política económica," *Progreso*, 22 Dec. 1849.

39. For a synthesis of craft political economy, see Gootenberg, "Social Origins of Protectionism," esp. 338–342. Or see "Representación que han elebado los gremios antes la Cámara," *Comercio*, 17 Oct. 1849; "Los artesanos," *Comercio*, 3 Jan. 1859; J. Silva Santisteban, *Breves reflexiones sobre los sucesos ocurridos en Lima y el Callao con motivo de la importación de artefactos* (Lima, pam., 1859); and *Conciliador*, 15–18 Feb. 1832 (liberal congruence).

40. *La Gaceta del Gobierno Legítimo del Perú* (Cuzco), 8 Feb. 1822; "Los Artesanos," *Clamores*, 13 Mar. 1827; *Telégrafo*, 14 June, 20 July 1827, 26 Aug. 1829; *Gaceta* (Lima), 4 Mar., 6 June 1835; AGN H-1 250/7, 1836; AGN H-1 279/903, Memoria de Síndicos Procuradores, Oct. 1840; *Comercio*, 27 Feb., 10 June, 21 July, 13 Aug., 23 Sept. 1840, 10 Mar. 1843, 10 Sept. 1845, 17 Oct. 1849. A critical document (revealing the most organized guilds) is the artisan "tariff" of 1850: *Comercio*, 12 July 1850.

41. Palma, "Growth of Chilean Industry," ch. 2, for innovative view of industrialization prospects; "Comercio y fábricas," *Telégrafo*, May 1828; *Comercio*, 8 Aug. 1845, 17 Oct. 1849, 3 Jan. 1859; "Industria," *Peruano*, 13 Sept. 1848.

42. Casanova, *Ensayo sobre la industria algodonera; Comercio*, Aug.–Sept. 1845; basic factory data in Carrasco, *Guía de forasteros de 1849*, 82–83; AGN, Notariales, no. 226, 1849; AGN H-1 326/774, "Expedientes promovidos para el establecimiento de una fábrica de seda," 1846; AGN H-8-19, Concurso de E. Rossel, 1851.

43. *Peruano*, 23 Aug. 1845, 4 Mar. 1846, 15, 22 July, 13, 20 Sept., 21, 25 Oct., 8 Nov., 1848; *Comercio*, 29 Jan., 4 Feb. 1848, 27–30 Sept., 9 Oct. 1849, 29 July 1850, 4–5 Oct. 1851; "Industria nacional—protección a las máquinas de Lima," *Progreso*, 24 Nov. 1849.

44. See Gootenberg, "Social Origins of Protectionism," 351–357, for this clash; or *Comercio*, 4, 25 July 1850, 3–4 July, 5, 7, 14, 20–25 Aug., 5 Oct. 1851. For failures, see Fuentes, *Estadística de Lima*, 719–723, which most honestly faults "government indifference" after 1850.

45. See Woodward, *The Consulado de Comercio of Guatemala*, or Rector, "Merchants and Commercial Policy in Chile"; no comparable study exists for the prominent Lima consulado. The following section draws on ch. 2 of my "Merchants, Foreigners, and the State"; vital primary sources include the consulado's republican archive (AGN H-8, legs. 1–125, 1821–60) and surviving books of consulado "Actas" (AGN H-4 1556, 1821–23; AGN H-4 1584, 1825–26; AGN H-4 1707, 1829–35; AGN H-4 1838, 1842–45). The merchants' classic role as an economic interest is probed in Hirschman, *Passions and Interests*, 91–93.

46. Bonilla, *Guano y burguesía*, 43–45, 156; Yepes, *Desarrollo capitalista*, 38–43; Bollinger, "Bourgeois Revolution," 23–25; Pike, *U.S. and the Andean Republics*, 50–72; Macera, "Historia económica como ciencia," 33.

47. For example: "Resolución del Gobierno Supremo," *Conciliador*, 20 Jan. 1830 and 6 July, 15 Oct. 1831; "Compañía Asiática," *Comercio*, 4–11 Dec. 1839; F. L., *Manifiesto sobre reformar la aduana y comercio* (see Chapter 2, n. 25, above); Gamio, *Representación al Supremo Gobierno* (see Chapter 2, n. 38, above); *Peruano*, 28 Dec. 1839; or Gamarra's firsthand explanation to the U.S. chargé in T52/1, Larned to Van Buren, 8 Mar. 1830.

48. Countless sources address this question. See AGN H-4 1584, Consulado, Actas, 18 Mar., 22 Nov. 1825, 8, 17 June, 1, 20 July 1826; T52/2, Larned to

Livingston, 2 Jan. 1833 (esp. enclosed foreign-merchant memorials); CCC/3, Barrère, July–Aug. 1835; AGN H-1 279/888–917, "Proyectos del Reglamento de Comercio," Oct. 1840; "El art. 61 del Reglamento de Comercio," *Comercio*, 26 Apr., 13 May 1842; BN MS, D3013, "Expediente relativo al comercio por menor de los estranjeros," 18 June 1842; FO61/121, Adams to Palmerston, 12 Mar. 1849.

49. Céspedes, "Lima y Buenos Aires"; Melzer, "Kingdom to Republic in Peru"; Flores, *Aristocracia y plebe*, chs. 2, 3, 7.

50. See above-cited "Actas" (n. 45) for consulado mobilizations. For regional pressures, see AML PS, "Vecinos de la ciudad de Ica a la Junta Departamental de Lima," 6 July 1832; *Miscelánea* 4, 21 Sept. 1833; ARE 2-0-E, Prefecturas, Lampa, 12 July 1830; Gamio, *Representación al Supremo Gobierno*; and Congress debates, *Comercio*, 23 Aug., 15 Sept. 1845.

51. CCC/2, Barrère, 3 Jan.–5 Mar. 1833; CCC/3–4, 22 June, 12 Aug. 1835; CCC/6, Le Moyne, 30 Apr.–2 July 1842 (French conflicts). A massive "literature" surrounds auctions: [Pérez de Tudela], *Martillos o su utilidad pública* (see Chapter 1, n. 2, above); M. Rivera, *Publicación de recursos reclamando la revocación del decreto . . . por el cual se prohibe el establecimiento de las casas de remates* (Lima, pam., 1832); "Observaciones de un comerciante de la sierra a favor de la casa de martillo," *Telégrafo*, Sept. 1828; press battles in *Telégrafo*, Aug.–Sept. 1828; polemics between (nationalist) *Miscelánea* and (liberal) *Mercurio*, July–Sept. 1831; *El Genio del Rimac* (Lima), July–Oct. 1834; and on into the 1840s. Consulado mobilizations were striking on this issue: e.g., AGN H-4 1707, Consulado, Actas, 22 Jan. 1829, 6 June, 18 Aug. 1831, 20 June 1834.

52. On tariffs, see AGN H-4 1707, Consulado, Actas, 3 Apr. 1832, 18 July 1834; AGN H-1 233/587, Consulado, 13 Aug. 1834; *Genio*, 22 Aug. 1834; Quirós, *Colección* IV:458–459 (12 Apr. 1834); AGN H-4 1838, Consulado, Actas, 1, 21 July 1843, 22 July 1845.

53. For the Compañía Asiática, see *Comercio*, 2–17 Dec. 1839, 28 June–15 July 1841, 11–28 June 1842; *Bolsa*, July 1841, May–June 1842; AGN H-4 1838, Consulado, Actas, 11 June 1842; AGN H-4 0337, Consejo de Estado, 17 June 1842, 16 Jan. 1843; T52/6, Pickett to Forsyth, 13 Feb. 1843; and FO61/78, Wilson to Palmerston, 31 July 1841. The Ramo de Arbitrios is discussed at length in Chapter 5, below.

54. Commercial growth statistics are computed from twelve Lima business tax registers, "Matrículas de Patentes," of 1826–59 (Gootenberg, "Artisans and Merchants," 36–55, tables 12, 13, and app. I); see also Appendix Table 2.1, above. Consulado membership and elite trends are calculated from AGN H-4 1707, Consulado, Actas, Elecciones, 5 Jan. 1830; AGN H-1 198/1075–1076, Matrícula de Patentes de Lima, 1830; AGN H-8-3, Consulado, Elecciones 1839/40, Dec. 1839; AGN H-4 1798, Matrícula de Patentes de Lima 1839 (Gootenberg, "Merchants, Foreigners, and the State," table 5).

55. Merchant liberalization (and the exception of Peru's nationalist guano-export policies) are analyzed in depth in Chapters 4 and 5, below.

56. Census materials, *Prensa*, May 1828–Oct. 1829; "Estadística de Huaraz," *Comercio*, 14 Dec. 1839–16 Jan. 1840; Choquehuanca, *Estadística de Azángaro* (rural manufactures trade). "Política económica," *Acento de la Justicia*, Sept. 1829; N. García, *Comercio*, 6 June 1840; Congress debates, *Comercio*, 8 July, 23, 27 Aug., 15 Sept. 1845 (political impact).

57. AGN H-8-1, Consulado Republicano, 17–20 July 1826; AGN H-4 1838, Con-

sulado, Actas, 1 July 1843; 27 Feb., 22 July 1845 (encomenderos). For factory movement, see *Peruano*, 23 Aug. 1845, 4 Mar., 12 Sept., 10 Oct., 16 Nov. 1846, 7 Jan., 19, 22 July, 13 Sept. (editorial "Industria"), 21, 25 Oct., 15 Nov., 1848, 10 Nov. 1849; Casanova, *Ensayo sobre la industria algodonera*; and nn. 44, 52, above.

58. Melzer, "Kingdom to Republic in Peru," chs. 5–8; Stein and Stein, *Colonial Heritage*, chs. 2, 4 (for colonial monopoly systems). Also AGN H-4 1584, Consulado, Actas, 1825–26; AGN H-4 1556, Consulado, Actas, 1821–23.

59. Liberals' charges of monopoly were commonplace (*Miscelánea*, 8 Jan. 1833; *Telégrafo*, Aug.–Nov. 1834; *Comercio*, Dec. 1839, July 1841; [Távara], *Análisis y amplificación*) and repeated ad nauseam by consuls. Yet this very notion of "monopoly" became charged with ideological power in Peru (Gootenberg, "Artisans and Merchants," 123–134).

60. Table 5 ("Consulado Political Elite, 1830/1840") in Gootenberg, "Merchants, Foreigners, and the State," 170–171 (linking colonial-and republican-merchant election, tax, and loan records). For immigrants' role, see AGN H-8-1, Administrativo, 11 Apr., 11 Nov. 1825; or see "Informe del Consulado," *Comercio*, 17 Jan. 1840.

61. This risk model is a synopsis of ch. 3 of my "Merchants, Foreigners, and the State," based on consulado bankruptcy and tax archives (AGN H-8, Consulado Republicano, legs. 1–125, 1821–60).

62. BRT 1824, BRT 1827, BRT 1834, and BRT 1837 outline the evolution of these commercial structures, as do "Contenciosos/Concursos" (AGN H-8, legs. 8–20, 1822–54). Also see Proctor, *Narrative of a Journey across the Andes*, 290–292.

63. For eloquent testimony on this dilemma, see "Patentes: unos comerciantes," *Comercio*, 21 Aug. 1845; AGN H-4 1584, Consulado, Actas, 18 Mar., 25 Nov. 1825; *Conciliador*, 20 Jan. 1830; "Informe que dio el Tribunal del Consulado," *Telégrafo*, 9 July 1834; "Comercio," *El Limeño* (Lima), 29 Mar. 1834; "Los mismos peruanos," *Comercio*, 11 Dec. 1839; or personal accounts in "Contenciosos/Concursos" cited above (n. 62).

64. "Prisión por deudas," *Comercio*, July–Oct. 1845; AGN H-4 1584, Consulado, Actas, 18 Mar., 15 Nov. 1825; AGN H-1 279/884–918, "Proyectos y otros documentos del Reglamento de Comercio," 22 Oct. 1840; AGN H-4 1707, Consulado, Actas, 22 Jan. 1830, 6 June 1831; AGN H-4 0315, Hacienda, Comunicaciones a las Cámaras, 19 Sept. 1831; *Peruano*, 28 Dec. 1839; "Compañía Asiática," *Comercio*, 4–5 Dec. 1839.

65. Polanyi, *Great Transformation*, chs. 1, 12; market clarity and peace appear critical to this possibility of a "self-regulating market."

66. For an overview of the port system, see Denegri, *Historia marítima* VI, ch. 2; "Memorias del Gen. Mendiburu" I (1829–45). Regional risks are detailed in "Concursos" (AGN H-8); or see AML PS, "Vecinos de la ciudad de Ica a la Junta Departamental," 6 July 1832; *Miscelánea*, 4, 21 Sept. 1833; *Comercio*, 23 Aug. 1845.

67. For provincial response to risk, see Gamio, *Representación al Supremo Gobierno*; Quirós, *Colección* III:270 (4 Jan. 1830), III:300 (11 Feb. 1830), III:338 (7 Apr. 1830), III:381 (2 July 1830), IV:245 (12 Jan. 1833). Foreign census data from ARE, 2-0-D, Prefecturas, 1840; ARE, 2-0-E, Prefecturas de Departamentos, 1860; *Peruano*, 30 Jan. 1846.

68. Robinson, *Theory of International Trade*, summarizes the relevant Ricardian and neoclassical trade theories. See Kindleberger, "Rise of Free Trade in

Europe," 20–23, for distribution of rents in opening economies; BRT 1827 for price shifts; and "Reglamento de Comercio," *Conciliador*, 15 Oct. 1831, for striking perceptions of promised structural change and conflict.

69. Two models stressing concentration factors are Johnson, "A Model of Economic Nationalism," 165–185, and Pincus, "Pressure Groups of Tariffs," 257–279.

70. I thank Shane Hunt for his observations on these issues.

71. BRT 1827; Deustua, *Minería peruana*, 29–30; Gootenberg, "Price Levels in Peru"; or see price index in Appendix Table 2.1, above. Griffin, *Underdevelopment*, ch. 2, analyzes price and trade adjustment dilemmas in underdeveloped contexts.

72. See, for example, Robinson and Eatwell, *Modern Economics*, 5–8, on mercantilism. For Peruvian controversies, see *Busca-pique a la piña* vs. *Principios de Hacienda* (Larrea). Suggestions of special difficulties in H. Unanue, *Exposición sobre la Hacienda Pública del Perú, por el Ministro de ella* (Lima, pam., 1825), 10–11. (Debates linking trade deficits and money supply mark all the 1820s "Memorias de Hacienda.")

73. See Deustua, *Minería peruana*, chs. 2–3, table 2, or Appendix Table 1.2, above. Rojas y Briones, *Proyectos de Economía Política* (see Chapter 2, n. 32, above), is one northern protectionist statement for regional integration of mining zones. See Bonilla, "Coyuntura comercial del siglo XIX" for regional pattern of exports.

74. AGN H-8, Concursos, legs. 16–19, 1844–53; AGN H-4 1838, Consulado, Actas, 3 June 1845; BRT 1840 (for evolving market stability). Chapter 5, below, under "Wounds of War (1841–45), Liberal Medicines," explores transition amid heightened chaos. Jones, *European Miracle*, is a recent view of the general political "embeddedness" of economic change.

CHAPTER 4

1. Views on instability are summarized in Walker, "Myth of Chaotic Charisma"; or see the approaches in Pike, *Modern History*, ch. 3, and Bonilla, "Continuidad y cambio en el Estado independiente," 481–498. For a more structural analysis, see Tantaleán, *Política económico-financiera*, ch. 1 ("El estado caudillista"). See Safford, "Post-Independence Spanish America," 403–421, for a recent general survey of caudillismo.

2. Examples include "El art. 61 del Reglamento de Comercio," *El Comercio* (Lima), 26 Apr. 1842; [Távara], *Análisis y amplificación* (see Chapter 2, n. 7, above); Congress debates in *El Mercurio Peruano* (Lima), June 1828, and *Comercio*, July–Sept. 1845; Un Peruano [J. C. Ulloa], *El Perú en 1853: un año de su historia contemporánea* (Paris, pam., 1854), 15–16.

3. Close to that view is Bollinger, "Bourgeois Revolution," 26–28, or, overall, Frank, *Lumpenbourgeoisie*, ch. 4 ("Civil War: Nationalism versus Free Trade"); cf., synthesis of regionalism and caudillismo in Gootenberg, "North-South."

4. For theories on Peru's evolving state, see Berg and Weaver, "Reinterpretation of Political Change"; Gorman, "State, Elite, and Export"; Friedman, *The State and Underdevelopment*, chs. 5–6; Cotler, *Clases, estado y nación*, ch. 2; V. Villanueva, *Ejército peruano*, chs. 1–2.

5. Cf. Bonilla, "Perú entre Independencia y Guerra," 418, and Denegri, *Historia marítima* VI:40–41. For one protectionist mobilization, see FO61/24, Wilson

to Palmerston, 18 Dec. 1833; for liberals, *El Peruano* (Lima), 6 Feb., 24 Mar., 5 May 1841; FO61/100, Wilson to Earl of Aberdeen, 3 Apr. 1843. Or see nn. 9–16, below.

6. FO61/58, Wilson to Palmerston, 11 Mar. 1839 (see also 1 Feb., 27 Mar., and [Crompton] 21 Apr. 1839); FO61/52, H. Wilson to B. H. Wilson, 23 Jan. 1838. British support to Santa Cruz is detailed in BRT 1837, BRT 1838, and FO/61, vols. 37–53, Wilson to Palmerston, 1836–38.

7. List based on *Peruano*, Aug. 1838–1841 (esp. Huancayo Congress reports, Sept.–Dec. 1839); BRT 1838, BRT 1839, BRT 1840; CCC/5, Saillard, 1837–39.

8. [J. J. Osma], *Observaciones que sobre las medidas tomadas por el Sr. Ministro de Relaciones Exteriores relativas a la naturalización de los extranjeros hacen unos peruanos* (Lima, pam., 1840); [M. Ferreyros], *Contestación a las observaciones que bajo el nombre de "unos peruanos" se han publicado en un folleto contra las medidas del Gobierno sobre naturalización de extranjeros* (Lima, pam., 1840); *Comercio*, July–Aug. 1840; FO61/70, Wilson to Palmerston, 27 Sept., 4 Oct. 1840.

9. Blow-by-blow account in FO61/60 (all Wilson to Palmerston), 2 Sept. 1839; FO61/67, 11 Jan. 1840; FO61/70, 4 Oct., 28 Dec. 1840; FO61/77, 1, 21 June 1841; FO61/78, 7, 18 Aug. 1841.

10. *El Tribunal del Pueblo* (Lima), 1838–39; *El Rebeñique* (Lima), 1841; *Peruano* and *Comercio*, all Oct. 1841; FO61/78, Wilson to Palmerston, 1 Sept., 6, 11 Oct. 1841; FO61/80, 17 Nov., 24 Dec. 1841. Also CCC/6, Saillard, 27 Jan. 1841 (and Correspondance Politique, vol. 10); T52/5, Pickett to Forsyth, 6 Sept. 1840; M154/4, Bartlett to Forsyth, 5 Oct., 6 Nov. 1838.

11. FO61/64, H. Wilson to B. H. Wilson, 17 Aug., 31 Oct. 1839; BRT 1839; *El Mensajero de Tacna* (Tacna), 1839. Also CCC/5, Saillard, June 1839; CCC/1 (Arequipa/Arica), Villamués, "Mémoire sur le Départment d'Arequipa," Apr. 1846; Dávila, *Medios para salvar Moquegua*, 40–42.

12. *El Regenerador* (Arequipa), 12 Jan. 1841; *Peruano*, 12 Jan., 24 Mar. 1841; FO61/83, H. Wilson and Crompton (Tacna), 16 Jan., 3 Feb., 30 Mar., 5, 15 May 1841; "Memorias del Gen. Mendiburu" (see Chapter 2, n. 37, above), I:115–190 (1840–42).

13. *Peruano*, 24 Mar. (editorial) and 10 July 1841; or similar, later events in *Peruano*, 12, 27 Apr., 10, 19–20 May, 31 July 1843.

14. FO61/83, H. Wilson, 16 Jan., 3 Feb. 1841; FO61/76, 5 Mar. 1841.

15. CCC/6, Saillard, 5 Oct. 1841 (and 3 Apr. 1841); *Peruano*, 28 Apr., 5–8 May 1841 (H. Wilson expulsion). Vivanco would try again to dispute guano control in the 1850s (FO61/172–174, Jan.–June 1857) without foreign takers; instead, Britain and the United States offered Peru protectorate status, revealing their then full acceptance of the Lima state.

16. *Peruano*, Apr.–July 1843; FO61/95, Masterson (Bolivia), 1 Feb. 1842; FO61/98, Barton to Palmerston, 5–19 May 1843; FO61/100, Crompton to Palmerston, 22 May, 3–8 Apr. 1843; FO61/103, Adams to Palmerston, 25 June 1844; Basadre, *Historia* II:697–722.

17. On alienness of foreigners to caudillismo, see *Los Clamores del Perú* (Lima), Feb.–Mar. 1827; "Escandalosa infracción de las leyes," "Preguntas," *El Telégrafo de Lima* (Lima), 24, 27 Apr. 1829 (or 8–9 Feb. 1828); BRT 1834; M154/2, Tudor to Clay, 6 Feb. 1828, and Radcliff, 18 June 1829; T52/1, Larned to Van Buren, 20 Apr. 1830, 18 Apr. 1831, 19 Nov. 1832, 2 Jan. 1833. See Beezley, "Caudillismo," for a variant of the patrimonial theory extended here.

18. Tristán, *Peregrinaciones de una paria*, 350–351; FO61/28–29, Wilson to Palmerston, 13 Nov., 18, 23 Dec. 1833, 29 Apr. 1834; FO61/55, Crompton, 21 Dec. 1838; FO61/59, Wilson to Palmerston, 1, 14 Feb., 27 Mar. 1839; CCC/1 (Arequipa/Arica), Villamués, 17 May 1845; CCC/1 (Lima), Barrère, 23 Dec. 1831, 23 Feb. 1832; Manning, *Diplomatic Correspondence*, vol. x, Apr.–Nov. 1835, esp. 18 Aug., 13 Oct., 13, 16 Nov. 1835; V. Villanueva, *Ejército peruano*, 407 (caudillo origins); Basadre, *Historia* i:311.

19. Reference to this group is universal: e.g., FO61/76, Wilson to Palmerston, 4 Oct., 28 Dec. 1840; FO61/78, 7 Aug. 1841; T52/2, Larned to Livingston, 30 Aug. 1833; CCC/2, Barrère, 1 Mar. 1833; *Peruano*, 29 Apr., 8 May 1841. See, too, Memoria de J. Villa (Ministro de Hacienda y de Guerra y Marina), *El Conciliador* (Lima), 22 Mar. 1834; Memoria de R. Castilla (Ministro de Guerra y Hacienda), *Peruano*, 2 Nov. 1839.

20. Sources for Iguaín and his ilk also seem endless: FO61/58, Wilson to Palmerston, 14 Feb. 1839 (quote); FO61/78, 7, 16 Aug., 1 Sept., 6 Oct. 1841; FO61/109, Adams to Earl of Aberdeen, 5 Oct. 1845; *Rebeñique*, Sept. 1841; *Comercio*, Apr.–May 1842, Aug.–Sept. 1845, 20 Feb. 1846; *Peruano*, 16 Oct. 1841; [H. B. Wilson], *Refutación de los cargos que hace Gen. Iguaín al Sr. encargado de Negocios de S.M.B. en las notas de 23 y 25 de mayo, publicadas en el periódico oficial* (Lima, pam., 1845).

21. For "Rosas-style" caudillos, see Burns, *Poverty of Progress*, ch. 6; Véliz, *Centralist Tradition*, 174–178. For pacification and pressures, FO61/104, Adams to Palmerston, June–Sept. 1844; FO61/105, Crompton and H. Wilson, Jan., Dec. 1844; FO61/108, Adams to Palmerston, Jan.–June 1845. Also see Denegri, *Historia marítima* vi:163–186 ("La cuestión inglesa").

22. Hünefeldt, "Negros de Lima," 32–33; FO61/24, Wilson to Palmerston, 18 Dec. 1833; "Síndicos Procuradores," *Comercio*, 21 July 1840; "Un maestro sastre que protesta de la ropa que introducen los extranjeros," *Comercio*, 23 Sept. 1840; speech by Dep. Cabero, *Comercio*, 23 Aug. 1845; "Representación de los gremios ante las Cámaras," *Comercio*, 17 Oct. 1849; "Un maestro de artesano," *Comercio*, 12 Dec. 1849.

23. Fall of liberal caudillos: FO61/28, Wilson to Palmerston, Oct.–Dec. 1834; FO61/50, Jan.–Aug. 1838; FO61/75, Jan.–Mar. 1841; FO61/103, Adams to Earl of Aberdeen, Jan.–Aug. 1844. The principled British, U.S., and French efforts to run blockades were intended not only to preserve commerce, but no doubt also to ease military pressures on liberals.

24. For two views of Santa Cruz, see FO61/53, Wilson's "Report on the Trade of Peru in 1837" (BRT 1837), esp. sections analyzing "enemies" of the Peru-Bolivia Confederation, vs. *El Redactor Peruano* (Lima), 31 May 1836, and *Tribunal del Pueblo*, 12 Sept., 11 Oct., 20 Dec. 1839. Also see Flores, *Arequipa y el sur*, 54–57.

25. *Telégrafo*, 8–9 Feb. 1828; "Los zeladores del Congreso," *Telégrafo*, 21 Mar. 1828; "Comercio y fábricas," *Telégrafo*, May 1828; M154/2, Tudor to Clay, 6 Feb. 1828; AGN H-1 233/587, Consulado, 13 Aug. 1834; *El Genio del Rimac* (Lima), 22 Aug. 1834; T52/3, Larned to Lane, 20 Aug. 1834; for auctions, *Genio*, all Aug.–Oct. 1834, esp. "Movimiento mercantil," 25 Aug. 1834, or Chapter 1, nn. 1–11, above.

26. T52/2, Larned to Livingston, 2 Jan. 1833; CCC/2, Barrère, Jan.–Feb. 1833. Disappointment with liberal allies plagued the U.S. campaign: e.g., M154/1, Tudor to Clay, 24 Dec. 1826, 6 Jan., 3 Feb., 23 Mar. 1827; M154/2, 6 Feb. 1827; T52/1, Larned to Van Buren, 12, 16 Apr. 1830; T52/1, "Conference on

the Subject of Prohibitory Duties," 20 Apr. 1830; T52/1, 20 Sept., 19 Nov. 1832; T52/1, Larned to Livingston, 2 Jan., 22 Dec. 1833. The British were simply disgusted with local liberals: FO61/11, Ricketts to Canning, 11 May 1827.

27. FO61/44, Tristán to Wilson, 1, 17 Jan. 1837; FO61/50, Wilson to Palmerston, "Memo," 1 May 1838, and queen's commendation, 27 July 1838; FO61/52, 6, 19 Feb., 20 Mar. 1838; Tristán to "Ajentes diplomáticos en ese Capital," *El Eco del Protectorado* (Lima), 17 Aug. 1836; J. García del Río, "Estado miserable del Perú por su división," *Peruano*, 7 Sept. 1838; "Correspondencia curiosa entre el ajente de Santa Cruz en Londres y la Secretaria de Negocios Estranjeros de S.M.B.," *Peruano*, 3–13 Apr. 1839.

28. Striking expressions of this predicament: FO61/11, Ricketts to Canning, "Secret," 6 Feb. 1827; FO61/12 (London), 20 Dec. 1827. Also see BRT 1838; CCC/3, Barrère, 21 May 1834; and T52/6, Pickett to Forsyth, 31 Mar. 1841. Mathew, "Imperialism of Free Trade: Peru," 566; Platt, "Imperialism of Free Trade: Reservations," 299; and Doyle, *Empires*, 222–226, give wider context.

29. See the discussion under "Wounds of War (1841–45), Liberal Medicines" in Chapter 5, below.

30. Mathew, "A Primitive Export Sector" and "Gibbs and the Peruvian Government"; "Memorias del Gen. Mendiburu" I:122–124, 191–196, 253–267 (1841–44); CCC/7, Le Moyne, 1845–46.

31. FO61/108, Adams to Earl of Aberdeen, 30 May, 14 June 1845; FO61/109, 5 Oct. 1845 (esp. Paz Soldán to Adams, 3 Sept. 1845); T52/7, Jewett to Buchanan, 3 Sept. 1845; CCC/8, Le Moyne, "Rapport por l'Etat y la Condition des Etrangers au Pérou," 1 Nov. 1846; *Peruano*, 27 Aug. 1845. For fuller treatment, Gootenberg, "Merchants, Foreigners, and the State," 383–393. Except for suggestions in Berg and Weaver, "Reinterpretation of Political Change," 69–84, and Friedman's *The State and Underdevelopment*, chs. 6–7, no work analyzes the twilight of caudillismo in Peru.

32. For British obsession with commercial monopolies, see FO61/70–89, Wilson to Palmerston, all 1840–42, esp. May 1842. Also see CCC/6, Le Moyne, 3 Apr., 5 Oct. 1841, 10 Feb. 1842; AGN H-8-15, Consulado, Concursos, 1841 (of Quirós y Allier, Bland, Barroilhet, and McClean Rowe); and AGN H-1 271/434 510, Consulado, 12 Dec. 1839.

33. Mathew, "Imperialism of Free Trade: Peru" and *Gibbs and the Guano Monopoly*. For one such struggle (the "Lobos" affair), see T52/9, Clay to Webster, June 1852–Jan. 1853.

34. Bonilla, *Guano y burguesía*, ch. 1 ("Los consignatorios del guano y el problema de la burguesía nacional en el Perú"); Yepes, *Desarrollo capitalista*, 60–84; Cotler, *Clases, estado y nación*, 100–102.

35. "Empréstitos," *Peruano*, 15, 19, 29 Sept. 1849; *Comercio*, all Sept.–Oct. 1849, esp. "Empréstitos" (Congress debates), 27–29 Sept. 1849; AGN H-4 0335, Hacienda, Comunicaciones, Aug.–Nov. 1849.

36. "Huano: dictamen de la Comisión de Hacienda del Senado," *Comercio*, 26 Sept., 27 Oct. 1851; *La Bolsa* (Lima), 20 June 1842 (Asiatic Co. members); *Peruano*, 27 Oct. 1849; "Empréstito," *El Progreso* (Lima), 30 Mar. 1850. On group trajectory, see Bonilla, *Guano y burguesía*, 45–65, or Camprubí, *Historia de los bancos*.

37. Oviedo, *Colección*, vol. IV (Ministerio del Gobierno), 1849–54, reveals the range of state privileges (or see *Comercio*, 22–23 Aug. 1852, on tariffs alone). Quiroz, *Deuda defraudada*, chs. 4–5, masterfully contrasts favors for the

elites vs. liberalism for the masses, issues which are analyzed below in Chapter 5.

38. Hunt, "Growth and Guano" (1973), 84–85: the major finding that overturns "enclave" models of the guano age.

39. F. Quirós, *A la Nación* (Lima, pam., 1845); F. Bilbao, *El Gobierno de la Libertad* (Lima, pam., 1855), which calls for linking free trade and civil rule; *Progreso*, all 1849–50 (esp. Aug. 1849, 27 July 1850), Mar. 1851 ("Nuestro actual estado político" and "Economía Política"), 6 Apr. 1851 ("Empréstito"); Basadre, *Historia* II:717, 917–918, 927.

40. Bonilla, *Guano y burguesía*, 50–65; Basadre, *Historia* IV:1911–1913 and chs. 81–82. Gorman, "State, Elite, and Export," suggests some long-term effects of civilismo's early base.

41. Instituto Riva Agüero, "Actas de los Congresos del Perú desde el año de 1822" (1928), vols. I, VI, 1822–52; *Mercurio*, Aug., Dec. 1827, June 1828; *Telégrafo*, Feb.–Mar., June 1828; M154/2, Radcliff to Clay, 30 Aug., 28 Nov. 1828, 26 Feb. 1829; CCC/1, Barrère, 29 July 1830.

42. *Mercurio*, Oct. 1831–Dec. 1832; *Telégrafo*, 1832, "Exposición del proyecto de Reglamento de Comercio que el Ejecutivo ha sometido al examen y sanción del Congreso," *Conciliador*, Sept. 1832–Jan. 1833; T52/1, Larned to Van Buren, 4 July 1831; T52/2, Larned to Livingston, 20 Sept., 13 Nov., 13 Dec. 1832, 22 Dec. 1833; Huancayo debates in *Peruano*, Oct.–Dec. 1839; full 1845 Congress debates in *Comercio*, July–Sept. 1845 (reproduced as *Extracto de las sesiones*).

43. Impressive coverage in *Comercio*: Jan.–Feb. 1848 (esp. 4–5 Feb.), Sept.–Dec. 1849 (esp. "Representación de los gremios ante las Cámaras," 17 Oct.); Jan., July–Aug. 1850; July–Oct. 1851 (esp. 19–23 Aug.); Jan.–Mar. 1852. Also see Consejo de Estado, "Proyecto de reforma del Reglamento de Comercio y varios otros documentos con que el tiene relación," *El Rejistro Oficial* (Lima), Aug. 1851. For 1850s shift, consult *Comercio*, 24 Dec. 1858–Jan. 1859; or see *Dictamen de la Cámara de Diputados sobre las representaciones de los gremios de Lima y Callao* (Lima, pam., 1859).

44. M154/1, Tudor to Clay, 2 Nov. 1826; M154/2, 6 Mar. 1828; M154/2, Radcliff to Clay, 30 Aug., 28 Nov. 1828, 26 Feb., 3, 18 July 1829; T52/1, Larned to Van Buren, 5 Mar., 20 Apr. 1830, 4 July, 25 Oct. 1831; T52/2, Larned to Livingston, 17 Feb., 7 Aug., 20 Sept., 13 Nov., 13 Dec. 1832, 2 Dec. 1833; T52/3, Larned to Forsyth, 5 July, 15, 20 Aug. 1834; CCC/1, Barrère, 29 July, 16 Oct. 1830, 11 May, 1 July, 26 Aug., 10 Oct. 1831.

45. For example: speeches by Deps. Farfán and Rodríguez, *Telégrafo*, 17 Dec. 1827; by Deps. Alegre, Cabero, and Ponce, *Comercio*, 8 July, 23 Aug., 27 Aug. 1845; by Sen Ugarte, *Comercio*, 20 Aug. 1851; and Saavedra, *Comercio*, 24 Dec. 1858.

46. Dancuart, *Crónica parlamentaria*, vols. I–III, even details committee assignments. Analyses of agrarian protectionism: CCC/1, Barrère, 19 July 1830 (dividing Congress into landholders wanting "complete prohibitions" vs. liberal landowners wanting merely "prohibitive duties"), 16 Oct. 1830, 11 May, 1 July, 26 Aug. 1831; CCC/6, Le Moyne, 18 June 1840, 12 Feb. 1843; CCC/7, 15 May 1843, "Demarches faites par M. Le Moyne sur obtenir au Pérou des diminutions de droits sur les vins et l'eaux de vie"; CCC/8, 17 July 1847; "Prohibición de importar harinas," *Progreso*, 15 Dec. 1849.

47. *Telégrafo*, June 1828; *Comercio*, July–Aug. 1845 and Sept.–Dec. 1849. For explicit recognition, see "El Reglamento de Comercio en el Senado," *Co-*

mercio, 5 Aug. 1851 (also see 25 Nov. 1849, 5 Jan., 19–20 Aug. 1850, 4 July 1851); "Política económica: Reglamento de Comercio," *Progreso*, 6 July, 17 Aug. 1850; and Silva, *Reflexiones sobre los sucesos con la importación* (see Chapter 3, n. 39, above), 31.

48. "Comercio y fábricas," *Telégrafo*, Feb.–Mar. 1828, 8 Oct. 1832; Congress debates, *Comercio*, Aug. 1845; "Representación de los gremios ante las Cámaras," *Comercio*, 17 Oct. 1849 (also 30 Oct., 7–8 Nov., 14, 20, 27 Dec. 1849). Or see M. Guzmán's poem celebrating one nationalist Congress: "El Triunfo de los Artesanos, Perú libre en su Progreso, Viva el nombre de García y las leyes del Congreso" (Biblioteca Nacional, Volantes, 1849). See, too, FO61/126, Adams to Palmerston, 12 Jan., 12 June 1850.

49. For autocratic politics, see M154/2, Tudor to Clay, 7 Nov. 1827, 6 Feb., 17 May 1828; FO61/11, Ricketts to Canning, 11 May 1827; FO61/45, "Petition of British Merchants in Lima," 28 June 1837; FO61/62, Wilson to Palmerston, 31 Dec. 1839; "Reglamento de Comercio," *El Amigo del Pueblo* (Lima), 14 May 1840; and *Comercio*, 6–8 May 1840, 23 July 1850, 21–26 Aug. 1851.

50. For in-depth analysis and documentation of this episode, see Gootenberg, "Social Origins of Protectionism," 351–356.

51. "Unos cursantes de economía política," *Comercio*, 23 July 1850; "Consejo de Estado," *Comercio*, 22 July 1850; "Leyes prohibitivas," *Comercio*, 25 Nov., 27 Dec. 1849, 5 Jan., 4, 22–24 July 1850, 16 Aug. 1851; and esp. speech of Sen. Seone, *Comercio*, 19 Aug. 1851, and "El Reglamento de Comercio en el Senado," 5 Aug. 1851. Also *Progreso*, 6, 13 July, 10, 17 Aug. 1850; *El Intérprete del Pueblo* (Lima), 5 Mar. 1852.

52. For Jacobinism, see *Comercio*, 26 Oct., 14, 29 Nov. 12–14, 27 Dec. 1849, 4–7 Jan., 7–18 Feb., 29 July 1850, and esp. "Un maestro de artesano," 12 Dec. 1849. French influence was conceivable: Leguía, "Las ideas de 1848."

53. "A la Representación Nacional," *Comercio*, 30 Dec. 1858. Note artisan awareness of own marginalization: "Comunicados," *Comercio*, 25 July 1850; "Unos artesanos," *Comercio*, 29 Nov. 1851 (and 19–20 Dec. 1850); or "Estado de los artesanos de Lima," *El Correo de Lima* (Lima), 16 Oct. 1851. For later marginalization, see *La Zamacueca Política* (Lima), Jan.–Feb. 1859; *Artesanos* (Lima, pam., 1859); or Gootenberg, "Artisans and Merchants," 41–43, 78–90, 163–170.

54. *Comercio*, 14, 23 Aug.–24 Oct. 1851, and esp. "Reglamento de Comercio," 4 Mar. 1852; *Rejistro*, "Proyecto de reforma del Reglamento de Comercio y varios otros documentos del Consejo de Estado," 12 Aug. 1850; "Informe de Comisión de Hacienda del Senado," *Rejistro*, 13 Mar. 1852; BN MS D2182, "Reforma del Reglamento de Comercio expedida por el Congreso de la República y referendado por el Presidente de la República," 13 Oct. 1851. Hunt, "Growth and Guano" (1973), 106–111, traces the effects of inflexible ad valorem policy.

55. For parallels, see Semmel, *Rise of Free Trade Imperialism*, ch. 7; Kindleberger, "Rise of Free Trade in Europe"; or, a superb study for Chile, Romero, *Sociedad de la Igualdad*.

56. Queries on this theme include Caravedo, "Problema del centralismo"; Mariátegui, *Seven Essays*, ch. 6; and the still suggestive 1931 observations of Basadre ("El centralismo y la subversión de las provincias") in *Problema y posibilidad*, ch. 10.

57. *La Minerva del Cuzco* (Cuzco), 4, 21, 22 June 1831, 26 May, 16 June, 14 July 1832; *Conciliador*, 27 June, 11 Aug. 1832; León, *Mensaje del Prefecto del*

Cuzco (see Chapter 3, n. 11, above); Rivera Serna, "Juntas Departamentales durante Gamarra"; for regional aspirations of independence, Fisher, "Royalism, Regionalism, and Rebellion"; for sierran protectionism, Denegri, *Historia marítima* VI:38–40.

58. AML PS, "Comisión de agricultura a la Junta Departamental," 16 Sept. 1829; AML PS, "Proyecto de agricultura," 18 July 1831; AML PS, "Vecinos de la ciudad de Ica a la Junta Departamental de Lima," 6 July 1832; AML, Cabildos, "Actas de la Municipalidad," nos. 46–47, 1827–30; AGN H-4 1707, Consulado, Actas, Apr. 1832; "El apuntador," *Mercurio*, 26 July 1831; *La Miscelánea* (Lima), 3–9 July 1830; "Proyecto," *Comercio*, 13 Jan. 1843.

59. *Conciliador*, Oct.–Nov. 1830 (esp. "Conciliador extraordinaria," 9 Oct. 1830); *Miscelánea*, 26 Sept.–26 Oct. 1830; T52/1, Larned to Livingston, 10 Aug.–Dec. 1830 (and dozens of attached documents); A. G. de La Fuente, *Manifiesto del Jeneral La-Fuente* (Santiago, pam., 1831); Távara, *Historia de partidos*, 78–81; T52/1, Larned to Livingston, 18 Apr., 17 May, 1831.

60. Basadre, *Historia* II:519, 536–539: rightly noting the odd behavior of liberals toward the juntas.

61. For port systems, BRT 1827; "Memorias del Gen. Mendiburu" I:115–146 (1840–44), III:517–528 (1850–52); AGN H-4 1707, Consulado, Actas, "Juez Diputado de Comercio de la Provincia de Tacna," 17 May 1831; AGN H-1 225/568, "Diputaciones Departamentales de Comercio," Jan. 1833; AML PS, "Vecinos de Ica," 7 July 1832; *Comercio*, 16 June 1840, 23 Aug. 1845.

62. BRT 1838; BRT 1839; BRT 1840; AGN H-1 302/101–119, Hacienda, 18 Aug. 1843; *Peruano*, 2, 30 Jan. 1841, 15 Apr., 10, 20 May 1843; Dávila, *Medios para salvar Moquegua*, 14–15, 45–46; Dancuart, *Anales* II:14–16, III:39.

63. BRT 1837; "Estadística de Huaraz," *Comercio*, Dec. 1839–Jan. 1840. For a region's decline, cf. "Estadística de Puno," *Comercio*, 1 July 1840, with earlier Choquehuanca, *Estadística de Azángaro*, and prefect reports (*Prensa*, 11 Oct. 1828). Also see estimates of Dep. Cabero for Ayacucho, *Comercio*, 23 Aug. 1845, following Larrea's statistics of 1826; Bustamante, *Apuntes y observaciones civiles*, 29–32, 82–83. Our only detailed study of a regional transformation is Jacobsen's "Landtenure and Society in Azángaro," esp. ch. 2; cf. Blanchard, "Change in Ica."

64. For 1820s regional shift, cf. "Comercio y fábricas," *Telégrafo*, May 1828 (or Congress debates, *Mercurio*, Aug., Dec. 1827, May–June 1828) with tariff debates in *Conciliador*, May, 30 July, Sept.–Nov. 1831, Jan. 1833; *Eco del Protectorado*, 7 Sept. 1836. For Lima and guild economy, see Chapter 3, n. 39, above.

65. [A. Gamarra], *Mensaje del Presidente provisorio de la República al Congreso* (Lima, pam., 1839) (in FO61/59, 17 Sept. 1839); "Reglamento de Comercio," *Peruano*, 1 Apr. 1840; "Aduanas," *Peruano*, 2 May, 16 Dec. 1840; "Reglamento de Comercio," *Peruano*, 2 Jan. 1841.

66. Speech by Dep. Ponce (Ayacucho), *Comercio*, 27 Aug. 1845 (or protest of the regional merchant García, 17 June 1840); full debates in *Comercio*, 8 July, 8, 9, 23, 27 Aug., 15 Sept. 1845 (or *Extracto de las sesiones*, 6–9, 23, 80–82, 104, 108–116, 120–122, 139–140, 189–190); "Seis mil camisas de tocuyo," *Comercio*, 19–25 Nov. 1846 (last military contracts).

67. *Comercio*, 25, 27 Aug., 15 Sept. 1845; Rivero, *Memoria sobre la industria agrícola*, 25–64 (with yet some protectionist overtones); Ledos, *Sobre la agricultura* (another compendium of possible exports); J. Bovo de Revello, *Brillante porvenir del Cuzco o exposición de las esperanzas de engrandecimiento*

de este departamento (Cuzco, pam. 1848); Dávila, *Medios para salvar Moquegua*, 47–59, 70–77; Távara, *Abolición de esclavitud* (see Chapter 3, n. 10, above), 18–22; Aréstegui, *Padre Horán* I:108–111. See Burns, *Poverty of Progress*, 18–32, for analogous developments.

68. *Los Intereses del País* (Cuzco), 18 Apr., 13 Sept. 1849; *Peruano*, 30 Jan., 15 Apr. 1841; *Comercio*, 19 Aug. 1850, 21 Aug. 1851; *Documentos legislativos sobre el establecimiento y la mejora de las vías de comunicación en el Perú* (Lima, pam., 1856). On port pressures, see esp. Congress debates in *Comercio*, 12 Aug. 1845; CCC/7, Le Moyne, Sept.–Dec. 1845; or n. 70, below.

69. Jacobsen, "Landtenure and Society in Azángaro," chs. 2–4; "Informe del Consejo de Estado sobre el proyecto presentado por el Ministro de Hacienda," *Comercio*, 14 Aug. 1850; Hünefeldt, "Los extrangeros y el siglo XIX," secs. 1–2; Engelsen, "Social Aspects of Agricultural Expansion," ch. 2.

70. AGN H-1 302/1011–1093, 18 Aug. 1843; AGN H-1 326/286–330, "Acta de los comerciantes de Tacna," 30 July 1846; "Memorias del Gen. Mendiburu" I:115–146 (1840–41), III:517–538 (1851–52). Port liberalization: *Peruano*, 30 Jan. 1841, 22 Apr., 3 July 1843, 12, 14 Feb., 22 Sept., 15 Nov. 1845, 26 Feb. 1846, 18 May 1848; *Bolsa*, 14 Mar., 6 Apr. 1841; *Comercio*, 16 June 1840, 21 July, 9, 12 Aug., 20 Sept. 1845; CCC/9, Le Moyne, "Loi relative à la marine merchant du Pérou," 23 Jan. 1848.

71. "Política económica," *Progreso*, 10 Aug. 1850; "Rápida ojeada sobre las causas jenerales que han determinado la suerte del Perú o sea ensayo de Economía Política," *Progreso*, 27 Apr., 11, 18 May 1850; "Reglamento de Comercio: unos cursantes de Economía Política," *Comercio*, 23 July 1850; "Política económica," *Comercio*, 30 July 1850; "Representación del comercio de Arequipa al gobierno," *Comercio*, 15 Aug. 1850; "Informe del Consejo de Estado," *Comercio*, 14 Aug. 1850. Also Blanchard, "Change in Ica" (Elías' roles).

72. See speech of Sen. Osores, "Igualdad de derechos en los puertos," *Comercio*, 12 July 1851 (and all July 1851); AGN H-1 367/19, Hacienda, 15 Jan. 1851; "Representación del comercio de Arequipa al gobierno," *Comercio*, 15 Aug. 1850; "Informe del Consejo de Estado," *Comercio*, 14 Aug. 1850; "Comercio de Arica," *Comercio*, 5, 7 Aug. 1851; "Reglamento de Comercio," *Comercio*, 27 Sept. 1851, and esp. 4 Mar. 1852. Also see Dancuart, *Anales* V:100–104 (1851), for pressures on officials; Basadre, *Historia* II:950, for Echenique's continuing concern.

73. Quiroz, "La consolidación," 247–267, superbly analyzes those regional revolts. See, too, V. Villanueva, *Ejército peruano*, ch. 2 (centralizing caudillismo), p. 407 (caudillo origins). "Federalist" critiques of guano-age liberalism later emerged: Cisneros (1866), *Ensayo sobre cuestiones económicas*, 28, 38–40, and Copello and Petriconi (1876), *Estudio sobre la independencia económica*, ch. 9.

74. Burns, *Poverty of Progress*, ch. 6; Beezley, "Caudillismo"; and Wolf and Hansen, "Caudillo Politics," are these theorists. Note Burns's unusual use of the term "inorganic democracy" (p. 86), following an Argentine writer, José Luis Romero.

CHAPTER 5

1. Exceptions are Tenenbaum's meticulous *Politics of Penury in Mexico* and Deas's "Fiscal Problems of Colombia." See Wolf and Hansen, "Caudillo Politics," for the dominant model of caudillo economics.

2. The present chapter uses extensive data found in ch. 5 of Gootenberg, "Merchants, Foreigners, and the State"; for another view, see Tantaleán, *Política económico-financiera*, "Las finanzas del estado caudillista," 44–63.

3. For depictions of caudillo crises, see García del Río, "Estado miserable del Perú por su división," *El Peruano* (Lima), 7 Sept. 1838; editorial, *La Prensa Peruana* (Lima), 4 Dec. 1828; [Orbegoso], "Mensaje a la Convención Nacional," *El Redactor* (Lima), 13 Aug. 1834; or any of 1820s "Memorias de Hacienda": e.g., L. Bazo, *Manifestación que hace al Pueblo Peruano de las medidas adoptadas por el Ministro de Hacienda en los seis meses que lo desempeñó* (Lima, pam., 1829), 7–18.

4. Pando, *Memoria de Hacienda 1830* (see Chapter 2, n. 30, above), "Presupuesto de gastos" and app. 5 ("Estado que manifiesta lo debido cobrar y cobrado en las contribuciones directas por un año"); "Estado de débito en que se hallen las Subprefecturas de los Departamentos por contribuciones," *Prensa*, 4 Dec. 1828; AGN H-1 175/770, Hacienda, "Empréstito interno del año de 1828: actas y otros documentos" (esp. Presupuesto de Tesorería General de Lima), 11 July 1828; AGN H-1 216/367, [J. Serra], "Memoria sobre las contribuciones directas," 1832; "Ministerio de Hacienda," *El Conciliador* (Lima), 24 Nov. 1832. See also 1837 "budget" in FO61/50, 14 June 1838. For European comparisons, see Kennedy, *Great Powers*, chs. 3–4; Peru's percentage of military spending is not as unusual as its deficit.

5. Bonilla, "Perú entre Independencia y Guerra," 418–420; Tantaleán, *Política económico-financiera*, 51, 61; Yepes, *Desarrollo capitalista*, 43; Hunt, "Growth and Guano" (1973), 104; Boloña, "Tariff Policies in Peru," 44–48; Dobyns and Doughty, *Peru*, 161–162.

6. Ministerio de Hacienda, *Memoria del Ministro de Hacienda contestando al dictamen de los cuatro vocales de la junta consultora en que se preponen arbitrios para reunir un millón de pesos para los gastos que tendrá que invertir la República en ciertos objetos de su interés sin perjudicar los ingresos de sus rentas* (Lima, pam., 1828); *Informe de la Comisión Principal de Hacienda sobre el estado de la deuda interior y exterior reconocida y por reconocer, y medios de amortizarla* (Lima, pam., 1828). For Santa Cruz's efforts, *El Eco del Protectorado* (Lima), 7 Sept. 1836; BRT 1837; FO61/50, Wilson to Palmerston, "Memo," 1 May 1838; *Peruano*, 7 Sept. 1838; "Memoria de Guerra y Hacienda," *Peruano*, 2 Nov. 1839; "Aduanas: contrabando," *Peruano*, 6 May 1840.

7. AGN H-1 185/1207, Prefecturas, Dec. 1828–Jan. 1829; FO61/24, Wilson to Palmerston, 26 Aug. 1833; T52/1, Larned to Van Buren, 8 Mar. 1830; CCC/3, Barrère, 10 Apr., 22 June 1835; "Respuesta del Cuerpo Diplomático relativo a la lei sobre empréstitos extranjeros," *Peruano*, 6 Dec. 1845; Palacios, *Deuda anglo-peruana*, ch. 1.

8. These sources are the scores of "Tesorería General de Lima" reports (the era's true budgetary records), published monthly in official gazettes: *Prensa* (1827–29), *Conciliador* (1830–34), *El Redactor Peruano* (Lima) and *La Gaceta del Gobierno* (Lima) (1835–38), *Peruano* (1839–45). Similar accounts are held in AGN H-1, under "Tesorería General," 1827–45. For a typical response to the monthly deficit, see "Ministerio de Hacienda," *Redactor*, 31 Dec. 1834.

9. For example: "Crédito público," *Peruano*, 22 Apr., 3 July 1843; "Empréstito," *Peruano*, 6 Dec. 1843; "Exposición del proyecto de Reglamento de Comercio," *Conciliador*, esp. 28 Nov. 1832; "Voto particular de los individuos de la

Comisión de Hacienda," *El Mercurio Peruano* (Lima), 23 May 1828; *Memoria contestando a los cuatro vocales*, 9–11, 26–27, 40; BRT 1837; BRT 1838.

10. See Appendix Table 3.1, above. Calculations are from "Razón nominal de las amortizaciones hechos con derechos de aduanas comprensivas desde agosto de 1827," *Prensa*, 12 Apr. 1828; "Amortizaciones con dinero y derechos," *Prensa*, 30 Oct. 1828; AGN H-1 175/770, "Empréstito interno del año de 1828," 24 July 1828–17 Jan. 1829; AGN H-4 1638, Tesorería General, "Libro de cuentas corrientes de cantidades que en dinero efectivo y villetes amortizados han enterado diferentes comerciantes . . . ," July 1828–Jan. 1830.

11. BRT 1834; BRT 1837; *Prensa*, 15, 17 Mar. 1828; "Voto particular," *El Telégrafo de Lima* (Lima), 22 May 1828; "Leyes sobre comercio," *Telégrafo*, 11 Jan. 1831; "Exposición del proyecto de Reglamento de Comercio," *Conciliador*, Nov. 1832; *Memoria contestando a los cuatro vocales*; "A los aboneros," *El Comercio* (Lima), 1, 3 Apr. 1843; *La Miscelánea* (Lima), 24 Aug. 1831; *El Genio del Rimac* (Lima), 14 July 1834; "Memorias del Gen. Mendiburu" (see Chapter 2, n. 37, above), I:252–257 (1844–45).

12. Early projects included D. de Orúe, *Proyecto presentado al Soberano Congreso* (Lima, pam., 1824); Tribunal del Consulado, *Proyecto de un banco de rescate que presenta al Soberano Congreso el Tribunal del Consulado* (Lima, pam., 1832); J. V. Galecio, *Proyecto o plan de arbitrios* (Lima, pam., 1832); *Miscelánea*, 17 June 1830.

13. See Appendix Table 3.2, above (or, for more detail, Gootenberg, "Merchants, Foreigners, and the State," app. ["Data and Methods on Emergency Finance, 1820–1850"]). The hundreds of sources on loans include the Consulado's archive (AGN H-8, esp. legs. 1–6); newspaper listings (e.g., *Conciliador*, 1–14 Mar. 1834); monthly Ramo de Arbitrios reports in the official press (e.g., "Prestamistas," *Peruano*, 16 Mar. 1839); and esp. the Hacienda's archival loan registers (e.g., AGN H-1 279/637, "Razón de las cantidades entregadas en dinero al Estado," 23 Dec. 1840).

14. "Proyecto para la instalación del Tribunal del Consulado en esta Capital," *Prensa*, 23 Sept. 1829; AGN H-1 175/770–776, "Empréstito interno del año de 1828," July 1828; AGN H-1 198/712, Consulado, 14, 20 Jan., 6 Feb. 1830; BN MS D902, D1358, "Ordenes para levantar empréstitos," 1829, 1831; Bazo, *Manifestación* (n. 3, above), 7–13; or Gamarra's explanation to the U.S. chargé in T52/1, 8 Mar. 1830. See Melzer, "Kingdom to Republic in Peru," chs. 3–5, on colonial precedent.

15. *Redactor*, 1–5 Mar., 5 Apr. 1834; AGN H-1 241/564, Consulado, 31 Dec. 1834; "Tribunal del Consulado," *Peruano*, 2 Jan. 1840. The most accessible Arbitrios fund "history" is M. del Río, *Memoria que presenta el Ministro de Hacienda del Perú al Congreso de 1847* (Lima, pam., 1847), 18–24.

16. AGN H-1 277/641, "Razón de los acreedores al Ramo de Arbitrios por las cantidades que reconoce de empréstitos levantados desde el año de 1834 hasta sept. de 1840," 26 Sept. 1840; AGN H-1 233/588, "Estado que manifiesta lo adeudo y gastado de los derechos del Ramo de Arbitrios," July 1834; AGN H-4 1735, Tesorería General, Ramo de Arbitrios, 1835; *Gaceta*, 4 Mar. 1835. See Appendix Table 3.3, above, for long-term Arbitrios debt.

17. Hacienda to Consejo de Estado, *Redactor*, 31 Dec. 1834; AGN H-1 241/564–696, Consulado to Hacienda, Jan.–Feb. 1835.

18. *Gaceta*, Prefectura, 4 Mar. 1835; AGN H-4 1735, Consulado, Ramo de Arbitrios, 2 Jan., 30 Mar., 25 Apr., 27 Sept., 31 Dec. 1835; AGN H-1 241, Consulado to Hacienda, 25 Mar. 1835 (Actas) and 2 Apr. 1835; AGN H-1 240/960,

Prefectura, 25 Aug. 1835. See also AGN H-1 271/495, "Razón de accionistas al Ramo de Arbitrios," 1839.

19. AGN H-1 279/637, "Razón de las cantidades entregadas en dinero al Estado por empréstito y de las en documentos," 23 Dec. 1840; AGN H-1 303/290, "Deudas y empréstitos del tiempo de la Restauración," 1843. For policy justifications, see AGN H-1 279/891, "Proyectos y otros documentos del Reglamento de Comercio," 22 Oct. 1840, no. 1; AGN H-4 1584, Consulado, Actas, 5 Mar., 22 Nov. 1825, 1 July 1826; *Gaceta*, 11 June 1835; *Peruano*, 7 Sept. 1838, 26 Oct. 1839, 1 Apr. 1840; *Comercio*, 25 Jan. 1840, 26 Apr., 20 May 1842, 21 Aug. 1845.

20. For merchant pressures, see AGN H-1 240/856–960, Prefectura, Feb.–Aug. 1835; AGN H-1 241/564–762, Consulado, Feb.–Apr. 1835; FO61/31–35, Wilson to Palmerston, 7 Apr., 24 June, 7 Aug. 1835, and Humphreys, 16 Apr. 1835; CCC/3, Barrère, 6 Apr., 22 June 1835; and T52/3, Larned to Forsyth, 7 Apr., 24 June, 18 Aug. 1835. Also see "Compañía Asiática," *Comercio*, 5–11 Dec. 1839; "Estanco nacional de tabaco," *Comercio*, 12 Dec. 1839.

21. See Appendix Tables 3.2 and 3.3, above; AGN H-1 255/456a, "Razón de las personas que se han presentado en quiebra que tiene noción el Tribunal del Consulado," 1837; AGN H-1 264/753, "Razón de los acreedores del Estado por empréstitos reconocidos por el Ramo de Arbitrios," 22 Dec. 1838; "Lamentable crisis comercial," *Telégrafo*, 6 Sept. 1838; FO61/45, Wilson to Palmerston, 31 May 1837.

22. AGN H-4 0446, Consulado, Correspondencia General, 21 Dec. 1839; AGN H-4 1781, Consulado, Expedientes, 2 Aug. 1838; AGN H-1 271, Consulado, 21 Feb. 1839; "Tribunal del Consulado," *Peruano*, 4 Jan. 1840 (and 2 Nov. 1839, 26 Dec. 1840).

23. AGN H-1 271/434–510, Consulado, 10 Sept. 1839; *Comercio*, 16 June 1842; FO61/78, Wilson to Palmerston, 31 July 1841. Similar problems plagued a tobacco monopoly: AGN H-1 271/434–510, 22 Oct. 1839; *Comercio*, 12 Dec. 1839.

24. "Ramo de Arbitrios," *Peruano*, 9 May 1840 (and 8 Aug. 1840); AGN H-4 1781, Consulado, "Reglamento de Arbitrios," 14 Aug. 1840; Huancayo Congress, *Comercio*, 10 Sept., 4 Nov. 1839 (and 8, 10 Feb., 2 Apr., 10 Aug. 1840).

25. "Tribunal del Consulado," *Peruano*, 4 Jan. 1840; "Reglamento de Comercio," *Peruano*, 1 Apr. 1840 (and 1 Feb., 2 May 1840); AGN H-1 279/514, Consulado, 28 Jan., 26 Mar. 1840.

26. FO61/75, Wilson to Palmerston, 27 Dec. 1840. See FO61/58–90, Wilson, all 1839–42, for antiforeign pressures (or BRT 1839; BRT 1840; CCC/6, Saillard, 18 June, 7 Dec. 1840, 5 Aug. 1841).

27. AGN H-1 279/884–918, "Proyectos y otros documentos del Reglamento de Comercio," 22 Oct. 1840; "Aduanas," *Peruano*, 2 May 1840; "Tribunal del Consulado," *Peruano*, 27 Dec. 1840. For artisan and procedural protests, see *Comercio*, 7, 8, 27 Apr., 6, 8, May 1840; "Síndicos Procuradores," *Comercio*, 21 July, 13, 18 Aug., 23 Sept., 1840; and "Reglamento de Comercio," *El Amigo del Pueblo* (Lima), 14 May 1840.

28. "Tribunal del Consulado," *Peruano*, 4 Jan. 1840; Huancayo Congress, *Peruano*, 15 Feb. 1840; "Aduanas," *Peruano*, 2 May 1840; "Ramo de Arbitrios," *Peruano*, 9 May 1840; *Informe de Hacienda sobre deuda interior y exterior*, 8–12.

29. "Ramo de Arbitrios," *Comercio*, 12 Jan. 1841; AGN H-1 303/291, "Razón de

las deudas pasivas contra el Estado desde la Restauración," 1843; *Peruano*, 20 Feb. 1841; *Comercio*, 12 July 1841.

30. AGN H-1 287/320, Consulado, Jan. 1840 (or *Comercio*, 23 Jan. 1841); AGN H-1 287/308–363, Consulado, "Oficio dirigido al Ministro de Hacienda," 23 Jan., 4 Mar. 1841 (reply in *Comercio*, 25 Jan. 1841); AGN H-1 285/1113–1115, "Distribución de los $10,000 que puede entrar los prestamistas extranjeros," 24–25 Jan. 1841; AGN H-1 295/597–598, "Razón de los abonos pendientes librados por adelantos de aduana," 18 Aug., 2 Nov. 1842.

31. *Peruano*, 26 June 1844. For merchant pillage and protests, see AGN H-1 295/300–349, Consulado to Hacienda, 11 Feb., 19 May 1842; AGN H-4 1838, Consulado, Actas, Apr. 1842; AGN H-4 0336, Hacienda, Comunicaciones, Jan.–Mar. 1842; *Comercio*, 26 May 1843; *La Bolsa* (Lima), 28 June 1843; and *Peruano*, 26 Oct. 1844.

32. "Monopolio de Ana," *Comercio*, 22 June 1842; "Compañía de Asia," *Comercio*, 10 June 1842; "Consejo de Estado," *Comercio*, 23 June 1842; AGN H-4 0337, Consejo de Estado, Comunicaciones, 17 June 1842, 17 Jan. 1843; CCC/7, Le Moyne, 30 June 1843. The phrase "Compañía Asiática" becomes forever synonymous with "betrayal": *Comercio*, 19 Sept. 1849, 25 July 1850.

33. *Peruano*, 26 June 1844; "Patentes: unos comerciantes," *Comercio*, 16–21 Aug. 1845; AGN H-4 1838, Consulado, Actas, 24 Dec. 1842; AGN H-8, legs. 14–16, Consulado, Concursos, 1839–46 (esp. bankruptcies of A. García and A. P. de Oliveira). Cf. AGN H-4 1835, Lima, Matrícula de Patentes, 1842/43, and AGN H-1 313/1442–1563, Matrícula de Patentes de Lima, 1844.

34. "Respuesta del Cuerpo Diplomático relativo a la lei sobre empréstitos extranjeros," *Peruano*, 6 Dec. 1845; or see speech of Dep. Alegre, *Comercio*, 8 Aug. 1845. Best censuses of foreign-merchant growth: FO61/123, Barton, "British Mercantile Houses (Lima, Callao, Tacna, and Arica), 1842/49," 1849; FO61/119, Islay, "List of British Mercantile Houses, 1842/48," 1848; cf. AGN H-1 342/1339, "Razón de los extranjeros que pagan patentes de industria," 1848.

35. "El art. 61 del Reglamento de Comercio," *Comercio*, 26 Apr. 1842; see other expressions of this theory in [Távara], *Análisis y amplificación* (see Chapter 2, n. 7, above), I:17, 52–56; "Empréstitos," *Peruano*, 6 Dec. 1845; and "Estranjeros," *El Progreso* (Lima), 29 Aug. 1849. Also see Hirschman, *Passions and Interests*, pt. II ("How Economic Expansion Was Expected to Improve the Political Order").

36. "Consejo de Estado: informe del Sr. Río," *Comercio*, 13 May 1842 (and *Bolsa*, 12 May, 26 Apr. 1842); BN MS D1645, 25 Apr. 1842; BN MS D3013, 18 June 1842; BN MS D1784, 22 Sept. 1846; *Comercio*, 8 July 1845; AGN H-4 1838, Consulado, Actas, 8 Mar., 9 and esp. 20 Apr. 1842.

37. "Prisión por deudas," *Comercio*, 8–29 July 1845; AGN H-4 1838, Consulado, Actas, "Causas de comercio," 3 July 1845; AGN H-1 400/1199-1235, "Almacén de vestuarios para el ejército," 1846. Other collaborative realms are seen in *Comercio*: "Seis mil camisas de tocuyo," 19 Nov. 1846, 9 July, 8–17 Aug. 1850; "Estado de abonos," "Emisión de abonos," 1, 24 Dec. 1844; "Carpentería," 10 Mar. 1843; 23 Oct. (the "Bolsa") and 6, 9 Nov. (railroads) 1840. Also see Oviedo, *Colección* XVI:407–410 (1845–46 tax strikes).

38. AGN H-4 1838, Consulado, Actas, 14 Feb. 1843, 24 Dec. 1845 (quote); AGN H-4 0227, 1842, Matrícula de Patentes de Lima, 329–345; "Banco de empréstito," *Comercio*, Dec. 1843; "Patentes: unos comerciantes," 16, 21 Aug. 1845; *Peruano*, 2 Aug., 24 Dec. 1845. For an excellent source on merchant blending

with foreigners, see the detailed business biographies in Regal, *Historia de ferrocarriles*, chs. 3–4.

39. Congress debates, *Comercio*, 8 July 1845; "Patentes," *Comercio*, 16 Aug. 1845; "Consejo de Estado," *Comercio*, 7 Sept. 1846; "Empréstitos," *Comercio*, 4 Oct. 1849, 15 Aug. 1850; "Reglamento de Comercio," *Comercio*, 4 Feb. 1852; "Gremio de cigarreros," *Comercio*, 20 Sept. 1853; *El General José Rufino Echenique a sus compatriotas* (Lima, pam., 1858), 109–110.

40. Gootenberg, "Artisans and Merchants," chs. 1–2, and app. v for methodology and sources (based on Matrículas de Patentes of Lima, 1840–61). For start of trend, "Un peruano arruinado," *Comercio*, 18 Aug. 1840; BN MS D1645, "Oficio dirigido por el Ministro de Hacienda," 25 Apr. 1842.

41. See Appendix Tables 2.2 and 2.3, above (but note slight difference with use of real incomes there). Useful documents include AGN H-1 342/1339, "Razón de los extranjeros que pagan patentes de industria," 1848, and Matrículas of 1830, 1839, 1844, 1850, and 1857. Other relevant census data are found throughout Córdova y Urrutia, *Estadística de pueblos de Lima* (1839), and Fuentes, *Estadística de Lima* (1858).

42. "Estado de los artesanos de Lima," *El Correo de Lima* (Lima), 16 Oct. 1851; Silva, *Reflexiones sobre los sucesos con la importación* (see Chapter 3, n. 39, above); *La Zamacueca Política* (Lima), Jan.–Feb. 1859; "Extranjeros," *La Revista de Lima* (Lima), 1 June 1860; J. J. Salcedo, *Memoria que presenta al Congreso de 1860 el Ministro de Hacienda y Comercio* (Lima, pam., 1860), 33; Giesecke, *Masas urbanas y rebelión*, 87–117.

43. See Appendix Table 2.3, above. Chief sources for these calculations (table 13 in Gootenberg, "Artisans and Merchants") are Matrículas de Patentes, 1844–61, and AGN H-1 342/1339, "Razón de los extranjeros que pagan patentes de industria," 1848. Such evidence might soften recent regional views of national merchant survival: e.g., Halperín-Donghi, *Historia contemporánea*, 142–152, or Ridings, "Foreign Predominance among Overseas Traders."

44. For applications of the "intermediary" class concept, see Pásara, "Rol del derecho," or Bollinger, "Bourgeois Revolution," 23–25.

45. For a sterling example, see Silva, *Reflexiones sobre los sucesos con la importación*. For Mexico, see the reactive liberalism described in Sinkin, *Mexican Reform*; Coatsworth, "Orígines del autoritarianismo"; or, in trade policy per se, Potash, *Mexican Government and Industrial Development*, ch. 7 (here, 1830s political instability also dooms protectionist experiments). For all Latin America, see Love and Jacobsen, *Guiding the Invisible Hand*.

46. For example: AGN H-1 287/308–363, Consulado, 23 Jan. 1841; AGN H-1 285/1113–1115, Prefectura, "Distribución entre los prestamistas extranjeros," Jan. 1841; *Comercio*, 23 Jan. 1841; *Peruano*, 113, 27 Mar. 1843; AGN H-4 0335, Hacienda to Prefectura, "Empréstito estranjero," 18 Sept. 1843.

47. "Empréstito," *Peruano*, 10 May 1843. In *Peruano*, also see "Crédito público," 22 Apr. 1843; and 20 May, 3 July, 25 Oct. 1843, 10 Apr., 20 July 1844.

48. AGN H-4 1838, Consulado, Actas, 24 Dec. 1845; CCC/7, Le Moyne, 28 Nov. 1843; CCC/8, "Rapport por l'Etat y la Condition des Etrangers au Pérou," 1 Nov. 1846, 30 Aug. 1847; FO61/109, Paz Soldán to Adams, 3 Sept. 1845; T52/ 7, Jewett To Buchanan, 3 Sept. 1845; *Peruano*, 27 Aug. 1845; "Lei sobre empréstitos extranjeros," *Peruano*, 6 Dec. 1845; "Lima," *Comercio*, 29 Aug. 1845. A useful general source on receding foreign discrimination is Coronel Zegarra, *Condición de estranjeros*, esp. app. 1.

49. See Appendix Table 3.1, above. Sources for my estimates include AGN H-1

NOTES TO CHAPTER 5

295/597, "Razón de los abonos pendientes librados por adelantos de aduana," Nov. and Dec. 1842; "Razón de cantidades exhibidas durante la administración anterior sobre los productos de la aduana de Callao," *Peruano*, 25 Mar. 1843; "Estado que manifiesta los abonos librados contra la aduana del Callao desde 1841 hasta 1844," *Comercio*, 1 Dec. 1844. "Memorias del Gen. Mendiburu" I:251–257 (1844–45), analyzes war debts.

50. Mathew, "Foreign Contractors at the Outset of Guano," "Gibbs and the Peruvian Government," and *Gibbs and the Guano Monopoly*, chs. 3–4; Hunt, "Growth and Guano" (1973); Levin, *Export Economies*, ch. 2; Bonilla, *Guano y burguesía*; Rodríguez, "Contratos del guano y sus efectos en las finanzas."

51. A huge pamphlet polemic surrounds this question: e.g., P. J. Carillo, *Memoria sobre la negociación del huano* (Lima, pam., 1845). Cf. Bonilla, *Guano y burguesía* and Tantaleán, *Política económico-financiera*, with Mathew's studies of the consignment system (n. 50 above).

52. See Appendix Table 3.4, above. Despite efforts by Mathew (and Tantaleán), we still have no clear accounting of this early guano finance. See Hunt, "Growth and Guano" (1973), 62–63, for total state revenues.

53. Mathew, "Imperialism of Free Trade: Peru"; while these accounts of foreign behavior coincide, my interpretations of motive differ. For overseas recognition of new influence (and interest) with guano, see FO61/87–89, Sealy to Canning, 22 Jan. 1842, May 1842; FO61/108, Adams to Palmerston, 4 Jan. 1845; T52/6, Pickett to Webster, 10 Dec. 1844; T52/7, Jewett to Buchanan, Sept. 1845, 28 Feb. 1846; CCC/6, Le Moyne, 5 Oct. 1841, 5 Feb., 5 Apr. 1842; and CCC/7, 12 May 1845. For "Lobos," T52/9, Clay to Webster, June 1852–Jan. 1853.

54. For Peru's paradoxical state autonomy, see discussion under "A Guano-Age Leviathan?" below; or Berg and Weaver, "Reinterpretation of Political Change"; or, as a striking policy example, "Huano: dictamen de la Comisión de Hacienda del Senado," *Comercio*, 26 Sept. 1851.

55. "Empréstito," *Peruano*, 10 May 1843; "Crédito público," *Peruano*, 22 Apr. 1844; "Memorias del Gen. Mendiburu" I:252–266 (1844–45). Consular reports are silent on these very fundamental issues; see Mathew, *Gibbs and the Guano Monopoly*, ch. 2, for some foreign insights.

56. Castilla as seen in FO61/104, Adams to Palmerston, Sept. 1844; FO61/108, 14 Jan. 1845; Mathew, "Gibbs and the Peruvian Government," 344; Dancuart, *Anales* IV:70–71 (5 Feb. 1846).

57. Quiroz, *Deuda defraudada*, ch. 2. For debt pressures, see Río, *Memoria de Hacienda 1847* (n. 15, above); M. del Río, *Memoria presentada a las Cámaras reunidas en sesiones extraordinarias en 1849 por el Ministro de Hacienda sobre la situación actual de ésta y las causas que la han motivado* (Lima, pam., 1849), pts. 1, 3; *Extracto de las sesiones*, 157, 189 (Oct. 1845); Dancuart, *Anales* III:46–51.

58. "Memorias del Gen. Mendiburu" I:252–266 (1844–45); budget debates in *Comercio*, 9 Feb. 1846; "Congreso extraordinario," *Comercio*, 19 Jan.–15 Feb. 1848, June 1849; *Informe del Consejo de Estado sobre el proyecto de presupuesto formado por el Ministro de Hacienda para el bienio de 1850 y 1851 remitido a la H. Cámara de Diputados* (Lima, pam., 1849); "Proyecto de reforma del Reglamento de Comercio para facilitar el Consejo de Estado," *El Rejistro Oficial* (Lima), 12 Aug. 1850, Notas.

59. Hunt, "Growth and Guano" (1973), table 6 (revenues); Mathew, *Gibbs and*

NOTES TO CHAPTER 5

the Guano Monopoly, 52, 69–70, 75–76, 80; *Peruano*, 24 Mar. 1846; Basadre, *Historia* II:800–806; Mathew, "First Anglo-Peruvian Debt."

60. Basadre, *Historia* II:810–816, covers many developments. Also see Río, *Memoria de Hacienda 1847*, 2–10; "Empréstito," *Peruano*, 27 Feb. 1850, Apr. 1850; Mathew, "Gibbs and the Peruvian Government," 351–353.

61. *Peruano*, May 1849; *Comercio*, 25 June–July 1849; Basadre, *Historia* II:740–741, 748–754. See Dancuart, *Anales*, vols. IV–V (1846–55), for major policy documents.

62. "Crédito público," *Peruano*, 20 Mar. 1850; editorial, *Peruano*, 27 Mar. 1850; Tantaleán, *Política económico-financiera*, pt. II ("Las transformaciones del estado caudillista"); Friedman, *The State and Underdevelopment*, 170–173; Hunt, "Growth and Guano" (1973), 59–85.

63. FO61/109, Paz Soldán to Adams, 3 Sept. 1845; *Peruano*, 27 Aug. 1845; *Comercio*, 29 Aug. 1845; Coronel Zegarra, *Condición de estranjeros*, app. 1 (11 Nov. 1845); CCC/8, Le Moyne, "Rapport por l'Etat y la Condition des Etrangers au Pérou," 1 Nov. 1846.

64. Mathew, "First Anglo-Peruvian Debt"; CCC/8, Le Moyne, 30 Aug. 1847; CCC/9, 26 Apr., 24 Aug. 1848, 29 Sept. 1849; CCC/10, 23 Dec. 1849, 6 Feb. 1850; T52/7, Jewett to Buchanan, 25 Oct., 27 Nov. 1845, 28 Feb. 1847 (Jewett, for his efforts, was finally expelled); T52/8, Clay to Webster, 12 Jan., 11 Aug. 1849, 12 Feb., 20 Oct. 1850; FO61/121, Adams to Palmerston, 29 Mar. 1849; FO61/130, 9 Nov., 8 Dec. 1851.

65. Palacios, *Deuda anglo-peruana*, chs. 1–3. Quiroz, "La consolidación" (and *Deuda defraudada*), is the revisionist study; much of the argument here follows that superb research and analysis. For views of the debt consolidation, see Basadre, *Historia* III:1012–1028; Bonilla, *Guano y burguesía*, 26–36; Cotler, *Clases, estado y nación*, 95–101; Tantaleán, *Política económico-financiera*, ch. 6; Yepes, *Desarrollo capitalista*, 61–64; and Engelsen, "Social Aspects of Agricultural Expansion," 55–65.

66. *Peruano*, 26 June 1844, 3 June 1846; BN MS D1780, 21 Mar. 1845; Río, *Memoria de Hacienda 1847*, 18–24; Congress debates, *Extracto de las sesiones*, 157, 189 (Oct. 1845), and *Comercio*, 7–16 Feb. 1848; AGN H-4 0336, Consulado, Comunicaciones, Jan., 29 Oct. 1845, 18 Sept. 1846, all 1847, Oct. 1848, Feb. 1849.

67. Quiroz, *Deuda defraudada*, ch. 2; Basadre, *Historia* II:819–822; "Memorias del Gen. Mendiburu" I:259–261 (1844); AGN H-1 326/322, "Razón de los acreedores del Ramo de Arbitrios," 1846; AGN H-1 333/367–415, Consulado, July–Oct. 1847. Consulado books after 1845 deal overwhelmingly with Ramo de Arbitrios functions: e.g., AGN H-4 1849, Ramo de Arbitrios, 1843, to AGN H-4 1986, Consulado, Caja de Consolidación, 1852.

68. Quiroz, *Deuda defraudada*, 58–60, 105–108; Palacios, *Deuda anglo-peruana*, 81–90; CCC/10, Le Moyne, 8 Feb., 13 July 1850; F. Casós, *Para la historia del Perú: revolución de 1854* (Cuzco, pam., 1854).

69. Río, *Memoria de Hacienda 1847*, 15. For loan requests, see AGN H-4 0336, Consulado, Comunicaciones, Oct. 1844, 19 Aug. 1848, 17 Aug., 15 Oct. 1849, 15 Apr. 1850; Mathew, *Gibbs and the Guano Monopoly*, ch. 2. For civil politics, see Quirós, *A la Nación* (see Chapter 4, n. 39, above); "Necesidad de un tercer candidato dedicado al estado de la Hacienda Pública," *Progreso*, 10 Aug. 1850 (or "Programa político," 29 Dec. 1849).

70. Quiroz, *Deuda defraudada*, chs. 3–7, traces the new elite. See Chapter 3, above, on Lima's missing liberal lobby of the 1820s–40s.

204

71. "Reglamento de Comercio," *Comercio*, 4 Feb. 1852 (and 14 Aug. 1851). For foreigners in consulado, see "Tribunal del Consulado," *Progreso*, 29 Dec. 1850; *Rejistro*, 25 Oct. 1851; AGN H-8-3, Consulado, "Elecciones," 1849–55, and Fuentes, *Estadística de Lima*, 702.
72. Quiroz, *Deuda defraudada*, 38–48, 71–93, for bond depreciation, transfers, and concentration; AGN H-4 1849, Ramo de Arbitrios, 1843; AGN H-1 333/307–415, Consulado, "Amortizaciones," 1847; Río, *Memoria de Hacienda 1847*, 18–24; AGN H-8-3, Consulado, "Elecciones," 1849–55 (foreign inroads).
73. Basadre, *Historia* II:748–749, 813–814, 817–822, 979–990; Palacios, *Deuda anglo-peruana*, 75–88; Gootenberg, "Social Origins of Protectionism," 347–358; Bonilla, *Guano y burguesía*, ch. 1; Yepes, *Desarrollo capitalista*, 60–64. Consult Dancuart, *Anales*, vol. v (1850–55), for official documents of the clash.
74. *Peruano*, May, 15–29 Sept., 12, 28 Nov. 1849; "Empréstitos," *Comercio*, 25 June–July, 14 Sept., 11 Oct. 1849; esp. Congress debates ("Empréstitos"), *Comercio*, 27–29 Sept. 1849; "Empréstito," *Progreso*, 30 Mar., 6 Apr. 1850; FO61/121, Adams to Palmerston, Mar. 1849; T52/8, Clay to Webster, Aug. 1849.
75. "Emprésitito—Comercio Nacional," *Comercio*, 29 Sept. 1849, and Melgar reports, *Comercio*, 29 Oct., 5–6 Nov. 1849; or see AGN H-4 0335, Hacienda, Comunicaciones, Aug.–Nov. 1849.
76. *Peruano*, 12 Nov. 1849 (Gibbs contract, debt laws); "Empréstito," *Peruano*, 27 Feb. 1850. See esp. "Huano: dictamen de la Comisión de Hacienda de Senado," *Comercio*, 26 Sept. 1851, and "El Presidente de la República a la Nación" (Echenique), *Peruano*, 20 Apr. 1851. Also Mathew, *Gibbs and the Guano Monopoly*, 99–110.
77. See Appendix Tables 1.2 and 3.4, above, for guano trade; N. Piérola, *Memoria que presenta al Congreso de 1853 el Ministro encargado del Despacho de Hacienda* (Lima, pam., 1853); Hunt, "Growth and Guano" (1973), 61–65; Basadre, *Historia* II, ch. 43 ("La afluencia fiscal entre 1851–53").
78. Mathew, *Gibbs and the Guano Monopoly*, 186–198; Quiroz, "La consolidación," 84–87, 125–130, 208, 211; *Echenique a sus compatriotas* (n. 39, above); *Comercio*, Feb., Nov.–Dec. 1850 (elections). "Memorias del Gen. Mendiburu" III:512–528, 572–600 (1850–54) is the outstanding source, for Mendiburu was intimately involved in all developments: the consolidation, guano contracts, commercial reform, and diplomacy.
79. See Chapter 4, above, under "A Congress of Protectionists," for the tariff battle. Fiscal arguments dominate the Melgar report in *Comercio*, 29 Oct. 1849. Also see "Leyes prohibitivas," *Comercio*, 25 Nov. 1849; "Rápida ojeada sobre las causas jenerales que han determinado la suerte del Perú," *Comercio*, 16 May 1850; "Consejo de Estado—Reglamento de Comercio," *Comercio*, 22 July 1850; "Unos cursantes de Economía Política," *Comercio*, 23–24, 30 July 1850; "Informe del Consejo de Estado," *Comercio*, 14 Aug. 1850; Senate debates, *Comercio*, 18–23 Aug. 1851; "Reglamento de Comercio," *Comercio*, 27 Sept. 1851, 4 Mar. 1852; or parallel debates and reports in *Peruano* and *Progreso* 1849–51.
80. Basadre, *Historia* II:979–990; Hunt, "Growth and Guano" (1973), table 8, 69–71; Dancuart, *Anales*, vol. v (1850–55). See *Echenique a sus compatriotas*, 90–110, for another view of new economic forces.
81. Hunt, "Growth and Guano" (1973), 86–96; Levin, *Export Economies*, ch. 2

("Peru in the Age of Guano"); Bonilla, *Guano y burguesía*, 119–159; Maiguashca, "Reinterpretation of Guano Age."

82. D. Eliás, *Memoria que presenta el Ministro de Hacienda de la República del Perú a la Convención Nacional de 1855* (Lima, pam., 1855), 15–24, anexo (tax reforms); Hunt, "Growth and Guano" (1973), 61–81; McQueen, *Peruvian Finance*, 1–10.

83. Hunt, "Growth and Guano" (1973), 97–107; Corden, "Booming Sector and Dutch Disease"; Gootenberg, "Artisans and Merchants," chs. 3–5 (on manufacturing possibilities).

84. For liberalism during 1870s crises, see J. M. Osores, *Conferencias sobre materias económicas dadas en el Club Literario* (Lima, pam., 1876), or M. A. Fuentes, *Catecismo de economía política* (Lima, pam., 1877). For concepts of rentier economy and class, see Hunt, "Growth and Guano" (1973), 110–112; Bonilla, *Guano y burguesía*, chs. 1, 3.

85. Silva, *Reflexiones sobre los sucesos con la importación; Comercio*, 20–31 Dec. 1858; Giesecke, *Masas urbanas y rebelión*, for a look at midcentury elite/mass politics.

86. Moore, *Social Origins of Dictatorship*; Coatsworth, "Orígines del authoritarianismo"; Véliz, *Centralist Tradition*, chs. 6–7; Gootenberg, "Artisans and Merchants," 52–65, 176–185, 220–221, and Gorman, "State, Elite, and Export" for ideas on evolving political culture.

87. Camprubí, *Historia de los bancos*, for a study of fiscal elites and ideology. See, too, Quiroz, *Deuda defraudada*, chs. 4–7, on liberal-statist nature; Yepes, *Desarrollo capitalista*, 60–67; and Bonilla, *Guano y burguesía*, 40–43.

88. Camprubí, *Historia de los bancos*, pt. III ("La intervención del estado—la crisis bancuaria"); Maiguashca, "Reinterpretation of Guano Age," ch. 6.

89. For relevant notions of state autonomy, see Berg and Weaver, "Reinterpretation of Political Change"; Coatsworth, "Obstacles to Growth," 94–100. Varied versions of social effects are in Skocpol, *States and Revolution*; North and Thomas, *Rise of Western World*; and Jones, *European Miracle*.

90. And fanciful plans: "Reunión de 7 de feb. de la Sociedad de Economía Política sobre el empleo más ventajoso que podría hacer el Perú de los recursos financieros que le ofrece extraordinariamente y temporalmente el huano," *Comercio*, 16 May 1856. For some other plans, see Casanova, *Ensayo sobre la industria algodonera*; Cisneros, *Ensayo sobre cuestiones económicas*; and Copello and Petriconi, *Estudio sobre la independencia económica* (a study of the 1870s crisis, as well). See Gootenberg, "Artisans and Merchants," 185–187, for some nationalist currents in the guano age.

91. Hunt, "Growth and Guano" (1973), 107–110; Maiguashca, "Reinterpretation of Guano Age," ch. 6.

CHAPTER 6

1. For recent approaches to Peruvian state-building, consult Gorman, "State, Elite, and Export"; Berg and Weaver, "Reinterpretation of Political Change"; Tantaleán, *Política económico-financiera*; Friedman, *The State and Underdevelopment*; and Saulniers and Revilla, "Economic Role of Peruvian State."

2. Gilpin, *Political Economy of International Relations*, ch. 3, for elaboration of Kindleberger's notion of "hegemon"; or McKeown, "Hegemonic Stability Theory and Tariffs Levels." For trade policy and state-building, see Gerschenkron, *Backwardness in Perspective*; Polanyi, *Great Transformation*; or

the Latin American studies in Love and Jacobsen, *Guiding the Invisible Hand.*

3. Bonilla and Spalding, "Independencia en el Perú." A running controversy, rather than a full revisionist portrait of independence, has emerged: see Fisher, "Royalism, Regionalism, and Rebellion," 232–240; Bonilla et al., *Independencia en el Perú,* 2nd ed. (1981), "Presentación"; Bonilla, "New Profile of History," 216; or Flores, *Independencia y revolución.*

4. Frank, *Lumpenbourgeoisie.* Bollinger, "Bourgeois Revolution," 34–36 ("The Origins of Dependency Theory in Peru") underscores the impact of Haya de la Torre, but not of Mariátegui's *Seven Essays.* Also see the approach to Latin America's bourgeoisie in Véliz, *Centralist Tradition,* chs. 6–8, 12–13; or see Hirschman, "Rival Views of Market Society," 124–132, for the paradoxes of "feeble bourgeoisie" theories.

5. Most criticisms of dependency focus on its "feudal"/"capitalist" dichotomy, overlooking the dilemmas of its theory of nationalism, or of the "dependent" bourgeoisie. And curiously, dependentistas themselves have made little attempt overall to defend their suggestive theory. For a few of the countless critiques, see Staniland, *What Is Political Economy?* ch. 5 ("International Political Economy"); Cardoso, "Consumption of Dependency Theory"; Halperín-Donghi, "Dependency and Historiography"; Brenner, "Origins of Capitalist Development"; and Palma, "Dependency: Theory or Methodology?"

6. Questions implied in recent "state-building" and "nationalism" literature: e.g., Tilly, *Formation of National States;* Breuilly, *Nationalism and the State;* B. Anderson, *Imagined Communities;* Corrigan and Sayer, *Great Arch.* While they are largely separated in Latin Americanist studies (e.g., Buisson et al., *Formación del Estado y Nación*), some convergence of dependency and state-building views occurs in Torsvik, *Center-Periphery and Nation-Building,* and Arnaud, *Estado y capitalismo en América Latina.*

7. Bonilla, "Perú entre Independencia y Guerra," and *Siglo a la deriva;* Cotler, *Clases, estado y nación;* Ycpes, *Desarrollo capitalista;* Tantaleán, *Política económico-financiera.*

8. See the discussion under "Liberal Peru and the Historians," Chapter 1, above; or, in general, the issue of socioeconomic alternatives posed in Burns, *Poverty of Progress,* and Albert, *South America and World Economy.*

9. For example: "Reglamento de Comercio," *El Comercio* (Lima), July 1850; Silva, *Reflexiones sobre los sucesos con la importación* (see Chapter 3, n. 39, above); *Dictamen de la Cámara sobre gremios* (see Chapter 4, n. 43, above); Peru, Congreso, *La protección y la libertad: debates del Senado* (Lima, pam., 1868); or (much later) in Bertram, "Garland: The Ideologist."

10. Hirschman, *Passions and Interests:* a work influenced by, but rarely applied to, Latin America. For the region's long-term liberal hegemony, see Love, "Structural Change in Latin America and Romania"; for another "social conflict" view, see Mallon, "Peasants and State Formation."

11. These conclusions verge on suggestions in Friedman, *The State and Underdevelopment* (which treats external dependency as a response to internal, state-building crises), and diverge from the more positive views of caudillismo in Beezley, "Caudillismo," and Burns, *Poverty of Progress.*

12. Thorp and Bertram, *Peru,* analyzes these cycles, which are analogous to Malloy's political stages of delayed development (*Authoritarianism and Corporatism,* 5–13). For even more baffling policy cycles, see Hirschman, "Political Economy: Exercises in Retrospection," 22–34.

13. For example, Zeitlin, *Civil Wars in Chile*, 1–20, 218–237 (and note the work's suggestive subtitle). Burns, *Poverty of Progress*, chs. 6–7, remains cautious on the generation of historical alternatives.

14. White, *Paraguay's Autonomous Revolution*; Williams, *Rise and Fall of the Paraguayan Republic*. Dependency fatalism evident in Stein and Stein, *Colonial Heritage*, based, of course, on the region's long-term history of colonized elites.

15. E. Laclau suggested this Gramscian distinction to me; see Cotler, *Clases, estado y nación*, for a recent fusion of Gramscian and dependency sociology. For the variety of nationalism typologies, see Kohn, *Nationalism*; Seton-Watson, *Nations and States*; Gellner, *Nations and Nationalism*; Whitaker, *Nationalism in Latin America*; A. Smith, *Theories of Nationalism*; Tivey, *The Nation-State*; or Eley, "Nationalism and History." The continuum employed resembles Stepan's dichotomy of "exclusionary" and "inclusionary" corporatism (*The State and Society*, pt. i), another conception based on Peru.

16. Andrews, "Independence: A Structural Analysis"; Skocpol, *States and Revolution*; but see, for example, our most complex case of nationalism in Sinkin, *Mexican Reform*, and Katz, *Secret War in Mexico*.

17. Chaplin, *Peruvian Nationalism*; Stepan, *The State and Society*; or historical analysis in Pike, *U.S. and the Andean Republics*. Also see Thorp and Bertram, *Peru*, ch. 15 (which treats the Velasco regime as a failed attempt at a nationalist "dependency" program).

18. See Halperín-Donghi, "Dependency and Historiography." Frank, in "Dependence Is Dead, Long Live Dependence," has fun with the theory's political puzzles. See Staniland, *What Is Political Economy?* ch. 5, for "world systems" praxis; Cotler, *Democracia e integración*, 12–17, as one "nationalist project" view.

19. To my knowledge, no analytic interpretation of dependency theory (or, for that matter, neoclassical trade theory) exists; both possibilities are intriguing.

20. *Los Clamores del Perú* (Lima), Feb.–Mar. 1827, for initial popular protectionism; Gootenberg, "Social Origins of Protectionism," 355–357, for later class differentiation around tariffs.

21. For example, Bonilla, "Clases populares y crisis colonial." Mallon, *Defense of Community*, chs. 1–2, not only specifies class roots of elite reaction, but (ch. 3) analyzes its impact on "nationalism" (a peasant variety, reactive to foreign invasion).

22. Breuilly, *Nationalism and the State*, for analysis of the elite/conservative thrust of European nationalist movements. Voluntaristic projections of reformist expectations onto Peru's nineteenth-century elites (e.g., Bonilla, *Guano y burguesía*, 26–65, or "Perú entre Independencia y Guerra," 470–472) have recently drawn criticism: Gilbert, *Oligarquía peruana*, 25; Rochabrún, "La visión del Perú," 72–73.

23. Two influential analyses of modern dualism as an obstacle to reform are Webb, "Policy and the Distribution of Income," and Fitzgerald, *The State and Development*.

24. Three classic works on economic and political dilemmas of defensive ("late") nationalism are Gerschenkron, *Backwardness in Perspective*; Moore, *Social Origins of Dictatorship*; and Hirschman, "Political Economy of Industrializa-

tion" (whose "late-late" developers and nationalism suffer the extra burdens of revolutionary social expectations).

25. Anna, *Fall of Royal Government*; Fisher, "Formación del Estado Peruano"; Bonilla, "Continuidad y cambio en el Estado independiente." Peru appears extreme even when compared to another reactive, "embryonic" nationalism: Brading, *Orígenes del nacionalismo mexicano*.

26. On the locus of liberalism, see Graham, *Independence in Latin America*, ch. 3; Safford, "Commercial Crisis and Economic Ideology," esp. 6–7. Cf. Peru with Argentina: Burgin, *Economic Aspects of Argentine Federalism*.

27. Flores, *Aristocracia y plebe*; Pike, *U.S. and the Andean Republics*, 50–72, analyzes this Hapsburg/Bourbon rift, yet locates Lima as the coastal core of Peruvian liberalism; cf. Palmer, *Peru: The Authoritarian Tradition*, ch. 2, for the impact of colonial "penetration."

28. For consulado rebirth, *La Prensa Peruana* (Lima), 23 Sept. 1829; Tribunal del Consulado, *Representación al Congreso sobre el cumplimiento de la ley de 26 de nov. de 1829 que manda la restauración del Tribunal del Consulado* (Lima, pam., 1832); *La Gaceta del Gobierno* (Lima), 15 Mar. 1835; and esp. BRT 1839.

29. For example: AGN H-1 248/647–656, Consulado, "Documentos referentes a los mercachifles," Aug.–Sept. 1836; *Gaceta*, June 1835. The wider effect was a kind of institutional "feudalism" depressing all market activities until the 1850s: Basadre, "Interpretación del Código Civil de 1852," 48–72; Gootenberg, "Patterns of Economic Institutional Change."

30. For recent conceptions of these conflicts, see Coatsworth, "Limits of Colonial Absolutism," 25–53; Glade, *Latin American Economies*, chs. 2–4; and Véliz, *Centralist Tradition*, chs. 6–7. For Peru's resistance to the Bourbons, see Fisher, *Government and Society in Peru*, and Wibel, "Evolution of Arequipa, 1780–1845," chs. 1–8.

31. Stein and Stein, *Colonial Heritage*, chs. 5–6; Halperín-Donghi, *Historia contemporánea*, chs. 3–4; cf. view of nineteenth century in Coatsworth, "Obstacles to Growth," 95–100, or "Orígenes del autoritarianismo."

32. Consult any of the many collections: notably, Pike and Stritch *The New Corporatism* (esp. Schmitter, "Still the Century of Corporatism?" 85–131); Malloy, *Authoritarianism and Corporatism*; Wiarda, *Corporatism and National Development*.

33. For further analysis of merchants as a "ruling class," see Gootenberg, "Merchants, Foreigners, and the State," 61–67, 143–155; or see Quiroz, "Estructura de la clase dominante."

34. Relevant recent analyses of relations among merchants, states, and modes of production include Genovese and Fox, " 'Janus Face' of Merchant Capital"; Gintis and Bowles, "State and Class in Feudalism"; P. Anderson, *Lineages of the Absolutist State*; or, wider still, Wolf, *People without History*.

35. Hirschman, "Ideologies of Development," 4–9; Macera, "Historia económica como ciencia" (and "Algodón y comercio exterior"); Whitaker, *Nationalism in Latin America*, 16, 20–22; Véliz, *Centralist Tradition*, ch. 8 ("Outward-Looking Nationalism and the Liberal Pause"). Burns, *Poverty of Progress*, ch. 5, while similar, also stresses an early elite antiliberalism.

36. Three of countless acts of official Peruvian resistance: FO61/11, Ricketts to Canning, "A Few Remarks Connected with the Commerce of Peru," 11 May 1827; T52/2, Larned to Van Buren, "Conference on the Subject of Prohibitory

Duties," 20 Apr. 1830; CCC/6, Le Moyne to Charun, 19 Apr. 1842. See Chapter 3, above, for nationalist projects.

37. See Safford's query on ideologies in "Commercial Crisis and Economic Ideology," 3–4, 13–14, 24–27. Recent economic nationalists are embracing a similar discourse: A. García, "Discurso del Presidente de la República" (to Latin American labor leaders, Lima), *El Peruano* (Lima), 16 Aug. 1986.

SELECT BIBLIOGRAPHY

ARCHIVES

Peru

Archivo General de la Nación, Lima
    Section H-1, Archivo Histórico de Hacienda, OL 1–422, Comunicaciones del Ministerio de Hacienda, cartas/oficios, 1821–58 (Tribunal del Consulado, Tesorería General, Aduanas, Prefecturas, Municipalidad de Lima, Empréstitos, Comisiones de Hacienda, Expedientes y Solicitudes, Patentes, Hospitales Militares)
    Section H-4, Libros Manuscritos Republicanos de la Sección Hacienda, 1821–61. (Tribunal del Consulado, Matrículas de Patentes, Cámara de Diputados, Consejo de Estado, Ramo de Arbitrios)
    Section H-8, Tribunal del Consulado (Republicano), Legajos 1–125, 1821–60 (Administrativo, Elecciones, Empréstitos, Libros de Cuentas, Contenciosos/Concursos)
    Notariales, Siglo XIX
    Periódicos Oficiales

Archivo General del Ministerio de Relaciones Exteriores del Perú, Lima
    Section 2-0-D, Prefectura de Lima, 1821–60
    Section 2-0-E, Prefecturas de Departamentos, 1821–60
    Section 6, Servicio Diplomático Extranjero, Legaciones de los Estados Unidos, Francia, Italia, 1828–45
    Section 9, Servicio Consular Extranjero, Legaciones de los Estados Unidos, Francia, Italia, 1830–44
    Archivadores (papeles sueltos)

Archivo de la Beneficencia Pública de Lima
    Hospitales, Libros de Cuentas, 1821–66

Archivo Municipal de Lima (Biblioteca Municipal de Lima)
    Libros de Cabildos, Actas de la Municipalidad, Libros 45–49, 1821–39
    Papeles Sueltos (Municipalidad, Junta Departamental, Policía), 1822–40
    Paquetes 22, 47, 64, 1829–39
    Censo General de Lima, 1831
    Periódicos Oficiales, 1828–55

Biblioteca Denegri Luna, Lima
    Memorias, newspapers, pamphlets

Biblioteca Nacional del Perú, Lima
    Colección de Manuscritos, Section D, 1828–60
    Hemeroteca (newspapers)
    Colecciones Zegarra, Porras (pamphlets)
    Volantes (broadsides)

Instituto Riva Agüero, Lima
    Actas del Congreso del Perú, 1822–52
    Newspapers

Museo Nacional de Historia, Lima
  Manuscritos Republicanos
  Pamphlets

France

Archives du Ministère des Affaires Etrangères, Paris
  Correspondance Consulaire et Commerciales, Lima, vols. 1–12, 1821–60
  Correspondance Consulaire et Commerciales, Arequipa/Arica, vol. 1, 1844–48
  Correspondance Politique, Pérou, vols. 1–16, 1798–1847

Great Britain

Public Record Office, London
  Foreign Office, Series 61, Correspondence between British Diplomatic and
    Consular Officers in Peru and the Foreign Office
  FO61, vols. 1–187, 1823–60
  British Reports on Trade, 1824, 1827, 1834, 1837, 1838, 1839, 1840

United States

National Archives, Washington, D.C.
  Record Group 59, General Records of the Department of State (film microcop-
    ies of records in the National Archives)
  M154, Dispatches from United States Consuls in Lima, vols. 1–6, 1823–54
  M155, Dispatches from United States Consuls in Callao, vols. 1–5, 1845–61
  T52, Dispatches from United States Ministers to Peru, vols. 1–16, 1826–61
  T781, Records of the United States Consulate at Callao-Lima, vols. 1–8,
    1825–64

Sterling Library, Yale University
  Manuscripts, newspapers, pamphlets

Newberry Library, Chicago
  Travelers' accounts

NEWSPAPERS
(*indicates official periodical)

El Acento de la Justicia (Cuzco), 1829
El Amigo del Pueblo (Lima), 1840
La Bolsa (Lima), 1841–42
Los Clamores del Perú (Lima), 1827
El Comercio (Lima), 1839–60
*El Conciliador (Lima), 1830–34
El Correo de Lima (Lima), 1850–51
El Eco de la Opinión del Perú (Lima), 1827
*El Eco del Protectorado (Lima), 1836–37
El Estandarte (Lima), 1836–37
*La Gaceta del Gobierno Legítimo (Lima), 1822–25
*La Gaceta del Gobierno (Lima), 1835
El Genio del Rimac (Lima), 1833–35

Los Intereses del País (Cuzco), 1848–51
El Intérprete del Pueblo (Lima), 1852
El Limeño (Lima), 1834–35
El Mapa Político y Literario (Lima), 1843–44
El Mensajero de Tacna (Tacna), 1839
El Mercurio Peruano (Lima), 1827–32
La Minerva del Cuzco (Cuzco), 1831–32
La Miscelánea (Lima), 1830–33
El Nacional (Arequipa), 1844–45
El Peruano (Lima), 1827, 1838–51
La Prensa Peruana (Lima), 1827–29
El Progreso (Lima), 1849–51
El Rebeñique (Lima), 1841
El Redactor (Lima), 1834
El Redactor Peruano (Lima), 1836–38
El Regenerador (Arequipa), 1841
El Rejistro Oficial (Lima), 1851–54
El Repertorio Peruano (Lima), 1843
La Revista de Lima (Lima), 1860–62
El Rimac (Lima), 1850–51
El Telégrafo de Lima (Lima), 1827–39
El Tribunal del Pueblo (Lima), 1838–39
La Zamacueca Política (Lima), 1859
El Zurriago (Lima), 1848

SECONDARY WORKS

Abel, Christopher, and Colin Lewis, eds. *Latin America, Economic Imperialism, and the State: The Political Economy of the External Connection from Independence to the Present*. London: Athlone Press, 1985.

Albert, Bill. *South America and the World Economy from Independence to 1930*. London: Macmillan, 1983.

Anderson, Benedict. *Imagined Communities: Reflections on the Origin and Spread of Nationalism*. London: Verso, 1983.

Anderson, Perry. *Lineages of the Absolutist State*. London: New Left Books, 1974.

Andrews, George Reid. "Spanish American Independence: A Structural Analysis." *Latin American Perspectives* 12 (1985): 105–132.

Anna, Timothy E. *The Fall of the Royal Government in Peru*. Lincoln: University of Nebraska Press, 1979.

Aréstegui, Narciso. *El Padre Horán*. 2 vols. Lima: Editorial Universo, 1969.

Arnaud, Pascual. *Estado y capitalismo en América Latina: caso de México y Argentina*. Mexico: Siglo XXI, 1981.

Baltes, Peter. "José María Pando: colaborador de Gamarra." Tesis de Bachiller, Pontificia Universidad Católica del Perú, 1968.

Basadre, Jorge. "Hacia una interpretación histórica del Código Civil de 1852." *Revista de Derecho y Ciencia Política* (Lima) 1 (1942): 48–72.

———. *Historia de la República del Perú*. Rev. 5th ed. 11 vols. Lima: Editorial Peruamérica, 1963.

———. *La multitud, la ciudad y el campo en la historia del Perú*. Lima: Imprenta A. J. Rivas, 1929.

Basadre, Jorge. *Peru: problema y posibilidad*. Lima: F. y E. Rosay, 1931.

Beezley, William H. "Caudillismo: An Interpretive Note." *Journal of Inter-American Studies* 11 (1969): 345–353.

Berg, Ronald, and Frederick S. Weaver. "Toward a Reinterpretation of Political Change in Peru during the First Century of Independence." *Journal of Inter-American Studies and World Affairs* 20 (1978): 69–84.

Bertram, Geoffrey. "Alejandro Garland: The Ideologist of 'Desarrollo Hacia Afuera.' " MS, Oxford, 1974.

Blanchard, Peter. "Socio-Economic Change in the Ica Region in the Mid-19th Century." Paper presented at 46th International Congress of Americanists, Amsterdam, 1988.

Bollinger, William S. "The Bourgeois Revolution in Peru: A Conception of Peruvian History." *Latin American Perspectives* 4 (1977): 18–57.

———. "The Evolution of Dependence: U.S.-Peruvian Trade, 1824–1923." MS, University of California–Los Angeles, 1973.

Boloña, Carlos A. "Tariff Policies in Peru, 1880–1980." D.Phil. thesis, Oxford University, 1981.

Bonilla, Heraclio. "Clases populares y Estado en el contexto de la crisis colonial." In *La Independencia en el Peru*, 13–76. 2nd ed. Edited by Bonilla et al. Lima: Instituto de Estudios Peruanos, 1982.

———. "Continuidad y cambio en la organización política del Estado en el Perú independiente." In *Problemas de la formación del Estado y de la Nación en Hispanoamérica*, 481–498. Edited by I. Buisson et al. Cologne: Böhlau Verlag, 1984.

———. "La coyuntura comercial del siglo XIX en el Perú." *Desarrollo Económico* 46 (1972): 305–331.

———. "La emergencia del control norteamericano sobre la economía peruana: 1850–1930." *Estudios Sociales Centroaméricanos* 5 (1976): 97–122.

———. "La expansión comercial británica en el Perú." *Revista del Museo Nacional* (Lima) 40 (1974): 253–275.

———, comp. *Gran Bretaña y el Perú: informes de los cónsules británicos*. 5 vols. Lima: Instituto de Estudios Peruanos and Banco Industrial del Perú, 1977.

———. *Gran Bretaña y el Perú: los mecanismos de un control económico*. Lima: Instituto de Estudios Peruanos, 1977.

———. *Guano y burguesía en el Perú*. Lima: Instituto de Estudios Peruanos, 1974.

———. "The New Profile of Peruvian History." *Latin American Research Review* 16 (1981): 210–225.

———. "Peru and Bolivia from Independence to the War of the Pacific." In *The Cambridge History of Latin America* III:539–572. Edited by Leslie Bethell. Cambridge: Cambridge University Press, 1985.

———. "El Perú entre la Independencia y la Guerra con Chile." In *Historia del Perú* VI:395–473. Edited by Juan Mejía Baca. Lima: Mejía Baca, 1980.

———. *Un siglo a la deriva: ensayos sobre el Perú, Bolivia y la guerra*. Lima: Instituto de Estudios Peruanos, 1980.

Bonilla, Heraclio, Lía del Río, and Pilar Ortiz de Zevallos. "Comercio Libre y crisis de la economía andina: el caso del Cuzco." *Histórica* (Lima) 2 (1978): 1–25.

Bonilla, Heraclio, and Karen Spalding. "La Independencia en el Perú: las palabras y los hechos." In *La Independencia en el Perú*, 15–65. Edited by Bonilla et al. Lima: Instituto de Estudios Peruanos, 1972.

Brading, David A. *Los orígines del nacionalismo mexicano*. Mexico: Fondo de Cultura Económica, 1973.

Brenner, Robert. "Origins of Capitalist Development: A Critique of Neo-Smithean Marxism." *New Left Review* 104 (1977): 25–92.

Breuilly, John. *Nationalism and the State*. New York: St. Martin's Press, 1982.

Buisson, I., G. Kahle, and H.-J. Konig, eds. *Problemas de la formación del Estado y de la Nación en Hispanoamérica*. Cologne: Böhlau Verlag, 1984.

Burga, Manuel. *De la encomienda a la hacienda capitalista: el valle del Jequetepeque del siglo XVI al XX*. Lima: Instituto de Estudios Peruanos, 1976.

Burgin, Miron. *The Economic Aspects of Argentine Federalism, 1820–1852*. Cambridge: Harvard University Press, 1946.

Burns, E. Bradford. *The Poverty of Progress: Latin America in the Nineteenth Century*. Berkeley: University of California Press, 1980.

Burr, Robert N. *By Reason or Force: Chile and the Balancing of Power in South America, 1830–1905*. Berkeley: University of California Press, 1974.

Bustamante, Juan. *Apuntes y observaciones civiles, políticas y religiosas con las noticias adquiridas en esa segunda viaje a la Europa por el Peruano D. Juan Bustamante*. Paris: Imprenta de Lacrampe Son y Cía., 1849.

Camprubí Alcázar, Carlos. *Historia de los bancos en el Perú (1860–1879)*. Lima: Editorial Lumen, 1957.

Caravedo M., Baltazar. "El problema del centralismo en el Perú republicano." *Análisis* (Lima) 7 (1979): 19–51.

Cardoso, Fernando Henrique. "The Consumption of Dependency Theory in the United States." *Latin American Research Review* 7 (1977): 7–25.

Cardoso, Fernando Henrique, and Enzo Faletto. *Dependency and Development in Latin America*. Translated by M. Urquidi. Berkeley: University of California Press, 1979.

Carpio, Juan. "Rebeliones arequipeñas del siglo XIX y configuraciones de la oligarquía 'nacional.'" *Análisis* 11 (1982): 33–45.

Carrasco, Eduardo. *Calendario y guía de forasteros de la República Peruana para el año de 1849*. Lima: J. Masías, 1848.

Casanova, Juan Norberto. *Ensayo económico-político sobre el porvenir de la industria algodonera fabril del Perú*. Lima: J. Masías, 1849.

Céspedes del Castillo, Guillermo. "Lima y Buenos Aires: repercusiones económicas y políticas de la creación del virreinato del Río de la Plata." *Anuario de Estudios Americanos* 3 (1946): 667–874.

Chaplin, David, ed. *Peruvian Nationalism: A Corporatist Revolution?* New Brunswick, N.J.: Transaction Books, 1976.

Choquehuanca, José Domingo. *Ensayo de estadística completa de los ramos económicos-políticos de la Provincia de Azángaro en el Departamento de Puno de la República Peruana del quinquenio desde 1825 hasta 1829 inclusive*. Lima: Imprenta M. Corral, 1833.

Cisneros, Luis Benjamín. *Ensayo sobre varias cuestiones económicas del Perú*. Le Havre: Tipografía del Comercio, 1866.

Clayton, Lawrence. "Private Matters: The Origins and Nature of U.S.-Peruvian Relations, 1820–50." *The Americas* 62 (1986): 377–419.

Cleven, N. Andrew. "Dictators Gamarra, Orbegoso, Salaverry, and Santa Cruz." In *South American Dictators during the First Century of Independence*, 289–

334. Edited by A. Curtis Wilgus. Washington, D.C.: George Washington University Press, 1937.

Coatsworth, John H. "The Limits of Colonial Absolutism: The State in Eighteenth-Century Mexico." In *Essays in the Political, Economic, and Social History of Colonial Latin America*, 25–51. Edited by Karen Spalding. Newark: University of Delaware Press, 1982.

———. "Obstacles to Economic Growth in Nineteenth-Century Mexico." *American Historical Review* 83 (1978): 80–100.

———. "Los orígenes del autoritarianismo moderno en México." *Foro Internacional* 16 (1975): 205–232.

Collier, David., ed. *The New Authoritarianism in Latin America*. Princeton: Princeton University Press, 1979.

Copello, Juan, and Luis Petriconi. *Estudio sobre la independencia económica del Perú*. Lima: Imprenta de El Nacional, 1876.

Corden, W. M. "Booming Sector and Dutch Disease Economics: Survey and Consolidation." *Oxford Economic Papers* 36 (1984): 359–380.

Córdova y Urrutia, José María. *Estadística histórica, geográfica, industrial y comercial de los pueblos que componen las provincias del Departamento de Lima*. Lima: Imprenta de Instrucción Primaria, 1839.

Coronel Zegarra, Félix C. *La condición jurídica de los estranjeros en el Perú*. Santiago: Imprenta de la Libertad, 1872.

Corrigan, Philip, and Derek Sayer. *The Great Arch: English State Formation as Cultural Revolution*. Oxford: Basil Blackwell, 1985.

Cortés Conde, Roberto, and Stanley J. Stein, eds. *Latin America: A Guide to Economic History, 1830–1930*. Berkeley: University of California Press, 1977.

Cotler, Julio. *Clases, estado y nación en el Perú*. Lima: Instituto de Estudios Peruanos, 1978.

———. *Democracia e integración nacional*. Lima: Instituto de Estudios Peruanos, 1980.

Dancuart, P. Emilio, comp. *Anales de la Hacienda Pública del Perú: historia y legislación fiscal de la República*. 24 vols. Lima: Imprenta Gil, 1902–26.

———. *Crónica parlamentaria del Perú*. 4 vols. [1821–57]. Lima: La Revista, 1906.

Dávila, Tomás. *Medios que se proponen al actual Congreso Constitucional del Perú y al Gobierno Supremo para salvar de su total destrucción la casi-arruinada agricultura de la importante Provincia de Moquegua*. Arequipa: Imprenta de Francisco Ibáñez y Hermano, 1853.

Deas, Malcolm. "The Fiscal Problems of Nineteenth-Century Colombia." *Journal of Latin American Studies* 14 (1982): 287–328.

Denegri Luna, Félix. "La antigua controversia sobre el Libre Comercio en el Cuzco de 1829." *Banca* (Lima) 2 (1982): 77–81.

———. *Historia marítima del Perú*. 2nd ed. Vol. VI: *La República, 1826 a 1851*. Lima: Instituto de Estudios Históricos-Marítimos del Perú, 1976.

Deustua, José. *La minería peruana y la iniciación de la República, 1820–1840*. Lima: Instituto de Estudios Peruanos, 1986.

Dobyns, Henry F., and Paul L. Doughty. *Peru: A Cultural History*. New York: Oxford University Press, 1976.

Doyle, Michael W. *Empires*. Ithaca, N.Y.: Cornell University Press, 1986.

Duncan, Kenneth, and Ian Rutledge, eds. *Land and Labour in Latin America: Essays on the Development of Agrarian Capitalism in the Nineteenth and Twentieth Centuries*. Cambridge: Cambridge University Press, 1977.

Eley, Geoff. "Nationalism and Social History." *Social History* 6 (1981): 83–108.

Engelsen, Juan Rolf. "Social Aspects of Agricultural Expansion in Coastal Peru, 1825–1878." Ph.D. diss., University of California–Los Angeles, 1977.

Esteves, Luis. *Apuntes para la historia económica del Perú*. Lima: Imprenta Huallaga, 1882.

Evans, Peter, Dietrich Rueschmeyer, and Theda Skocpol. "On the Road Toward a More Adequate Understanding of the State." In *Bringing the State Back In*, 347–366. Edited by Evans, Rueschmeyer, and Skocpol. Cambridge: Cambridge University Press, 1985.

Extracto de las sesiones de la Cámara de Diputados publicados en el "Comercio" de Lima. Lima: Imprenta del Comercio, 1845.

Fisher, John R. "La formación del Estado Peruano (1808–1824) y Simón Bolívar." In *Problemas de la formación del Estado y de la Nación en Hispanoamérica*, 465–480. Edited by I. Buisson et al. Cologne: Böhlau Verlag, 1984.

———. *Government and Society in Colonial Peru: The Intendant System, 1784–1814*. London: Athlone Press, 1970.

———. "Royalism, Regionalism, and Rebellion in Colonial Peru, 1808–1815." *Hispanic American Historical Review* 59 (1979): 232–258.

Fitzgerald, E. K. *The State and Economic Development: Peru since 1968*. Cambridge: Cambridge University Press, 1976.

Flores Galindo, Alberto. *Arequipa y el sur andino: siglos XVIII–XX*. Lima: Editorial Horizonte, 1977.

———. *Aristocracia y plebe: Lima, 1760–1830 (Estructura de clases y sociedad colonial)*. Lima: Mosca Azul Editores, 1984.

———, ed. *Independencia y revolución, 1780–1840*. 2 vols. Lima: Instituto Nacional de Cultura, 1987.

———. "El militarismo y la dominación británica (1825–1845)." In *Nueva historia general del Perú*, 107–123. Edited by C. Araníbar and H. Bonilla. Lima: Mosca Azul Editores, 1979.

Frank, André Gunder. *Capitalism and Underdevelopment in Latin America: Historical Studies of Chile and Brazil*. New York: Monthly Review Press, 1969.

———. "Dependence Is Dead, Long Live Dependence and the Class Struggle: A Reply to Critics." *Latin American Perspectives* 1 (1974): 89–106.

———. *Lumpenbourgeoisie and Lumpendevelopment: Dependency, Class, and Politics in Latin America*. New York: Monthly Review Press, 1972.

Friedman, Douglas. *The State and Underdevelopment in Spanish America: The Political Roots of Dependency in Peru and Argentina*. Boulder, Colo.: Westview Press, 1984.

Fuentes, Manuel A. *Estadística general de Lima*. Lima: Tipografía Nacional, 1858.

Furtado, Celso. *Economic Development of Latin America: A Survey from Colonial Times to the Cuban Revolution*. Translated by S. Macedo. Cambridge: Cambridge University Press, 1970.

Gallagher, J., and R. Robinson. "The Imperialism of Free Trade." *Economic History Review*, Second Series 6 (1953): 1–15.

García Vera, José Antonio. "Aduanas y comerciantes: Trujillo 1796–1836." MS, Buenos Aires, 1987.

Gellner, Ernest. *Nations and Nationalism*. Oxford: Basil Blackwell, 1983.

Genovese, Eugene, and Elizabeth Fox. "The 'Janus Face' of Merchant Capital." In Genovese and Fox, *Fruits of Merchant Capital*, 3–27. New York: Oxford University Press, 1983.

217

Gerschenkron, Alexander. *Economic Backwardness in Historical Perspective.* Cambridge: Harvard University Press, 1966.

Giesecke, Margarita. *Masas urbanas y rebelión en la historia: golpe de estado, Lima, 1872.* Lima: CEDHIP, 1978.

Gilbert, Dennis. *La oligarquía peruana: historia de tres familias.* Translated by M. Mould de Pease. Lima: Editorial Horizonte, 1982.

Gilpin, Robert. *The Political Economy of International Relations.* Princeton: Princeton University Press, 1987.

Gintis, Herbert, and Samuel Bowles. "State and Class in European Feudalism." In *Statemaking and Social Movements: Essays in History and Theory,* 19–52. Edited by Charles Bright and Susan Harding. Ann Arbor: University of Michigan Press, 1984.

Glade, William. *The Latin American Economies: A Study of Their Institutional Evolution.* New York: Van Nostrand, 1969.

Gleason, Daniel M. "Ideological Cleavages in Early Republican Peru, 1821–1872." Ph.D. diss., University of Notre Dame, 1974.

Gootenberg, Paul. "Artisans and Merchants: The Making of an Open Economy in Lima, Peru, 1830 to 1860." M.Phil. thesis, Oxford University, 1981.

———. "Beleaguered Liberals: The Failed First Generation of Free Traders in Peru." In *Guiding the Invisible Hand: Economic Liberalism and the State in Latin American History,* 63–97. Edited by Joseph Love and Nils Jacobsen. New York: Praeger, 1988.

———. "Carneros y Chuño: Price Levels in Nineteenth-Century Peru." *Hispanic American Historical Review* 70 (1990) (Forthcoming).

———. "Fabricks and Flours, Hearts and Minds: A United States Imperialism of Free Trade in Peru, 1825–1840." MS, Boston, 1987.

———. "Merchants, Foreigners, and the State: The Origins of Trade Policies in Post-Independence Peru." Ph.D. diss., University of Chicago, 1985.

———. "North-South: Trade Policy, Regionalism, and Caudillismo in Post-Independence Peru." MS, Boston, 1988.

———. "The Patterns of Economic Institutional Change in Nineteenth-Century Peru." B.A. thesis, University of Chicago, 1978.

———. "The Social Origins of Protectionism and Free Trade in Nineteenth-Century Lima." *Journal of Latin American Studies* 14 (1982): 329–358.

Gorman, Stephen M. "The State, Elite, and Export in Nineteenth-Century Peru: Toward an Alternative Reinterpretation of Political Change." *Journal of Inter-American Studies and World Affairs* 21 (1979): 395–419.

Gosselman, Carl August. *Informes sobre los Estados Sudamericanos en los años de 1837 y 1838.* Translated by Ernesto DeThorey. Stockholm: Instituto de Estudios Ibero-Americanos, 1962.

Graham, Richard. *Independence in Latin America: A Comparative Approach.* New York: Alfred A. Knopf, 1972.

Griffin, Charles C. "Economic and Social Aspects of the Era of Spanish American Independence." *Hispanic American Historical Review* 29 (1949): 170–187.

Griffin, Keith. *Underdevelopment in Spanish America.* London: Allen & Unwin, 1969.

Halperín-Donghi, Tulio. "Dependency Theory and Latin American Historiography." *Latin American Research Review* 17 (1982): 115–150.

———. *Historia contemporánea de América Latina.* Madrid: Alianza Editorial, 1969.

Harth-Terré, Emilio, and Alberto Márquez Abanto. "Las bellas artes en el Virreinato del Perú: perspectiva social y económica del artesano virreinal en Lima." *Revista del Archivo Nacional del Perú* 26 (1962): 352–446.

Helmer, M. "Commerce et industrie au Pérou a la fin du XVIIIᵐᵉ siècle." *Revista de Indias* 10 (1950): 519–526.

Herrera Alarcón, Dante. *Rebeliones que intentaron desmembrar el sur del Perú*. Callao: Colegio Militar Prado, 1961.

Hicks, John. *A Theory of Economic History*. Oxford: Oxford University Press, 1969.

Hirschman, Albert O. "Against Parsimony: Three Easy Ways of Complicating Some Categories of Economic Discourse." In Hirschman, *Rival Views of Market Society and Other Essays*, 142–163. New York: Viking, 1986.

———. "Ideologies of Economic Development in Latin America." In Hirschman, ed., *Latin American Issues: Essays and Comments*. New York: Twentieth Century Fund, 1961.

———. *The Passions and the Interests: Political Arguments for Capitalism before Its Triumph*. Princeton: Princeton University Press, 1977.

———. "The Political Economy of Import-Substituting Industrialization in Latin America." *Quarterly Journal of Economics* 82 (1968): 2–32.

———. "The Political Economy of Latin American Development: Seven Exercises in Retrospection." *Latin American Research Review* 22 (1987): 7–36.

———. "Rival Views of Market Society." In Hirschman, *Rival Views of Market Society and Other Essays*, 105–141. New York: Viking, 1986.

Humphreys, R. A., comp. *British Consular Reports on the Trade and Politics of Latin America, 1824–1826*. London: Royal Historical Society, 1940.

Hünefeldt, Christine. "Cimarrones, bandoleros y milicianos: 1821." *Histórica* 3 (1979): 71–88.

———. "Los extranjeros y el siglo XIX: Perú." MS, Lima, 1980.

———. "Los negros de Lima: 1800–1830." *Histórica* 3 (1979): 17–51.

Hunt, Shane J. "Growth and Guano in Nineteenth-Century Peru." Discussion Paper 34, RPED, Woodrow Wilson School, Princeton University, 1973.

———. "Growth and Guano in Nineteenth-Century Peru." In *The Latin American Economies: Growth and the Export Sector, 1880–1930*, 255–319. Edited by Roberto Cortés Conde and Shane J. Hunt. New York: Holmes & Meier, 1985.

———. "Price and Quantum Estimates of Peruvian Exports, 1830–1962." Discussion Paper 33, RPED, Woodrow Wilson School, Princeton University, 1973.

Hunt, Shane J., and Pablo Macera. "Interpretive Essay." In *Latin America: A Guide to Economic History, 1830–1930*, 547–571. Edited by Roberto Cortés Conde and Stanley J. Stein. Berkeley: University of California Press, 1977.

Imlah, Albert. *Economic Elements in the Pax Britannica: Studies in British Foreign Trade in the Nineteenth Century*. New York: Russell & Russell, 1969.

Jacobsen, Nils. "Landtenure and Society in the Peruvian Altiplano: Azángaro Province, 1770–1920." Ph.D. diss., University of California–Berkeley, 1982.

Jaramillo, Juan Diego. *Bolívar y Canning, 1822–1827*. Bogotá: Banco de la República, 1983.

Johnson, Harry G. "A Theoretical Model of Economic Nationalism in New and Developing States." *Political Science Quarterly* 80 (1965): 165–185.

Jones, E. L. *The European Miracle: Environments, Economies, and Geopolitics in the History of Europe and Asia*. Cambridge: Cambridge University Press, 1981.

Katz, Friedrich. *The Secret War in Mexico: Europe, the United States, and the Mexican Revolution.* Chicago: University of Chicago Press, 1981.

Keen, Benjamin, and Mark Wasserman. *A History of Latin America.* Boston: Houghton Mifflin Company, 1988.

Kennedy, Paul. *The Rise and Fall of the Great Powers: Economic Change and Military Conflict from 1500 to 2000.* New York: Random House, 1987.

Kindleberger, Charles P. "The Rise of Free Trade in Western Europe, 1820–1875." *Journal of Economic History* 35 (1975): 20–56.

Kohn, Hans. *Nationalism: Its Meaning and History.* Princeton: Princeton University Press, 1955.

Ledos, Carlos. *Consideraciones sobre la agricultura.* Lima: J. Masías, 1847.

Leguía, Jorge Guillermo. "Las ideas de 1848 en el Perú." In Leguía, *Estudios históricos,* 113–144. Santiago: Ediciones Ercilla, 1939.

Levin, Jonathan V. *The Export Economies: Their Pattern of Development in Historical Perspective.* Cambridge: Harvard University Press, 1960.

Liss, Peggy K. *Atlantic Empires: The Network of Trade and Revolution, 1713–1826.* Baltimore: Johns Hopkins University Press, 1983.

Louis, W. R., ed. *Imperialism: The Robinson and Gallagher Controversy.* New York: New Viewpoints, 1976.

Love, Joseph L. "Structural Change and Conceptual Response in Latin America and Romania, 1860–1950." In *Guiding the Invisible Hand: Economic Liberalism and the State in Latin American History,* 1–34. Edited by Love and Nils Jacobsen. New York: Praeger, 1988.

Love, Joseph L., and Nils Jacobsen, eds. *Guiding the Invisible Hand: Economic Liberalism and the State in Latin American History.* New York: Praeger, 1988.

Lynch, John. *The Spanish-American Revolutions, 1808–1826.* New York: W. W. Norton, 1973.

Macera, Pablo. "Algodón y comercio exterior peruano en el siglo XIX." In Macera, *Trabajos de historia* III:275–296. Lima: Instituto Nacional de Cultura, 1977.

———. "La historia económica como ciencia en el Perú." In Macera, *Trabajos de historia* II:21–71. Lima: Instituto Nacional de Cultura, 1977.

———. "Las plantaciones azucareras andinas (1821–1875)." In Macera, *Trabajos de historia* IV:9–310. Lima: Instituto Nacional de Cultura, 1977.

McGreevy, William P. "Recent Research on the Economic History of Latin America." *Latin American Research Review* 3 (1968): 89–118.

McKeown, Timothy J. "Hegemonic Stability Theory and Nineteenth-Century Tariff Levels in Europe." *International Organization* 37 (1983): 73–91.

McQueen, Charles A. *Peruvian Public Finance.* Trade Promotion Series, no. 30. Washington, D.C.: U.S. Department of Commerce, 1926.

Maiguashca, Juan. "A Reinterpretation of the Guano Age, 1840–1880." D.Phil. thesis, Oxford University, 1967.

Mallon, Florencia E. *The Defense of Community in Peru's Central Highlands: Peasant Struggle and Capitalist Transition, 1860–1940.* Princeton: Princeton University Press, 1983.

———. "Economic Liberalism: Where We Are and Where We Need to Go." In *Guiding the Invisible Hand: Economic Liberalism and the State in Latin American History,* 177–186. Edited by Joseph Love and Nils Jacobsen. New York: Praeger, 1988.

———. "Peasants and State Formation in Nineteenth-Century Mexico: Morelos,

1848–1858." Paper presented at Latin American Studies Association, Boston, October 1986.

Malloy, James, ed. *Authoritarianism and Corporatism in Latin America.* Pittsburgh: University of Pittsburgh Press, 1977.

Manning, William R., comp. *Diplomatic Correspondence of the United States Concerning the Independence of the Latin American Nations.* Vol. III. New York: Oxford University Press, 1925.

————, comp. *Diplomatic Correspondence of the United States: Inter-American Affairs, 1831–1860.* Vol. X. Washington, D.C.: Carnegie Endowment for International Peace, 1938.

Mariátegui, José Carlos. *Seven Interpretive Essays on Peruvian Reality.* Translated by M. Urquidi. Austin: University of Texas Press, 1971.

Mathew, W. M. "Antony Gibbs and Sons, the Guano Trade, and the Peruvian Government, 1842–1861." In *Business Imperialism, 1840–1930: An Inquiry Based on British Experience in Latin America,* 337–370. Edited by D.C.M. Platt. Oxford: Oxford University Press, 1977.

————. "The First Anglo-Peruvian Debt and Its Settlement, 1822–1849." *Journal of Latin American Studies* 2 (1968): 81–98.

————. "Foreign Contractors and the Peruvian Government at the Outset of the Guano Trade." *Hispanic American Historical Review* 52 (1972): 589–620.

————. *The House of Gibbs and the Peruvian Guano Monopoly.* London: Royal Historical Society, 1981.

————. "The Imperialism of Free Trade: Peru, 1820–1870." *Economic History Review.* Second Series 21 (1968): 562–579.

————. "A Primitive Export Sector: Guano Production in Mid-Nineteenth Century Peru." *Journal of Latin American Studies* 9 (1977): 35–57.

Melzer, John T. S. "Kingdom to Republic in Peru: The 'Consulado de Comercio' of Lima and the Independence of Peru." Ph.D. diss., Tulane University, 1978.

Moore, Barrington Jr. *Social Origins of Dictatorship and Democracy.* Boston: Beacon Press, 1966.

Moscoso, Maximiliano. "Apuntes para la historia de la industria textil en el Cuzco colonial." *Revista Universitaria* (Cuzco) 122 (1962/63): 67–94.

Nolan, Louis Clinton. "The Diplomatic and Commercial Relations of the United States and Peru, 1826–1875." Ph.D. diss., Duke University, 1935.

North, Douglass C., and Robert P. Thomas. *The Rise of the Western World: A New Economic History.* Cambridge: Cambridge University Press, 1976.

Ospina Vásquez, Luis. *La industria y protección en Colombia 1810–1930.* Medellín: Editorial Santa Fé, 1955.

Oszlak, Oscar. "The Historical Formation of the State in Latin America: Some Theoretical and Methodological Guidelines for Its Study." *Latin American Research Review* 16 (1981): 3–33.

Oviedo, Juan., comp. *Colección de leyes, decretos y órdenes publicadas en el Perú desde el año de 1821 hasta 31 de diciembre de 1859.* 16 vols. Lima: F. Bailly, 1861–72.

Owen, Roger, and Bob Sutcliffe, eds. *Studies in the Theory of Imperialism.* London: Longman, 1972.

Palacios Moreyra, Carlos. *La deuda anglo-peruana, 1822–1890.* Lima: Librería Studium, 1983.

Palma, José Gabriel. "Dependency: A Formal Theory of Underdevelopment or a

Methodology for the Analysis of Concrete Situations of Underdevelopment?" *World Development* 6 (1978): 896–907.

———. "Growth and Structure of Chilean Manufacturing Industry from 1830 to 1935: Origins and Development of a Process of Industrialization in an Export Economy." D.Phil. thesis, Oxford University, 1979.

Palmer, David Scott. *Peru: The Authoritarian Tradition*. New York: Praeger, 1980.

Pásara, Luis. "El rol del derecho en la época del guano." *Derecho* (Lima) 28 (1970): 11–33.

Paz Soldán, Mariano Felipe. *Historia del Perú independiente: 1819–1839*. 4 vols. Lima: Imprenta El Havre, 1868–70.

Perú, Cámara Nacional de Diputados. *Historia del Parlamento Nacional: Actas de los Congresos del Perú desde el año de 1822*. 4 vols. [1822–28]. Lima: Cámara de Diputados, 1928.

Piel, Jean. "The Place of the Peasantry in the National Life of Peru in the Nineteenth Century." *Past and Present* 46 (1970): 108–133.

Pike, Fredrick B. *The Modern History of Peru*. New York: Praeger, 1967.

———. *The United States and the Andean Republics: Peru, Bolivia, and Ecuador*. Cambridge: Harvard University Press, 1977.

Pike, Fredrick B. and Thomas J. Stritch, eds. *The New Corporatism: Social-Political Structures in the Iberian World*. Notre Dame: University of Notre Dame Press, 1974.

Pincus, J. J. "Pressure Groups and the Patterns of Tariffs." *Journal of Political Economy* 83 (1975): 757–779.

Platt, D.C.M., ed. *Business Imperialism, 1840–1930: An Inquiry Based on British Experience in Latin America*. Oxford: Oxford University Press, 1977.

———. "Dependency in Nineteenth-Century Latin America: An Historian Objects." *Latin American Research Review* 15 (1980): 113–131.

———. "The Imperialism of Free Trade: Some Reservations." *Economic History Review*. Second Series 21 (1968): 296–306.

———. *Latin America and British Trade, 1806–1914*. New York: Harper & Row, 1973.

Polanyi, Karl. *The Great Transformation: The Political and Economic Origins of Our Time*. Boston: Beacon Press, 1957.

Ponce, Fernando Agustín. "The Social Structure of Arequipa, 1840–1879." Ph.D. diss., University of Texas–Austin, 1980.

Potash, Robert. *The Mexican Government and Industrial Development in the Early Republic: The Banco de Avío*. Amherst: University of Massachusetts Press, 1983.

Proctor, Robert. *Narrative of a Journey across the Cordillera of the Andes and of a Residence in Lima and other Parts of Peru, in the years 1823 and 1824*. London: Colburn & Bentley, 1825.

Quirós, Mariano Santos de, comp. *Colección de leyes, decretos y órdenes publicados en el Perú desde su Independencia en el año de 1821 hasta 1854*. 12 vols. Lima: J. Masías, 1831–54.

Quiroz, Alfonso W. "La consolidación de la deuda interna peruana, 1850–58: los efectos sociales de una medida financiera estatal." Tesis de Bachiller, Pontificia Universidad Católica del Perú, 1980.

———. *La deuda defraudada: consolidación de 1850 y dominio económico en el Perú*. Lima: Instituto Nacional de Cultura, 1987.

———. "Estructura económica y desarrollos regionales de la clase dominante,

1821–1850." In *Independencia y revolución* II:201–268. Edited by Alberto Flores Galindo. Lima: Instituto Nacional de Cultura, 1987.

Ramírez, Susan E. *Provincial Patriarchs: Land Tenure and the Economics of Power in Colonial Peru.* Albuquerque: University of New Mexico Press, 1988.

Randall, Laura. *A Comparative Economic History of Latin America, 1500–1914.* Vol. IV: *Peru.* New York: Institute of Latin American Studies, Columbia University, 1977.

Rector, John L. "Merchants, Trade, and Commercial Policy in Chile, 1810–1840." Ph.D. diss., Indiana University, 1976.

Regal, Alberto. *Historia de los ferrocarriles de Lima.* Lima: Instituto de Vías de Transporte, 1965.

Ridings, Eugene W. "Foreign Predominance among Overseas Traders in Nineteenth-Century Latin America." *Latin American Research Review* 20 (1985): 3–27.

Rivera Serna, Raúl. "Las Juntas Departamentales durante el primer gobierno del Mariscal Don Agustín Gamarra." *Boletín de la Biblioteca Nacional* (Lima) 17 (1964): 3–18.

Rivero, Francisco de. *Memoria o sean apuntamientos sobre la industria agrícola del Perú y sobre algunas medios que pudieran adoptarse para remediar su decadencia.* Lima: Monterola, 1845.

Robinson, Joan. *Reflections of the Theory of International Trade.* Manchester: University of Manchester Press, 1974.

Robinson, Joan, and John Eatwell. *An Introduction to Modern Economics.* London: McGraw-Hill, 1973.

Robinson, Ronald. "Non-European Foundations of European Imperialism: Sketch for a Theory of Collaboration." In *Studies in the Theory of Imperialism*, 117–143. Edited by Roger Owen and Bob Sutcliffe. London: Longman, 1072.

Rochabrún, Guillermo. "La visión del Perú de Julio Cotler," *Análisis* 4 (1978): 69–85.

Rodríguez, José M. *Estudios económicos y financieros y ojeado sobre la Hacienda Pública del Perú y la necesidad de su reforma.* Lima: Imprenta Gil, 1895.

———. "Historia de los contratos del guano y sus efectos en las finanzas del Perú." *El Economista Peruano* 6 (1921): 85–129.

Romero, Emilio. *Historia económica del Perú.* Buenos Aires: Editorial Sudamericano, 1949.

Romero, Luis Alberto. *La Sociedad de la Igualdad: los artesanos de Santiago de Chile y sus primeras experiencias políticas.* Buenos Aires: Instituto Torcuato DiTella, 1978.

Safford, Frank. "Commercial Crisis and Economic Ideology in New Granada, 1825–50." Paper presented at Latin American Studies Association, Boston, October 1986.

———. "Politics, Ideology, and Society in Post-Independence Spanish America." In *The Cambridge History of Latin America* III:347–421. Edited by Leslie Bethell. Cambridge: Cambridge University Press, 1985.

Salas, Miriam. "Los obrajes huamanguinos y sus interconexiones con otros sectores económicos en el centro-sur peruano a fines del siglo XVIII." In *The Economies of Mexico and Peru during the Late Colonial Period, 1760–1810*, 203–233. Edited by Nils Jacobsen and Hans-Jürgen Puhle. Berlin: Colloquium Verlag, 1986.

Salvucci, Richard J. *Textiles and Capitalism in Mexico: An Economic History of the Obrajes, 1539–1840.* Princeton: Princeton University Press, 1987.

Saulniers, Alfred, and Julio Revilla. "The Economic Role of the Peruvian State: 1821–1919." Paper presented at Latin American Studies Association, Mexico City, September 1983.

Schmitter, Philippe C. "Still the Century of Corporatism?" In *The New Corporatism,* 85–131. Edited by Fredrick B. Pike and Thomas J. Stritch. Notre Dame: University of Notre Dame Press, 1974.

Schmitter, Philippe C., John H. Coatsworth, and Joanne Fox Przeworski. "Historical Perspectives on the State, Civil Society, and the Economy in Latin America." MS, University of Chicago, 1976.

Semmel, Bernard. *The Rise of Free Trade Imperialism: Classical Political Economy, the Empire of Free Trade, and Imperialism, 1750–1850.* Cambridge: Cambridge University Press, 1970.

Seton-Watson, Hugh. *Nations and States: An Enquiry into the Origins of Nations and the Politics of Nationalism.* Boulder, Colo.: Westview Press, 1977.

Silva Santisteban, Fernando. *Los obrajes en el Virreinato del Perú.* Lima: Museo Nacional de Historia, 1964.

Sinkin, Richard. *The Mexican Reform, 1855–1876: A Study in Liberal Nation-Building.* Austin: University of Texas Press, 1979.

Skidmore, Thomas E., and Peter H. Smith. *Modern Latin America.* New York: Oxford University Press, 1984.

Skocpol, Theda. *States and Social Revolutions: A Comparative Analysis of France, Russia, and China.* Cambridge: Cambridge University Press, 1979.

Smith, Antony. *Theories of Nationalism.* New York: Holmes & Meier, 1971.

Smith, Tony. *The Pattern of Imperialism: The United States, Great Britain, and the Late-Industrializing World since 1815.* Cambridge: Cambridge University Press, 1981.

Staniland, Martin. *What Is Political Economy? A Study of Social Theory and Underdevelopment.* New Haven: Yale University Press, 1985.

Stein, Stanley J., and Barbara H. Stein. *The Colonial Heritage of Latin America: Essays on Economic Dependence in Perspective.* New York: Oxford University Press, 1970.

———. "D.C.M. Platt: The Anatomy of 'Autonomy.' " *Latin American Research Review* 15 (1980): 131–146.

Stepan, Alfred. *The State and Society: Peru in Comparative Perspective.* Princeton: Princeton University Press, 1978.

Stevenson, W. B. *A Historical and Descriptive Narrative of Twenty Years' Residence in South America.* 3 vols. London: Hurst, Robinson & Company, 1825.

Tantaleán Arbulú, Javier. *Política económico-financiera y la formación del Estado: siglo XIX.* Lima: CEDEP, 1983.

Távara, Santiago. *Historia de los partidos* [1862]. Lima: Jorge Basadre and Félix Denegri Luna, 1951.

Temperley, Harold. *The Foreign Policy of Canning, 1822–1827: The Neo-Holy Alliance and the New World.* London: Archon Books, 1966.

Tenenbaum, Barbara A. *The Politics of Penury: Debts and Taxes in Mexico, 1821–1856.* Albuquerque: University of New Mexico Press, 1986.

Thorp, Rosemary, and Geoffrey Bertram. *Peru, 1890–1977: Growth and Policy in an Open Economy.* London: Macmillan, 1978.

Tilly, Charles, ed. *The Formation of National States in Western Europe.* Princeton: Princeton University Press, 1975.

Tivey, Leonard, ed. *The Nation-State: The Formation of Modern Politics.* New York: St. Martin's Press, 1981.

Torsvik, Per, ed. *Mobilization, Center-Periphery Structures, and Nation-Building.* Bergen: Universitets Forlagt, 1981.

Tristán, Flora. *Peregrinaciones de una paria* [1836]. Translated by E. Romero. Lima: Editorial Cultura Antártica, 1946.

Ugarte, César Antonio. *Bosquejo de la historia económica del Perú.* Lima: Editorial Cabieses, 1926.

Urrutia, Jaime. "De las rutas, ferias y circuitos en Huamanga." *Allpanchis* 18 (1983): 47–65.

Valdivia, Juan Gualberto. *Memorias sobre las revoluciones de Arequipa desde 1834 hasta 1866.* Lima: Mariano Murga, 1874.

Véliz, Claudio. *The Centralist Tradition in Latin America.* Princeton: Princeton University Press, 1980.

————. "La mesa de tres patas." *Desarrollo Económico* 3 (1963): 231–247.

Villanueva, Victor. *Ejército peruano: del caudillaje anárquico al militarismo reformista.* Lima: Mejía Baca, 1973.

Villanueva Urteaga, Horacio. *Gamarra y la iniciación republicana en el Cuzco.* Lima: Banco de los Andes, 1981.

Von Tschudi, J. J. *Testimonio del Perú, 1838–42* [1846]. Translated by Elsa de Sagarta. Lima: Biblioteca Peruana, 1966.

Walker, Charles. "The Myth of Chaotic Charisma: Caudillismo in Post-Independence Peru." MS, University of Chicago, 1986.

Weaver, Frederick S. *Class, State, and Industrial Structure: The Historical Process of South American Industrial Growth.* Westport, Conn.: Greenwood Press, 1980.

Webb, Richard. "Government Policy and the Distribution of Income in Peru, 1963–1973." In *The Peruvian Experiment,* 79–127. Edited by A. Lowenthal. Princeton: Princeton University Press, 1973.

Whitaker, Arthur P. *Nationalism in Latin America.* Gainesville: University of Florida Press, 1962.

White, Richard A. *Paraguay's Autonomous Revolution, 1810–1840.* Albuquerque: University of New Mexico Press, 1978.

Wiarda, Howard O. *Corporatism and National Development in Latin America.* Boulder, Colo.: Westview Press, 1981.

Wibel, John Frederick. "The Evolution of a Regional Community within the Spanish Empire and Peruvian Nation: Arequipa, 1780–1845." Ph.D. diss., Stanford University, 1975.

Williams, John Hoyt. *The Rise and Fall of the Paraguayan Republic, 1800–1870.* Austin: University of Texas Press, 1979.

Wolf, Eric R. *Europe and the People without History.* Berkeley: University of California Press, 1982.

Wolf, Eric R., and Edward C. Hansen. "Caudillo Politics: A Structural Analysis." *Comparative Studies in Society and History* 9 (1967): 168–179.

Woodward, Ralph Lee Jr. *Class Privilege and Economic Development: The Consulado de Comercio of Guatemala, 1793–1871.* Chapel Hill: University of North Carolina Press, 1966.

Yepes del Castillo, Ernesto. *Perú 1820–1920: un siglo de desarrollo capitalista.* Lima: Instituto de Estudios Peruanos, 1972.

Zeitlin, Maurice. *The Civil Wars in Chile (or the bourgeois revolutions that never were).* Princeton: Princeton University Press, 1984.